C000148004

Gift Aid

20   70827283   6318

THE SCOTTISH MOUNTAINEERING CLUB JOURNAL 2017

View from the North Ridge of Clach Glas. Photo: Tom Prentice.

THE SCOTTISH MOUNTAINEERING CLUB JOURNAL 2017

Edited by Peter Biggar

Volume 45

No. 208

THE SCOTTISH MOUNTAINEERING CLUB

THE SCOTTISH MOUNTAINEERING CLUB JOURNAL 2017
Volume 45 No 208

Published by the Scottish Mountaineering Club 2017
www.smc.org.uk/

ISSN 0080-813X
ISBN 978-1-907233-08-1

Typeset by Noel Williams

Printed and bound by Novoprint S.A., Barcelona, Spain.

Distributed by Cordee Ltd, 11 Jacknell Road, Hinckley, LE10 3BS.

CONTENTS

The North Face of the South Peak of the Cobbler. Photo: Des Rubens.

THE BELAY, MAGRATHEA

By Steve Perry

I KNEW ABOUT THE ROUTE long before seeing it in the flesh. Yes, the rumour mill had been busy with talk of Julian Lines spending the last few years taking huge falls from some blank wall high on Creag an Dubh Loch, and the only thing saving him from disaster were a few RPs you wouldn't hang your coat on! The whole thing had quickly spiralled into climbing folklore on the Highland scene and was often talked about down the wall or at the crag. There were even pictures in print of him on the route, though it had yet to be climbed. With all this in mind I still never really knew what to expect when agreeing to give him a belay – I just hoped in my heart it wouldn't be some sort of horror show.

Slowly passing the flat wall whilst abseiling in I soon realised that 'seeing it in the flesh' was quite an apt turn of phrase; the impeccable granite appeared completely bare of anything mere mortals would describe as holds and to be honest looked utterly unclimbable, yet at the same time, that impossible looking first pitch is just so aesthetically perfect.

On that occasion Jules had made it to the jug which signified the end

Jules Lines on an earlier attempt on Magrathea (E9 7a) at Creag an Dubh Loch.
Photo: Dave Cuthbertson, Cubby Images.

of difficulties, but finding himself under such outstretched body tension was unable to grasp it. A nail-less crucifixion. This new high point of substantial success had then suddenly become a new high point for potential disaster! Being so focused on catching his gravity fuelled mass, nothing else existed. I was inside a bubble and the earth had stopped spinning. The fall screamed silently whilst my brain tried desperately to compute his momentum into force, but somehow the gear held once more and Jules avoided the bone crunching narrow ledge we both quietly tried to ignore. Frustrated for him I finally breathed and the planet rotated again.

We were walking in to the Dubh Loch once more but everything felt different this time. Jules explained how he had been back to the cliff just a few days ago and made a simple change to his sequence approaching the jug. I could tell that this had unlocked something, not just on the climb but in his mind and he was now radiating a real confidence that was quite contagious.

On reaching the far end of the loch Jules stripped and walked in to the water, sinking deeper and deeper until completely submerged. The water resembled black ink under the overcast sky and as I sat and ate, I shivered at the thought of how cold it must be. Maybe this was part of some asceticism or just a way of offering himself to the cliffs in the hope of good luck. In a few short hours we'd be back at this loch and I wondered just what would happen before and what would be going through his mind on our return. Only time and Creag an Dubh Loch could give those answers.

We were perched on a narrow ledge a few hundred metres above the loch. Above is this sheet of featureless rock so out of character with the overhanging cliffs looming much higher and then I realised – I was still unsure of where the upper pitches actually went – but quickly decided I could worry about that later.

Standing beneath this route was a real conversation killer and so I just did my thing while Jules stood looking out, then he turned and there was the smile and a nod – OK let's do this.

There had been some cunning plans put in place to help him climb this pitch, beginning with leading up and placing all the gear then down climbing back to the ledge. We then moved the entire belay so as to load the gear differently in case of a fall. I got myself well anchored down which wasn't dynamically great as that would increase the load on the gear, but a compromise had to be made between that and me being lifted then Jules hitting the ledge.

The physics and geometry were all a worry.

I watched Jules chalk his hands and quietly contemplate everything above him, then he left the ledge and prowled cat-like through the opening moves. There was a real hunger in his climbing this time and the meat still to come. The pace steadied as he levitated upwards and then rightwards passing the cluster of gear I was eyeing nervously but this time

The start of the final pitch of Magrathea. Photo: Steve Perry.

none fell out: a novelty. Here now started the ballet section where he moved with a grace honed by years of deadly solos, dancing through this sequence of crimps, further and further into the red with only fear for a partner. The dance was reaching its finale and I willed him on, astounded as his feet floated past invisible edges, fingertips gripping the tiniest of nubbins. Then came the crux, and the elusive jug, he was all but there when the music stopped! Jules held the rock in the crucifixion, trapped by lateral forces he could only stare at the jug. I held my breath for what felt like minutes but then came the lunge and there was the grip, and will it stay on, please stay on and YEEESSS! The victory shout echoed around the Dubh Loch.

We laughed and talked, surmised and joked, whilst Jules built a belay and I stripped mine, all the time relief washing over me in a warm glow.

I now realised that even though we were connected by this single rope, the monolithic rock separating us may as well have been a light year of space in terms of me climbing it to him. I tried anyway but quickly realised the start section I had presumed would be doable wasn't at all and so resorted to aiding up the abseil line. On reaching the cluster of gear I was really taken aback at how it looked and realised then how much he had risked in leading that route. Immense self-belief and bravery came to mind. Once at the belay ledge I could tell Jules wasn't really there, he was away on a higher plane you only get to visit with a massive sense of achievement. Years of effort and hardship mixed with endless bouts of frustration all dispersed by a few minutes of sublime and death defying climbing.

The next section looked as if geology and climbing had joined forces to create a magnificent pitch. Jules set off and for the first time ever I saw him faff on a route. He was still blown away by his own success but soon enough the climber in his soul clicked back into control and he cruised up to the next belay. I had no doubt I'd blow this pitch having just travelled from a two week trip offshore with virtually no sleep and therefore decided I'd nothing to lose. The ropes disappeared up a snaking crack-line, very gritstone like in nature and truly delightful to climb. Each time I thought this was my zenith somehow I pushed on and finally with lots of encouragement reached the belay. Wow!

I was so made up with that!

Jules was now back in full-on climbing mode and set off up what was the final pitch, which like the rest, looked such a gem. A rising traverse led to a vicious corner crack and then I was lost in the moves, never wanting it to end but it did: it was done, it was real. (*Magrathea*, E9 7a)

Descending we talked of what was next and what had been done before, of places to visit and climbs that must be done. I looked across at the cliffs and saw so many routes, so many journeys that had gone years before, and on reaching the loch shore and dipping my hand in, I looked at Jules and knew the answers.

OSSIAN'S CAVE PREVISITED
A Likely Story

By Ian Crofton

'IF YOU BELIEVE THAT, you're an even bigger fool than I took you for.' The Honorary Archivist was having none of it. He may well have been right. And yet, the circumstances of my discovery (or 'discovery' as the Hon Archivist would put it, firmly within inverted commas) still leave me believing that the letter just might be genuine.

I should start at the beginning – or at least one of the beginnings of this strange tale. A few months ago I received the news of the death of a distant cousin, second at least and somewhat removed. Unmarried and childless, he had lived in the old house his family had inhabited for generations in north Somerset, in the village of Porlock, a few miles west of Minehead. This cousin had made little mark upon the world, spending his working life as a bank clerk, eventually rising to the position of branch manager. His long retirement was devoted to cataloguing the family archives, apparently hoarded over generations in a musty linen press. He had virtually completed this onerous task when, in his 92nd year, pneumonia knocked on the door, took his hand and led him quietly away. The news of his death came in the form of a letter from his solicitors, in which I was informed that I had been left a modest legacy, together with an old letter that my cousin had found in the family papers, which he had thought might interest me.

Now I must begin at the second beginning, which finds us, not at a beginning at all but *in medias res*, on 1 September 1803, in a rough drovers' inn close to the upper ends of Glens Coe and Etive:

> This Kingshouse, from the rancid moorland peat, smells like a dirty macquerel with bilge-water. Nine miles every way from all dwelling. Vile troop of drovers, with fiddle and dancing, and drinking, kept it up all night…

So wrote Samuel Taylor Coleridge in his journal[1]. One might have supposed that he would have welcomed the meagre hospitality of the Kingshouse more than he did, given the day he'd had, walking all the way from Glen Falloch, a distance he estimated at 40 or 45 miles. 'For eighteen miles there are but two habitations! and all that way I met no sheep, no cattle, only one goat!' Just as he was unimpressed by the Kingshouse, so he was similarly underwhelmed, or so he said in a letter to his wife, by the neighbouring mountains:

'Glencoe interested me, but rather disappointed me. There was no

---

[1] S.T. Coleridge, journal, 1 September 1803. He was accompanied intermittently on his Highland tour by William and Dorothy Wordsworth. Regarding the Kingshouse, the latter wrote, 'Never did I see such a miserable, such a wretched place'.

superincumbency of crag, and the crags not so bare or precipitous as I had expected.'[2]

He was, it seems, a difficult man to please, topographically. A few days before he'd complained on his walk up Loch Lomond that 'everywhere there is a distressing sense of local unrememberableness'[3]. However, he gave a rather different account of Glen Coe in his journal than he had in that letter to his wife, describing how the 'higher and craggy' mountains rose up into 'turrets, steeples, sugarloaves, and often bulls' brows, brows savager than those of urus or byson'[4].

That would have been that as far as our understanding of Coleridge's experience of Glen Coe is concerned had it not been for my 'discovery' (I hereby, with my inverted commas, nod towards the Hon Archivist's scepticism).

The letter I have in my possession, dated 3 September 1803, signed 'S.T.C.' and addressed to '———— —————, The Grange, Porlock, Somersetshire'[5], gives us an insight into the early history of mountaineering in Scotland, or, more precisely, an account of perhaps the first rock climb made in Scotland that was not for such utilitarian purposes as harvesting birds' eggs or rescuing a crag-fast sheep.

The year before his Scottish tour, Coleridge had made what is generally regarded as the first purpose-free rock climb in England, when he descended from the summit of Scafell via Broad Stand, became for a time crag-fast, then found his way down, probably by the narrow crevice known as Fat Man's Agony, until at last he arrived safely on the col of Mickledore.[6]

That might have proved the end of Coleridge's career as a cragsman, had not a dramatic rock feature caught his eye as he walked down Glen Coe. In the letter I have before me, the poet describes how he passed under 'the greatest and sternest of three great bulwarks that jut out and down towards the valley from the loftier peaks above and behind them'. This 'greatest and sternest' bulwark is undoubtedly Aonach Dubh, the third, as one descends the glen, of the Three Sisters (a name not coined until the Victorian era).

This identification is confirmed by Coleridge's more detailed description:

> As I passed under this horrid horn of rock, I felt at any moment it might bear down and crush me, as a bull would a person. I was for long moments too affrighted to lift my eyes, but lift them I did and

---

[2] S.T. Coleridge, letter to Sara Coleridge, 2 September 1803.

[3] S.T. Coleridge, journal, 25 August 1803.

[4] S.T. Coleridge, journal, 2 September 1803.

[5] This and all subsequent quotations from letter dated 3 September 1803, MS in the possession of the author.

[6] As described in his letter of 6 August 1802 to Sara Hutchinson, the sister of Wordsworth's wife, and the woman with whom Coleridge was long in love.

saw, oh wonder, that the front of the grim bastion was slit, high up, by a vast fissure, a cave or cleft of some kind, a dark inroad into the mountain's inner darkness.

It is clear that Coleridge was looking up at Ossian's Cave, although, according to the Hon Archivist, the name is not known in print until it appeared in an advertisement in the *Inverness Courier* of 18 July 1843.[7]

Coleridge continues his journey along the northern shore of Loch Achtriochtan – not named but dubbed a 'gloomy, unreflecting lake wherein one might picture the dead dreaming their dreary dreams'. He saw himself as Aeneas, 'perched on the shore of Avernus', the crater lake in Campania supposed by the ancient Romans to be the passage to the Underworld.

At the farther end of Loch Achtriochtan he came to a 'rude shepherd's cot...

...One of the denizens – I assume from his long grey beard and glittering eye[8] he was the patriarch of the house – appeared like a ghoul from the black interior and beckoned me over, as if he would tell me something. At first he could only utter the barbarous noises of the Gael, but when he saw my visage blank and uncomprehending he broke into what might pass as English. 'Whhhat brings thee to these parts, sir?' he began. I explained I was on a tour. 'A tour? Whhhhy would thee be on a tour?' I told him I was a poet, a celebrator of nature and of liberty. 'Ah, a poet art thou? Long, long ago whee had a poet here, a *bard* whee say. He lived up there, high on the Black Aonach, in the cave. Thou wilt haff passed under it.' I said indeed I had, but questioned how anybody, let alone a person as refined as a poet, could possibly live in such a harsh and airy place. What was your poet's name, I asked him. 'Osheen,' he replied without hesitation. 'Thou might haff heard his name. He was back in fame some years ago after Mr Macpherson put him into his books.'[9]

Macpherson, I inwardly fumed, that notorious fraudster and scoundrel! 'As gross an imposition,' wrote the great Dr Johnson of the Ossian forgeries, 'as ever the world was troubled with.'[10] As I lost myself in indignation I was jerked back to the present by a tugging at

---

[7] Robin N. Campbell, 'Ossian's Cave and its Visitors', *SMCJ*, 44/207 (2016), p. 15.

[8] Cf. 'It is an ancient Mariner / And he stoppeth one of three. "By thy long grey beard and glittering eye, / Now wherefore stopp'st thou me?", Coleridge, 'The Rime of the Ancient Mariner', *Lyrical Ballads* (1798).

[9] In 1760 James Macpherson had published *Fragments of Ancient Poetry, Collected in the Highlands of Scotland, and Translated from the Gaelic or Erse Language*. Macpherson claimed that these 'fragments' were translations from the legendary bard Ossian or Oisín, son of Finn or Fionn mac Cumhaill. They proved immensely popular throughout Europe, but were later shown to be forgeries.

[10] Remark to 'Mr M'Queen', quoted by James Boswell in *The Journal of a Tour to the Hebrides with Samuel Johnson* (22 September 1773, first published 1785).

my sleeve. I turned to my host, who held me with his glittering eye. 'It is not a harsh and airy place, as thou hast mis-said,' he said. 'It is a fine place, the finest palace for a poet. Indeed, a stately pleasure-dome[11], I haff heard it said.' I questioned how this could be. 'My son will show thee,' he said. 'My son will show thee the wonders of Osheen's Cave.' My head was inclined to scoff, but my heart opened at the prospect. Marquis, for that was the name the old man gave me, called for his son.

A view of Glen Coe, after Robert Andrew Riddell, circa 1795. Above the skeletal conifer to the left of the bridge, the West Face of Aonach Dubh is clearly visible, with the North Face and Ossian's cave hidden in shade.

Regrettably, I am one of 'those ignorant members', so despised by the Hon Archivist, who has yet to make a visit to Ossian's Cave. So I am not in a position to comment upon the accuracy of Coleridge's account of his own ascent in the company of Young Marquis. This account is reproduced in full below.

'Young Marquis will take you,' Old Marquis said. The former was a stout fellow who stood at least a head higher than myself. The old man addressed some remark to him in Erse, whereupon Young Marquis grunted, dipped back into the hovel, and emerged with a long length of hawser wrapped round his shoulders. He set off at a trot towards the river called Coe, and when I did not follow, he turned round and

---

[11] Cf. 'In Xanadu did Kubla Khan / A stately pleasure-dome decree', the opening of Coleridge's 'Kubla Khan', written in 1797 (six years before his Glen Coe adventure), although not published until 1816.

gave a whistle. I understood that I was to stick to his heel like a dog. I did as I was bid, but when I came to the where Coe the ancient river ran down to a sunless sea[12], I paused, fearful of the deep waters. Young Marquis, seeing my hesitation, looked over my shoulder towards the hovel, put his hands to his mouth and let out a great bellow. I turned round to where he had directed his shout and saw a figure somewhat like him, tall and sturdy, come through the door. Had it not been for the fact that the figure was dressed in a long skirt, I would have taken this creature for Young Marquis's younger brother. As it transpired the creature was, in fact, Young Marquis's wife.

Another view of Glen Coe, after Turner, circa 1834–6, perhaps owing more to memory and imagination than topography.

In a few great strides she caught up with me on the bank of the Coe. Then she tucked up her skirts, crouched down, and gestured that I should mount her back. In this fashion I was carried across the river, the Great Dame finding sure footing at every step. At the far side, she allowed me to dismount, before wading wordlessly back across the river.

Young Marquis and I continued round the southern shore of Lake Avernus, and then once more along the bank of the Coe, under the ghastly gaze of the Black Aonach. This great bulwark, like a petrified giant, presented a horrid face of rotten crags and fissures, bristling with stunted trees. I could see no possible route of ascent, but after a distance Young Marquis pointed upward where a series of ledges formed some species of corridor upward and leftward through the obstacles.

---

[12] Cf. 'Where Alph, the sacred river, ran / Through caverns measureless to man / Down to a sunless sea'; from the same poem.

This corridor we followed, along a ridge suspended above a defile filled with waterfall upon cataract upon cascade. As we rose, our way steepened, and I clutched at the grass and any protuberance of rock I could lay my hands on. Young Marquis seemed little perturbed by the airy situation we found ourselves in, and would, on occasion, turn round and look down upon me with a visage that betrayed little pity and much scorn. Not a word passed his lips.

At a height more fitted to eagles or angels than mortal men, the defile beside us shallowed and the waterfalls diminished sufficiently for us to make our way across and achieve a long, broad shelf on our right-hand side. We followed this, still upward, until we came to what might be termed the nub or crux. Above us, the mighty Cave of Ossian stretched skyward, and at the same time bore down on us like some malevolent shade, its black interior boding nought but ill. Between us and its lower entry rose a perilous rock, rank with summer growth, while below us unseen cliffs tumbled down into the vale of Coe below.

The palsy of the limbs that had afflicted me on my descent of Scafell returned. I shook all over but otherwise could not move, my body fixed to the spot on which I stood. I was but dimly aware of Young Marquis's rough hands around my waist. Looking down, I saw that he had knotted one end of his hawser round my person. Looking up a moment later, I saw his thickset figure, like some Jack-a-Napes or Bab-boon at the fair, scurrying upward, pulling himself by any leaf, branch or rocky spur that came to hand, trailing the hawser – whose coils sat by my side – behind him. At last he came to a ledge on which grew a holly tree, little more than a sapling. To this frail stick he tied

Ossian, as imagined by Joseph Robert von Langer in 1823.

himself, looked down upon me, and gave a bark, or Eldritch cry. Numbed as I was by my fearful position I stood rooted to the spot. There was another bark, or perhaps a roar of disgust, and then a great tug at my waist dragged me upward. My hands fluttered for grips, my feet for purchase. I had no choice, the hawser at my waist informed me, but to mount upward, my belly bouncing across the rocks and tufts of grass and fern, my knees colliding with stone after stone. At the holly tree, the whole procedure was repeated, and then again, I think two more times, until we at last entered the portals of the Cave.

It was not, as Old Marquis had assured me, a stately pleasure dome. It was an awful place, worse than the worst Highlander's hovel, not fit for a beggar let alone a bard. With the floor rising at forty-five degrees, there was no place to set a table at which a bard might scribe; no place even to sit and rest without fear of sliding back down the steep slot into the fathoms of thin air between us and the hard vale bottom. This was not, I concluded, a place for poets; not somewhere where one could breathe in the breath of inspiration. No: the Cave of Ossian, I concluded, was never home to any bard, rather a sepulchre for the spirit, a place where fear not wonder seized the soul.

I barely had time to entertain my disappointment when I felt Young Marquis's hand on my shoulder, shoving me down a chute of grass to the Cave's mouth. Calculating in a moment that I must either descend or die up there alone, of hunger and anguish of spirit, I let the momentum of the push start me downward, happy that I was secured by the hawser from above. As I hastened, longing for *terra firma* once more, rocks shifted beneath my feet, and clattered into the abyss, releasing a stench of brimstone as stone dashed on stone; it was as if the *genii loci*, the local devils, were hastening me out of it; Your doom has not yet come, they seemed to say. In time – oh, and what a length of anxious, fretful time – we reached the foot of the Black Aonach once more. Young Marquis released me from his hawser, and I wandered lonely, if not o'er hill and vale as might a cloud[13], then along the happily flat bank of the Coe.

That is the letter, pretty much in its entirety as far as the matter of Ossian's Cave is concerned. I have taken it upon me to impose some orthographic consistency, regularity of punctuation and other minor editorial finesses. Such interference would not necessarily meet the approval of the scholarly world, but my aim here is to make the material available to a wider general audience.

We come at last to the question of authenticity. Could the letter be genuine?

---

[13] Coleridge appears here to be anticipating the lines of his friend William Wordsworth, 'I wandered lonely as a cloud / That floats on high o'er vales and hills, / When all at once I saw a crowd, / A host, of golden daffodils.' Wordsworth had had the experience on which the poem is based in 1802, but according to his own account he did not write the poem itself until 1804, the year after the Scottish tour.

First of all I must ask, Why would anyone, least of all my distant cousin, wish to hoax me? It is inconceivable that this person from Porlock[14] – a man as much free from levity as from dishonesty, as befits a branch bank manager – would ever have considered deceiving me, or, indeed, the world at large. At a glance, though I am no expert, the handwriting in the letter looks very much like the hand of Coleridge as seen in collections of his manuscripts from this period. But it would take a specialist scholar to confirm this, along with a statistical comparison of phrasings, vocabulary and so on – not to mention proper chemical analyses of the ink and paper used, to determine whether they could be dated to 1803 or earlier. To this end, it is my intention to donate the letter to the British Library. Once I have their judgement, I will publish it in a note in the Journal.

Recently doubt has been cast on the previously accepted first ascent of *Ossian's Ladder* (as the route up to Ossian's Cave from Sloping Shelf is named). It has long been attributed to the Glen Coe shepherd Neil Marquis in 1868 (although several sources insist that his name was actually Nicol Marquis)[15]. Since then, it has generally been agreed that the first certain ascent was by Godfrey Solly, Norman Collie and Joseph Collier at Easter 1894, a few days before their first winter ascent of Tower Ridge on Ben Nevis[16]. But could it be that this trio were beaten to it ninety years earlier by another shepherd called Marquis and the first known recreational rock-climber in these islands? We can only await the judgement of scholarship and science.

---

[14] 'On awakening [from an opium-induced dream] he ... instantly and eagerly wrote down the lines that are here preserved. At this moment he was unfortunately called out by a person on business from Porlock.' Coleridge's preliminary note to the first publication of 'Kubla Khan' in 1816 perhaps gives us a hint of the connection to the recipient of his letter of 3 September 1803, extensively quoted from herein.

[15] For example, William Douglas and Alex Fraser, *SMCJ*, 7/38 (May 1902), pp. 101, 109. Apparently the relevant Scottish census records include a Nicol Marquis (but no Neil Marquis) for 1861, 1881 and 1891. I am indebted to Noel Williams for the above information.

[16] Ken Crocket, *Mountaineering in Scotland: The Early Years* (2015), pp. 113–114; Campbell, op.cit., pp. 13, 15–16.

ETIVE SONNET (i)

By Donald Orr

We were coiling rope when the tourists arrived.
Granite cruise over and skinned knuckles
patterned with chalk. We could have been spied
from the road end car park, our helmets and harnesses.
A crowd of them, handbags and trainers, sportswear,
cigarettes in sunburned hands, holiday makers
in the cul-de-sac of Glen Etive's core.
They peppered us with demands
as to what it was like on the slabs,
the steep exposure of the rockband
above them was outlandish and eccentric.
They were young, happy and exotic.
We salted them with responses,
like beads and mirrors to natives.

ETIVE SONNET (ii)

By Donald Orr

He stood not far from Coupal Bridge,
a lay-by in summer evening sunlight,
folding kit away, stacking gear on the ledge
and looking across the river at the day's rite,
performed in heat on the upper crags of Creise.
The river crossing on roaring currents,
the bog-walk and climb to a place
of space and light above the spread of Rannoch.
The cracks and holds of the upper buttress
the runnels and fissures, faces and ledges
of the day's journey to clear air and the endless
memorial held in skin and sinew; the abraded edges,
the roughened hands the price of rockhood;
the cost to the body, the price of remembrance.

AND SOA, IT CAME TO PASS

By Chris Dickinson

THE MERITS OF CLIMBS on Erraid, Ross of Mull and Iona are now widely acknowledged. The beauty of this wild corner of Mull draws many, not just for the quality of the climbs, but for the backdrop of perfect white sandy beaches, islands and skerries, the wildlife and the highlights of Iona and Staffa.

A few years back I had the pleasure of discovering fine new climbs on islands off the coast of Erraid, in particular Eilean nam Muc. Climbing here in good weather feels a bit like being transported to somewhere like Sardinia. I have spent days on sun baked granite where eventually the heat begins to take its toll. The area lends itself to travel by kayak, amongst seals and basking sharks. The sun shimmering on a sea dotted by the magnificent array of the Torran rocks is the backdrop.

In June 2015 I enjoyed another stay at the fine camp site on the shore at Fidden. I had been exploring some of the islets in the sound of Iona by kayak, winkling out the odd climb. On the morning of my departure, the sea was flat calm. Away out to the southwest, there is an island that is rather more than a quick paddle across a narrow strait. I decided to make a quick dash out across the 6km to Soa. My curiosity had finally got the better of me. Soa is slightly closer to the south end of Iona than to the Ross of Mull. However, Fidden is in fact the closest point that you can reach by car, southern Iona being devoid of roads in any case. Having only a plastic river kayak with me for tootling about, the flat sea made a quick dash out there a practicality.

Coming ashore in the sheltered north-west bay of Soa. Photo: Chris Dickinson.

On arrival at the island, I paddled anti-clockwise around it to check out the cliffs on the southern, hitherto unseen, half of the island. To my delight I paddled past a number of fine and solid cliffs gazing out into the Atlantic Ocean, some with platforms at their base and a couple that fall directly into the sea. A fine lagoon guarded by small skerries creates a degree of shelter from south-westerly swells. I then landed at the main beach, a tombolo that divides the island into two, from the east side and took a quick 20 minute hike to the major cliffs I had just seen from the kayak. Excited by what I had photographed, I jumped back into my kayak and headed back to Fidden. On the way I was aware I was beginning to ship some water. On arrival at the beach I discovered that I had an 45cm long crack in the underside of the hull! It must have cracked open whilst I was sliding off the rocks on Soa. I was lucky I had not swamped. The kayak had simply failed that day, perhaps, after a hard life on some rocky river runs.

In recent years I have tried to undertake cragging trips that involve sea kayaks. I messaged the usual suspects and only Anthony Walker was ready for this wee Soa adventure. A posting on Facebook brought an interested response from Billy Hood, someone I knew from a way back but had never actually climbed with. In August 2015, we arrived at Fidden together and set up a luxurious campsite looking out to Soa.

Soa lies about 3km south of the south end of Iona and a similar distance west of Eilean nam Muc. It is really two islands, joined by the tombolo beach and this means that it can be approached by a sheltered bay on each side. It is a heavenly spot and would in make a great spot for an offshore camp. There are some small grassy spots that would take a tent or two. The island is un-grazed and has a beautiful array of flowers and lush vegetation. The southern half of the island is very rugged indeed, a paradise of ancient gneiss, with ponds of rainwater trapped on its surface. At its highest point it rises to 35m above the sea.

The southern coast is where all the significant climbing possibilities lie. The rock is beautiful Lewisian gneiss and reassuringly solid, having been pounded by the Atlantic. From the cliff top one looks out over a spectacular array of rocky islets known as the Torran Rocks. This spectacular stretch of sparkling sea and rugged rocks, also washed by tidal streams, is treacherous for seafarers. For this reason the Dubh Artach lighthouse was built in 1867 on Dhucartach Rock at the end of the Torran series. It lies 23km south-west of Iona and is visible from Soa. It is one of only four lighthouses that lie more than ten nautical miles off the Scottish coast. Notwithstanding the light, in April 1912, a steel steamship, the Cathcart Park carrying a cargo of salt from Runcorn to Wick, ran aground on or near Soa. The crew of 11 all escaped in two small boats.

On a beautiful sunny day on Sunday 16 August, we headed out past Eileans Dubh and Muc, scene of previous adventures and then made the open water crossing to Soa. A gentle glassy swell was rolling in from the southwest. This time the journey was in sea kayaks, far better suited to the crossing and the location.

The team on Soa – Billy Hood, Chris Dickinson and Anthony Walker. Photo: Dickinson.

Leaving the kayaks at the beach, we shouldered rucksacks and clambered over the rough southern half of the island to the cliffs we had just inspected from the sea. We made for the obvious cove which is the centrepiece of the south coast cliffs of Soa. We named this Dubh Artach Cove. Here there is a beautiful overhanging wall, like the prow of a great ship, with a very fierce-looking right hand face of banded gneiss. This wall is bounded by a great corner running the full height of the island and right of that is a huge slab This is bounded on the east by a fine arête and then a steep wall, somewhat shorter with excellent rock. Ledges beneath the routes gave easy access.

I plumped for the great central dièdre as a start to our rockfest. The dièdre starts as a fault rising out of the sea, chimney width. The early moves offer no protection until the cleft narrows to become a crack. The gneiss was brilliantly solid. Occasional footholds on the slab aided progress. The dièdre led right to the summit of the island. We spent a wonderful first day climbing all the lines from the *Dubh Artach Dièdre* eastwards, taking it in turns to lead a climb. Lunch break saw us basking like lizards in the sun on the shelf below the prow. The sun came full onto the cliffs in the afternoon and the hardest part was to stay well hydrated.

Anthony Walker enjoying the fine crack of Kwivering Kormorant. Photo: Dickinson.

We had fun thinking up names for the climbs and went for alliterations like *Perfect Penguin*, *Happy Hoody* and *Chunky Chimney*. One of last routes that day was *Book at Bedtime*, led by Billy Hood, a perfect and classic V-shaped corner towards the east end of the Dubh Artach Cove

area. At the end of a very satisfying day we paddled up towards Iona before crossing the sound back to Fidden. It was a brilliant evening back at Fidden, watching the sunset from the shore and the vista out to our playground on Soa and Iona.

Emboldened by a day of climbs gradually increasing in difficulty, Monday morning saw us paddle direct to Soa to try our luck on the main and wildly leaning Dubh Artach Wall.

I decided to tackle the steep fault that leads up left to the jutting prow above the huge

Billy Hood easing his way up Book at Bedtime (HVS 5a). Photo: Dickinson.

Chris Dickinson reaching the tiny finishing holds on Groaner's Groove (E1 5b).
Photo: Anthony Walker.

lower overhang, at the east end of the wall. This climb gained exposure rapidly as the fault led literally out along the lip of the overhang. There was enough protection to give encouragement and once on the prow I was relieved to find good placements to tackle the final steeper moves up the soaring arête. The final moves up the hanging arête were very exposed, but on reassuringly big holds.

It is a great feeling to have to commit and then discover those all-important final holds that will provide the key to success. I called the route *Singing Seals* (VS 4c) in honour of the seals by now singing in the lagoon below. Belayed on top, I surveyed the special scene, fine cliffs stretching away on either side, sparkling sea, a rash of skerries and views to the hills of Islay and Jura. The west coast of Scotland has given up so many rock climbing gems in recent decades and it was amazing to reflect that in 2015 it was still giving.

The remainder of the day allowed us to lead one further climb each and the quality and character of each was inspiring. A small hanging ramp breached the top of the overhanging wall to the left of the prow. It was a compelling line and gave Billy a very fine lead. The route follows a diagonal fault that leads all the way to the final ramp. Since the whole wall was overhanging, the trick was to find holds and protection in the fault that allowed him to make progress rightwards to gain the ramp. The final moves were exciting and unlikely as the impending wall tried to push us off the ramp and the holds were certainly well spaced. It was a lovely feeling of relief to grasp the top of the wall and pull onto the belay. Billy called the route *Mighty Minke*.

Anthony Walker and Billy Hood enjoy the end of another perfect day on the south coast of Soa. Photo: Dickinson.

Around the corner from the main Dubh Artach Wall to the west, I tackled the fine, but rather brutal overhanging crack line. Attracted less by the brutality and potential suffering and more by the promise of sound placements in the perfect rock and crack, I had to make some wild bridging moves to get established. Here I came to an awkward narrowing where the footholds for bridging appeared to run out completely. Great determination was needed to reach tiny holds that brought my suffering to a close and this fine tussle to a happy ending. *Groaner's Groove* seemed an appropriate name by way of acknowledgement of the groans and grunts from myself and Billy who climbed it. We rounded off our fantastic two-day exploration with a climb above the deep cleft east of Dubh Artach Cove, led by Anthony He followed the beautiful wide but easy crack line up the cliff that avoids the birdy ledges that characterise the ledges on the central section of this cliff, occupied as they were by quivering and somewhat bemused cormorants. The crack led up into a fine steep corner to finish. True to our theme the climb became *Kwivering Kormorant*.

Soa had given generously. It was a happy and fulfilled crew who reluctantly paddled home and left the Banded Wall and the western cliffs for another time or perhaps other visitors. Further west, and separate from the Dubh Artach area is another steep prow and cliffs overhanging the sea and the cliff also overhangs a cleft that almost cuts right through the southern half of Soa. This cliff has some fine potential for some hard climbs, but also sees nesting birds in spring and summer. We left this and the more broken crag on the north side of the beautiful half moon bay to the left for a future visit.

Note: the climbs completed on Soa are listed in *SMCJ*, 44/207 (2016), 138–40.

REQUIEM FOR A CLIMBER

By Gavin Anderson

A SOLITARY GULL SWOOPED and sailed above the choppy waters, its wing tips brushing the crest of the white horses as it wheeled and dipped, banking this way and that like a pedigree showing off its paces while it floated in and out between the broken spars of ice littering the loch. Suddenly the white bird beat its wings as aided by a rising updraught of air it was borne away to vanish in the crags and icy gullies enclosing the waters.

The men standing at the edge of the lochan at the foot of Creag Meagaidh were cold. The keen wind blew flakes of ice, harbingers of storm, into their faces, but they had eyes only for their three colleagues clad in bright red oilskins wading thigh deep trying to fish out an object bobbing in the water. So thick was the ice and snow crusted round it that it was difficult to make it out as a girl's body. A broken crampon hanging from the boot made a tiny almost bell like tinkle when it bumped into any of the wind drifted ice floes. Slowly they steered the corpse in, then dragged her out of the water. A last wave lapped over what was just recognizable as a woman's face.

The bearded man on the shore said,

'Oh my Christ!' Then stood back as the others carefully strapped the girl's body to the stretcher. 'She was guy bonny, they say.'

'Not so you'd know now.' For mercifully the face was covered by a mask of ice.

'What do you reckon's happened?' This was another member of the team, who was gently tucking in the enshrouding blanket.

'Difficult to say. She's been missin' a week.' The leader looked at the thickly plastered cliffs. 'She could have fallen off a route, who knows, or been avalanched off from there into the lochan. He pointed to a pile of massive chunks of snowy rubble fringing the lochan. 'There's your evidence of an avalanche if you want it.'

'What a place to do it in.' This came from another hooded figure huddled against the wind, guarding the stretcher.

'You mean she…?'

'Maybe she was trying for a solo ascent.'

'Unlikely.' The old man shook his head. 'Anyway is there a difference?'

'I'm telling you fair besotted she was wi' her Himalayan guy. He dumped her for her best friend – some best friend.' This was the old man in the hooded cagoule again. He pointed upwards to the huge shining pillar of ice that was the *Centre Post* of Creag Meagaidh. 'Centre Post Direct. 200ft of vertical ice. A tour de force by Robertson in the sixties. One and only ascent. He had to chop steps all the way up.'

'You're forgetting the one last year.'

'Aye and mind wha that was, then?'

'Ye ken fine. It was yon Himalayan guy, whose name seems to have slipped our minds, and his new missus…Surely not? That could do it.'

'You know what they say. Murder, you kill one person. Suicide, you kill everyone.'

'A very cold revenge.'

'Whatever. But it's sad for her, sad for hers and sad for us that have to pick up the bits.'

A general murmur of assent greeted this, more due to the arrival of the threatened blizzard than anything else. A sudden scud of snow flew horizontally across the surface of the loch, its blast jostling the group into one another.

Having made up their minds as to the cause of death they now closed them, to concentrate on getting out. Wading through knee-deep snow under a battering head wind was enough of a problem without the distraction of weighing the fine distinction between soloing and suicide.

They dropped into the streambed of the Allt Coire Ardair. Its high retaining walls shielding them from the wind, as they stumbled in the deep snowdrifts, now and then their feet slipping into the burn's unfrozen stream. Without the stream bed's protective cover, progress would have been impossible through the deep snow in the prevailing conditions.

There was a great bend in the valley. It was further down the hillside and so less windswept. Here the rescue team emerged from the burn trench and carried their burden past a copse of spacious evergreens across a boggy field till they reached the farm, where an ambulance was waiting, its headlights burning as a homing device. When they reached the ambulance the rescuers gently handed their burden over to the ambulance men. The crew took over, placed the body into the van without ceremony, almost roughly. No word of thanks or appreciation was given to the men who had borne the girl's body that long trudge from mountain to roadhead.

The van driver in farewell said, 'You'll hae to wait. The polis want to talk to youse.' He waved, shut his window and drove off to Raigmore hospital in Inverness. They stood there scuffling their feet in the snow. 'Maybe we should say a few words.' They were cold; they were miserable standing backs into the storm. They weren't irreligious, but none of them could think of anything to say. These few moments of quiet were girl's requiem. To break the awkward silence the youngest said, 'If we followed this burn where would it lead to?'

'To the bloody sea ye daft loon!' This was the old grey beard in charge. He could feel the cold in his bones. He was angry with the ambulance men, and deeply depressed about the girl, about the whole day. He regretted snapping at Jamie. In softer tones he said, 'From the mountains to the sea, Jamie, bypassing uncounted hills through a lochan down a pass or two. It never stops. Let's gang tae the pub, at least it'll be warm for the polis to talk to us. And we can look at the map to satisfy Jamie's enquiring mind.'

Meanwhile behind the farm, the burn, notwithstanding its important role in the evacuation and indifferent to the muddy concerns of mankind, rustled and susurrated over a barrier of blanched washed stones on its way down to Loch Laggan.

MIDGIES ON ARRAN

By Gordon Jarvie

An itchy wee sonnet?

Wee sleekit biting bliddy beasties,
how did ye like yer midnight feasties?
Luik at ma airms, ma face, ma ankles –
aa chowed tae bits, ma bed in fankles!

The very Monarchs o the Glen
can staund nae mair, an this is when
they flit alang Lochranza's shore
because they canna thole NO MORE!

Intae the briney sea they gang
jinking thir nippit antlers sair,
roaring thir heids aff. It's no fair.
The enemy they canna see
maddens thaim jist lik thee or me.
May the salt sea-tangle set thaim free.

GOING BIG DOWN UNDER
Adventure Skiing and Major First Descents in New Zealand

By Ross Hewitt

Tom Grant and I spent three weeks exploring the Aoraki/Mount Cook range finding out that New Zealand has some incredible adventures to offer and skiing a couple of big first descents along the way.

The approach to the East Ridge of Mount Cook. Photo: Ross Hewitt.

Kiwiland, or Skiwiland as New Zealand's Southern Alps quickly became known, is home to big wild mountains, snowy ridges and elegant ice arêtes. It's no wonder that Edmund Hillary was the right man to 'conquer' Everest with Sherpa Tenzing Norgay. Rapidly changing weather and depressions bring incessant gusty wind. However, once you get to grips with taking advantage of the weather windows, New Zealand has such a unique, spectacular, rugged and colourful landscape that will have you check yourself several times a day and wonder how it was created. As an island with the main divide only 50km or so from the Tasman Sea, the 'sou'westerer' storms roll in heavily laden with moisture and drop snow over the high ground. There is nothing but ocean between the South Island and Antarctica and the snowfall is nearly three times what the Northern Alps receive and generally stabilises fast in spring.

The mountains have a plethora of faces bigger than 800m and all the ski features you could want plastered with snow: spines, ridges, faces, hanging glaciers, couloirs, and of course low angled glaciers. The range is split east and west by the main divide formed by a chain of impressive

The West Face of Elie de Beaumont. The picture which inspired the ski descent from the right shoulder. Photo: Cam Mulvey.

peaks that include Aoraki / Mt Cook and Tasman. The best way to utilise your time is to spend the money on a ride in a ski plane or heli to the huts and avoid travelling on miles of unstable moraines at all cost.

A few weeks prior to the trip an Instagram photograph of Elie de Beaumont's West Face revealed a line that instantly caught my attention. The line is complex, burly yet elegant, isolated and unskied. Local opinion was the line I wanted to ski was a rock slab with several overlaps that wouldn't go on skis. Although discouraging this didn't put me off the idea completely but the difficulties were not limited to the skiing but also the logistics of getting back from the bottom of the face. Without a convenient hut west of the main divide, the plan was to traverse the mountain, ski the face on sight, and then find a way back over the divide. Our experience of the gusty wind induced too much fear at the thought of basing ourselves over on the west in a tent so that option was quickly dismissed.

Altogether there were a number of unknowns that we would have to solve en route. Without the luxury of climbing or even seeing the face, we would just have to deal with what we found. Our second big unknown was the state of the glaciers below the face for re-crossing the divide and whether they would offer an easy passage or leave us stranded in a crevasse maze. On reflection this seemed a far out plan with low chance of success and every chance of becoming a prolonged epic due to one of the unknown factors baring its teeth. Quite a daunting thought when you are used to planning every last detail, but the line in the photo had been enough to motivate us to fly half way round the world.

Tom Grant skiing the West Face of Elie de Beaumont. Photo Ross Hewitt.

Once the next rip-roaring sou'wester cleared we waited at the airport from dawn for a ski plane back into the Tasman Saddle hut. Frustrations were running high after getting bumped back a few flights. We eventually landed at noon and were greeted with perfect conditions of cool temps and light wind. The opportunity was too good to miss and besides I was feeling too excited and nervous to sit around waiting in the hut all afternoon. We dumped our gear, ate a snack and downed as much water as possible before racing up Elie to catch corn time on the west face. On the climb we wallowed up the steep east facing slopes onto the summit ridge in hideous crust and deep unconsolidated snow that was still undergoing transformation.

As we arrived on the broad summit ridge the view expanded across the stunning west face and, beyond the mountains, stretched out to the sub tropical jungle tucked in under a sea of clouds. The sun beat down onto the slope from the west and the corning snow below the ridge confirmed our timing was right. We changed in silence feeling the pressure build in our chests but knowing to take our time to make sure things were done right, boots in ski mode, binding surfaces de-iced and skis locked on. Below the slope rolled over in a vast expanse with no obvious feature to orientate us on our photo. Doubts about finding the right line added to my pre-ski nerves as the face has some serious obstacles we needed to avoid. The cloud was bubbling up towards the face from the west and for want of a better strategy we decided to ski back along the summit ridge and simply handrail down the left side of the mountain. There was a still niggling worry in the back of my mind that we would encounter some kind of unskiable overlap that would require down climbing due to New Zealand's characteristic 'Weetabix rock'. Would the route go sweetly or turn into some time-consuming mountaineering nightmare landing us in a crevasse maze below?

Low angled but exposed turns down the summit ridge help loosen the muscles and sharpen the coordination for what lay ahead. We paused briefly above a band of rime ice at the top of the face and without saying a word checked each other's body language for psych levels. The brief moment allowed my brain to register the tension rising. Anxiety, doubts, fear all trying to sabotage the day and make you turn back towards the safety of the hut. The driving forces of logic, excitement, desire, inquisitiveness battle to keep you on track. For me the battle line between the two warring camps advances and retreats with my daily biorhythms and energy levels and equates to the overall level of psych. With the seconds passing it was time to focus the mind and become centred as we committed onto the face itself. After skipping the band of rime, sweet corn provided delectable skiing as we descended in sensually fluid turns. The slope continued to roll over finally reaching a maximum sustained pitch of about 45°. To our amazement and relief the line of snow kept coming and led us cleanly off the face onto the Times Glacier with no obstacles to overcome. Skiing is just so much sweeter when the flow isn't broken.

Now the second major unknown section of our journey lay ahead. As we surveyed the surroundings for a route back over the main divide we decided to forgo the heavily crevassed trad route to the Divers Col via the Stevenson Glacier and instead take the north-west couloir on Mt Walter. It was baking hot on the Times Glacier and we soon ran out of water. However, the sun was moving off our couloir and with the cloud level building our anxiety lay around losing visibility and navigating unknown complex terrain east of the main divide.

We made quick progress up onto the watershed but before we could get our skis on the cloud rolled in and our visibility was reduced to a few metres. I had taken photos of the descent terrain on our way up Elie and these were crucial for us to determine the escape line – a beautiful knife-edged arête that connected our hanging glacier to easy ground on the Tasman glacier below. With the sun low in the sky our anxiety levels rose again since skiing the arête in the dark was not an option. We window-shopped and skied as fast as possible until we had to stop and wait for the next window. Eventually we located the start of the arête. Visibility started to improve, allowing us to relax a little and enjoy intermittent spells of golden evening light.

The arête provided some incredibly exposed turns with tails breaking through on the crusty side and icy snow on the other. We stayed on the crusty side as it gave our skis more support and slowly found our way down to the Tasman Glacier. From there it was an easy hour skinning back to the hut and after the fast pace and challenges of the day it was the first opportunity reflect. Fatigue, thirst and hunger quickly made themselves known and slowly a warm glow of satisfaction started to flood through me upon the realisation of an outrageous idea that had been inspired by a photo.

'...a beautiful knife-edged arête that connected our hanging glacier to easy ground on the Tasman Glacier below.' Tom Grant pictured.
Photo: Ross Hewitt.

TO RIDE A LOG

By Hamish Brown

DURING OUR FIRST ATLAS WINTER in 1965 four of us set off to cross the range north to south, starting at the Neltner (Toubkal) Hut on the familiar north side then, from the tizi (col/pass) at the head of that glen, the Tizi n' Ouanoums (3664m) head down to the Lac d'Ifhi (2312m), the only *lac* in the massif and a remarkable sight. We'd follow the Oued Tifhout on out from the *lac* due south. The Tifhout becomes the Oued Sous which turns west once on the southern plains to eventually reach the sea at Agadir.

The crossing went well and the bivouac by the *lac* was a delight but, on waking, the sky showed all the marks of a storm coming in, and we knew what that could mean. We packed up and fled for 'home', back over the Tizi n' Ouanoums. After the stony flood plain, that route entailed 1350m of slog up an ever-narrowing gully. Nearing the top one of the party gave an icicle the size of a rugger forward's thigh a whack only to have it topple and shoot off down the fall line. Yells of 'Below!' Quiet, in the falling snow, then 'Missed!' The storm was in full force by the *tizi* and in the maelstrom we nearly missed the hut (3207m) shades of the CIC. One of the weary party fell asleep at supper and gently lowered his face into his hot, very hot, soup. Only amusing later. The crossing went on the bucket list for the following year.

Quite illogically we decided to go for the N–S crossing while away west of Toubkal, climbing at the Lépiney Hut, and then set off in the opposite direction to first relish the equally-desired weird world of the Tazarharht Plateau: a 'desert de pierres, plat, nu, vide, si haut perché qu'on n'apercoit rien sous le ciel'. We gained this by a mere 900m gully up through the cliffs, hard labour with heavy packs, but worth it to relish the weird stony void. Many exhausted Bath Whites and a few Painted Ladies were flopping about and others had sunk into the snow, sad corpses in their little pits. We had already spent quite a bit of time marking these butterflies for Bristol University and some would turn up in the grounds at Clifton. They make an astonishing migration from West Africa, over the Sahara, over the Atlas, over the Bay of Biscay to end up in the West Country. Marking entailed a colour-coded dot of paint on a thorax. We did wonder what the local shepherd boys reported home when they saw us rushing around like madmen with our huge nets.

What followed were days of wandering eastwards, all up and down against the grain of the land. What I now remember were two contrasting nights, the first in a poor hamlet, the other a magical bivouac high above the Lac d'Ifni. In the hamlet we were given a room to sleep in. The day's sun made this room an effective night-storage heater and we lay gasping and sweating on our airbeds. I felt something crawl across my face. I wrote in my log, 'Bugs … crawling, scuttling into every fold of flesh or clothing. Attacked, they exploded pop, leaving a smudge of blood (ours) and a smell which hangs horribly in memory. Scores scuttled into cracks in the walls when I shone a torch on them. There were long, hairy ones which fell onto us from the ceiling. They waded through the DDT powder we fought them with. Only the cold of dawn stopped the assault. In the early light you could see the squashed remains and the smell lingered. Our bites were real and irritated for weeks.' (This was to be the only such Atlas experience in over 50 years of wanderings.)

Our objective of a north-south crossing by re-visiting the Lac d'Ifni to continue south eventually meant one last haul to a *tizi* which proved a fine crossing with a 1370m descent to the *lac*. Before this effort we stopped to make a proper meal: soup, corned beef and veg. We could have rolled over and slept there and then. A shepherd took the empty tin as treasure trove. He refused any food. He kept shouting, determined, however unintelligent we appeared, to get his message through. Waving at the water and then the sky rather suggested rain. The last thing we wanted was a storm with the chance of blizzards on high and flash floods and washed-out tracks below.

A pinnacle on the col never seemed to draw nearer. The rocks were vividly tinted, one immense wall above would have given weeks of rock climbing, and it was only a flanking crag. As our energy ebbed, the tide of day also slipped away; the valley vanished darkly behind us and the ragged gendarmes above our heads seemed to grope up like hands to set the twinkling stars in their places. At last, the col, over 3350m up, with the last shimmer of dusk seeping away ... The sky had cleared again and the moon blazed the ragged rim of peaks with light. Jbel Toubkal (4167m) swept down and down in junior summits to the Lac d' Ifni which lay like a clouded mirror still thousands of feet below. Duvets and crampons were donned.

We descended steep snow for about 600m before we found a stream. Crampons squealing on the iced rocks we scrambled over for long, welcome drinks. Before long we sat in bed, under a huge boulder, mugs in hand, looking out on the moon-washed desert landscape, the night breathlessly cold and magical. Here surely was Obadiah's 'nest among the stars'. The perfect bivouac.

When Toubkal's summit was caught in dawn's 'noose of light' we wended on down (another 600m) to the valley of boulders to reach the Lac d' Ifni. We set up the stove in expectation of a second breakfast. It soon arrived: three small trout which we swopped for half a box of matches. Rolled in oatmeal and cooked in butter they were delicious. One of the fishermen then started beating the ground with his pole and came over to show us his trophy, a large adder. He said transport was possible down the Tifhout-Sous from Assarag, our intended exit. To escape the *lac* a tenuous path wiggled over 90m sheer cliffs to gain the natural dam of red rocks which held this well secreted, stretch of water.

We picked up a *seguia* (water channel) the finest ever seen, stone-lined, five feet deep and the same across. Walnut trees began though we were still over 1830m up and the landscape became two-tone thanks to the magic of water: above the *seguia* was starkly barren, below was green and prosperous, 'the water of life' made plain. The *seguia* ran for many miles, now and then through a village, sometimes cascading down to a lower level of terraces. The chunky red boxes of the villages in that verdant setting rather mimicked a landscape by Cezanne. The women went unveiled and wore brightly-coloured garments. They greeted us with smiles by their washing troughs or when passing with bony cows. This rich world glowed too with a frothy pink mist of almond blossom. It was beautiful beyond the singing of it.

Assarag, 4½ hours we'd been told, but we took most of that just to reach the first big stream draining much of the world east of Toubkal – a temptation in the sweltering heat to return 'home' to the cooler, snowy north side of the Atlas. No. We had to complete a real crossing. The only N–S crossing I knew of was by Robin Fedden and party who wrote telling how they crossed from the Neltner Hut *tizi* down direct to the *lac* and on for Assarag. They arrived at 6.30 p.m. but 'out' transport always departs early in the day. We hoped so.

We toiled up to a village, Tisgui, hoping to purchase eggs and maybe eat before going on in the evening coolness and were at once invited into a house, kicking off our dusty boots and collapsing on the cushions in the cool guest room. The ceiling was painted like a mediaeval castle at home. Our host spoke a bit of French. A tray appeared with bread, butter and hard-boiled eggs. It was salty bread, curling and hot from the ashes – baked since our arrival while we sipped a coffee. We then sat back for mint tea and with commendable discipline refused invitations to stay the night.

We were told Assarag only had one bus a week, leaving *at night*. We had to get out my log book to find what day it was. The bus left that very night! Did we make a dash for it? Our host was emphatically against this. 'Non! Non! Assarag – fini. Allez d'Imlil à Tidili.' We found Imlil was the next village where our Oued Tifhout became Oued Sous but of Tidili we found no trace. The conversation became repetitive. We must go to Tidili.

'Un piste a Tidili?'

'Oui.'

'Est-ce qu'il est possible d'y aller en voiture?'

'Oui.'

'À Assarag?'

'Non! Non! Assarag fini. A Tidili.'

Our gracious host came to the edge of the village to set us on our way. The last two hours before dusk were always cool and enjoyable for walking. We would walk in companionable silence, savouring the delicious solitude. There was another big village across the valley with a *kasbah* and a succession of threshing floors. After half an hour we turned a corner. There was the expected Imlil and, beyond, a wide red ribbon of road with a lorry standing on it!

The lorry had a huge log on the back and we dreaded the thought that it might go off, even as we watched. No one appeared for a while and Roger suggested we bivvy under it to make sure. 'They might not see us and drive off,' Clive muttered. We decided it had to be going somewhere useful – no doubt to Assarag. The driver came eventually and agreed to give us a lift, departing at first light.

'Allez vous a Assarag?'

'Non. Tidili.'

We groaned.

'Ou est Tidili?'

He pointed eastwards. I began reading names off the map, one or two received nods but there was no Tidili.

Tidili however was in the direction of the Tizi n' Tichka road over the Atlas from Ouarzazate to Marrakech and we could walk to it from wherever Tidili was. But why go east? Struggling up to 2400m to escape this valley and traversing endless ridges all along the Atlas. We gave up. We would take the adventure. We slept out on a threshing floor. The night was cold with a huge ripe moon which faded the lesser stars but left the constellations swinging the night hours through.

Behind the driver's house was a monstrous machine, bulging with wheels and long arms, used for dragging the trunks of walnut down to Imlil. Walls, ravines, terraces, were nothing to its determined progression and were simply rebuilt afterwards. Our transport had ten wheels, on three axles, some of the wheels were cruelly ripped and cratered. A thick log was chained on the back with a smaller one loose alongside. Everything was built with massive strength: the metal cab, front fender, winch and heavily protected lights; twenty feet of gargantuan machinery powered by a Perkins engine.

Our morning departure was leisurely; crowbars, jacks and so on were heaved aboard, then baskets of food, then the co-driver appeared and after him, a third person for the cab armed with a rifle.

'Riding shotgun,' Clive suggested.

I managed to sit on our rucksacks between the log and the cab while Roger and Clive straddled the log. I had qualms at the first bend but survived the journey without being squeezed into the cab by the log. The pace was slow, but at least required no physical effort on our part. Mentally it left us both exhausted and exhilarated.

For several hours we groaned eastwards, up-valley. The road was simply scoured out and in places, as we passed, the edge crumbled beneath us to slither away suggestively out of sight. At some of the bends we had to reverse for a second attempt, the co-driver leaping out to place a wedge under the rear wheels before they reached the edge, or to yell before the stern of the battleship ran back into the bank.

The countryside was bleak but there were villages where the windows had eyes that followed our passing. Some villages were perched on outcrops, some hidden in the side valleys which sent us into sweeping detours. Eventually we stopped outside a house. We were invited in: carved beams, good carpets and silver teapot. In a corner on a stand there was a Victorian monstrosity of artificial fruits and flowers under a glass dome.

Everyone seemed to be armed with rifles and bearing curved daggers. Our host made mint tea and the lorry driver brought out bread and sardines from a basket. Several tins were emptied into a dish and the bread broken and distributed. We dipped it in the common dish as usual. Sardines never tasted as good at home. A transistor blared. We produced Kendal mint cake which was broken and passed round. The drivers thawed, or simply were awake now, for it was still only ten o'clock, and began to ask questions – and satisfy our curiosity.

The timber went on from Tidili to Marrakech and thence all over the world. Our driver lived in Marrakech but for several years had been working for this French timber company who were extracting valuable walnut trees from the south of the Toubkal massif. Each day he took a load from Imlil to Tidili, returned, loaded and then the next day repeated the process. His name was Bourgemâa ben Amou, a charming person, independent, friendly and kind. He posed with his lorry and we took the photographs which we later posted to Marrakech.

We climbed aboard again and drove on up to the watershed, over 2400m, with magnificent views in every direction: northwards, the scruffy scree slopes of Jbel Iferouane, 4001m, filled the near view; west we looked back to the country we had walked through, a landscape of troubled reds and purples below gathering storm clouds; east we looked down to a great valley and further mountains and south to scrub-studded slopes which continued to the distant volcano of Jbel Siroua.

We dipped to splash through a stream and the branches of a tree nearly decapitated the pair on the log. The landscape became bare red sandstone over which we juddered. For a mile or two there were road gangs out; they ranged from young children in flimsy rags to toothless crones in accumulated *djellabas*. One or two workers had limbs missing, some had swollen goitres and others eyes glazed with trachoma. Many bore arms and there was great yelling and shouting as we passed.

The going was downhill now, a gradual descent in spirals and sweeps over every surface imaginable, through the odd village and finally onto a big plain. It was all very reminiscent of a Western movie. We clattered into the last outpost in a cloud of dust. It could have been down Mexico way with the swarthy, armed figures and adobe-style buildings.

'Tidili.'

'It's real then.' Roger whispered.

Bourgemâa pointed east to the next range; the pass through it led to the Tizi n' Tichka road, a day's tramp he reckoned. We were profuse in our thanks. I got Bourgemâa aside and asked him if I could offer payment at all. He would have none of it but the gesture was appreciated for he invited us to 'come along in' and perhaps someone would take us on the next stage.

We went into the biggest house and stumbled up a dark stairway. Soon a dozen of us were sitting or squatting around a table eating a gigantic *tagine*. There was the usual fresh bread to dip in the gravy. A laver went round and then we shared out the rest of our Kendal mint cake. French, Italian, English, Scots, Arab and Berber were grouped together in the Tidili Transport Cafe. Bourgemâa tipped off his load and roared off for Imlil in a cloud of dust.

We were invited onto an even larger lorry which took two big logs and with a giant of a driver to match, we set off over a desert plain to a distant sneck in the hills. On our left lay Taska n' Zat (summits up to 3900m) stretching ridge after ridge ahead, rimmed still with snow but the southern slopes dizzy in the heat shimmer. Once into the pass we were over 1800m again, the road swinging in constant bends, demanding endless fast handling of the heavy wheel. The guard slept. We hung on, unimpressed now by the impressive, drugged with a day of thrills, punch-drunk with heady shocks. The whole sky had clouded over and the heat was weighted with threat. The old shepherd had warned us; he was only a couple of days out.

We came out to the blessed main road in the late afternoon, jumped down, shook hands all round, and watched the huge lorry grind off for the 2260m pass of the Tizi n' Tichka and Marrakech. We followed in a bus an hour later, a bit of an anticlimax, but feeling smug too. It rained all the way over the Atlas, and the streets of Marrakech were awash.

CLASSIC DAYS ON COOK AND TASMAN

By Alan Hunt

THE TRAVERSE OF MOUNT COOK and Mount Tasman are two of New Zealand's finest outings. This account goes back to New Year 1984 and recounts the events that I still remember very clearly, it was an absorbing adventure.

'It's always like this on Saturday night', the girl from Dunedin said with indifference as the bar doors flew open and a well aimed fire hose swept the grunting combatants out onto the pavement. As the staff replaced the hose and restored the upturned seats we resumed our chat.

Grand Plateau landing below the East Face of Mount Cook. All photos: Alan Hunt.

Two weeks earlier, my wife Fi, and Mike, a Kiwi bee farmer we had met up with some days earlier, had left the Hermitage bar in The Mount Cook National Park as the New Year's Eve festivities livened up and dancing on the hotel lawn began. The Southern Cross and companion stars were sharp and bright emphasizing the clear outline of the surrounding mountains against the night sky, the weather was looking fine and conditions on the hill should be good. If we stayed for the inevitable all night celebrations and consequent hangover we would miss out on the approaching weather window. We left there and then and early next morning took an early flight in the tiny three-seater plane to Mount Cook's Plateau Hut, with food for a week.

We landed on the Grand Plateau, the large flat glacier basin that sits below the East Face of Mount Cook and Tasman and after a short walk we were sorting gear in the convenient nearby Plateau Hut. It's a full day's walk from the road head to the hut with a normal rucksack load, yet here we were less than an hour after leaving the valley emptying our bulging loads and not a streak of sweat to show for it. So much for the 'Long Walk in'!

On the approach we had flown under the sweeping 2000m Caroline Face of Cook first climbed in 1970 by John Glasgow and Peter Gough and still a prized route, then, under the East Face before spiralling down to the glacier landing strip. The excitement generated by the awesome sight of so much challenging snow and ice was palpable and we all felt apprehensive about the thought of a major route.

It had so far been a poor season, Cook had not been climbed from this side since November and the hut was empty, not for long though, all day the wee plane kept buzzing in and out and by evening the hut was full and atmospheric chatter about route choices bounced around. As a safety measure most of the National Park huts had two way radios installed and a regular check-in was requested by the Park staff, so we made the obligatory evening call and they updated the weather forecast. Two days of settled conditions were expected.

What to do? This might be the only chance of a route on Mt. Cook. Three other parties were going for the Zurbriggen Ridge, a classic and a preferable route to the crevassed and serac threatened but technically easier Linda Glacier approach.

The East Ridge separates the long and sustained ice climbs of the East Face from the plunging, avalanche threatened, Caroline Face and is one of the great classic routes on the mountain, first climbed in 1936 by a young Dan Bryant and Lud Mahan, a big outing in the days of step cutting with long axes. The height difference from bottom to top is 1500 metres and to reach the start meant traversing under the East Face, ground that is constantly at risk from avalanche and falling ice so an early start was essential.

We left the hut at 10 p.m. as the night frost began to bight and hopefully cement everything in place. We needed a long day anyway to complete the route, traverse the summit ridge and descend the Linda Glacier to the hut. The approach was on ghastly, strength sapping, knee-deep breaking crust. Only wee Fi managed to stay smugly on the surface. We moved as quickly as possible under the objective dangers lurking above.

'Glad that's behind us,' said Mike, expressing the relief we all felt as dawn broke. Now for the challenge of the ridge. It turned out to be in excellent condition, hard névé and ice at about Scottish grade 3/4 or Alpine Difficile and we made rapid progress over clean rock outcrops, ice gullies and narrow snow arêtes until we reached the final steeping slopes below the summit. Here the ice was hard and steep but we chose to move together to save time. With aching calves and taught nerves, we stopped for our first real rest on the summit crest of Middle Peak and anxiously observed the heavily corniced ridge that led to the main summit of Cook.

Fiona, the author's wife, on the East Ridge of Mount Cook.

In places the cornice was huge: an enormous unstable looking mass overhanging the East Face emphasizing the dangers of the traverse we had made below it on the approach which seemed a long time ago. We learned later that the whole lot eventually collapsed taking a large section of the ridge down the face in a calamitous avalanche! There was no question of strolling along the crest we had to traverse the steep ice slope of the West Face that glistened wickedly in the pink light of the setting sun.

The day was growing old and we would have to move quickly to avoid a night out. Although the weather looked stable and the forecast had been good, the mountain is notorious for rapid changes. In 1982 two young Kiwi climbers Mark Inglis and Phil Doole had reached this point only to be faced with the full force of a screaming Nor'wester, New Zealand's version of an Atlantic depression. Below the summit ridge lies an enormous crevasse ironically called 'The Middle Peak Hotel' and this was to be their home for two desperate weeks before they were daringly plucked to safety by a small private helicopter. This brought an end to a long drawn out saga of rescue attempts including the crashing of a NZAF helicopter. Such was the frenzy of media attention over the incident the Prime Minister, affectionately known as 'Piggy' Muldoon, threatened to ban mountaineering, happily it remained only a threat.

Sadly, both Phil and Mark had their frostbitten feet amputated, but amazingly we had left Phil the previous evening going off to attempt the Zurbriggen Ridge. It was probably the thought of his difficulties negotiating that breaking crust that spurred us on during our approach.

We traversed the steep slope below the ridge moving together or short-roping as it is called in modern parlance. This is manageable on snow but on ice it gives a false sense of security.

'What happens if one of us slips?' said Mike. A slip was unthinkable. I might hold diminutive Fi but not a burly Kiwi farmer as well. Serious concentration was needed and we reached the summit both mentally and physically drained. Mike had been here before and with Antipodean confidence assured us he could find and link up the mandatory abseils.

In the fading light we began the descent of the ridge leading to the Linda glacier where we could just make out the trough in the soft snow made earlier by others; if we could reach it we could descend the rest by torch light. We hesitated at the last abseil, we couldn't make out the ground below, the wrong way could leave us in very unpleasant territory so we decided to bivouac for the night, glad to have at last stopped moving.

I had brought a cocoa and sugar mix along to add to melting snow as a rehydrating treat during the day and it had worked well but now the snow was frozen hard and when I tried to lick the dried mixture with a very dry tongue a lot of the powder seemed to miss my mouth and finished up all over my face and there it stayed to the amusement of the others next morning. When we regained the hut we learned that since Phil and Mark's epic, climbers had been avoiding the East Ridge! The consensus was that ours was a bold early season effort. 'Nice one!' a local guide said, we agreed.

Mike had to go and look after his bees so he caught a flight out and then two days of bad weather followed and Fi went to bed and slept like she does. I spread our smelly gear round the now almost empty hut, then the evening radio check once again promised a further spell of fine weather

Fiona Hunt on the Syme Ridge of Mount Tasman.

so we decided to go for the traverse of Mount Tasman via the Syme Ridge, yet another Dan Bryant classic this time with Rod Syme in 1933. Bryant was a member of a new group of young impecunious amateur New Zealand climbers who made many fine pre-war first ascents.

The route is approached by what the guide book encouragingly referred to as 'The Mad Mile': an area covered by serac debris. So next morning we charged across this aptly named ground thankful that the Kiwi mile seemed to be substantially shorter than the UK version.

Once across we climbed a superb snow ridge that led to the 'Great Divide', the watershed ridge system that culminates at the summit of Tasman. Once on the ridge the route to the summit involved climbing over snow mushrooms; traversing narrow ice arêtes with only the odd corniced section where we had to drop off the crest. Conditions were good and we made good time to the summit where, in contrast to Cook, we stopped for a break.

Far below the Pacific surf was breaking on the South Island shore in contrast to the Alpine view along the Divide of seemingly limitless peaks that promised days of adventure for those who are prepared to make the long and arduous approach they usually require.

Fiona descending the corniced ridge of Tasman late in the day.

The descent was down hard steep ice with an unforgiving drop down the Balfour Face as a run out so we faced in and carefully down climbed with occasional abseils until we reached easier ground above the Linda Glacier. On the glacier we were joined by two unroped Australians retreating from one of the steep ice routes on the Balfour Face and they prudently followed our path through the complex of dripping crevasses and creaking snow bridges.

Suddenly there was a muffled curse, I looked around and all I could see was the top of a blue hard hat, the rest of him had slipped in to a concealed 'slot', the Kiwi term for the evil narrow concealed crevasses that do their best to exercise a form of visitor control over mountaineers. Being roped up I was not in danger of following him too far, nevertheless I began to think light as the sagging surface creaked under me. Once on firmer ground I passed him a bight of rope as a hand hold and he slithered out of the hole like the victim of an Eskimo seal hunt on the pack ice.

Next day we caught a flight back to the valley and signed out at Park H.Q. We had been really fortunate with the weather and the choice of routes had given us a chance to sample two of New Zealand's many fine classic mountain climbs.

A week later after a three-day retreat from Mount Aspiring that involved the crossing of dangerously swollen rivers resulting from ceaseless rain, we finished up in the nearest township and that night saw us in the local bar ready for a quiet drink. 'It's always like this on Saturday night', she said!

Ten years later I did climb Mount Aspiring on my own in perfect weather but that's another story.

THE BULLROAR INCIDENT

By Ken Crocket

IN SCOTLAND, THERE SEEMED to be a pause following the Marshall-Smith week on the Ben in February 1960; some might have said it was more of a stunned silence, though Alex Small, a long time and enthusiastic mountaineer in his own right, commented that it was due more to there being few climbers around who could fully appreciate this tour de force. Winter conditions too could have been one of the reasons that exploratory climbing in Scotland dipped for a while in the early 1960s.

There were of course noteworthy exceptions, one being a fine ascent of *Vanishing Gully* (200m V,5 ***) on Nevis by Graham Tiso and Ronnie Marshall on 15 January 1961. Tiso led the crux pitch, often a vertical or bulging wall of ice taking an obvious line on Secondary Tower Ridge. There is an interesting entry in the CIC Hut Logbook for 21 January 1961 – '*Attempting new stuff on Carn Dearg Buttress. Got gripped & came down after 200 ft. A. Wightman & D. Haston.*' In fact Wightman had taken a leader fall of over 30m onto a poor belay. Haston must have been keen on *Route II*, as he was up the next day with Robin Smith. Both failed on this line, eventually climbed in winter in February 1978 at VI,6 *** and described as one of the finest mixed routes on Ben Nevis. The attempts are mentioned in the Cruickshank biography.[1]

The major ascent in the summer of 1961, at least in the west of the country, was *The Bullroar* (285m HVS ****) on Ben Nevis, from the hand of the master, Jimmy Marshall, aided and ably abetted by Jimmy Stenhouse. This great rock climb, making an exhilarating traverse across the great slabs of Càrn Dearg Buttress, has been regarded as Marshall's finest summer addition to Ben Nevis, if not Scotland. The outstanding move on the route is while on a descending traverse of a slab above the lip of an overhang. Those who are keen on good protection may advise their second to use a back rope, otherwise you emulate the late Doug Lang and swing across the slab, ending up hanging down the overlap below.

The name is taken from the *bullroarer*, the ancient ritual musical instrument, examples of which have been found in many parts of the world including Scotland. Basically it is a rectangular thin slat of wood attached to a cord. This cord is given a slight twist and the roarer is swung in a large circle, vertical or horizontal. When the cord unwinds it will begin alternating its twisting, and the roarer will make its characteristic roaring vibrato sound. Indeed, it has been used for long-distance communication, made possible by the low-frequency component of its sound.

There is a very amusing and personal story attached to this route, and its name, until now untold in print. One August weekend the author and

[1] Cruickshank, Jimmy. *High Endeavours – The Life and Legend of Robin Smith* (Edinburgh, 2005, Canongate.) pp. 182–3.

Càrn Dearg Buttress: a climber is just visible starting the first traverse pitch of The Bullroar in pleasant sunny conditions. Photo: Noel Williams.

his climbing partner were the sole occupants of the CIC Hut. On the Saturday they decided to climb *The Bullroar*, the rocks being dry and the weather looking good.

After a few pitches however, clouds started to form, menacing, and not your happy, fluffy white ones. By this time we were past the crux and high on the slabs, about to cross the line of Centurion. I made my misgivings clear and suggested we think about bailing out. My companion, who was in a stubborn set of mind, refused. He insisted we continue.

We climbed on. The sky became darker and spots of rain began. Again I suggested a retreat, and again he refused. It was August, and still warm, but the clouds were looking more menacing by the minute and the drops of rain more frequent. I strongly suggested a retreat a third time, but no.

It was my lead, and we had effectively finished the traversing and were on what was probably the last steepish, if easy pitch, when all meteorological hell broke loose. There was a massive crash of thunder, it became very dark, and within a minute or two I was literally ankle-deep in water running over the steep slab I was on, some 20ft or so above the belay. I had runners in, but climbing higher was impossible through the torrent. I sacrificed a big nut and was lowered to the belay. I recall watching the water pour out the bottom of my breech legs (we were still wearing breeches then), and wondering whether it would be better to fasten the breeches below the knees, or keep them open. Both of us were shivering, as the rain quickly cooled us down. We decided to abseil.

I will try to keep this brief, but basically after a couple of steep abseils, with my turn to go, I peered over the brink of what was a vertical or steeper wall. I thought I could just make out a faint ledge way down in the murk, at the limit of visibility, and chucked down the ropes. Down I slid, until I came opposite a ledge. I could just touch the rock with outstretched toes, and when I spotted an old peg, I shouted up the good news and began to swing in to the ledge. I am fairly sure it was a section of what became known as the Patey Traverse, following one attempt by the Aberdonians to gain access to the Sassenach chimney.

The grim one followed and joined me on the ledge, with one more abseil remaining before ground zero. Then the ropes jammed. Experienced alpinists may know the feeling well at this point. Naturally we had checked that they were running before we abseiled, and we can only surmise that they had jammed lower down. It happens, you know. One of the ropes, mine, had been bought the week before, but, considering a trip to the Alps, I had taken out insurance through a deal some mandarin in the club had helped set up. We had still to get down however.

It was now dark, there was no one around, and it was up to us alone. *'What do we do now?'*, asked the grim one. I replied that we had to cut the rope, pulling down with its stretch as much as we could. *'How do we cut it?'* he asked. *'Simple'*, I replied, placing the edge of a blade peg across the tensioned ropes and hitting it with a peg hammer. Two blows and the deed was done. Three more mini abseils and a lot more gear (it was our necks after all) and we finally reached the ground.

And the amusing twist to the story? It seems that in Aberdeenshire and Kincardineshire the bullroarer was known as a *'thunner spell'*, and was thought to protect against being struck by lightning[2]. They were made by farm-servants and villagers. In Aberdeen, for example, it was also known as a *'thunder-bolt'*. As might be expected, they were also a toy and nuisance maker for children. Well, we were gratefully spared the lightning, but that night, safe on my bunk in the hut, I awoke suddenly with a nightmare in which I was falling...

Oh, and the insurance? I placed my claim and received from the insurers a letter of disbelief. Why were we not able to walk off they asked. I dashed off a reply, complete with a photograph of the 'Great Buttress', the line of the route and appropriate scales included. The cheque eventually arrived, and I returned to the climbing shop for the other half.

As the final insult, a party of Aberdonians were on the buttress soon after, making a large and unexpected haul of gear. The ropes remained in situ for several years, hanging in space where the free

The unfortunate rope hanging on Ken Crocket's wall. Photo: Ken Crocket.

abseil had occurred, a memorial to Scottish stubbornness. Years later, Dave Cuthbertson kindly dropped into my lap the piece of rope that had been at the belay, and in my study it swings still, though mutely.

---

[2] Haddon, Alfred C. *The Study of Man* (London. Bliss, Sands & Co 1898) p. 222: 'It was believed that the use of this instrument [thun'er-spell] during a thunder-storm saved one from being struck with "the thun'er-bolt."'

PARISHES OF THE INFINITE

By Steve Hindley

*But at least you have had a fine moment, and looked down upon all
the kingdoms of the earth. And whether it was wise or foolish, tomorrow's travel will carry you, body and mind, into some different
parish of the infinite.* (Robert Louis Stevenson, Walking Tours)

MOULIN. IT WAS LUNCHTIME in mid-October and the morning had trickled
away in a succession of frustrating occurrences. It was a chill 1°C and the
mist was almost solid but maybe I could make something of the day after
all. I poured a coffee and slowly got suited and booted. As the level in the
cup decreased so did the level of my frustration.

In a mountain hut, on another continent, so recent I still had the suntan,
I'd had a conversation about Ben Vrackie but it was a conversation I was
poorly qualified to embark upon because it was a hill I knew nothing
about. I'd never climbed it. Maybe today I could put that right.

An avenue of golden leafiness led me away and since I was alone I
could kick my way through great piles of leaves without fear of
embarrassment, amusing the child within. I revelled in their richness and
shades of colour, shades to make Monet weep, standing out vividly in a
world of monochrome misty numbness, and as more leaves fell I walked
on through a shower of autumn, out on to the slopes beyond.

There were people on the hill but the dampness and the gloom of the
leaden sky, the weight of the mist pressing down into the ground, had the
ability to subdue mood as well as noise and we passed with nothing more
than a quiet hello, as if wary of disturbing the silence.

Working its way upwards the well-made and well-signposted path
wriggled round little knolls and past little cliffs to a lochan beneath the
final swell of the hill. I couldn't see it but the map assured me the hill was
there. A couple of stepping stones hopped across the outflow and I
followed them hopefully. Immediately, the path rose like a staircase. It
was very steep and climbed in regular steps. Ideally I'd prefer it not to be
there at all but on a hill so popular its presence is probably a necessity.
From below it was invisible and having accepted its necessity I was
grateful for its quality.

The pull up the hill soon started to make me feel a little warm so I
stopped to remove a layer. As I did so there was an almost imperceptible
lightening of the world, a hint that there was something other than mist
and coldness. The sun was close. Just a few more steps took me into that
world of sparkling brilliance that lives where the sun meets the mist. Go
lower and all is gloom; go higher and the world shows you other things.
But to be there, at the boundary of the two – now! That's the place for the
jaded soul! The light plays such tricks and oh, the feeling of rejuvenation

it gives! If I could've bottled it; if I could have carried it with me, on into the rest of life, through what are usually quiet humdrum days earning a living, that feeling would have sustained me.

I'm not sure what time I arrived at the summit but it didn't actually matter. The view was all that mattered and it was both immense and incredibly impressive. To the east was just the most perfect sea of cloud, absolutely, without a doubt, the best cloud inversion I'd ever had the privilege of observing in almost forty years of wandering the hills and mountains of these blessed isles. It was dazzling in its intensity and inviting in its apparent softness.

The merest bump, complete with radio mast, gave away the location of Mount Blair. Across the trench of Glen Garry, from the depths of which the lochan occasionally winked up at me as the sun reflected from its placid surface, stood Schiehallion. The Farragon hills, the Lawers group, and Ben More and Stob Binnein, those inseparable twins, were all in view, and any other number of hills too; hills too numerous to mention. They rose clear, blue, and silent from their beds of glistening white softness and all the while the cloud-sea ebbed and flowed around and between them, repainting the picture at a moment's notice and isolating each group from its neighbour. The continuation up Glen Garry towards Drumochter was hidden but away to the west, and clear as a bell at fifty miles, stood Ben Nevis and the Glen Coe peaks, all in rather a jumble but there nonetheless. For all that, the dominant feature of the view was Beinn a' Ghlo, where all the peaks stood clear above Shinagag.

'It was dazzling in its intensity and inviting in its apparent softness.' Photo: Steve Hindley.

I didn't know which way to turn or where to point the camera. This was a visual feast such as is granted only rarely: and all I did, for hours, was sit and soak it all up. There were a couple of subsidiary summits and I wandered from one to the other, sitting long and drinking it all in. It was the kind of scene you wish you could implant in your memory; a scene so rich that it brings into play all the senses because it gives rise to feelings so intense all the senses are stimulated: the softest breeze that would normally go unnoticed is felt by every hair on your face; the harsh sharpness of the rock upon which you sit and the lush growth of grass beneath your feet are savoured; in places like this there's always a meadow pipit to be heard, usually at the limit of hearing, but it's there just the same and appreciated all the better for the moment; the raven's croak is a shout of joy, and if you're blessed with total silence you can hear the sound of the life flowing through your veins. And have you ever noticed how life itself has a smell? You can smell it whenever you're far enough away from the works of man and if you're doubtful on that point then take a walk in a Caledonian pine forest in the springtime or on a Hebridean beach after a summer storm.

At such times of heightened awareness all the senses are stimulated simultaneously and the poor old brain has to deal with it all. The result is a stupor, a conflict of emotions that demands the time to be savoured. Maybe this is why days like this have such a profound effect on us. I suspect, although I don't know, that I climb mountains for days like this. It's my spirituality; my attempt to connect with the unseen and to know that which cannot be known but is sometimes shown.

In such a place and on such a day is silence but in that silence is a sound. It's the sound of the omnipresent pulse of life that 'civilisation' seeks to drown out for fear you'll ask the big questions; it's the sound of your heart beating in time to the rhythm of the universe, and it's the sound that comes with the contentment you feel as your soul bleeds out into eternity. It's the sound of the infinite and this is your church, the church where you are the intoxicated supplicant, and on such a day you see that what you seek is not outside of you at all. On such a day you see there are infinite parishes of the infinite; that you carry them all within you, and that you are free to come and go as you please.

If ever there was a day to sit on a mountain top and wait for the sunset this was it but when I checked my bag I saw I'd not got my head-torch. I left it as late as I dared before heading off down. On the way I passed some people going up. Theirs was the prize as each one climbed alone into the sunset in search of their infinity.

UPS AND DOWNS

By Mike Dixon

THE FIRST ADULT I saw openly weeping was during my initial year at primary school. Miss Hughes, a probationer who taught the class next door to mine, was being comforted by my own teacher as we were returning from afternoon break. When I later described this incident at home no specific reason was offered for her being upset but I was asked whether I and my peers had been misbehaving to cause it. This shows it was a long time ago. Most modern parents don't entertain the possibility of any wrong-doing by their kids.

On the variable picture on our first black and white TV which the budgie would disturb by perching on the portable aerial, grainy pictures brought news of an almighty slippage of coal waste onto a primary school in one of the South Wales valleys. The Aberfan Disaster resulted in the death of 116 children and 5 adults from Pantglas Junior School. It emerged that Miss Hughes had done a placement there during her teacher training course.

Three years later I was allowed to stay up late one school night to watch a major sporting event. Man Utd., playing in an all blue strip, beat Benfica in the European Cup Final. Amongst the celebrations and parading of the cup around Wembley, Bobby Charlton, the captain, was crying when he embraced the manager Matt Busby. I was puzzled but was told that this was not always a sign people were unhappy. Charlton had been lucky to survive the Munich air crash ten years previously unlike several of his team mates. Victory must have been especially poignant for him. Emotions were not straightforward things. There was a blurred dimension on occasions.

Growing up, events closer to home caused you to ponder your own mortality. The first death associated with steep places was when a boy the same age as me, in his teens, fell while fishing on the Little Orme. Convex grassy slopes turned to cliffs plunging into the sea which were by then attracting attention from climbers like Rowland Edwards. Announced in Monday's Assembly several girls were crying. Kevin had captured a few hearts as well as a few virginities. In the aftermath, suspicious fingers were pointed at his companions on the day, quite unwarrantedly. Not surprisingly his parents closed down their business and moved permanently from the area.

The late teenage period brought a premature death from a terminal illness and someone killed in the military. Climbing ended a few lives early. If the mountains didn't get you old age would mop things up eventually. Some can't give up the hills or climbing, others do because they can't compromise with diminishing grades or failing flesh. Some reinvent themselves to accommodate the changes: easier days, cycling among the hills, taking pictures of them. Reinvention is a battle for others.

Ruadh Stac Mòr (l) and A'Mhaighdean (r) in Autumn. All Photos: Mike Dixon.

The unfortunate end up with limited mobility, dogged by illnesses and a questionable quality of life. Luis Bunuel didn't climb but made films. He summed it up perfectly: 'In the name of Hippocrates, doctors have invented the most exquisite form of torture ever known to man: survival.'

In October 2016 the hills were a golden blaze and I took the opportunity of superb weather, but dwindling daylight, to visit the Fisherfield area from Poolewe. Even with bike access it still felt a long way. One of the diciest stretches involved crossing the windswept causeway near Carnmore. This short concrete section was quite the gustiest spot of the whole day despite its lowly altitude. With white horses rearing up on the Dubh and Fionn Lochs I wobbled across mindful of some metalwork and spikes in the water. If I came off, I might be impaled on them perhaps creating a first in the mountain accident reports and a gruesome but somehow fitting incident for upcoming Halloween.

The north-west ridge of A' Mhaighdean is the finest non-technical way to climb the mountain but ahead of me was a stalking party. The leader of the trio didn't make any attempt at communication. Either he thought I was staying on the track and heading for Shenavall or he was going to teach me a lesson and shoot me later for disturbing his clients' sport. They crossed to the lower reaches of the ridge whereas I continued a little higher before heading out of sight for the same feature. I was soon padding up delightfully gneiss slabs while the molten disc of Fuar Loch Beag came into view in the mini, crucible-like coire to my left. It forms a hidden sanctum within this gigantic, wilderness retreat.

Further up the format went into cinemascope to reveal the loch's larger relative, with a backdrop comprising the cone of Beinn Dearg Bheag and

The Beinn Deargs and An Teallach seen over the shoulder of Ruadh Stac Mòr, with Fuar Loch Mòr in the foreground, from the North-west Ridge of A' Mhaighdean.

the drama of An Teallach's jagged ridge. And that was just the view in one direction. All the Munro baggers after the Big 6 (or Big 5 now Beinn a' Chlaidheimh has been demoted to Corbett status), usually from Shenavall, don't know what they're missing. At least they get the summit view down the Fionn Loch to Beinn Airigh Charr, Trotternish and Harris beyond. Water, mountains, sea and islands, that magical fusion, the signature of the North West.

Suddenly a gun went off from below but no bullet seemed to have entered me so I continued. The gneiss gave way to sandstone, a Norman-like square tower to turn, and soon after the top.

From there I headed to Ruadh Stac Mòr to complete the circuit. Eight weeks ago James Edwards had been here. I'd met him when he was doing supply teaching. Unluckily he'd ended up with a 'challenging' bunch (PC-speak for 'little fuckers') and at lunch break looked frazzled. At 3 o'clock he seemed to have visibly aged. He'd rather be guiding clients up Grade V/VI routes than a life of this he confessed. But he was youngish, resilient and grinned a lot, with many classroom and mountain days ahead of him. He liked big walks as part of the climbing day which is what the Fisherfield is all about. As I looked at the broken sandstone hillside I wondered what had happened to him on that day. The terrain doesn't need to be that steep or technically difficult for one slip to break your body. Four days prior, a lack of concentration and some slippery rock nearly made me a statistic on the East Ridge of Lurg Mhòr heading out to the top of Meall Mòr. I tempted fate further by some worrying moves to retrieve an errant walking pole.

And on that day amongst the glory of the Fisherfield I thought of exactly one year ago to the day when a family member's body finally shut down. Worn-out, bed-ridden, immobile, mostly asleep at the end but weak smiles still punctuated the infant-like stares.

Less than two months later and with the benefit of reading an obituary, I was staring up at a mountain where James Edwards had left his mark, on the South Face of Mount Aspiring in New Zealand's Southern Alps. A picture of his appears in the current New Zealand Alpine Club's Mount Aspiring Region guide. It's of an earlier attempt on what later became a direct line up the centre of the face. The following day I was peering over the top of this feature after completing a more pedestrian route up this beautifully sculptured peak encased in ice formations more typical of South America.

By February of 2017 I'd transferred to the North Island and was driving round the Bay of Plenty and the East Cape down to the bottom of Hawke's Bay. Huge sweeps of empty sand with tangles of driftwood at their backs, vivid Maori carvings, colgate-white churches and magnificent horses and foals which approached you with absolute trust. Three days in a semi-dreamscape, lubricated by the fine local wines. And scattered amongst all this beauty there is poverty and its associated issues. In Gisborne I witnessed domestic violence in the street by a man on a woman and child. All that can be said in his defence is that the fist became an open palm when he turned his attention to the girl. 'It happens all the time,' commented a local lady in a desensitised, matter of fact tone, pausing to

Descending the North-west Ridge of Mount Aspiring.

allow her dog to pee on a nearby car tyre before resuming their evening stroll.

The next day on the Mahia Peninsula, on a beach easing out to shallow child friendly waters, families were picnicking, swimming, creating sculptures in the sand and playing cricket with sticks acting as wickets. It was the last day of freedom before New Zealand pupils returned to school after the long summer holiday. There were buckets, spades and rubber rings with not a smart phone or iPad in sight. It could have been a scene from my own childhood. Then a growling, black, 4WD vehicle with dark glass pulled up. A woman, heavily pregnant, got out and proceeded to slug on a lager bottle and chain smoke. Her partner had arms as big as my thighs with six skull tattoos on one. Any comments directed at the slack health practices of the woman might be the prompt for another visit to his tattooist for skull number seven. Anyone who is sceptical that inequalities begin in the womb should observe something like this. In five years time the woman will be enrolling her child at a local school. The Kiwi James Edwardses will have big challenges ahead of them.

Further south the city of Napier is a homage to art deco architecture. One of the most famous frontages shouldn't be taken at its glitzy face value. It's the one-time headquarters of the National Tobacco Company as the sign still proclaims. Behind the jazz age spangle and opulence of Long Island, Jay Gatsby had a past he wanted to hide. In New Zealand the Hawkes's Bay wineries and plush restaurants aren't far from the towns with their posters about domestic abuse. At least we were seeing an aspect

The National Tobacco Company Building in Napier.

Mount Cook from 35,000 feet.

not revealed in the glossy tourist literature. Places and people are never that black and white.

From Christchurch to Inverness involves a lot of air time. Seeing the world from a great height always reawakens the notion of existence being a cosmic joke. Harry Lime via the words of Graham Greene and the charisma of Orson Welles developed his own take on this theme: 'Look down there. Tell me. Would you really feel any pity if one of those dots stopped moving forever? If I offered you twenty thousand pounds for every dot that stopped, would you really, old man, tell me to keep my money, or would you calculate how many dots you could afford to spare? Free of income tax, old man. Free of income tax.' Substitute money for religious fundamentalism and Lime's sentiments have a chillingly modern ring.

The flight began with a south-west course over the Southern Alps and a perfect end to my antipodean tour: Mount Cook living up to its Maori name Aoraki by piercing through a sea of cloud. Then the plane headed south, shadowing the west coast and there was the triangle of Aspiring poking out too. Zoom in and those dots who play on its flanks all have hearts, histories and families. Since my ascent at the beginning of December there had been a death on it to someone I'd had a pint with one balmy evening in Wanaka and a pair had tumbled together from high up the South-west Ridge leaving them seriously injured. If the medical student from Dunedin does pull through he'll have a lot of personal experience to inform his career. And James Edwards must have had one

The South Face of Mount Aspiring seen from Glendhu Bay.

hell of a grin when he emerged from the South Face after completing his new route on the second attempt, to which he and his two partners gave the name 24 Hour Party People.

It's not easy to shut out the negative memories associated with a place. I watched all the Aberfan documentaries to commemorate the fiftieth anniversary of the disaster. A muted anger pervaded them: 'Buried alive by the National Coal Board,' 'corporate manslaughter.' Most of the victims were too young for their families ever to experience closure. Places which evoke sadness and joy can become more hallowed for some. The Little Orme, Cadair Idris, Stob Coire Albannaich and now Mount Aspiring all have this quality for me.

Mixed emotions swirled around after one of the best holidays ever. I drifted off to sleep and awoke woozily to see a familiar shape below in soft focus: Bonar Bridge, nearly home. But Bonar Bridge has no white armadillo shaped building close by. Hours and hours more of air conditioned, cramped, cattle truck class to go. However there is the opportunity to imbibe an inordinate amount of free booze from Sydney to London. Time passed very pleasantly. I looked forward to one final opportunity for more of the same on the last leg from Heathrow. But since my outward flight, British Airways had gone the way of Sleazy Jet and had started charging for food and drink on its internal flights. Ah, the vicissitudes of life.

A BAPTISM OF EGGS

By Mike Jacob

*There are hard men with pieces of fencing wire for fuses in their
nervous systems*

Iain Smart ('A Tree for Each Season')

IN THE ARCHIVES OF the ornithological section of the National Museum of
Scotland, Edinburgh, are two ordinary-looking box files with no great
apparent appeal. They contain treasure, however, in the form of the only
remaining personal diaries from Harold Raeburn's formative years. That
they should have lain un-researched for nearly 90 years would seem to
be a bit of a mystery; presumably they were thought to be a somewhat
dry catalogue for an activity that today is considered to have been rather
shameful – the collection of birds' eggs. It is an appropriate co-incidence
that these diaries, along with Harold's egg-collection, should have ended
up in the depths of this imposing building overlooking Chambers Street,
an area of the city which would have been very familiar to Harold with
its proximity to the Raeburn family brewery in nearby Merchant Street.

Harold's collection, accompanied by the 19 diaries, was donated to the
museum in 1929, three years after his death, by his sisters Ethel and Ruth,
who were the executors for his estate. Raeburn (born 1865) showed an
avid interest in natural-history and the museum still holds a grey partridge
(from Hoperig, East Lothian) and a ptarmigan (from Ben Cruachan)
donated by Harold himself in 1888 and 1896 respectively. Bob McGowan,
Senior Curator (Ornithology) at the Museum when I visited a few years
ago, wrote to me:

*His interest was clearly a serious one, as the eggs were neatly side-
blown with a single hole, in the 'professional' manner, and inscribed with
locality and date of collection and initialled 'HR'. It is unclear who
schooled Raeburn in his preparation technique and note-taking although
egg collecting was a very widespread pastime at that time. Collections
were often built up through the purchase of eggs, often singles, from
natural history dealers. Collections of full clutches, personally-collected,
complemented with collection data tended to be more unusual and were
indicative of more methodical and determined individuals. Raeburn's
collection is a good example of this type of 'scientific collection' and it is
only clutches with accurate collection data that have any true scientific
value today. Not only did Raeburn inscribe his eggs but he recorded much
useful information in a series of associated notebooks. This is generally
in the form of chronological observations on clutches collected as well
as detailed descriptions of the nests' breeding colonies. More unusual is
one notebook recording a series of fresh weights of eggs during the period
1885–95.*

The diaries, as one would expect, are of more interest to an ornithologist than a mountaineer but some of the material provides an interesting insight into the late-Victorian world of the youthful Raeburn. In the following digest, all *quotations* are taken from his entries – it is notable that even within his private writing the grammar is perfect – with the need only for the addition of some occasional punctuation to improve the flow. A graphic presentation of his egg-collecting activities is given below:

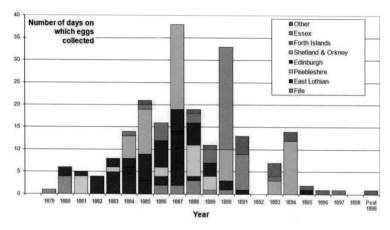

TABLE 1
(by Hal Jacob)

Various geographical areas have been amalgamated for clarity and convenience. Harold tended to visit the same places in successive years and the main ones were (using his spellings):

EDINBURGH – Costorphine, Craiglockhart, Dalmahoy Crags, Fernieness, Duddingston, Longniddrie, Ravelston, Ratho, Gogarburn, Moorfoot, Gladhouse, Thriepmuir, Pentlands, Harperrig.

FIFE – Redwellswood, Kingask, Tentsmuir, Largo Bay, Bonnytown, St Andrews, Troy Wood, Kinshaldy Wood.

PEEBLESHIRE – Fruid, Tweedsmuir, Kingledores Glen, Lyne, Talla, Auchencorth, Manor, Blackhope, Coalyburn, Mossfennan.

SHETLAND & ORKNEY – Unst, Tethaland, Tingwall, Yell, Bressay, North Roe, Papa Stour, Noss, Lyra Skerry, Fugla, Walls, Coul Head.

EAST LOTHIAN – Dirleton, Belhaven Bay, Haddington, Gullane.

FORTH ISLANDS – Isle of May, Bass Rock, Inchmickery, Lamb Island.

ESSEX – Romford, Southminster, Hornchurch, Hadleigh, Blackmore, Hainholt, Chignall, Laindon, Ingrebourne, and various parks and woods.

The collection itself consists of nearly 500 sets of either single or clutches of eggs which were taken predominantly in the nesting-season months of April, May and June.

Raeburn's boyhood interest in birds is confirmed by the earliest eggs in the collection, which were removed from the nest of a Sandwich Tern on the Farne Islands, Northumberland, in June 1874 when he was 9 years old, which suggests a family holiday perhaps. Like most youngsters, for whom collecting useless things is an obligatory stage of childhood, Harold probably put the eggs on a shelf and forgot about them. In the early 1880s, he renewed his interest in ornithology with eggs collected from various species of birds in and around Edinburgh, using local trains or his bicycle to make the journeys. He was not averse to shooting, for on New Year's Day, 1885 he … *went down to R. to shoot …shot a pigeon and dug out a rabbit* and a few days later *went to St. Andrews and shot a cormorant and several ducks*. Later, he makes it plain that he grew to despise the indiscriminate killing of such magnificent birds as ravens, ospreys and golden eagles, preferring to do his shooting with a camera.

Harold's approach to his subject was not one of a casual enthusiast but that of a diligent and objective scientist, basing his work upon accurate observation and record-keeping. He carefully weighed his eggs *from 1890 nearly all on chemical balances … before being blown* and the results of his painstaking research were later published in learned periodicals of the time. Of particular note is that he was elected to membership of the Royal Physical Society of Edinburgh on the 18 March 1885, a few months before his twentieth birthday. This distinguished and august Society was instituted in 1771, with Royal Charter in 1778, and was inaugurated 'for the promotion of Zoology and other branches of Natural History.' Membership was very exclusive and candidates, fairly typically for the 1880s, required several proposers and seconders from amongst existing Fellows and had to submit details of their personal background and their achievements and interests. Being a member of a successful business family would certainly have helped and Harold Raeburn could well have been the youngest ever to gain admittance to this select organisation.

The first diary of real interest is a self-titled *Journalistic, Literary and Personal* notebook which includes memos about items he had seen in publications, such as 'The Field' magazine. A noted ornithologist of the day was Dr H. Saxby, who had lived and worked on Shetland. He contributed seven papers on ornithological subjects to the 'Zoologist', a monthly natural-history journal, between 1861 and 1871, and was author of *The Birds of Shetland*. The precocious Harold, showing the questioning mind of a seasoned scientist, queries some of Saxby's remarks and descriptions, which differed from his own observations, for he too was fascinated by Shetland. This decade-long association started in 1884: a period notable for his solo explorations on lonely crags and sea-cliffs in search of eggs and which provided the foundation for his remarkable mountaineering career.

The distant northern island archipelago that makes up Shetland may seem a rather strange choice as a regular destination for a young man living in Edinburgh. However, the main attraction would have been the wealth of bird-life, with migrant sea-birds flocking to the islands to breed and the great advantage, at latitude 60°N, of long hours of summer daylight.

A typical visit was made towards the end of May, 1887. *He left Leith at 6.30am by the St. Magnus* with the boat calling in at Aberdeen before stopping *at St. Margaret's Hope* (South Ronaldsay, Orkney) *during the night, nothing to be seen for fog and a good deal of rain falling at intervals all day* before arriving at Lerwick. He usually stayed, for some of the time at least, at the home of the Scott family who lived at Melby, Walls in West Mainland. Within sight was Papa Stour, one of the most fertile islands in Shetland, with an indented and precipitous coastline featuring remarkable wicks and geos, columnar stacks and sea-caves.

Detailed observations were made about the birds that he saw on his walks. The difficulties encountered during his solitary wanderings over the unfrequented cliffs and sea-shore are illustrated by a day in early June. He *left Walls at 9am and went first to GrassW. where he swam out to one holm ... seven or eight nests of the L.B. gull but only 1 egg.* The following day he *went over to Papa Stour and arranged to go round the cliffs and stacks but the weather got worse and the wind shifted to the S.W. bringing a nasty sea on the west side of the islands, so had to give it up. The weather got worse ... a very heavy rain ... driven by a strong gale ... it was nearly impossible to face it. The tide was out and a stack near the shore accessible from below so, seeing a couple of pairs of the Greater Blackbacked gulls were nesting on the flat summit, I had a try at scaling it. I got up to within 20ft of the top when a sheer piece of rock stopped all progress. Got a herring-gull's nest about halfway up with three eggs. Mr. Scott sent a boat across for me with three boys but the wind had risen before we started to go back and the tide was running strong so we had to leave her and take a larger one. We managed to cut the tide with success and got into Melby all right. In the evening we went out to the big boat to secure her moorings, the wind was worse than ever and the tide was running strong. We ran out before the wind at a fine rate but had a stiff pull coming back. Mr. Scott says it is the worst night we have had this summer. It was fine to see the meeting of the wind and tide, the water leaping right up into the air.*

On his trips, Harold met, and obtained information from, fishermen, crofters and other ornithologists, and continued to explore the islands, particularly the spectacular cliffs where he could admire the wheeling, soaring flight of such perfectly adapted birds as gannets, skuas and eagles. The fascination of this solitary wandering, peering round ledges on lonely cliffs and scrambling over sea-washed boulders, is succinctly described by Adam Nicolson –

If puffin and gannets are from different worlds, the shags are from another universe. It is an all-power meeting with an extraordinary, ancient, corrupt, imperial, angry, dirty, green-eyed, yellow-gaped, oil-skinned, iridescent, rancid, rock-hole glory ... they are ... ancient beyond any sense ...the shag, or something very like it, flew over seas in which the ichthyosaurs swam. Your head comes over the lip of rock, and there ... you see the couple of young, half-formed embryonic creature, shag chicks, rat-birds, serpentine, leathery, hideous.

Nowadays, the collecting of birds' eggs in Britain has long been outlawed. However, during the nineteenth century, there was an explosion of interest in the natural world and the capture of animals, dead or alive, was considered to be a perfectly legitimate method of obtaining information. In the 1860s, the Victorian obsession with collecting anything – minerals, butterflies, botanical specimens, eggs – and shooting wild animals for sport, particularly birds, reached a peak.

It may seem difficult to understand the attraction of such pastimes; however, I was shown one of these old private collections displayed in specially-built mahogany cabinets in the NMS – and it is an eye-opener. Row upon row of beautifully coloured and perfectly-matching patterned eggs, arranged in clutches in nests of cotton-wool, allow one to understand the attraction of the labour and the passion of the protagonists.

Harold gave a reading to a meeting of the Royal Physical Society of Edinburgh on 18 April 1888 entitled 'The Summer Birds of Shetland, with Notes on their Distribution, Nesting and Numbers.' Even then, the White-tailed Eagle (Erne or Sea-Eagle) was near extinction in Shetland but Harold was privileged to see one of these *fine birds...though they are very much reduced from what they were fifty years ago.* What is quite clear, however, is that Harold both approached and researched his subject with a remarkable maturity for someone so young.

In 1889, Harold, nearing the completion of his academic studies, succeeded in obtaining two eggs from the eyrie of a golden eagle; a kind of ornithological Holy Grail and an accomplishment which presumably sorted the 'bird men' from the 'bird boys'. He doesn't say exactly where this was, other than near Forfar, but it was probably one of the crags in Glen Mark or Glen Lee. Obviously, the hunt for eggs took place in the early months of the year, on this occasion it was 12 April (the only day in 1889 in the OTHER category; see Table 1):

...while searching a snow covered range of cliffs for the nest of the Golden Eagle I used quantities of snowballs to put off the sitting bird as she might happen to have her nest in any of the ledges into which I could not see. I afterwards climbed to one of the ledges thus bombarded and just as my eyes rose above the level of the ledge the female eagle scrambled off the nest and shuffled to the edge of the cliff opening her enormous wings the while and launched out easily into the air. Several of the snowballs must have whizzed past her head and shattered on the rock immediately behind her. Although small avalanches were continually dropping from the cliff above, still the eagle must have known avalanches do not fall up, besides, though she could not see me, or I her owing to the breadth of the ledge, the male eagle had seen me and probably given her notice. After being put off the nest she sailed straight away, disappearing in a few seconds in the mist and snow and I saw nothing more of either

her or her mate. The eggs were only 3 or 4 days old. Neither of the eagles uttered a sound the whole time.

Not everyone whom he encountered in the glens welcomed the presence of the stranger. After hunting for peregrine falcons on a crag at the head of the Manor Water, Peeblesshire *a man came up to me calling himself the under-keeper and told me that if I came again I should have to go to Peebles. I said "hardly that, I think" and asked him what he did with the young ravens. He refused to tell me, when I said "Sell them, I suppose"*

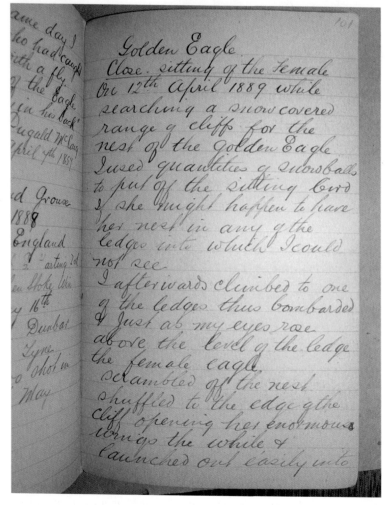

Raeburn's account of the collection of the Golden Eagle's eggs in 1889.
Photo: Noel Williams.

*The very eggs: clearly showing Raeburn's initials and the date in the fainter writing.
Photo: Noel Williams.*

*but he looked sulky and wouldn't say. He also said he should inform Mr.
Scin next morning. The poor fellow forgot that he had nothing to tell Mr.
Scin, not even my name. Later, Harold wrote that Mr. E. tells me today
(April 30th) that Mr. Scin is the Earl of Wemyss' keeper and has no
business whatever with the Bitch Craig. It appears Lord Arthur Cecil
wants young peregrines and Scin is to get them for him for a
consideration.*

The New Routes section of the 2016 *SMCJ* has several entries for the
Bitch Craig but the preceding paragraph reveals, as might be anticipated,
that Raeburn was exploring there over a century earlier.

By this time, Harold was in regular correspondence with some leading
naturalists and ornithologists of the day, such as John Harvie-Brown
(1844–1916). Harvie-Brown made numerous expeditions throughout
Scotland, visiting remote islands in his yacht, the Shiantelle. Although
he wasn't a climber, Harvie-Brown was interested in the Scottish hills and
became a member of the SMC in 1891, two years after its formation, and
contributed notes to the SMC *Journal* from time to time.

In 1890, Harold visited Shetland and Papa Stour again and, fortunately,
left an interesting account of his findings in a scientific article published
the following year in the 'Zoologist'. He wrote – *In the old times the men
of Papa had a reputation as climbers little inferior to those of Unst or
Foula, but for many years past climbing has been almost entirely given
up, and I was informed that only two men on the island are now able to
make the ascent of the Lyra Skerry. I was fortunate enough, on the
occasion of my second visit, to secure the services of the best of these men.
He rejoices in the name of "Long Peter", and certainly deserves the*

adjective, standing some 6ft. 3in. in his "rivlins" (raw cowhide shoes worn by the Shetlanders). I had a good illustration, during the course of the day, of the great advantage his enormous reach gives him in cliff climbing ... the all but inaccessible Lyra Skerry. This, to which we now pulled, is very incorrectly termed a skerry, which means, strictly speaking, a low wave-washed rock. It is really a huge "stack" of porphyritic rock, 180ft. high and about a quarter of a mile in circumference. It lies between Fogla and the cliffs of Papa, from which it is distant about a furlong, and has two fine outlying stacks or pillars on either side, called respectively "Snolda" and the "Fit." Lyra is perpendicular, or overhanging, on all sides except one small portion at the S.E. corner, just to the right of the magnificent sea-floored cavern that passes through the island. This was pointed out to me as "the road up."

Peter now took a coil of codline in his hand and, watching his opportunity as the light boat rose on the swell, jumped clear of the water on to a dry ledge. Though I did not relish the look of the said "road up", there was no other way of getting to the top; so I followed him. Peter now explained to me that there were only two "bad bits" – one about half-way up, and the other just at the very top. The first of these is where the rock projects so far as to overhang the sea below, and from where – the men were careful to inform me – a climber had fallen some years before but, striking the water, was picked up by his comrades in the boat, escaping with a broken arm and a severe shock from a fall of 90 feet. They added, perhaps unnecessarily, that he did not again attempt the ascent.

The last fifteen feet, however, according to Peter, was the only really difficult bit. I had on a pair of indiarubber shoes, which are capital for rock-climbing as long as they are dry; but when I had got up fifty feet or so I followed Peter's example and took to stockings, as they afford much greater freedom for the toes.

The ascent for the first 90 feet is comparatively easy, for the rock, though almost perpendicular, is firm. At this place occurs the first "bad bit," as it is necessary to round a point which projects clear over the water, and the ledges have a nasty outward slope. However, the finger grip is good and, watching where my guide put his feet, we were soon both past this. Above this part the climbing is comparatively easy till the top is neared. Here, within fifteen feet of the summit, we brought up against what appeared to me a totally unscaleable piece. We were clinging in a sort of shallow niche of the cliff, which above our heads narrowed to a crack about eight inches wide. If it had been a foot wider the ascent would have been comparatively easy by bracing the body against the sides, but its narrowness precluded this. I now watched Long Peter's movements with interest, and here was the point where his great height and long arms stood him in good stead for, stretching himself up the left-hand edge of the crack, he seized a small ledge nearly eight feet above the niche we stood in, and slowly and carefully he drew himself up, finding a crevice for his toes, and, getting another grip higher up, he was at the summit in a few seconds. He then passed the doubled codline down to me, which I fastened under my arms and, Peter putting a 56 lb. strain on it, I swarmed up the edge of the crack, and stood beside him on the top.

How Raeburn measured the amount of tension given by Peter is anybody's guess. An ascent of the cliffs, possibly a repeat of Long Peter's route, is described in the SMC's Northern Highlands (North) guidebook, page 442, where it is called Lyra Skerry, graded Severe, climbed in 1992.

Around this time, Harold developed an interest in photography and became a member of the prestigious Edinburgh Photographic Society (founded in 1861) of which another well-known Edinburgh mountaineer, William Inglis-Clark, was an active member. He visited the Shetland Islands again in both 1893 and 1894, and noted an eagle's nest on some huge sea cliffs at the Noup of Noss – *the nest looking a hopeless affair but I went down my 60ft rope as far as possible to try to see if anything could be made of what looked like a ... grassy ledge.* He retreated and tried the next day. The rope that Raeburn used was probably his own and would have been made of 3-stranded hemp or manila fibre. Unlike modern nylon rope there was no stretch in it, so that any shock-loading would have been transmitted directly to the belayer. The cliff was ... *extremely rotten ... hummocks giving way at the touch of the foot and B. several times let out about 6ft of slack rope so that I was obliged to do all my own holding on with the knowledge that if a tussock did give way the jerk I should give would inevitably have the effect of persuading Mr.B.S.* (Baigrie Sutherland) *to try a race with me to the bottom of the Noup, which as I should have about 100ft or so less to go, would probably result in a win for me, B.S. a good second as he is a 13stone man. The problem is given –*

> *13 stone falls from the height of 600ft*
> *10½ stone falls from 500ft*
> *Which gets there first?*

(For readers familiar only with the metric system, *stone* here refers not to a large pebble but to the imperial system of measurement).

Although he must have had nerves of steel, Raeburn's precarious predicament on this huge, dangerous cliff may have addled his scientific mind and made him forget the findings of Galileo and Newton – that gravity exerts the same force on all objects and that, ignoring wind-resistance, he would most certainly have reached sea-level before his companion. In the event, the question was not answered by practical experimentation for he succeeded in climbing back up ... *B.S. hauling of course as at several places the sandstone crops through, forming small overhanging bits not possible of ascending unaided.* He came to the conclusion that he needed a *good solid 300ft rope and a couple at least of good men above and a windlass to haul up and even then I doubt if one could get in to the nest as it appears to be in a deep recess and a good deal overhung.* By now, his long-suffering belayer had grown tired of his cliff-top duties and *then went off to attend to his sheep.*

Harold was also experimenting with different photographic methods; he mentions the use of a telephoto lens, and sounds rather intolerant of S. (presumably, Mr. Sutherland) who ...*stupidly forgot the iron tripod head* ... and, over the coming years, he pioneered ways to use a camera to capture the drama of birds and nests in their natural surroundings. A few years on, in Jan, 1901 he gave a lecture to the Edinburgh Photographic Society on 'Birds' Nest Photography'. Parts of the presentation and their expression reveal Raeburn's extreme confidence in his views. Like a modern-day, blustering politician, the mere force of his certainty would have been enough to persuade any doubters as to the authority of his argument and anyone prepared to challenge him would have had to be on top of both their facts and their debating skills. This is illustrated, for example, when he compares different types of camera ... *for this class of work a stand-camera is absolutely essential and a snapshot camera utterly useless*. A less-sure person may have used more considered language, but who would take issue with someone who pursued his interest with such dedication that he took his weighty camera to *the topmost boughs of some lofty tree, on the quaggy bottom of some reedy lake, or precariously clinging to a very inadequate ledge of a dizzy cliff*?

His younger brother, Norman, was also present on Shetland on this occasion, although it would seem that he did not travel there with Harold, and they both contributed articles about their observations to the *Annals of Scottish Natural History* in 1895. Harold continued to write to Harvie-Brown, the last-dated letter in 1907, mostly about sightings of birds in the Scottish hills. He also corresponded, in 1898 and 1899, with Hugh Macpherson, another well-known ornithologist, about his observation of eagles on Skye, whilst walking between Sligachan and Coruisk.

One obvious question from a study of Table 1 is why Raeburn should have been collecting eggs from the flatlands of Essex? The answer is that he lived in Romford for reasons to do with his training as a brewer. Romford, then, was a small market town and not part of the greater suburbia which now surrounds London, brewing being the town's main industry. He noted, however, that ... *the opposite (Kentish) side of the Thames is far more interesting than the Essex side*. He travelled and explored ... *went a long round today on the cycle. Roads in fairly good condition and a beautiful day. Distance covered about 50 – 60 miles* and visited London Zoo, which he admired in general, but felt sorry for the peregrines and ravens confined in their cages.

Table 1 also demonstrates that, after his visit to Shetland in 1894, his egg-collecting waned as mountaineering gradually took precedence although he always maintained his interest in ornithology. However, Harold Raeburn was also accomplished in yet another surprising sporting context (it wasn't sailing) and I hope that the Hon. Editor will allow me to provide further details in the next issue of the *Journal*.

HOT ROCKIN' IN THE COSTA BLANCA

By Smiler Cuthbertson

It HAD BEEN OVER twenty years since Clare and I had been on my first and only visit to Calpe. When we had seen the superb Peñon de Ifach, the *Via Valencianos* was my most wanted route, but I realised it did look a bit too hard for her.

12 April 2016 – We were heading once again for Benidorm, myself and Richard, a great friend and past client over 15 years, he lives near Durham. We joined up with Geoff Lowe from Inverness and Ian Innes from my village, Dores, to revisit this fashionable bolt-clipping paradise and see what Hot Rockin' was all about. My big concern was: would the chronic arthritis which had plagued me for a year ease with the heat? Richard had strict instructions, you lead, OK!

Day 1. Landing at midday in Alicante, we followed Geoff and Ian's usual routine, grabbing the hire car and heading straight for Sella. Wow, after Inverness it was hot but a couple of single pitches later, we were getting the hang of climbing in the sun. The lads said 'first and every day, around five or six pitches would be the task', and so it turned out, we had real fun. From the very start, standards weren't pushed: 5+ was enough for us.

Sella was great climbing, just a little polished at times. The lads picked out the routes, and Richard and I led each climb after them. Mostly 4s with the occasional 5 or 5+, it was nice just getting our daily quota in. Like all bolt-clipping climbs however, one soon forgets some names, but at the 'Sector Competición' at Sella, *Desbioquea que No* (5) stood out for quality. Everyone belayed each other, the leader lowering off and exchanging leads, often leaving quickdraws in place to get as much climbing in as possible, and pausing only occasionally for some water or shade. Yes, superb, just as I remembered my routes with Clare those many years ago.

Around five-thirty the lads remembered the cheap but nice nine-story hotel we were booked into in Benidorm started serving meals at half-past-seven. I was still surprised but happy with my initial successes on the sharp end, and pleased to see Richard going very well.

We drove towards the concrete jungle that is Benidorm, the Spanish countryside flashing by. The consensus was a beer or two was required. I hadn't had any alcohol for a year with my condition, so I stuck to Cola, and Richard joined me. The lads were happy to quench their thirst with beers. The bar opposite the hotel is run by a nice Yorkshire couple, who were, as expected, very amenable to us. A bonus was the box of film CDs on the bar for sale, to thumb through, at a ridiculously cheap price (three euros each).

The self-service routine at meal times suits climbers, with an initial urge to gross out on vast quantities of food, but as the week passed by, I think

Richard Jolley abseiling in to the ill-fated Magical Mystery Tour. Photo: Smiler Cuthbertson.

Richard following the Magical Mystery Tour. Smiler was already several pitches too far.
Photo: Smiler Cuthbertson.

we all tempered slightly and usually it was good three-course food. The breakfasts were equally scrumptious with the added bonus (if one was careful) of nabbing day food off the counters.

Day 2. We decided on Toix Ouest. I only had a faint memory from my first and only other visit, but the climbing didn't let me down. Very similar routes to Sella except more open, on a long ridge of steep slabby faces. The crags, many of them, were as accessible as Sella, with an abundance of routes of all grades, especially the Grade 5s we were after, and there were even some two-pitch routes.

In his younger days, Geoff had spent a few years living here, working as an unofficial rock climbing guide (quite legal those years ago). His friend and past 'employer', Richard Mayfield, still runs the Orange House, a hostel favoured by climbers. In the past it was possible to have free lodgings, in exchange for doing chores each day around the hostel. Sadly that's out nowadays. Later in the week we were to meet up with Richard M. and one instantly took a liking to this guy.

Toix Ouest was good. *Green Route 2, Espolon Limaban* and *Red Route 11* (all 5s) are the routes I recall: some great climbing. We all were very happy just clipping the bolts and having fun. We'd be back.

Day 3. Marin was chosen from the many crags available, for its main face has as the guidebook says, 'the best selection of lower grade routes in the Costa Blanca'. Neat routes of our preferred standard, set at an altitude higher than previously, it meant a cooler and very acceptable temperature, at least until the midday sun took over. Even then, the slight breeze cooled us in the warm sunshine. Out of the four or five good routes we did, *Kiki* (5+) stood out as a real classic. Marin is a nice little slabby crag.

Day 4. Richard and I had plans for the south face route on the Peñon de Ifach, the *Via Valencianos* 5+ and 240 metres long, this huge centre piece of the Costa Blanca. This stunning tower sits proudly on a short peninsula and majestically overlooks Calpe. We'd been told there were fewer Brits likely to be on the route on a Saturday, as it was a hotel 'changeover day'.

I'd seen the tower before, some routes around a 1000 feet long, but on my first visit, I hadn't wanted to push Clare into trying any of these huge climbs, and we had just gazed at the huge walls. I'd missed out on the Peñon route on my first visit to Calpe, but now with Richard, I could do it! However, after sixteen years since it was first climbed and hundreds of ascents it appeared some damage had been done to the route in terms of polished rock. We had two guidebooks, mine and Ian's scruffy copy. I originally thought his was much older than my 2005 version, but it was actually from 2013 and well used. Both guidebook versions of the *Via Valencianos* route do specifically mention how the crux pitch is very polished but, unlike Ian's guide, mine doesn't mention that some aid may be necessary! Richard was offering to lead the pitch so I put my concern out of my head.

The first two pitches went easily enough at V. Diff/Severe but we were then confronted by an slightly overhanging, curving corner crack, with a single bolt runner. The limestone all around the bolt was very polished. After a couple of tentative moves above the bolt, Richard discovered a short 9mm perlon sling hidden away in the crack. A high runner! All he needed. He was up! It was a determined effort from Richard. I followed, but I hadn't his strength to free it, so I aided the polished area and put it to the back of my mind. Pitch 4 was my lead. I was still shaking slightly after the exertion of the hard pitch as I walked across an easy ledge for twenty feet to the base of huge slabs, split by cracks. This was the main feature of the route. A steep start would soon be followed by easier climbing up the cracked slab with what looked to be plenty of good holds.

After a fingery start on my first attempt, I realised I'd lost a bit of strength after the struggle on Richard's pitch. I felt I'd better step back down, rest and put some gear in! A good solid flake to my right took my Camelot 3. Now I had a good runner quite close to me. After a few minutes break I set off again and pulled on the small finger holds. I could see what to do, lock off and shoot my left foot out onto that sloper and I'd be up!

Bang! I slid off the very polished sloping foothold and ended up a few feet lower, upside down, unhurt but hanging by the Cam! Fortunately Richard had smartly stopped me and quickly lowered me the few feet to the start. A few minutes recovering and this time, there'd be no messing around with this polished rock. A Rock Three in the crack, a sling to stand in and I had gained the easier angled slab. Fifty metres later, I belayed and brought Richard up. As he was quite a distance below me at the start, I couldn't really see where he was climbing. When he reached the belay, I learned a local climber was also using our route to get to the harder climb further right, and on reaching where I'd started, this guy had gone out right and into a big corner. This was much less polished and Richard wisely did the same.

The long slabs we were on were all full runouts, and we were now hundreds of feet above the sea. The last slab pitch took Richard to the famous horizontal crest, a much photographed place where you look over to the whole of Calpe one way and the ocean the other. A superb sight. When I reached Richard I said that I must have one picture from here so I leaned over the arête using my elbows over the edge with both hands on the camera shot.

Horror! The battery compartment opened and down the other side of the ridge onto rough grassy ground went both batteries! On a rescue mission I did get one battery back, but I couldn't find the other. Annoyed, I returned to the stance and Richard took the shot.

We were now on easier ground and after a few steep moves it was plain sailing with a couple of easy runouts. We eventually moved together to the summit.

Several tourists had made the long (and slippery) walk up from the town for the views. Now with our trainers back on, we hurried down the tricky and polished rock of the track. It took about an hour or so until we could cut through the suburbia near the base and were soon sitting with cokes and ice creams. A quick call told us Geoff and Ian were on their way to collect us. Stories rang out long and loudly and I remember later having two glasses of wine that evening!

Day5: Guadalest was next. The place was not recorded in my old guidebook but Ian's copy had it. A quaint little village with a nice cafe, which gave us lovely morning *cafe cón leche*. Richard and I had promised a leisurely day after the exertions on the Peñon. After we all did a few straightforward climbs, the huge tower at the right-hand end of the crag attracted Geoff and Ian. Watching these two lead the route called *Carabassa* (5+) inspired me so Richard and I led it as well.

The usual quota of grade 4s and 5s succumbed to the team, including a prolonged attack on a 6a, *Borrosca de Neu*, which finally gave way to a determined attempt from Ian. He had pulled on some very tiny holds to succeed, so well done to him. Geoff and Richard weren't interested in top roping it, so I did it (badly) just for the tick. I reckoned it was full-on 6b!

Day 6. *The Magical Mystery Tour* fiasco. A re-visit to Toix Ouest was selected. Richard and I wanted to do a bit of exploring and decided to try the reputedly easy but good *Magical Mystery Tour*, a 5a (HVS) sort of sea-level traverse. The other team decided to stick to the upper cliffs. We drove to a café for our morning fix of *cafe cón leche*.

As we sat in the warm, morning sunshine, scoffing pastries, Ian suddenly realised he'd left his rock shoes on the veranda of the hotel room. The lads decided to drop us off first at the parking spot for Toix Ouest, but not before we called at a nearby supermarket for some day food and drinks. While we were buying these snacks, who should turn up but Geoff's old friend from earlier times, Richard Mayfield, owner of the Orange House and (I think) an MIC or at least MIA. He had a lady client that day and was also heading for the same traverse. After introductions we said we'd follow the pair along the route. This would allow me to discard my heavy Costa Blanca guidebook.

Geoff and Ian duly dropped us off at the car park some fifteen minutes after the Orange House team had gone, and Richard and I followed the track along and down to the cliff edge overlooking the sea. We found their rucksacks and the in situ abseil rope, and we were happy to use the prepared descent. I went first, steeply down for some 6 to 7m until I came across an old wooden ladder fixed to the wall. Abseiling past this, I soon discovered the wall overhung dramatically, and I followed an extremely dodgy-looking steel ladder. This rusting pile of steel dropped around eighty to a hundred feet down the overhanging wall. I now recalled my old guidebook mentioning 'some ancient ladders can be found, leading down to ledges above the sea'. I was now hanging quite a way from the rock face and I clearly viewed the full length of this spectacular abseil. Reaching the base ledges, I called for Richard to come down, taking a couple of great photos of him in mid-air, together with the rusty ladder.

We sorted the gear out and started the traverse. It was virtually walking country at first, but soon I was regretting not bringing the guide book. The climbing got more spectacular, more difficult, and soon I was leading some intricate and steeper ground, occasionally following a downward line which, because of the lack of bolts and trad gear, proved quite exciting for Richard to second.

Following my nose and the very occasional rusty bolt, the climbing continued to be exciting. After around four lengthy pitches, using rather tenuous nut and Friend belays, I remembered we somehow, somewhere had to go upwards! I followed the odd old bolt, and at last a pillar of rock, covered in seagull poo, led upwards. This was not easy but there was one bolt runner. With some effort, and no other gear, I reached an alcove with a rusty bolt. I added in a couple of poor nuts and belayed as best I could. Richard came up and we didn't take long to realise we were maybe out of our depth.

We made a rapid decision to retreat. This was serious country indeed. Above us, a bulging wall looked pretty difficult, with just one old bolt showing around thirty feet above the stance. The deciding factor for me was that the very steep wall led into a huge scooped area above which there was some pretty overhanging stuff. This reminded me of the Cornice area on Derbyshire limestone. I was climbing OK, but not well enough for this. We'd have to go back and escape by those ladders.

The ropes snaked down for around eighty feet before hitting some ledges above the sea. I made a mental note that one of our two ropes was destined for the briny, but realised there wasn't much choice. Eyeing up the rusty bolt with some concern, I murmured quietly to myself 'get on with it'. The abseil went without incident and soon we were reversing our approach line. We did alternative leads along familiar ground and in an hour or so the steel ladder appeared.

There was little choice but to escape by the ladders. I offered to do the ascent, me being lighter in weight than Richard, and deep down I was ready for the upper section as well. Richard thoughtfully removed any excess weight of rock gear I wouldn't need, and with lots of conviction, I stepped onto the bottom rung. Nothing moved! Ever so slowly and steadily, I moved up this vertical pile of rust! I even attached quickdraws to rungs every fifteen feet or so, with the idea that if the top disconnected itself, the fall would somehow be slowed by a one by one collapsing effect as the ladder broke into sections.

Some hope, but I added the runners anyway. Ten fairly serious minutes later and I reached the upper ledge. Tying on to the bottom of the wooden ladder, which at least wasn't rusty, I added as much trad gear as I could find around me. Richard came up without incident. It was now after 4 p.m. so there was little time to waste. Relieving Richard of all the trad gear, I climbed easily up the rickety ladder and added a dubious sling to the last rung. What followed was desperate.

After fifteen feet of steep and careful climbing, some crimps and side

The only way out: Smiler's troubles began where the ladder ends. Photo: Richard Jolley.

holds with only just adequate footholds, I found my only real runner, a Friend Two in a shallow hole. I shoved it in hard, completely unconcerned as to whether it would ever come out again, and I viewed the final climbing. There would be no way back! I could see the moves. Reach across left to the rounded edge of the groove we'd originally abseiled down, lay-away with the left hand, smear with the right foot, push the left foot across into the groove, swing the right hand across and up onto another lay-away, and trust there was something to go for after that.

That's what it looked like, and there wasn't any more gear! I poised for a minute or so and then made the moves. There was certainly no way back. I found a small jug high up in the groove and with a huge sigh of relief I pulled onto the top and the abseil point. I was 'too pooped to whoop' but apparently I did let out some sort of expletive. Wow! That was as hard and as serious as I'd led in forty years. Shaking slightly after the effort, I fixed the perfect double steel spike belay and sat gratefully down.

Richard was climbing well, but he admitted to having real trouble on the lay-away moves, as I had expected. Even on a top rope it would be difficult, pushing at least E4 and 5c (British) on the crux, but with a minimal amount of slack he finally emerged onto the ledge. He gave me considerable credit for the lead. As he neared the top, my mobile rang from inside the rucksack, stashed about 5m away from me. I shouted to him:

'That'll be the lads wondering where we are.' It was well after six o'clock now. I had been expecting some concern from them. With Richard now up, I returned Ian's call, not mentioning just yet any problems we may have had. The lads, after retrieving the missing rock shoes, had been climbing at Sella again, and with no contact from me all day, they were rightly concerned.

After talking things over with the Orange House, they drove back to Toix Ouest. They had just reached the parking spot when they received my call. Forty minutes later and back at the car, Richard and I finally relaxed. After a short resume of our epic, dinner in the hotel beckoned and Geoff sped us back. There were quite a few stories told over my pints (that's plural) that evening. Of course, the biggest error was not taking our own guidebook with us. We'd have read that after no more than a couple of pitches of traversing from the ladder's base, we should have started to turn upwards, thus finishing with the final two steady pitches, grade 4 and 5. Secretly though, after a year's arthritic lay-off, I was pretty pleased with the lead on that exit pitch. I still haven't found if it has ever been done. There were no signs of traffic or in situ protection and plenty of suspect rock that should have gone with time.

However, it has been done now, and with care, the ladders could provide the escape route someone might need. That last 7 to 9m though? Well....?

SUMMER SEAS TO WINTER WOES

By Phil Gribbon

ONCE UPON A TIME I took my old, decaying double canoe to the summer meet at the Allt Dearg cottage that nestles on the moor above the hotel at Sligachan. The decline in my uphill power meant that it was easier to be faintly strenuous at a slow and steady pace on the lowest available altitude. To be on a wide, watery expanse on the ruckled surface of a restless sea and gently paddling my canoe would fulfil this condition admirably.

Why not take her over to the nearby Isle of Scalpay? It lies on the far side of the narrow kyle by Strathaird and presents an uninspiring bare hillside of grass and heather above a formal block of monotonous conifers. It seems devoid of any possible attractions, but the district guidebook to the Islands of Scotland claims that Scalpay is surprisingly hilly and that to reach the highest point the going is rough from almost any direction.

Let's go, Mike, a bit of paddling won't go amiss, and for the asking we will have an exploratory outing that combines a seagoing voyage with a little bit of gentle mountain walking, plus the tantalising prospect of gaining a brief foothold on an isolated island that is normally beyond the reach of proletarian paddlers. It would be just a swift crossing from a convenient embarkation point at the ancient, disintegrating wooden quay close to the road.

We parked beyond Strollamus, then lugged the canoe bits to the water's edge and dumped them on a flattish myriad of boulders draped with slippery screeds of bladder wrack. It was a tedious business assembling the jigsaw of poles, frames and flexible features needed to construct a seaworthy canoe. We clambered into our orange waterproof gear, not being keen to drip wet drops off our paddles on to our dry trews, and tugged our craft closer to the water.

All this time we had been aware that a car had drawn up at the roadside. Its two occupants had got out and were talking animatedly at each other. They split up: one drove off westward, while the other with grace, style and poise shoved open the gate and walked towards us. She sported a smart, sleek crunchie bar-coloured two piece costume with delicate shoes, a dabble of jewellery and a matching handbag. This was not the normal garb for an inquisitive tourist. We stood our ground, awaiting developments.

'Say, fellas, are you here to take me over the water?'

She cast a deservedly scathing eye over our fragile craft, looked us carefully up and down, and exuding some justifiable disbelief. 'Go in that thing?'

We looked at each other, quite bewildered at her query. 'No, not at all. We are not ferrymen. We are here for pleasure, going off to explore the island.'

The author admiring one of the lochans on Scalpay with Dun Caan on Raasay in the background. Photo: Mike Jacob.

We realised that there must be a reason for her arrival at the quay so we asked the obvious question. 'Are you expecting someone?'

'Yes, that's for sure, and I'm expecting to be treated in a right dinky hunky-dory manner. Look how far I've come for this visit. I'm searching for where my great-great ancestors lived before they were forced away and emigrated to Australia. Doesn't happen every day, does it?'

Our visitor wasn't short on explanation. She also had rightly assessed us as irrelevant personages but who might have some link with her visit. 'Are you my welcoming party?'

Our conversation abruptly ended when a well-splattered Landrover drew up at the gate and the driver got out and came towards us. He was well groomed and affable, clad in a padded outdoor jacket in subdued country fare colours and wearing lightly the air of the factor or even the land proprietor, but we were wrong. He introduced himself as the one-time farmer on the island whose job was not only to keep the roaming herd of cattle in good fettle but also do everything else to keep the estate running smoothly. However for family reasons he had quit to be nearer the amenities of Broadford rather than be isolated on a sea-girt chunk of barren landscape. No one now was living on the island. Its big house was ill-frequented and used only by flitting summer visitors. Still standing proud, it had seen its days of glory slip away, an ostentatious mansion of lost, inherited privilege.

He had the responsibility now to ferry the dedicated ancestor hunter on to the island and take her to the ancient chapel and long abandoned graveyard where some of her distant forbears lay mouldering beneath a jungle of rank grass and tangled bracken.

However, there was still someone else needed to complete the boarding party. A small unpretentious sedate saloon was drawing up behind the grubby Landrover. A diminutive lady hopped sprightly out on to the gravel at the roadside, and without hesitation came towards us. It was obvious that she was at the apex of a pecking order. She possessed the air of high status in a long-established clan pattern of the island. She was going to be the hostess for the day.

It was time to introduce ourselves and explain our wish as reputable members of a well known mountaineering club to ascend to the highest point of the island to savour and admire the view. This was accepted without question, and things began to move. The ferryman slithered off round to the obscured side of the quay and returned towing a sleek white boat powered by a plenty all up and go- go engine. Skilfully he transferred his passengers on board, pressed the starter button, and the trio roared off to commune with the ghosts of a bygone age.

Our voyage was straightforward. Once seated in the cockpit, we pushed out into the current and rhythmically paddled across to the far shore. Grounded and with our canoe secured, we pulled on our boots and set off uphill. Our mountaineering day was under way.

Gentle stuff with as the book says 'especially fine views' of the rampant rolling Red Hills creeping overland towards our island and framed in the distance the seductive profile of Blàbheinn. Gray sun warmed slabs of scuffed bedrock protruded out of the short heather and in keeping with our mood we stepped blithely up on the dry eroded rock hide of the geological immensity of our mother earth sleeping below our feet.

We soon reached the bouldery summit of Mullach na Carn at the immense height of 389m and wondered what to do next. Before us was a contorted jumble of twisted lochans in a hidden bowl. We decided to explore them by skirting around their intricate shorelines. Excessive thickets of long untrammelled heather struggled against us as we staggered along the heaped tongues of moraine and followed the obstacle course towards a peculiar ruinous structure stuck on the furthest bank of the biggest lochan.

We approached this curious construction with interest. It grew into a well built round edifice, all open on the sunny side, and from its conical roof protruded a stump of corroded chimney pipe. It had the signs of long neglect with its fallen rock blocks and rusted metal barbecue appendages. Centrally placed beneath the hanging relic of a smoke cowl was a huge fire platform, a sacrificial grilling altar for all those over-sized fish that surely could never have lived in this diminutive lochan. We reckoned any

Same place, same climber, different conditions: Pete Biggar completing the abseil on the 3rd Pinnacle six years later. Photo: Roger Robb.

innocent hooked fish bound for the fiery altar might now have grown to be quite monstrous. No one appeared to have been there for years. We poked around and mulled over the times when the laird must have entertained his sporting guests as they dabbled hopefully on a midge-infested summer evening before retreating down the neglected footpath back to his big house.

We went down this path through skimpy old pine trees and emerged close to the house. There was no sign of the visiting Australian and her escort party. All was quiet. Perhaps they were all inside supping their morning coffee or had gone off to potter around the forsaken graveyard? Walking along the track we approached a sizeable house hidden behind a phalanx of shrubs. It was still in reasonable repair. We surmised that the occupants of the two cars parked at the road near the quay were holidaying in the house. We tried to sneak past quietly without disturbing anyone. We had nearly made it when a strident aggravated female voice issued through the bushes and in no uncertain tones asked what we as furtive interlopers were doing on the island. We had disturbed her peace and quiet, and not wishing further to spoil her day we nonchalantly paid little attention and walked on muttering to ourselves.

Yes, our day had turned out to be a most unusual and memorable outing, and quite free from toiling up another big hill. Thoughts of the evening ahead came and went as we walked back to our mighty ship. Our outing would make a gentle after dinner conversation piece while the venerable members, sitting glasses in hand, relaxed round the fire in the cottage. Mere dreams…

We reached our insignificant little ship, launched and paddled across the kyle, went through its dismantling, packing and loading, and drove off homewards. We rounded the curve close to the ferry terminal to Raasay and the last big hill that I had tried to climb on the Cullin ridge came slowly into view. Memories suddenly intruded of that crazy hiatus with rock and rope up there when we had to retreat deeply demoralised at our strange behaviour.

It didn't bear thinking about but that day had got into my head and it wouldn't go away. Here I was driving along side the sea loch in a dwam with the car controlled by subconscious responses; it was as if it was fortuitously imbued with an uncanny navigational sense taking us back to the cottage.

What had happened up there was really a very innocuous but salutary tale and makes one wonder how easy it is to make idiotic and irrational decisions. Peter and I had set off to go up the Pinnacle Ridge of Sgùrr nan Gillean. It wasn't the most inspiring of winter days, a better description would be a surprisingly uninviting bleak day, yet our unbridled enthusiasm had propelled us up into the damp clinging mist that shrouded the staggered sawbuck of pinnacles that ended on the singular top of the mountain. No uncertainty arose in our minds about a satisfactory outcome. We had often scrambled straightforwardly up the ridge of pinnacles in

Pinnacle Ridge of Sgurr nan Gillean. Watercolour by Helen Forde.

summertime and knew that its intimate variations might add interest to our traverse of the mountain. Never did we expect to fail so ignominiously.

We came to a short damp wall decorated with crudgey lumps of soggy snow and decided to put the rope on. After all it couldn't be far until we came to the third pinnacle, or was this it, where we would have to hurl the doubled rope into the depths in order to descend au rappel into the narrow slot separating the two biggest humps on the ridge. Before we realised it we were there and looking at the greatest collection of bits of old fading rope draped securely round their shared anchor point. It was just a question more of what colour do you fancy rather than how reliable do they look. We picked a happy pair of more youthful loops and having threaded and fed our friendly old green rope through our choice out of the multitude of slings we hurled the coils of doubled rope into the misty nebulous depths. In turn we then backed down the initial wee face and scuttled carefully across an incipient ledge system before back climbing down a cleft to just reach the snow bank bridging the notch. This was the moment to drag the rope out of its slings and haul it down to use for our ascent up another probable pinnacle at our backs.

However we were not the first foolish optimists to find that the rope refused to move. Curses subdued! Put in some more strength, please, so together we put our combined weight into increasing the tension on the jammed rope. Not a whit of difference did it make except to confirm that our tactics could not shift the rope, and were probably making the situation worse. We were flummoxed, baffled and unwilling to consider the option of free climbing back up the manky cliff without any reliable security. Under these unpleasant conditions, never! Instead we could descend eastward from the snowy gap, traverse under the east face of the ridge to regain its spine, climb up to free the rope, and retreat with our metaphorical tails between our legs. Hopefully but in low spirits we went on our downward traverse and regained the ridge somewhere and started back up again, all the time inwardly cursing our incompetence at our poor rope work and the blithe mindlessness that had assumed that everything would go smoothly.

We had reached the dreepy crudgey little wall when all motivation and rationality escaped our heads and fled into the droopy mists clinging above the rocks. Why this happened we would never know but we stopped, turned round and without adequate consideration started back down the ridge. With hindsight it wouldn't have been much further to retrieve his rope but we were abandoning it in disgust. He insisted that it didn't matter, it was a well used ancient rope and a nice glossy new one had been on the cards, and I, skinflint that I be, accepted his reasons without question, and besides I was getting cold. Our retreat went well, to weave down under the gloom. Someone else, someday, would get a surprise to find a fortuitously provided abseil rope draped down the obnoxious Third Pinnacle, and good luck to them!

We turned off by the Sligachan hotel, as the deep memory of that mountain failure faded, and the joyous feeling of the day's satisfactory sea paddle and pad came back. The turnoff to the Allt Dearg cottage had arrived, and we swung in and slowly bumped up the track. It was time for dinner....

ARDVERIKIE WALL – HALF CENTURY

First ascent : 24 June 1967
In celebration of 50 years climbing on Binnein Shuas

By Graeme Hunter

BEFORE THE 'MONARCH OF THE GLEN' and the BBC's Glen Boggle TV series, the south side of Loch Laggan was a quiet backwater seldom visited, and certainly saw few climbers. It was in the shadow of Creag Meagaidh which, understandably was the area's main attraction, particularly in winter.

However, in 1964, on a grotty winter's day while on a Carn Dearg Mountaineering Club meet, along with Tony Viveash and his faithful Jack Russell called Jim, we set off to explore the delights of the sodden south side of Binnein Shuas. Its craggy profile was clearly visible from the Creag Meagaidh camp site, and looked enticing. On first inspection I was

Doug Lang and Graeme Hunter on the 40th anniversary of the first ascent.

Photo: Hunter collection.

really impressed with the expanse of rock, and my research couldn't find any record of previous activity, not even a visit by Bugs McKeith who had been active not far away on Dirc Mhor. However Tony, who was an enthusiastic hillwalker, wasn't quite so tempted by the potential.

I returned the following year with Bob Devine (A micro-biologist from Dundee) to explore the potential. Bob turned out to be more an après climber than actual, so again he wasn't keen to explore the crag further, however we climbed Hidden Gully, as we called it. I was frustrated and keen to get to grips with this unexplored crag (Or so I thought. Tom Patey, unbeknown to me had also visited the crag in the summer of 1964, he climbed one route, but failed to realise the crag's potential, which was most unlike Tom!). I needed a partner.

Based in Dundee I had climbed with Davie Crabb and Dougie Lang, who were already an established team. However, I enticed Dougie to secretly visit Binnein Shuas with me with the promise of sunkissed, virgin rock, and excellent Howff accommodation at the base of the crag. Dougie was strategically important in this cunning plan as he had transport! A white Volvo 122s which was quite a sporty job, and with Dougie behind the wheel, it just flew up the A9, sometimes quite literally.

On a fine June Friday evening we hid the car away from prying eyes behind the keeper's cottage just over the bridge at the west end of Loch Laggan. We followed the estate road up to Lochan na h-Earba then picked

Doug Lang camping below the bridge over the outflow of Loch na h-Earba with Binnein Shuas back left.

Photo: Graeme Hunter.

an ascending line up to the crag to the splendid howff that I'd promised Doug. There was no path up to the crag at that time, so it was hard work crashing through the bog myrtle and heather. The huge overhangs of The Fortress were bathed in the setting sun as we worked our way to the howff nestling among the boulders. While it was an excellent shelter, the sleeping accommodation wasn't quite level and it appeared to have been a dining cave for a fox or a wild-cat, as the cave floor was strewn with old bones and bits of fur. Now Dougie was quite a dapper and fastidious character and was none too pleased with the quality of the accommodation. However, after much moaning and groaning he made it through the night. In the morning after a few brews of Earl Grey we lay in the heather looking up at the architecture of the crag, inspecting the detail through my small stalker's telescope. It became blatantly obvious that there was a stunning clean line right up the centre of the crag, but it looked a bit thin and quite hard.

Anyway, we geared up, which didn't take long as we didn't have a lot of gear. Some of my nuts were home made. We were concerned that we didn't have anything small enough for protection on this compact rock type. I was now resplendent in a brand new pair of EBs which replaced my worn out tatty Masters which had seen better days. We couldn't see any obvious belay on the wall above a prominent nose, but reckoned it would be a long run out, so I climbed up and belayed on the right under the black nose, then Doug tackled the grooves on the nose. While steep, they were well protected. He disappeared over the top and up the slab above and shouted gleefully that he had found a great belay stance and a huge flake in exactly the perfect position.

It was a beautiful sunny day and the views up and down the loch below were stunning. Greatly encouraged by the quality of the rock, I tackled

Graeme Hunter after the first ascent of Ardverikie Wall 24 June 1967.

Photo: Doug Lang.

the next steep slab pitch which had a rounded corner to the right, which didn't tempt me. There were plenty of small holds on the slab so I just made a direct line up the slab aiming for the top corner under a small overhang where I got my first protection, I pulled over on good holds and found yet another excellent stance, in exactly the right place again – amazing.

The next pitch was a right traverse on delicate holds then up a scoop to

Sandy Allen on Ardverikie Wall. Photo: Andy Nisbet.

a spike belay. The climb continued up to the Heather Terrace followed by an easy slab to the top. Dougie and I were delighted with the quality of the rock and the amazing architecture of the route. We agreed that the route's appearance certainly belied its difficulty and awarded it a Mild Severe. We both also felt that it was such a plumb classic line with great situations, it deserved a classic sounding name. So *Ardverikie Wall* seemed totally appropriate, named after the Castle and Estate.

During the summers of 1967/8 we had Binnein Shuas to ourselves and added a total of 17 new routes to the cliffs. On 24 June 2017 it will be a half century since Ardverikie Wall's first ascent, and I've climbed it many times since (even in big boots). It's a magic place with a truly remote big mountain feel. Tom Patey graciously admitted later that it was 'the best route he'd ever walked past'. Ironically, it's now reckoned to be one of the most popular rock routes in Scotland.

Tragically, Dougie was killed in an avalanche in Coire Fee in Glen Doll on 19 March 2011. We were both there for the 40th anniversary of Ardverikie Wall and we'd talked about the upcoming 50th. Well, I hope to be there on the day, I might not get up the route with my titanium hips, but I'll celebrate the occasion with a wee tipple and a slice of Dundee Cake to Dougie's memory, and partnership.

Margaret and Graeme Hunter at Ardverikie Castle 2016. Photo:Hunter Collection.

HIGH ON BRAERIACH

By Raymond Simpson

THERE ARE MORNINGS IN April when I can't be at peace. An anticyclone will be holding mist in the glens and I know the stars have been out and the frost has transformed the remains of the winter. Yes, I know the rest of the world has forgotten about winter and is looking forward to Spring; buds on the apple trees, flies hatching on the river, roe bucks getting horny. I should be on the field getting the onions and tatties planted but I need to be somewhere else...

I called Greg, Brian, Rob, Mick and Mungo but none were available...or did they think I was daft? So after a morning working at the field, I left the Cairngorm car park in the late afternoon and was soon bypassing the Great Slab on the right and cramponing into the Couloir. There was even a wee icy section below the toe of Ewen Buttress. I emerged onto the plateau into thick mist and a biting north-west wind. A bit different from that day in the '60s when I took off my wet dachsteins to dry in the sun whilst I belayed at the top of left branch Y Gully. I still have the groove on my hand from No2 laid nylon rope!

Out with the compass, as from experience I know that, left to my own devices, I walk anticlockwise in the mist. Located the top of Allt a' Choire Mhòir but not enough snow to slide down tonight so stumbled down to

The Garbh Choire Hut in April 2017. Photo: Raymond Simpson.

the Lairig and across the flats to what remains of the Garbh Choire hut. Lovely alpenglow on Càrn a' Mhaim and the Southern Cairngorms and a stormy mackerel sky with scudding cloud above Angel's Peak. The hut is now sadly neither wind nor water tight but someone has made a bench to sit on. Got the stove going, not the purr of the old primus but a lighter silent meths burner, copious brews and a hot meal washed down with half the Singleton. I was glad to snuggle down into the bivi bag as the wind roared and gusted through the holes in the fabric and ghosts and fitful dreams filled the stormy night.

Although the stone shelter was built by the Lairig club in the '60s, the hut became popular with younger Aberdeen climbers, early or late in the season to avoid the massive cornices that sculpted the lips of the Garbh Choire. From the age of 15, I climbed here, often approaching in deep snows of early winter via climbs on Sputan Dearg or the Northern Corries, finding the hut by moonlight and exploring the rich potential of the Garbh Choire's classic winter routes and finding some new ones.

Latterly we learned that if you got up early enough, the best conditions were to be found at Easter during what became known as the 'Braeriach High'. We must have made more than twenty winter ascents in the late '60s and early '70s. These are stories to be told by garrulous old men over a dram but then...It was not just the climbs but the epic overnight approaches over the plateau or ridges and drunken aftermaths in the Fife Arms...the joys of finding perfect snow and ice conditions; a huge variety of climbs in four or five corries, from short hard ice routes in Mòr to long mixed mountaineering routes in Brochain and alpine like faces on Angel's peak. I still remember the exhilaration of pulling over steep snowy ribs or snouts of cornices into the sun and the joys of festering by the hut in the afternoons, a better high than I got from most things I did in the '60s!

Not many stars showing in the first misty grey light but enough moon to get going after a quick brew. Snow reached almost down to the creaking ice on Lochain Uaine and ptarmigan were strutting out of their snow holes leaving their morning ablutions behind. After a couple of hundred feet, the slope became steep enough to need crampons. Choosing a central line through the light mist obscuring the face, I found myself drawn to a rocky barrier over which an attractive mantle of blue ice flowed. This gave an interesting pitch; it's a long time since I cut handholds but the swan neck of the single modern axe I carried made this easy. I often wonder why we took so long to figure this out?

Above, some mixed climbing led to the final steep snow slopes. I trended right to avoid the remains of cornices and pulled out by the cairn of Angel's Peak. A raw icy wind was depositing rime on me and the rocks so I gave up on traversing blind round the plateau to Braeriach and went with the wind to Cairn Toul scattering snow buntings before me. On the way, I passed a curious window formed by two massive slabs of granite which I hadn't noticed before. The summit cairn gave little shelter and I followed hard snow down the top of the north ridge. As I descended, the mists cleared and I had fine views of the mosaic of ice flows breaking up on Lochain Uaine.

I paused above the loch and revisited memories, events and folk I had not thought about for many years...Graham and myself, a couple of schoolboys climbing *Anchor Route* on Sputan, then finding the hut in a snowstorm and next morning, climbing the iced up waterfall and Angel's ridge; Jim and I crossing from Einich in a sleety thaw and forcing our limbs into frozen ventile at dawn to do a fine new line in the Corrie of the Chokestone Gully; Johnnie and I settling down for a New Year's dram with Bob Scot in Luibeg when the phone rang and Bob sent the pair of us up to the Garbh Choire on a wild night ahead of the Rescue team to 'get that loon doon intae yon hut afore he dees oot there in the snaw'; Alan, Jimmer and Spunk, with Greg and I very much apprentices, exploring the rock climbing in Garbh Choire Dhaidh. Many, many wonderful anticyclonic April days with Brian, Greg, Rob and Johnnie targeting the previous generation's summer routes and turning them into winter classics. Later in the '80s, skiing in with Rob Ferguson or John Eames to climb and ski and all too rarely since then.

Descending to the hut in the sunshine, I had my first glimpse of the Garbh Choire Mòr, laden with snow to the corrie floor even in this relatively snowless winter. Brochain held less with only West gully completely white. I spread out the gear to dry and lay on the moss for an hour drinking multiple brews and finishing the Singleton, I swear I could hear in the wind the distant banter of gallus loons.

On the walk out, frogs and insects were busy in the pools of snow melt. I enjoyed the fine new path through the Lairig. Beyond the March I found a burn leading up to the meadow above Lurchers. It provided almost 1000 feet of steep snow plodding on the way back over to the ski road...so, finally after a poor winter, I got my hit of snow and ice and more memories than I had bargained for.

THE QUIET METEOROLOGIST

By Robert Aitken

In July 1925 a goodly company of seven SMC members assembled with a couple of other friends at the Fafleralp Hotel in the upper reaches of the Lötschental in the Oberland, to constitute what was to all intents and purposes an Alpine Meet, though such a thing as a Meet on 'alien soil' was at that time in breach of the Club's constitutional precepts. After warming-up with some one-day ascents from Fafleralp, the party progressed eastwards over the cols and glaciers of the Aletsch, via Concordia to the Pavilion Dolfuss above the Unteraargletscher, and thence by the Strahlegg to Grindelwald. [1]

Despite the considerable collective experience of the participants, an element of mild farce marked the logistics of the expedition, which involved delivery of food in advance to the huts along their route. Problems with telephones, language, and religious holidays complicated these arrangements. The commissariat, as recorded in both the *SMCJ* and the *Alpine Journal*, came to rely unduly on beans of various sorts. 'This form of vegetable' as Percy Unna observed pointedly, 'has its special drawbacks.' Sandy Harrison noted that 'a certain excess of beans was bartered for tea at one of the huts.'

At the Strahlegg Hut the SMC party fell in with the crack team of Frank Smythe and J.H.B. Bell, fresh from a traverse of the Schreckhorn and Lauteraarhorn. These two had had their eyes on a new climb on the Fiescherhorn, but Dr Bell was temporarily out of action with a sprained ankle. After Sandy Harrison and Kenneth Douglas had set off for the ordinary route on the Schreckhorn, Frank Smythe, keen not to miss a day's climbing, caught them up, and persuaded them not only to let him join them, but to raise their ambitions to tackle the SW Ridge, the route he had followed with Bell a few days before.

The resulting adventure hardly needs a detailed account, as it is one of the most intensively recorded tales in the annals of mountaineering. Frank Smythe wrote up the climb in 'high astounding terms', and then re-cycled the story exhaustively – his son Tony Smythe, in his admirable recent biography, records 7 published versions over 20 years. Such, no doubt, were the pressures back then on a climber who aspired to make a living from writing and photography, but it no doubt provided ammunition for AC members of the Old School who regarded Frank Smythe as little more than a Grub Street hack. Despite all that, Smythe's is a vividly gripping account, well worth reading in any of its incarnations. [2]

In summary, when less than 200m below the summit, the party was hit by a savage storm squall with lightning and hail, and driven to take shelter under a convenient overhang for the better part of an hour. When that storm passed on, Harrison recalled, 'The meteorologist [Douglas] wisely decided to make quite certain of the weather before continuing, and it was soon apparent that really bad weather was about to set in.' The decision was for immediate retreat. Early on in what became an epic six-hour battle for survival in a ferocious *tourmente*, down vertiginous slabs ever more plastered in snow and ice, Smythe was struck by lightning and almost knocked off the mountain. Partially recovered, he moved to the front of the party to search out a line of descent through the storm: 'We were often unable to see each other, though separated by only a yard or two, and two or three times I felt Harrison's boot on my head as he moved down a step, quite unaware that I was immediately below.' But: 'Never did Douglas or Harrison falter, their progress was mechanical rather than human in its certainty.' Finally, after tumbling over the bergschrund to safety, 'we shook hands, not without feeling, for it had been a very close thing.' [3]

Unna, recording this SMC Meet That Was Not A Meet in the *AJ*, summarised these life-or-death events on the Schreckhorn as 'a very uncomfortable experience'. That exquisite understatement may well have met with the approval of C.K.M. Douglas. This was a man resilient in the face of danger and stress, and evidently not given to self-advertisement or to publicising his own notable achievements.

Charles Kenneth Mackinnon Douglas (1893–1982) – known to his family as Kenneth – was a member of the SMC from 1922 to 1933, and an active climber from 1922 to 1927. As far as we know, Douglas gave up climbing and resigned from the Club when he married, a failure of perseverance that of course means that he never attained that very modest degree of immortality conferred by an obituary in this *Journal*. But he deserves to be commemorated.

Douglas was the son of a doctor in the West End of Edinburgh, one of a distinguished and talented family. At Edinburgh Academy he showed sharp academic ability, particularly in mathematics. He was introduced to meteorology, which quickly became a passion, by a newly appointed science Master, McCallum Fairgrieve, and to geography and the Pentlands by Caleb G. Cash, a hugely energetic polymathic enthusiast for early maps of Scotland, and for the Cairngorms, a notable compiler of hill tables: a neglected figure in the history of Scottish orography [4]. Perhaps due to that stimulus, Douglas had ascended the four Cairngorm 4000-footers and Lochnagar before such activities were curtailed by the outbreak of War. That also cut short his studies in mathematics at King's College Cambridge, for which he had won an Edinburgh Academy Exhibition, at the end of his second year.

Predictably enough, by December 1914 Douglas had gained a commission in the Royal Scots, the Edinburgh infantry regiment. Less predictably, by June 1915 he had transferred to the nascent Royal Flying Corps and started training as an observer, later progressing to become a pilot. From the outset he took a keen practical interest in the scope for using aircraft as a means of monitoring and assessing atmospheric conditions, the formation of clouds and the evolution of air masses. He carried out these pioneering meteorological observations with basic instruments in the harsh conditions of an open cockpit, at first entirely in the intervals of more immediately pressing and sometimes seriously life-threatening military engagements. He published his first results on 'Weather observations from an aeroplane' as early as August 1916; in his absence they were proudly presented in a paper to the Scottish Meteorological Society by his former EA mentor Fairgrieve. Given the fortitude required just to fly in the flimsy planes of the time, much less to engage in aerial warfare, Douglas' courage and commitment is self-evident. His very survival is remarkable: he was several times wounded in air combat, and suffered injuries in a crash which seem to have troubled him for the rest of his life. The Air Force Cross he was awarded seems hardly adequate recognition. From May 1918 to August 1919 he served briefly in the first dedicated Air Force unit undertaking flights specifically for meteorological recording and monitoring in France, before he transferred to the Met Office.

Restored to civilian life, Douglas sent in a membership application to the SMC in October 1922, giving his address as his family home at 19 Chester Street in the West End of Edinburgh. The supporting signatures on his form are those of Ling and Sang, which means less than first appears, since it was common practice for the President and Secretary to endorse candidates who did not know other SMC members. The application has a very thin Scottish base: a mere 15 Munros, with minimal evidence of the experience of mountains under snow that was supposedly regarded as a *sine qua non*. A footnote addendum referring to 'Experience of snow conditions up to 2700ft in Southern Uplands, Jan–April 1922' is probably an acknowledgement of that deficiency. The Club Committee was probably ready to be lenient in its concern to rebuild membership after the War; besides, the more impressive content of Douglas's application was an Alpine season in August 1922, which showed him undertaking the usual introductory *courses* from Arolla, but then progressing to the Dent Blanche, the traverse of the Aiguilles Rouges, the Matterhorn by the Zmutt, and the Zinal Rothorn. Even if, as seems very likely, these climbs were undertaken exclusively with a guide, that rapid progression suggests that the guide found his client more than competent, and that Kenneth Douglas aspired to be a serious mountaineer. [5]

After his election to the Club Douglas attended three successive Meets: at Crianlarich (New Year 1923), Loch Maree (Easter 1923), and Blair Atholl (New Year 1924). All his outings at these Meets were in parties including Sandy Harrison; at the first two Meets John Harrison joined them. Sandy Harrison, just a few years older, may well have found Douglas congenial company. Both Edinburgh men, both had seen intense War service as junior officers in the Royal Scots before moving into highly hazardous specialisms, Harrison to the 'Suicide Club' – the Machine Gun Corps – and Douglas to the RFC.

At Crianlarich they ran through the standard winter ascents – More and

Stobinian, Y Gully on Cruach Ardrain and Central Gully of Lui; at Blair Atholl, Beinn a' Ghlo and Càrn a' Chlamain. From Kinlochewe at Easter they found rather more adventurous fare: besides traversing Liathach and the western tops of Beinn Eighe, they climbed the East Buttress in Coire Mhic Fhearcair and explored the west face of Slioch, which they found 'disappointing, being either very easy or loose and dangerous'. [6]

Unfortunately we have no knowledge of what other climbing Douglas may have done in Scotland, but we have records for five Alpine seasons between 1922 and 1927. In 1923, apparently with a guide, he started in the Oberland and made the season's first ascents of the Wetterhorn and the Schreckhorn, before flitting to Chamonix for an intense fortnight's climbing that included the Tacul, the Géant, and traverses of Charmoz, Grépon, and Dru – no mean programme. In 1924 he and Harrison were based in Zermatt and Arolla. In the first fortnight they employed a guide, though tellingly Douglas complains that he was 'perhaps inclined to be too cautious in uncertain weather', which thwarted much of their programme of big peaks. Snatching the Matterhorn by the Hörnli in threatening weather, they dropped the guide, picked up A.J. Rusk, and shifted westwards, collecting the Dent Blanche *en route* before rounding off with the traverse of the Aiguilles Rouges and Mont Collon.

1925 was the season of the Schreckhorn epic. We have no record that Douglas was in the Alps in 1926. In 1927 he spent a fortnight at Zermatt in early September. His record is somewhat cryptic in its first part: 'I traversed the Furgg Grat and Rimpfisch Grat with Joseph Biner, and the Wellenkuppe and Obergabelhorn with Adoph Schaller.' My reading is that those 'Grats' were merely training outings on the lower crests of the respective ridges; while it is not inconceivable that Douglas, who seems to have been a devotee of the Matterhorn, made a full ascent of the Furggen Ridge, it seems unlikely. [7]

Apart from confirming that Douglas was a solid, determined and energetic alpinist with a taste for big peaks, his Alpine record shows that by the time he and Harrison set off together for the Schreckhorn in 1925, they would have had a full understanding of each other's capabilities. It also shows that Douglas had done the Schreckhorn before; he seems to have liked to repeat, without guides, mountains he had first done behind a guide. And it makes it amply clear that Kenneth Douglas the meteorologist was not readily deterred by uncertain weather, and may even have relished the added challenge it presented. It's striking from Smythe's account that the party pushed on up the Schreckhorn despite an ominous eerie green light at sunrise that might have persuaded less venturesome parties to take their second breakfast back at the hut.

Despite being based in southern England, Douglas was elected to the SMC Committee from 1930 to 1933. However we have no evidence that he did any further climbing, and he appears to have resigned from the Club and given up climbing when in 1933 he married a lady he had met on one of his Alpine holidays.

From the mid-1920s onwards Douglas was employed in the Meteorological Office. With the benefit of contacts with Norwegian colleagues working in the same field, he developed an exceptional level of interpretive skill in working from synoptic charts. His peers came to regard him as the greatest synoptic forecaster of his time in Britain, and – since much of that process is now largely computer-assisted – perhaps the greatest of all time.

These skills were to become of national importance during WWII, when accurate weather forecasting was vital to naval and air operations, but particularly in the run-up to D-Day. The dramatic saga of the gestation of the crucial forecast for the Normandy landings has been often told, partly because the details are still warmly contested. Despite his mastery of synoptic charts, Douglas remained sceptical of the ability of forecasters to predict weather with any accuracy more than 36–48 hours ahead. He probably felt distinctly unhappy at the demands of his superior officers up to Eisenhower, who desperately needed reassurance that the invasion forces should have at least workable conditions of sky and sea. The already uncertain forecasting process was hindered by patchy and unreliable observations in the Atlantic, by an exceptionally unseasonal flux of weather systems for May and June 1944 in the Western Approaches, and even more by clashes of personality, culture, and scientific methodology among the three forecasting teams involved. Douglas' cautious approach was a vital counterweight to the uninhibited optimism of the US group. In the event, the forecasters between them accurately identified a narrow window of opportunity in the midst of a run of depressional storms which could readily have led to disaster. The Rest, as they too often say, Is History. But as the unassertive backroom boy, Kenneth Douglas got very little credit, while other forecasters picked up decorations from American, French and British authorities. Douglas, who already had an OBE awarded in 1941, received a letter of thanks from Eisenhower. [8]

Life for Kenneth Douglas thereafter was predictably less dramatic. He continued his work at the Met Office until he retired in 1954, his career crowned with awards from the Royal Meteorological Society for his outstanding and varied contributions to the science. He lived quietly in Devon till his death in February 1982; to the last, it is reported, he had pictures of the Alps, and particularly of the Matterhorn, on his walls.

As with our other notable meteorologist Club member, Professor Gordon Manley [9], Douglas made very limited contributions to the literature of mountain weather. Apart from a paper on 'Alpine cloud forms' in the *Quarterly Journal of the Royal Meteorological Society* in 1928, he contributed some data to Kenneth Hunter's chapter on 'The meteorology of the Scottish mountains' in the SMC *General Guide* of 1933, and an appendix on Alpine weather to Seligman's *Snow structures and ski fields* (1936).

Kenneth Douglas may have won his laurels in meteorology, but the

SMC can justly claim him as one of our own. His self-effacing reserve, extreme even by Scottish standards, has left him almost entirely unknown among our members, as among the wider public. He deserves better, not least because he clearly was a mountaineer of courage and resolve. Coming back full circle to the 'whirlwind and blizzard' on the Schreckhorn, we can leave the last word with Frank Smythe: 'I could not wish for two more stout-hearted companions than Harrison and Douglas.'

Sources and notes

C.K.M. Douglas is well served by a number of semi-biographical papers from historians of meteorology assessing his role in the development of the science. I have drawn heavily on a selection of these sources:

Brian Booth, 'C.K.M.Douglas and early meteorological research using aeroplanes as a platform for carrying instruments', *Royal Meteorological Society History Group Newsletter*, 1 (2013), 15–17.

M. Field, 'Meteorologist's profile – Charles Kenneth Mackinnon Douglas, OBE, AFC, MA.', *Weather*, 54/10 (1999), 321–7.

R.C. Sutcliffe, 'Obituary: Charles Kenneth Mackinnon Douglas, OBE, AFC, MA.', *Q.J.R. Meteorol. Soc.*, 108/458 (1982), 996–7.

[1] Good-humoured accounts of this 'Meet' were provided by Unna (*Alpine Journal*, 36/231 (1925), 304–5) and Harrison (*SMCJ*, 17/100 (1925), 227–9). The party comprised Donald, Douglas, Goggs, Harrison, Ling, Sang, and Unna of the SMC, with J.W. Brown of the Alpine Club and J. Kirkland (Brown joined the SMC the following year, and was Unna's regular Alpine partner for ten years thereafter). Solly and his wife, with a Miss MacLay, were also at the Fafleralp Hotel. Douglas came across country to Fafleralp from Kandersteg, and joined parties in climbing the Tschingelhorn, Lauterbrunnen Breithorn and Birghorn from the hotel.

The SMC's constitutional dictat against Meets outwith Scotland, which now seems at least a little jingoistic, was confirmed at the AGM in 1925 (*SMCJ*, 17/99 (1925), 145) when a motion from Secretary Sang to discard it was rejected by members. That may have been frustrating for Sang, who had been one of the Oberland party.

[2] Tony Smythe, *My Father Frank: unresting spirit of Everest*, (Sheffield: Bâton Wicks, 2013), pp66–7, 302. Readers of a pedantic turn of mind may find it mildly engaging to compare Frank Smythe's various versions and to relate them to Harrison's in the *SMCJ* (*supra*), as well as the paraphrase in Harry Calvert's *Smythe's Mountains,* (London: Gollancz, 1985). There are, as might be expected, minor discrepancies, but none of substance.

[3] This from the *AJ* version of Smythe's account: 'Thunderstorms in the Alps', *Alpine Journal*, 37/232 (1926), 91–9. It's grimly amusing to record that when Smythe and Sandy Harrison joined forces again in the Alps in 1929, they both got a violent shock from a lightning flash while standing on the metal threshold of the Torino Hut in their nailed boots (Tony Smythe *op.cit*. p115).

[4] Caleb George Cash (1857–1917) was born in Birmingham and undertook his teacher training in London, but became a passionate enthusiast for Scotland and its topography, and especially for Speyside, where among other interests he ruefully observed and recorded the persecution to extinction of the local ospreys.

His frequent contributions to the early *Cairngorm Club Journal* included tables of 2000' hills in the Cairngorms, as well as a listing of the hills visible from Arthur's Seat. He was also closely involved in the cataloguing of Pont's early manuscript maps, and worked with Sir Arthur Mitchell on Macfarlane's *Geographical Collections* and *A Contribution to the Bibliography of Scottish Topography* (1917). He has recently been brought to wider public notice by Kellan MacInnes in *Caleb's List: Climbing the Scottish mountains visible from Arthur's Seat*, (Edinburgh: Luath Press, 2013).

[5] Application form courtesy of Robin Campbell.

[6] *SMCJ*, 16/95 (1923), 254–8; 16/96 (1923), 301–7; 17/97 (1924), 48–52.

[7] *SMCJ*, 16/96 (1923), 334; 17/98 (1924), 107–8; 18/104 (1927), 123.

[8] A small sample of the literature on the Overlord weather forecasting saga:

C.K.M. Douglas, 'Forecasting for the D-Day landings', *The Meteorological Magazine*, 81/960 (1952), 161–71.

Lawrence Hogben, 'Diary', *London Review of Books*, 16/10 (26 May 1994), 21.

R.A.S. Ratcliffe, 'Weather forecasting for D-Day, June 1944', *Weather,* 49/6 (1994), 198–202.

J.M. Stagg, *Forecast for Overlord*, (Addlestone: Ian Allen, 1971).

[9] 'In memoriam: Professor Gordon Manley', *SMCJ*, 32/172 (1981), 195–6.

Acknowledgements
This fragment of history owes its origin and a good deal of its material to Brian Booth, a retired senior meteorologist who has carried out extensive painstaking research on the life and professional career of C.K.M. Douglas. Brian approached the Club some years ago seeking information and an assessment of Douglas' climbing career, but we learned far more from him. He must be exonerated from any errors of fact or excessively exuberant interpretation. I should also like to thank Tony Smythe for his advice and assistance. Further underpinnings of this note derive from the assiduous efforts of our indefatigable Hon. Archivist Dr Campbell.

LAST DAYS BELOW THE EIGER

A distant memory of Tom Carruthers
1936–1961 aged 25

By Bill Sproul

WHEN I WROTE TOM'S obituary for the SMC *Journal* in May 1963 I stated: 'Few people had heard of Tom Carruthers until he climbed the North Face of the Matterhorn.' At that time, a first British ascent of an alpine north face was a big deal, especially for a young Glasgow lad. This established his credentials in the climbing scene. Tom described his ascent of 1961 as 'a disagreeable/splendid climb…. on the face we found no definite pitch; everything is exactly like everything else. There is no security on this climb… we used belays purely for psychological reasons.'

Now, fifty-five years later, once again, few readers will know of him. I hope to provide here some historical context, personal details and understanding of the man. A memoir written so long after the events will be somewhat cloudy but many youthful Alpine adventures with my buddy I still see in full colour. Some, in more shadowy parts of recall, benefited from the stimulation of conversations with mutual companions or from reading historical accounts.

Placing Carruthers in the pantheon of Scottish climbers is fairly easy. Think of Marshall, Smith, Haston, Patey, Clough, Pyper, Robertson. Tom was a contemporary albeit a *lanterne rouge*, the last man in cycling terms. His reputation as a young tiger was emerging slowly at the time of his death and no doubt would have grown from his Matterhorn North Face ascent, which was bold for the time and had already been contested by a number of Brits including Smith and Haston who had attempted a first British ascent a few weeks earlier but bailed to the Hornli Hut. As was said of another climber also long dead 'a fire burnt within him' – he was absolutely determined to climb the mountain and no one knows better than I do how for several months he devoted his whole mind and to this objective. Carruthers' objectives after the Matterhorn were other North Face ascents. His tick list was inspired by books and articles, which stirred his imagination.

As young men we devoured mountaineering books, classics by WH Murray and his fellow club pals, Tom Weir's Himalayan stories, Tillman's trips by boat to distant ranges, Alastair Borthwick's kayaking in western islands – these and more modern ones: Lionel Terray, Gaston Rébuffat and Herman Buhl, and Harrer's thrilling *The White Spider*. Much of our mountain lore and possible future ascents were gathered from these authors and from SMCJ accounts of both new climbs and classics from the thirties and forties. We read of climbing partnerships and relationships; *Gervasutti's Climbs* was a well thumbed favourite: they fed our imaginations and gave us ideas of how and what to climb.

The author belayed by Tom Carruthers climbing above Loch Scavaig in Skye in 1962.
Photo: Tom Weir (Roger Robb collection).

The trajectory of Tom's climbing career was forged from these bookish tales and the history of great mountain epics. The great north faces of the Alps were laid out as a worthy challenge and the notion of climbing them seemed distant but attainable.

They made up the ultimate contemporary tick list for a couple of Glasgow boys. Whether or not these notions were foolhardy and over-reaching is debatable but no more so than the idea of some young laddie bashing his first Munros then realizing by reading early SMC guides that his world of mountains was unbounded.

From Munros to alpine north faces may seem a ludicrous leap but it was not so much a leap, more a ramp. Rock climbing summers in Scotland, ascents in the Alps, Dolomites and the Tatras, long distance walking, winter mixed routes – each added to our skills and turned us into strong and competent mountaineers. This and aerobic training throughout the year producing increased strength, provided that ramp. Evidence of this stage? In the period from July 1961 to August 1962, Tom climbed the north faces of the Matterhorn, Aiguille du Plan, Aiguille du Dru and the south face of the Midi. He attempted the Walker Spur on the Grand Jorasses and the North Face of the Eiger.

Tom was a successful amateur Time Trial cyclist, winning local races in Scotland. On occasion Tom would leave work in Glasgow on Friday, with his lightly loaded bike, and arrive late evening in Glen Coe. On Sunday after two days of rock climbing he would repeat the return trip. He poo-pooed the notion of being a tough guy and referred to the secretive Schmid brothers from Munich who made the first ascent of the Matterhorn North Face in 1931. They cycled from Munich to Zermatt, with their climbing and camping kit, made their climb and cycled back to Germany fully loaded then told their story. They were tough guys!

Cycling competitively is akin to climbing in some surprising ways. Train with clear objectives, be ready to suffer, push and drain your reserves. Stay focused as circumstances change, then execute your recovery plan. Tom understood and practised his cycling knowing that he could use this training to good climbing effect.

There is no surprise in knowing that with each generation any sport will change. Now plans are based on better information. Equipment, both tools and clothing, have made higher standards possible. The communication of information during the '50s and '60s was pretty slow paced, if one wanted information on a particular mountain or climb, one had to look in books and the SMC or Alpine journals. In the case of the North Face of the Eiger our knowledge was limited to information from *The White Spider* published in 1959, it did not come from other climbers. Tom found the 1938 route description to be inferior to the best information known to only a few.

The amount, reliability and access to climbing information today are so much better. A young hotshot can have route descriptions, topos, and timing for a new climb well before an ascent. Amateurs and professionals benefit from huge numbers of blogs and websites in English, from around the world. The advantage doesn't just apply to new routes but also to known climbs where a variation, a different finish, bivy sites, removal of pegs, and belay points can give the climber an edge. This is a vey different world from the early 1960s.

Tom and I spent much of 1962 climbing together throughout Scotland and the Alps. After my season ended Tom and I said our goodbyes at Chamonix rail station on 9 August 1962. After an accident we had managed to self-rescue off the Bonatti route on the Grand Capucin. I had a cast on my lower right leg and was headed back to Scotland. Tom was fit and ready for his next north face. Towards the end of August 1962 Carruthers travelled from Chamonix to Grindelwald to meet up with a number of climbing friends from Scotland.

Our buddies were camped below the Eiger North Face in the wooded area above Alpiglen. One of them pointed out to Tom a secluded campsite away from the gawking, walking tourists and the train tracks that headed higher to Kleine Scheidegg. The weather was generally fine – warm days, cold nights – and the long-range forecast was for a continuing pattern of settled weather for a couple of weeks. As summer started to wind down so, too, did the number of climbers diminish. His friends were starting to talk about making their way back home to jobs, wives and girlfriends. Now he was where he wanted to be – he was healthy, fit, rested and equipped for the Eiger, but without a companion. I am in no doubt that he was completely ready for the route.

Tom must have started to ask around the dwindling Alpiglen tents if someone was looking for a partner. Brian Nally, who had been Tom's rope mate on the North Face of the Matterhorn the previous summer had talked about the Eiger. Was he around? If so, Nally would be an obvious candidate. But Brian, after an aborted attempt on 24–25 July, was back in London having satisfied the news hounds that swarm to the mountain when disaster occurs.

Sadly, a few weeks before Tom's climb, Brian and his mate Barry Brewster got into difficulties on the face. Barry had been injured by stonefall on 24 July 1962, survived the night, probably with a broken back, and then was swept off his belay in a massive rock avalanche which killed him. Nally set off down the ice field while at the same time Don Whillans and Chris Bonington were retreating to escape a brewing storm. Nally was above them and looked as though he was assembling gear. They could see from the bottom of the second icefield that Nally was obviously in deep trouble. They climbed the icefield, reached a confused Nally and tied him into their rope. In awful, deteriorating weather they continued their descent. They were raked by stone fall and soaked in the cascades. The details of Whillans' and Bonington's rescue of Nally are harrowing and heroic. Nally was ushered off the mountain by Don and Chris watched by Swiss guides unwilling to expose themselves to the almost continuous stone fall bombardment. These actions took place before Tom arrived in

Alpiglen at the end of August and to what extent he knew about Nally and Brewster is not known.

Having climbed so many routes with Tom I know how he approached a big climb. His preparation was thorough; his gear selection and personal items were thoughtfully assembled. The following is what I have often imagined Tom would have thought and done before his fateful ascent of the Nordwand. Some of my imaginings are guided by Bonington's and Ian Clough's accounts of their interaction with Tom and also their descriptions of the day. I have taken literary licence to paint the picture of Tom's efforts to ascend the Heckmair 1938 route on The North Face of the Eiger.

Tom met Egon Moderedder in the Alpiglen Berghaus, where Egon was staying. Egon had an open face and a casual manner, an athletic build and Tom liked the look of him. Egon told Tom that he had climbed in the Eastern Alps and in the Caucuses. Egon had come off the face a few days before with his buddy who on reaching the daunting second ice-field elected to descend. Egon spoke German – his first and only language – Tom spoke a little German learned from an Austrian girlfriend; he and Egon agreed to meet the next day, ready for their ascent!

Next day the early weather was encouragingly clear and calm allowing Tom methodically to pack and repack his gear. Reaching the first avalanche cones of ice Egon indicated he wanted to put on his crampons. The lower rocks were wet, covered with rubble, generally down sloping and required attention. The lowest rocks were a scramble with occasional short walls. They took their time realizing that it would be better to have a comfortable bivouac lower on the face, rather than a probably cold one higher up. The Shattered Pillar with the Gallery window off to the right was straightforward and led them to the next section. Voices above, but no one in sight, the Difficult Crack ahead. They stopped, scanned ahead and saw a figure moving around on a ledge below the buttress.

'Hello,' came a voice, English thought Tom: shit! shit! Egon who was above Tom was replying in German. Who were these guys? There were two of them. Tom's reaction was first anger because they were English and competition, then irritation because the presence of another party could complicate things.

'Who the fuck are you?' asked Tom.

'Clough and Bonington' came the reply.

They scrambled up higher to settle on a ledge near the Englishmen, cleared rocks from the surface and unpacked their gear, then setup the stove and made a brew. They exchanged pleasantries, the Englishmen probing who Egon was and what had he climbed.

Tom knew the names. Clough was known in Scotland, had climbed with Tom Patey and been on many RAF rescues. Bonington was a friend of Hamish MacInnes. Maybe they weren't as bad as a couple of nondescript Continentals hell-bent on the summit?

Next morning by the time Egon and Tom were ready to climb, the

Englishmen had just completed the Difficult Crack and were out of sight. The rock climb was easy compared to expectations and was free of ice, up the crack and then a gully. The left traverse to the Hinterstoisser traverse was uneventful but slow going. Tom knew that he was being tentative in his climbing with a nagging feeling he was being ultra safe with each move. Egon was quiet and seemed ready to be guided by Tom and did not offer to take the lead.

The notorious high-angled traverse to the left was 40m long but dry with tatty ropes strung along its length all weathered and faded. The dry rock made the climb easier but with his pack pulling on his back Tom carefully edged across using the tension on his own rope and friction on his boots. The historical significance of this pitch was not lost on Tom and the last twenty feet were finished in a scramble of moves. Above they kept left to the start of the First Ice-field.

Tom's fatal route finding mistake happened next by following the Harrer description 'a vertical 70 feet to the Swallows' Nest…. Traverse left to the First Ice-field… straight up a perpendicular cliff separating the first and second ice fields…50 feet left … 40 foot rock-pitch… diagonal right to Ice Hose….then up to Second Ice-field….Diagonally leftwards to the top of 2nd Ice-field'.

Whereas Clough in his *AJ* 1963 account of the same day, just a few hours before Carruthers describes his route – 'scrambled on rocks up the side of the First Ice-field…then at the top of the Ice Hose, across bare rocks to the foot of the Second Ice-field.' Bonington had been on the face twice before with Don Whillans, and his knowledge of the route was impeccable.

The Eiger watchers on the Scheidegg terrace could see the pair as they climbed very slowly straight up the First Ice-field. Cloud started to form on the lower part of the face obscuring the climbers. The time taken by Carruthers from the First Ice-field to the Second was about three hours and on the Second Ice-field even longer. He chose the easier route diagonally across the second ice field and not straight up.

Tom and Egon were caught in the middle of the ice field where there was no shelter from avalanche and stones coming down thousands of feet. Here they died, swept off the face to end up as broken bodies at the foot of the face. Tom's watch stopped at 5:15. Clough recalls a massive avalanche of rocks as he and Bonington were about to climb The Spider. This may have been 'the' fatal rock fall. The Englishmen, shaken by the size and ferocity of the rockfall, prudently bivouacked, waiting till daylight before finishing their ascent.

One year before, almost to the day and time, Tom had sat on the summit of the Matterhorn, the first Brit to climb its North Face. Twelve months later he was swept to his death. Tom and Egon were unlucky. They were on a particularly exposed area of the face and were struck by a stone fall. According to Clough's account there was a…'tremendous crashing and roaring and an avalanche of rocks came thundering down the gully and screamed out into the void below. The sunshine which we were enjoying was loosening rocks from their icy clasps.'

Could Tom have done a better job of managing his climb? Absolutely.

He should have waited to find a more compatible companion. Someone speaking fluent English with whom he could have made a climb as a 'get to know each other' outing. The weather pattern was stable which often occurs in the Alps as summer merges into autumn. Weather should not have been an issue. Late season has had more ascents than any other season. The face was dry allowing a lightweight ascent.

Why were they so late in starting after the bivouac? Did they want space between them and Bonington and Clough? Why not have a true alpine start and avoid being caught in the most dangerous part of the face? What went wrong that they were slow out of the gate? Was this due to lost equipment – an ice axe dropped, a crampon dropped or somehow lost?

Some have supported the idea that Carruthers was not capable or experienced enough for the Eiger. I would emphatically disagree and point to the number of young alpinists who have successfully summited the 1938 route. I believe this view is taken because Tom was an unknown within UK climbing, primarily in England where many simply had little knowledge of what experience was required to succeed in executing an active high quality, high quantity winter season.

I have often reflected on what Tom could have achieved in the future of which we often talked. Climbs, mountains, routes and challenges, Tom's ambitions were never humdrum. I believe that, as in so many aspects of the man's accomplishments, he had the skills and tenacity to achieve his goals and become a preeminent mountaineer.

THE WRIGGLE PITON

By Gordon Smith

FOR MANY YEARS THERE was an old piton overdriven into the mica schist of the Polney Crag climb *Wriggle*, at the base of the shallow groove shared by *Wriggle*, *The Rut* and *The Groove*. It was in a crack just after the traverse out from under the initial overhang and the battle with the prickly bush. It would seem that it might still be there for I read about just such a piton not so very long ago on the UK Climbing website. Someone was complaining about it being there, and in the wrong place. No one, apparently, knew who had put it there. But I think I know. Me. And the year was 1969.

When I was twelve years old my early literary tastes matured from Enid Blyton's Famous Five and Secret Seven and I developed a grand, vicarious passion for mountaineering. I began, over the years, to read all the how-to books and all the classics in the Blairgowrie Public Library with a grand and voracious appetite: Bell's *A Progress in Mountaineering*, Murray's *Mountaineering in Scotland*, Terray's *Conquistadors of the Useless*. I read Frank Smythe and Gaston Rébuffat and Chris Bonington. I read about the ascents of Annapurna and Everest, Route Major and The Red Sentinel. Eventually I read about the North Face of the Grandes Jorasses, and about the immense struggles and the tragedies upon the North Wall of the Eiger as related by Herr Harrer and others; struggles and tragedies that had attended Hinterstoisser's Traverse and the three great ice sheets, shrouded in notoriety and storm and bombarded by falling rocks. I read wide eyed about *Death Bivouac* and the *Traverse of the Gods* and the *Spider*, and those last difficulties in the *Exit Cracks* where Corti,

The Wriggle piton: according to Grahame Nicoll, who took the photo, it is one of the most clipped pitons in Scotland and would still take a modest fall.

the Italian lone survivor, had hung from his long wire being drawn slowly centimetre by centimetre up out of the maelstrom on his rescuer's back. And back into bitter, slandered life.

On a happier note Smythe advised me that on the Brenva Face of Mont Blanc I should *stand four-square to the slope and hew from the shoulder* and Murray told me of the *fat blue spark* that had jumped from Dunn's bootnail as the latter had stumbled descending Curved Ridge on the Buachaille in winter, and how he had *gathered* Dunn to his bosom – as, without a doubt, every good ropemate should... Murray also had described MacAlpine's prowess in flowing up an icy gutter *like a persian cat to a milk saucer*. All this was grist, as they say, to the romantic mill, and indeed that cat became my ideal of perfection. *This* would be how *I* would climb icy gutters, smooth and focused as a stalking cat. Or so I intended.

The next winter, when I was thirteen, I climbed an insignificant hill near my parents' house. Booted in my wellies, I climbed it in the snow and gazed from the summit at the long white line of the Highlands stretching from Ben Vorlich in the west past Schiehallion to Glas Maol and the Broad Cairn to the north-east. All glittered in the frosty sunlight. I imagined them lofty Alpine and Himalayan Peaks, those little, rounded, unknown Scottish hills, and I transformed their gentle southerly and south-easterly slopes into icy north wall precipices. Deliciously I dreamed of dangers, of stormy strife and desperate struggle. I didn't know anyone who actually did climb mountains although twice I had gone with some school-mates on hill-walks, wearing kilts(!) and plimsoles and led by our head-master, to the Trossachs; once to the summit of Ben Vorlich above Loch Earn and once to the summit of Ben Ledi above Loch Katrine. The hot sun, heathery slopes, and the sweetness and purple stain of ripe blaeberries are all that I remember about those expeditions. And yet how deeply they influenced my future directions.

For my fourteenth birthday my mother bought me a bicycle: second-hand, single speed, blue frame, straight handlebars not the cissie ones which bent back like those on my sister's bicycle. I took to riding in the summer, always in the direction of Schiehallion which looked, from the direction of my little hill if not from any other, as the most mountainous of the mountains. And the name, ah the romance of that name! I never did reach Schiehallion but I passed several times an obvious cliff above the main A9 just north of Dunkeld.

I worked, that summer, on my mother shamelessly wheedling the poor woman into buying me, in a moment of later much regretted weakness, a pair of black leather Dachstein mountaineering boots, a 70 centimetre Stubai Aschenbrenner, and a rope; it was a #3 laid nylon rope, 120ft., white. I also saved my berry-picking money to buy a piton, two oval steel karabiners, a rock-climber's hammer on a length of string, and a length of #3 laid nylon rope, white, tied into a loop with a double fisherman newly learned especially for that purpose. I bought them from Banks the Outfitters, the outdoors shop in Perth. My books had spoken to me of ice-axes, of ropes and of slings and karabiners and piton-hammers. Now, I decided, having acquired them I was properly equipped and ready. I, myself, was a mountaineer.

On my first day of 'real' climbing, one Saturday late during the summer holidays, I set off from our house in Blairgowrie riding my bicycle across the B35 road to Dunkeld. I turned right at the junction with the A9 towards Polney Crag and came across members of a Dundee club, milling around and looking up at the climbs. I collared the youngest, Ally, just a boy of

Simon Yearsley on the Groove. Wriggle goes across the wrinkled slab to the right of the dark slot just below Simon's right-hand rope. Photo: Grahame Nicoll.

thirteen who also was looking to climb; but no-one would climb with him. He was too young and just a beginner. Like me.

I had the rope, I had the gear, and so I led. *Wriggle* (Very Severe) for our first rock climb. We had no guidebook, so we didn't know. I did know, from my books however, how to tie a bowline and thus we at least were able to tie ourselves onto the rope. I knew, also from my books, what calls we should use:

Climb when you're ready
Climbing

OK we chanted religiously although scarcely could I understand Ally's thick Dundonian (I was born and spent my early life in that most cultured of Indian cities, Calcutta, and therefore spoke English with a diction born of the Raj). And I knew, still from my books, the most important bit of knowledge in rock-climbing – at least in those days before climbing became just another sport – *the leader must never fall!*

I straggled through the bush, leaving it enwrapped with my precious sling and one of my two karabiners as I strained around the corner under the overhang. It was a series of tricky little moves, wobbling from large chalky flake, fingers jammed into a sharp-edged slot, to hands clamped over a rounded, greasy edge. And fighting that ferocious tree, of course. Thence into a shaky position out in the open, bridged in my new boots, across the shallow groove over the abyss. Knees a-tremble I pounded my precious piton into a pocket in a dirty crack, sprouting lichen and a few blades of grass, twenty five feet or so above the bottom of the cliff. I clipped my remaining karabiner to it. And by sheer good fortune I clipped the climbing rope through that sole karabiner in such a way that it ran, although reluctantly. I moved on heaving against its immense drag. I didn't fancy the look of the overhanging corner that continued straight above (*The Rut*) and so traversed rightwards under it across a wall, then straight up on sloping holds a further sixty feet to the summit of the climb, to grass and to bushes and trees. And to my salvation and the descent path. (*Wriggle*). Ally, when he followed, didn't have a hammer and so the piton remained. For many years.

Death, it must be observed, had hovered close upon my heels that day but I was ignorant. I was young then, foolish, and filled with a fine new passion. Today, almost half a century later and many years past my last adventures on crag and mountain-face, the lingering memory mocks me in my safe and studied, and regretful, ways:

> The Moving Finger writes; and, having writ,
> Moves on: nor all thy Piety nor Wit
> Shall lure it back to cancel half a Line,
> Nor all thy Tears wash out a Word of it.

The Rubáiyát of Omar Khayyám LI (trans. Fitzgerald)

IT WAS UPON A LAMMAS NIGHT

By Iain Smart

IT WAS UPON A Lammas night when corn rigs are bonnie that we drove up Glen Clova one fine evening to climb on a little crag on the sunny side of the glen. I remember the ash trees had already lost their leaves and their bare branches were hung about with heavy bunches of bronze keys glowing in the sunshine.

We did a few short climbs. They were strenuous and on one pitch I had to be pulled up by the rope, something unthinkable a few years ago, informing me that my tree of life had lost its leaves and I was sib with the ash trees.

As we lay out on the top of the crag while I recovered and my companion coiled the rope, a mighty Sea King helicopter flew low up the glen on some rescue mission. The noise shattered the tranquillity of the evening. The tree tops waved and even the grass was flattened by the mighty down-draught that kept five tons of metal in the air.

Once the hubbub had passed and the scattered pieces of the evening's stained glass had reassembled themselves we did another climb. This time I slipped and pendulumed off the crux, completing the ascent on another climb altogether. Life is full of surprises.

As I lay back luxuriously in the heather deprecating the lack of originality of people who stayed on one route from start to finish, our attention was directed to a kestrel hovering over the stubble field below us. The bird identified some small movement in the complex terrain beneath, swooped down a hundred feet onto a small creature, rose up with it clutched in its claws and made off to rend it apart and so maintain its being at the expense of some field mouse or, more explicitly, by utilising the energy stored in the chemical bonds of the little creature's tissues.

'Doesn't the feat it has just performed fill you with wonder?' I asked my companion, as he neatly twirled the end of the rope round the coils and threaded the end through the gap above the twirls.

'Not particularly, he replied, 'that's just what kestrels do.'

'Try replicating that with a computer the size of a bird brain.'

'Small drone aircraft can zap targets on the ground almost as accurately. It's a matter of miniaturisation.'

'You will never parallel what that kestrel has done with an electronic system, however miniaturised.'

'Why not?'

'Because there is a fundamental difference between the biological computer in that bird's skull and the electronic computer on your desk.'

I let the answer hang for a minute. He lent back comfortably, his head pillowed on his folded up rope and disclaimed any support.

'This is your field, you tell me. I am a philosopher.' he replied 'I know what the brain does, but not how it does it.'

'Well hold firm, I am about to make an intellectual pendulum from systems that work by electronic current to those that use ionic current.'

'Go ahead. It won't be the first time you've done that manoeuvre this evening.'

'The brain and a computer both process signals,' I began, 'but achieve their results using different substrates.'

'Explain what you mean by that, oh wise one.'

'An electronic computer is just that. It works by pushing electrons along wires and in so doing generates a lot of heat. In order to dissipate heat the components have to be far enough apart for a fan to blow a draught of cooling air over them. This sets a limit to miniaturisation. A computer with the processing capacity of the kestrel brain made from electronic components would generate a lot of heat and would therefore require a sophisticated cooling system. It would also need to carry a generator somewhere to provide the power required to drive electrons through its myriad components and to work the fans required to cool them. The actual signal processing done by a computer doesn't use much energy: it's the powering-up of the components that is expensive. Then the whole caboodle would have to be lifted off the ground and given the ability to hover, identify a tiny little animal in the grass, swoop down silently from a hundred feet and daintily pick it up.'

'Go on,' he said, 'so how does the kestrel do it?

'Kestrels, like all biological systems, use ionic current, not electronic current.'

'What in the name of the wee man is the difference between an electronic and an ionic current? They are both currents are they not? They both use electrons to pass signals?'

'Ionic current is much more subtle. It depends on separating charged ions of sodium and potassium along the membrane that covers the living protoplasmic strand that is a nerve fibre. A signal is transmitted by a breakdown in polarisation travelling along the outside of the protoplasmic strand. It is a slower way of passing a signal but generates less heat than pushing electrons along a wire of the same diameter. It needs some energy to separate the sodium and potassium ions, so the separation is a form of order and is thus an energy store. The passage of a nerve impulse is like toppling a row of dominoes. The change from ordered to disordered dominoes dissipates energy in the form of heat but not nearly as much as pushing electrons along a wire. Then of course you have to pay the bill. The dominoes have to be set up again, but much of the required energy is available locally from the heat released from the collapse of the dominoes. This of course is the principle of the Stirling Engine, discovered by biological systems aeons before the advent of humans.'

My leader looked baffled. He was a philosopher after all.

'So that solves the heat problem.' I explained: 'transmission of ionic nerve impulses is energy efficient. The brain is really "cool" in both senses. Practically it means that the cells in the kestrel brain can be crammed close together. The other trendy word that comes to mind is "neat".'

'If what you say is true, "cool" and "neat" are valid in both old and modern senses of these words,' he agreed philosophically.

'If we ever make a computer from electronic components with the capacity of the human brain – able to philosophise to itself and laugh at its own jokes – or even better able to understand what it's laughing at, it will be the size of an aircraft hangar and generate prodigious amounts of heat and require the energy content of millions and millions of mice.'

Our conversation was interrupted at this point by the return of the immense yellow Sea King helicopter. The noise was deafening, terrifying all the mice for miles around. It hovered near us as if we might provide some business. A man at the door gave us a wave. We gave him the thumbs-up. He looked disappointed. If necessary he could be lowered on a wire to pick up an injured climber, the analogue of the kestrel's mouse.

Later, as the evening fell gently on bonnie Glen Clova, a kestrel returned and showed us how a professional does the job, neatly and coolly.

'Aye, the wee craitur has the knack,' my friend admitted. 'But it took your biological systems millions of millennia to perfect an ionic computer. We have only been at it for a hundred years or so; we'll produce an analogue one day. Meanwhile let's go into Kirrie and pick up a neat fish supper and a nice cool beer.'

TO WP[1] ON PIZZO BIANCO: 17 JULY 1923

By Graeme Morrison

You found, like some Phoenician trader long ago,
Wide-scattered lands of song, lapped all by one great sea,
Heard horns of Elfland echo in the Odyssey,
Or in Byrhtnoth at Maldon saw Roland's valour glow;

And felt as deep delight on April days to go
On Arran's granite combs, and view from summit scree
Ridges white to the north, and islands in the sea,
Or weather Ardnamurchan in an onshore blow.

May Freya[2] and Poldores[3] haven your lifeless head,
For on the firn-sea now your mortal shell is spread,
While westwards Monte Rosa, dawn-lit, coruscates.

Enrapt a half-hour since, you deemed this spot most blessed;
Now at the sunrise flush, upon this sparkling crest,
For you, as for us all, the encircling ocean waits.

---

[1] William Paton Ker, 1855–1923. Literary scholar, Professor of Poetry at Oxford, and original member of the Club. 'One of the most endearing men that Glasgow ever produced,' his motto (from Horace) was *nos manet oceanus*.

[2] Freya Stark, 1893–1993. Acolyte of Ker, and in later life a celebrated travel writer.

[3] Poldores MacCunn, 1896–1983. God-daughter of Ker; subsequently a medical practitioner.

THREE TICKETS IN THE NATIONAL LOTTERY

By George Allan

The first ticket

IT FEELS LIKE A lifetime ago now, that winter a few years before the session in the Clachaig when Chouinard, Cunningham and MacInnes, over a few malts, confined the art of step cutting to the history books, or so the story goes. To be a man, and it was almost all men in those days, you had to possess the skills to fashion a neat step in neve with one swing of the axe and to cut a ladder in ice with the economy of a skinflint. I was really just a boy still but I wanted to be a man so I signed up for a winter climbing course with the Glencoe School of Winter Climbing. MacInnes was, of course, the presiding spirit and, at that point, Clough was his second in command.

Our small party was billeted at the Glencoe Youth Hostel for a couple of shillings a night. The first day was dawning fine and cold as we congregated outside awaiting our orders. They soon came, but not in the way we expected. A hillwalker had failed to return and Hamish, as the epicentre of all things mountain rescue in the glen, was mounting a search; he was rounding up volunteers and we were handy for the purpose, although our participation could hardly have been called voluntary. I was dispatched, by myself, to search the Lairig Gartain. The snow sparkled under a cobalt sky as I zigzagged up the glen, shouting out at regular intervals. It was a supremely beautiful day but my efforts, and those of the others searching elsewhere, were unsuccessful. Happily, the lost walker appeared under his own steam.

The next day provided what we came for. In Coire nan Lochan, we got to grips with the craft of winter climbing. We were taught well and returned to hostel pleased with our day of step cutting, bollard belaying and launching ourselves head first down the slope to perfect the art of axe breaking. We were half way through enjoying a well-earned meal when a message came through that another rescue was underway: we were wanted again. Little strings of torches bobbed their way up the path to Coire nam Beitheach; occasionally, high above us, arc lights pierced the darkness. Word started to come down the line that we weren't on a rescue mission, we were there to carry down the bodies. When we reached the coire the grisly part of the job had been done and the two young students were trussed up on stretchers with only their boots protruding from under rucksacks and canvass. Few words were exchanged as the stretchers were carried down the hill.

Next day, the clouds were down, the temperature was up and there were spits of rain in the air: a day for a snowless Clachaig Gully in Hamish's view. We had only scrambled as far as the bottom of the Great Cave Pitch when stones started rattling down. We beat a retreat. Once we were safe, Hamish outlined his solution. A section of the left wall was loose, he said, discharging debris from time to time – dynamite would solve the problem. I never did discover whether he carried out this threat.

The weather was much the same the following day with little snow visible beneath the cloud covered tops of the Three Sisters. We were becoming frustrated; we were half way through the week and had yet to get to grips with a winter pitch. To everyone's surprise, Hamish announced that we would learn to climb ice on the north face of Gearr Aonach. There were mumblings of dissatisfaction as we traversed round under the cliffs but we should have had faith: if anyone would know where there might be ice in Glencoe, it would be Hamish. He had judged it right, of course. As we rounded a corner, there, in a rocky depression, was a steep channel of ice. It seemed to emerge by magic from a small bay and disappear into a pile of boulders at its base but it was enough to allow us to spend the day chipping away contentedly on a top rope.

We descended by a different route, dropping more directly down steep ground till stopped by a short wall. Hamish threw a rope round a handy tree and announced that we needn't go to the bother of an abseil, using the rope as a handrail would allow a speedy down climb. Making quick work of this obstacle, my compatriots waited in a bunch below for the final man to descend. I hadn't been paying attention and, instead of using the rope as an extra hold, I leant back on it as if to abseil. The inevitable happened: I took flight. Landing on a shelf at the base, I grabbed out wildly and, by sheer luck, caught hold of the rope and steadied myself. Below, the heather dropped away steeply till the slope disappeared over another cliff. Hamish gave me a quizzical look, pulled down the rope and we all trooped off on a faint path which traversed round the hill.

The second ticket
It was a long time ago now. During those years when most people climb at their most intensive, I had stayed away from the hills. When I decided to return, I was desperate just be up there and, as luck would have it, I fell in with Chizzer, that character of the great outdoors, then resident in Aberdeen. I provided the enthusiasm and he reminded me which end of the rope was which and so it was that we found ourselves, on a sultry summer's day, half way up the Black Spout. *Route 2* on the Pinnacle was my idea: I was taken by the description of the long, exposed traverse on the second pitch. Chizzer fixed a belay at the base of the rib on the uphill side of the initial fault which I then proceeded to enjoy: steady climbing with well protected moves. Below, I could hear Chizzer passing the time of day with a couple of people descending the Spout. At the top of the chimney-crack, blocks, well jammed to all appearances, filled the corner and a slab slanted leftwards to the belay. I bridged up onto the slab, right foot on one of the blocks. It started as an ominous grinding sound, then everything went into slow motion, then a roar and finally a series of deafening explosions as block after block burst amongst the rubble in the Spout. When the noise of artillery finally stopped, an acrid smell filled

the whole gully. To my amazement I was still there, perched on the slab.

'Chizzer! Chizzer!'

'I'm okay – it all missed me.'

I closed my eyes and pressed my forehead against the slab and breathed deeply. Waves of relief flooded through me but they were short lived; with a sudden jolt, an ice cold finger ran down my spine – the guys down the Spout!

'Are you alright?'

My shouts echoed back up to me off the walls and then silence. 'Oh, God. I've killed them, I've killed them!'

Louder, louder, louder – 'Are you alright? Are you alright?'

Again the mocking echo and silence. At last an unmistakable sound – a tiny, distant voice rising from somewhere near the bottom of the gully.

'Yes – we-are-alright. Are-you-okay?'

I was pinned to the mountain, the rope being jammed behind boulders now wedged in the fault. With some jiggery-pokery, I made it to safety. We said little as we walked back across the corrie to the track and the waiting car.

There is a scene at the end of the film *Deliverance* when Jon Voight's character is back home after the horrific descent of the river. He has a nightmare in which the placid surface of the lake into which the river flows is suddenly broken by a human arm rising slowly out of the water. Over the following month, I kept waking in the darkest hours with a start. I swear that I heard a ferocious rumbling and that the room was filled with an acrid smell.

The third ticket

It was some years ago. It was mild, too mild, as John and I squelched up the Allt a' Mhuilinn, but with the Ben it is always worth persisting. The snow was soft and the temperature was hovering just above freezing as we ascended the left lobe of Coire na Ciste, however there was fat ice about. We choose *Five Finger Discount*. I was anticipating a not too demanding climb and a pleasant late winter stroll back across the plateau.

A river of ice topped by a channel of neve found me belayed in the right hand corner of a bay. On its opposite side, a short wall leads to a steep, but stepped, mixed section culminating in a sharp edge beyond which the route follows a gully. An hour later I was still at the same stance. Impatience was growing: 'Just go for that wall, John, it can't be that hard', I kept repeating under my breath. In that wonderfully old fashioned phrase once used by Don Whillans in a similar situation, he was going up and down 'like a bride's nightie'. John was trying to get purchase above that wretched little section of rock but to no avail. Then suddenly he made his move: axe in a sod of turf in a tiny alcove just to the right of the wall, feet up, left axe into good ice above the wall – problem solved. He was soon out of sight with the ropes paying out quickly as he climbed the gully.

Half an hour later, I was repeating John's performance for the umpteenth time. Up the wall I would go until I could just reach the top, but what I needed lay one foot above. I had tried sinking my axe into the turf sod but, while frozen, it vibrated alarming demonstrating all too clearly why he had been reluctant to use it. I had to find a better solution. With John well out of earshot, a tight rope was out of the question. A better climber would have discovered a way of utilising the thin, but hollow, skin of ice drooling down the wall but I could make no sense of it at all; a prudent climber would have pulled up on the rope but I wanted to do it cleanly. 'You can't stay here for ever', I thought 'it has to be the turf' – in went the pick, up went my left crampon, left arm swung towards the good ice – then the axe flew out, turf attached.

'A couple of feet, a jerk and I will stop' but there was no jerk and no stopping. Coire na Ciste, intensely coloured, accelerated towards me. Finally the jolt came and my plunge stopped. I was thirty feet below the bay. I righted myself, put in a screw and shook my limbs – 'Thank God, nothing damaged'. I looked up, the rope, taught as piano wire, was hooked over a small protuberance on the sharp edge – our connection with the Ben and with life itself.

A mumbling and groaning started in the gully beyond the rib to my left – 'The bloody belay peg ripped'.

Up the gully John went again. This time the belay was sound and I had a very tight rope. I led through on the easy final pitch. One of the ropes trailing behind me was trashed, elongated with the sheath torn exposing three metres of damaged core. Please don't let there be anyone at the belay! But there was, a climber completing *Burrito's Groove*. That sharp edge had saved us from death but not from the ignominy of having to explain how incompetent climbing and a poorly constructed belay had led to a mangled rope!

John and I had better days in the hills. I still occasionally give in to temptation and give the lottery a whirl. John is in a home, a prisoner of dementia: a ticket in a different lottery. The North Face of the Ben, austere and indifferent, looks down on us all.

OCEANO IRRAZIONALE

By Rob Adams

PERCHED HIGH ABOVE THE valley, looking up at the crux off width pitch of *Oceano Irrazionale*, I was feeling somewhat intimidated. My selfless and generous thoughts of offering the lead to my partner put aside, there was only one thing for it. Camelot 5 racked, I was on my way. French 6a+ can't be that hard, can it … ?

Val di Mello. Wake up to the sound of cow bells drifting down the alpine meadows with a light mist lifting from the tree lined granite walls. Forage for Porcini mushrooms amongst wildflowers in grassy pastures. Soothe your feet in cool glacial meltwater whilst relaxing in the warm sun on rest days. Enjoy butter and cheese polenta with locally made red wine, after a long day climbing in the high valleys. Besides that, it's also a traditional and alpine rock climbing paradise.

If you have visited, you may also remember the granite hulk that hangs over the entrance to the valley, may possibly remember trying to avoid direct eye contact as you walk past to find your route for the day, or maybe wiping sweaty palms after thinking for just a little too long about climbing the crack system that runs directly up the front face. That hulk of granite is the Asteroidi, and the crack system is *Oceano Irrazionale*, starting from a wooded ledge system which slashes through the crag half way up.

It had been eight years since I first set foot in the Mello. I was in the very early stages of my climbing career, and after a baptism of fire on *Il Risveglio di Kundalini* (my first multi-pitch rock climb), climbing something like *Oceano* seemed highly improbable, verging on eternally impossible. But that's how seeds are sown.

In September 2016, halfway through my six months away from the office, I was back in the valley, at the end of a productive two-month trip in Europe. I'd had the pleasure of spending the month of August with my brother Tom, climbing classic routes including *La Demande* in Verdon (at 6a or 'HVS' the biggest sandbag ever!), *Luna Nascente* in Val di Mello, *Via Cassin* on the Piz Badile and the *Westgrat* on the Salbitschijen ('possibly the best multi-pitch rock route anywhere,' to quote Mr A. Nisbet). We'd ascended 4000m peaks in Saas Fee, and completed one of the finest and most absorbing scrambles ever, the Lenzspitze-Nadelhorn traverse. I had enjoyed a week of alpine cragging, culminating in the super classic *Rébuffat-Baquet*, and then had two weeks climbing in the Dolomites with my wife Bex, including the superbly exposed *Piaz Arête* on the Vajolet Towers. It's fair to say that by the time I met my close friends, Sam and Clare in Val di Mello, whilst exhilarated and satisfied, my body was feeling a little tired.

The observant reader will have spotted that I'd been in Val di Mello already with my brother, and climbed *Luna Nascente*, a route so famous it has its own poster in the local campsite. Stunning crack climbing at

The Asteroidi above Val di Mello. All photos: Rob Adams.

around E2 culminates in a French 5a slab on the final pitch. I can hear your thoughts already: 5a? No problem, especially after completing the crux pitches lower down! I'm wearing my action shoes, and can climb two numbers harder; this will be a breeze. It turns out a breeze would have been nice. Twenty-seven degree heat, combined with shoes two-and-a-half sizes too small and 25m of unprotected slab resulted in the inevitable: excruciating pain with a side portion of terror. The kind of pain that makes you climb standing on your heels, or to take your shoes off before you set up a belay while trying not to vomit. We were delighted to have completed the route, but were in no hurry to climb anything else whilst it was that hot. After a day of being unceremoniously spat off single pitch 5b slabs we high-tailed it to higher altitudes and lower temperatures. Most importantly we went with a fine set of excuses not to tackle the obvious challenge. Glaciated granite can be a hard taskmaster.

Back to Mello a second time, the excuses had run out. I was going well, had a willing partner, and a good forecast for the mountains meant that Sam and I would be climbing *Oceano* the next day.

I knew we should be able to complete the route, but for some reason the intimidation factor was disproportionately high. Maybe it was that the route felt particularly committing, hanging high above the valley. Or perhaps it was that I felt a personal responsibility for success. Could it be that the route has a bit of a reputation, and I was worried we may befall the same fate as previous contenders? We've all be there, there's a gremlin sat on your shoulder, casting doubt over your ability and ideas:

'Are you sure you are climbing that well? What makes you think you

Sam Chinnery on the approach to the climb.

can climb this route? I don't think you're fit enough! I don't think you'll have enough time...' I realised that I was still looking up at *Oceano* through the eyes of the novice who finished *Kundalini* eight years ago, shell-shocked with bloodied hands; through the eyes that had witnessed a storm arrive late-afternoon, from the safety of the valley, and seen climbers frantically descending amongst torrents of water, head torches rolling down the face like shining raindrops.

I'd need to put aside those images of eight years ago and break the route down into a set of attainable goals. I'd need to employ tactics similar to those I use on Christmas Day – put five plates of food in front of me and I'd be a bit intimidated, but deliver them sequentially, and spaced out a little, no problem. So breaking this challenge down into sections, I did my best to transform the task into nice bite-sized chunks. And armed with the confidence and experience from the previous two months, and riding a temporary peak on the emotional wave, we set off (possibly an hour or two later than we should have done) for the climb. What's the worst that could happen?

After a relaxed start, we broke off the main track running up the valley and headed uphill. Two hours of adventurous approach, much of it nearing vertical and on frayed rope masquerading as Via Ferrata, meant that going up was fast becoming much more appealing than going down. After some too-ing and fro-ing from Sam on the initial unprotected chimney, we were on our way!

Climbing the soaring vertical flake above the first pitch I was in the zone and flowed upwards, reaping the benefits of two months on rock. I stopped only occasionally to place a secure Camelot, it felt like I couldn't

The soaring flake crack on pitch 2 of Oceano Irrazionale.

fall off. Sam climbed a technical groove, and, free climbing a variation through the pendulum noted in the guidebook, we arrived at the crux pitch.

The exposure was now dizzying. People in the valley below were reduced to the size of ants, going about their business unaware of the fine line being trodden between excitement and fear high above them. Beyond the off-width and capping roof above, easier climbing would lead us to the summit. It all came down to the next 30m.

Spurred on by rare positive encouragement from Sam, I set off, working my way up towards the roof. The uncertainty diminished and confidence grew. Soon I was changing direction, vertical grove transitioning to horizontal off- width, heart pumping fast, eyes and fingers searching for the next hold. The perfect vertical handholds of the vertical crack below were a distant memory, so a different tactic was required. The off-width devoured my leg to well above the knee and the Camelot 5 was deployed.

I paused to take in the situation. Beneath my feet the blank wall swept 120m down to the ledge below, then another 180m to the base of the crag. Fear gave way to pure enjoyment. Keep on moving. Insert leg a little higher. Slide the cam up a little further... Insert, slide, repeat.

As I withdrew my leg from the Asteroidi's granite jaws and swung up onto the belay ledge, I was met by a wave of emotions. Over the years I have aspired to many milestones and objectives, some big and some small. Subconsciously, climbing *Oceano* had become one of the big ones. Should I be ashamed to admit that euphoria and adrenaline almost brought a tear to my eye?

I made a mental note not to believe everything that guidebooks say

Sam traversing the off-width high on the route.

(cams up to size 4? Yeah right!), and whilst setting up the belay, I thought of the bold first ascentionists who climbed the route without modern camming equipment. I brought up Sam. He made some satisfyingly concerned mutterings about peeling off. I did have a bit of sympathy for him. Running the Camelot 5 up the crack as I climbed provided me with security; it also provided Sam with the prospect of a wild swing across the blank slab below, should he fall off. Fortunately, he held it together and we made a clean ascent.

After a slip on some grass on the 2b pitch above almost cost us the onsight, we embarked upon our summit bid with the crux pitches behind us. One pitch from the top I heard a cry from below; the Italians who had been following us throughout the day (apparently without my close friend the Camelot 5) had reached their psychological limit and were calling for a rope. Rescue complete, we topped out and began our onsight of the 8a... In reverse, to abseil to the base of the crag I should add.

Dusk fell quickly upon us and soon we were lost in the trees at the base of the crag, happy with our experience but wishing that we'd gotten up that little bit earlier... Back in the valley, we reaped the rewards of our rescue, with gifts of homemade speck (smoked ham), cheese and beer from our Italian friends.

NOT CRICKET AT THE CIC

By Noel Williams

PICTURE, IF YOU WILL, the CIC Hut on the morning of Christmas Eve. Willie and Chris are in residence. The weather is not encouraging and they are both enjoying a long lie-in. It is shortly before noon. They are trying to escape the false jollity and commercialism of the festive season. They are not miseries, far from it, but they also hope to have the 'hill' to themselves for a change.

Little do they know that as they lie dozing a strange duo are all the while approaching up the Allt a' Mhuilinn. One is the secretary of the local rescue team, the other is a reporter for Highland Radio. They try the door but it is locked. They knock loudly. Willie is half awake and can hear their voices. Then he spots them peering through a knot-hole in the shutters.

'I'm sure there's someone in there, but they're still dossing. Anyone in there? Open up, this is the rescue team.'

Willie gets up and opens the door.

'I'm Andy Nicol of Lochaber MRT. We're just up to do an interview about climbing on Ben Nevis.'

Willie notes that Andy is well kitted out, but the reporter seems to be wearing a leather motorcycle jacket and floppy fell walking boots. The pair then stand outside for some 15 minutes while the reporter records an interview with Andy. Andy names the main gullies and buttresses and points out some of the places where climbers come to grief. Willie soon loses interest and goes back inside. Anxious to lock the door Willie enquires, 'Are you coming in or what?' They eventually go inside. Willie offers them a cup of tea. They chat for a while.

'What are you doing up here at Christmas? What has the weather been like?'

At this stage the reporter's tape recorder is in his knapsack. 'Would you be prepared to give me an interview for Highland Radio?'

'No chance, but that man over there might.'

Chris amazingly is still asleep in his sleeping bag oblivious to all that has been going on.

'I believe you might be willing to give me an interview?'

'Uugh? What?'

Despite his dozy condition the reporter is anxious to interrogate him. 'Why do so many climbers get into trouble up here every winter?' Willie is tempted to butt in '...because they wear motorcycle jackets and Spanish fell boots.' However, he doesn't want to be drawn into the interrogation, so bites his tongue and goes outside. For the best part of an hour Chris attempts to answer a string of inane questions. Eventually the two residents are left in peace again.

Time passes.

Two days later the weather improves slightly though it remains far from perfect. Willie and Chris have the mountain to themselves or so they think. They set off for *Comb Gully*. As they rope up for the first pitch proper Willie spots a lone figure way down in the corrie below.

Willie eventually arrives below the crux chockstone. Water is flowing down the back. He can't find a belay but eventually excavates a stance. He manages to finagle a poor nut placement and jams himself between the wall and the chockstone. Then he starts to bring up Chris.

Once Chris is installed at the stance, Willie leads out and over the crux chockstone. He soon reaches a stance and knocks in a peg for a belay.

Chris shouts up, 'This guy's soloing up behind us. He's only got one axe.'

Willie can't see their side-kick at this point, but he shouts down: 'Hey pal. This next bit's rather thin. Do you want a top rope?'

'No, I think I'll be alright.'

'Well I think you'd better tie on. Hold on there a moment.'

Chris uses one of his ropes to tie on their strange companion. Willie takes in the slack. Chris then has quite a struggle following Willie around the chockstone.

When their companion eventually tries to second the pitch he falls off at the chockstone and Willie is pulled off the stance. Eventually he has to be hauled up bodily onto the snow slope above.

As the guy comes into view Willie can hardly believe his eyes. He's using a walking axe with a straight pick and is wearing oiled mitts. He has on very bendy boots, but no crampons. He seems to be wearing just a cricket jumper for a top. The pink skin of his chest is exposed in the V of the white jumper's neck. He's carrying an enormous rucksac with side pockets. He has no head covering of any sort and is wearing John Lennon specs.

'Don't you think you're a bit foolhardy trying a route like this with only one axe?

'I was only out for a walk and I saw your tracks. You seemed to know where you were going, so I decided to follow you.'

Chris leads through to the top. When Willie eventually extracts his angle peg from the stance he sees that it has split under the shock load.

They all gather on the plateau and coil the ropes. The cricketer bids his farewell and starts heading off uphill towards the summit. When asked where he's going, he replies, 'To my tent in Glen Nevis'.

Willie and Chris have a friendly word and guide him in the direction of the Red Burn. They watch him disappear into the mist before making their way to the top of Number 4 Gully.

THE GRAHAMS – BOTHIES, BOGS AND SCORPIONS

By Alison Coull

WITH THE RECENT PUBLICATION of an SMC guidebook on the Grahams and Donalds it seems an appropriate time to reflect on the merits of a round of the Grahams.

The Grahams still seem to be an acquired taste but with the SMC book already a best seller and due for a re-print, the number of registered compleationists is creeping up.

Kenny Robb enjoying the evening light on Beinn nan Lus, Argyll. Photo: Alison Coull.

I was definitely a late convert to the Grahams. The Munros had been completed on 1 January 2000. At that time it felt extremely important to finish on millennium day (anyone remember now what that was all about?). I started working my way through the Corbetts. I hadn't heard of Grahams. My partner Kenny had done three rounds of the Munros, a round of the tops and a Corbett compleation when he discovered the existence of another hill list in Scotland. This was a revelation. A new list to tick. Kenny set about the Grahams with the enthusiasm that only comes from having fresh summits to visit. He was now working a nine day fortnight so there was plenty of scope for day trips to tick off the central belt classics. But they were not for me. 'Nope, I am definitely not doing the Grahams. It's a waste of time. Count me out.'

However as the SMC book shows there are a surprising number of Corbetts that can be combined with Grahams. So the Corbett bagging trips inevitably became combined with a Graham or two. Then there were the bash up and down half day jobs just for a leg stretch or when the weather was poor or for some hill fitness. Then there were the ones that were worth doing in their own right. Then there were the ones that involved a trip to an unvisited area or an interesting bothy trip and you may as well go up the Graham while you are there. Then you count up how many you have done and decide that you may as well just finish them.

So it was as part of that process we found ourselves at Over Phawhope bothy near to Hawick for a rare three Graham day. It was a bit excessive to stay at Pawhope Bothy. It is only a 15 minute walk from the road end but it was November. It allowed an early start and provided more interest for the weekend. The short approach did carry the risk that such a convenient bothy near to Hawick would be packed with party goers.

The bothy was immaculate and there was nobody there. Great. We got the fire going and settled down. At around 10 p.m. the door opened and a huge, shavenheaded man in camouflage clothing came in – a Phawhope regular we were informed. He disappeared back to the track to get some fence posts for fire wood and returned with 12 full-size posts strapped to his back. He took out a small axe from his rucksack and proceeded to chop cut the posts into stove sized chunks of wood each with a single stroke. The fire was fair blazing now. He stripped to the waist and settled himself down in front of the fire as we tucked in at the side. A bottle of

.Over Phawhope Bothy, November 2009. Photo: Alison Coull.

rum appeared and he swigged straight from the bottle. We made polite conversation although it has to be said that the conversation was mainly oneway. He had been in the army but was feeling a bit traumatised by the experience. Most of his friends had committed suicide or were suffering from PTSD. None of the stories seemed to quite add up.

The conversation took on slightly more sinister tones: 'If you met me in the street, you wouldn't speak to me would you?' Looking at this towering giant of a man with his shaven head and the ring of seven scorpions tattooed round his neck, it was difficult to disagree with this statement. Eventually the bottle of rum was finished. Scorpion man passed out in his chair and we retired to bed. It was hard to sleep. Getting up in the night Kenny tiptoed to the door. Scorpion man rolled over. 'Who's that?' he shouted. 'It's all right, it's just me' – Kenny's reply came out in a high pitched squeak. 'No it's not f…..g all right' came the bawled reply. But then Scorpion man rolled over and went back to sleep.

In the morning Scorpion man said he had not slept very well. He had had a nightmare about an intruder getting into his house. We sympathised but said we were in a bit of a hurry and left for the Grahams. It was a beautiful day but we had to return to the bothy to pick up our stuff. Oh well hopefully he would be gone. The bothy was in sight. We saw that the fire was still going. We prepared for re-entry. 'Ah you are back'. 'I thought you would like a cup of tea'. 'You must come back at New Year – we have a great party here'. We thanked him for the tea, assured him we would consider the New Year party and packed up our stuff.

Then there was the wild boar incident on Alladale estate. We were on our way back from the Graham and I stopped at the side of the track. Unknown to me a wild boar was approaching from the other side. Kenny watched mesmerised thinking surely she has seen the boar. But no, I didn't notice its presence until it was almost taking the sandwich out of my hand. It was massive. I am not sure what the proper etiquette is when confronted with a wild boar but let's just say that it didn't involve facing it down.

Another wildlife incident came on the round of the Moidart bog hell that is Croit Beinn and Beinn Gair. A dead deer came to life dramatically causing both of us to have a mini heart attack. The movement turned out to be a brown coloured badger enjoying a feast of venison.

Not all Graham expeditions were as exciting. It was more usual for interest to be provided by the difficulty of the terrain and absence of anything resembling a path. A trip to Cowal involved an epic ascent through head high bracken and bracken crevasses. Dempster's book notes that this is a rarely climbed summit that will reward the determined walker. The term 'one for the connoisseur' came to be used to describe this sort of horror show. Alternatively 'classic Graham terrain'.

We were now aiming for a joint Graham compleation. I had a bit to do to catch up with Kenny. This meant a rather unwelcome number of repeats for him, particularly around the central belt. But there were a few choice Grahams that came into the category of 'you are on your own for that'.

Alison on the remote Graham, An Cruachan with the Mullardoch ridge in the background. Photo: Kenny Robb.

Fortunately the Edinburgh Mountaineering Club has a few Graham baggers who could be recruited for that remote or elusive summit. Two of these baggers joined me for an Iron Lodge backpacking trip to the remote summits of An Cruachan and Càrn na Breabaig. We met two other Graham baggers doing these hills that weekend. I wonder if those hills have ever had so many ascents in a single day.

Finally, it was nearly all over, the remaining stragglers had been bagged and the Joint compleation was scheduled for November 2014 on Blackhope scar, the nearest Graham to Edinburgh and definitely classic Graham terrain. However, for Kenny a niggle over the last four years developed into a sudden inability to walk in July 2014 and a hip replacement operation. The Graham compleation was on hold until the following November to coincide with publication of the SMC guidebook. A typically soggy affair and the first hill I have climbed where somebody carried an umbrella the whole way.

So that's it. No more lists. Back to the Munros and proper paths, although, there are still the tops to do and then there are the Donalds and the Marilyns…

And what was the significance of the scorpion tattoos? Well, Scorpion man informed us that each one represented a member of the Srebenican special forces that he had killed. The 'Scorpions' being a Serbian paramilitary unit involved in war crimes.

NEW ROUTES

The deadline for sending route descriptions to the New Routes Editor is 30 June each year. Descriptions of some crags and routes have not been included here, but can be found on the New Routes section of the SMC website. In general this applies mainly to short routes and remote crags.

OUTER HEBRIDES

LEWIS SEA-CLIFFS
Uig, Mangarstadh, The Hooded Wall:
Learning to Crawl 35m E4 5c *. Mark Garthwaite, Rab Anderson. 4 Jun 2017.
This climbs the extremely steep finishing groove which forms the hood over this section. Start at the foot of the abseil line (*Bare Black*) and climb the obvious stepped line rightwards up the back wall to a ledge. Draw breath and climb the groove up right to exit; the wedged boulder at the top of the cliff is just above.

Àird Uig, Geòdha Caol-rinneach:
It's Frothy, Man 35m E3/4. Mark Garthwaite, Rab Anderson. 2 Jun 2017.
The central corner; start as for *Backslip Way* (SMCJ 2001), or abseil to the start.
1. 15m Follow *Backslip Way*, then go up left to ledges below the corner.
2. 20m 5c Place a high wire on the left, then move up and right to holds (gear) to gain the ledge at the foot of the upper corner, which is climbed to the top.

Àird Uig, Chapel Geòdha:
Rock Over to Prolapse 30m E2 5c *. Mark Garthwaite, Rab Anderson. 2 Jun 2017.
Climb to ledges partway up *Cor Blimey Corner*, then climb the crack in the right wall until forced out right, where the edge leads to the top.

Àird Uig, Geòdha Ruadh:
(NB 044 385)
This large inlet is situated on the west side of Gallan Head. Go through Àird Uig to the last house (a cafe called 'The Edge') and park just before a gate (NB 0483 3832). Walk up the road for 200m before heading off left for a further 200m.
   Most of the routes lie on the obvious slabby face on the north-west side of the geo. The climbing is better than it looks and the rock is excellent.

South-East Face:
(NB 0448 3853) Non-tidal North-West facing
This fun excursion follows the obvious pegmatite intrusion which rises from left to right across the face. Mainly easy climbing on good rock in a fine position. Approach by abseiling down a grassy gully direct to ledges at the start of the route.

You're So Vein 55m Severe *. Andrew Wielochowski, Noel Williams. 11 May 2017.
1. 40m 4a Follow the pegmatite band rightwards via a steep step which requires care with protection. Belay on a comfortable horizontal ledge.
2. 15m Continue traversing over a few easy steps to the top.

North-West Face:
(NB 0445 3855)   Non-tidal   South-East facing
Approach: Either by scrambling down in a southerly direction and traversing in (one awkward step), or by abseiling from the cliff-top. For all but the first route it is best to belay in a deep crack which slants across the easy-angled lower section of the slab.

Quite Gnice   25m   Diff. Andrew Wielochowski. 7 May 2017.
From a flat area at the left end of the easy slab, climb up leftwards at first before slanting rightwards to join an obvious crack system which is followed to the top.

Gnice   30m   V.Diff *. Andrew Wielochowski, Noel Williams. 8 May 2017.
Slant leftwards from the bottom crack towards the left-hand end of a thin tapering overhang. Climb a thin crack system direct to the top.

No More Mr Gnice Guy   30m   VS 4c *. Andrew Wielochowski, Noel Williams. 11 May 2017.
Go up to a short left-facing corner below the right end of the thin tapering overhang. Climb up directly at first, then traverse right on small flakes with difficulty before continuing up to a prominent overhang. Either surmount this direct using excellent flake-pockets or step left and cross it without difficulty above a pale flake. Continue easily to the top.

Really Gnice   30m   H.Severe 4b **. Andrew Wielochowski, Noel Williams. 8 May 2017.
Slant slightly right from the bottom crack to the left-hand side of a small black slab. Climb a thin crack system direct to the upper overhang. Arrange a belay on the right before finishing direct on amazing holds.

Gnice Enough   30m   H.Severe 4b *. Andrew Wielochowski, Noel Williams. 8 May 2017.
Slant rightwards from the bottom crack to the right side of a small black slab. Climb a thin crack system direct to a small grass ledge. Finish more easily just to the right of a right-facing corner.

Àird Uig, Geòdha Gorm:
(NB 0646 3808)   West facing
This large bay lies 1.5km east of Àird Uig. There is a conspicuous slabby intrusion of pink rock some 80m high on its eastern side. This first route is an adventurous outing with some scary rock and limited belays. It starts well above the sea from a fairly comfortable grassy bay a little above the base of the slab at the bottom right of the face (looking up). From there it gains and follows the left-hand arete. Approach: From a parking area beside on old building (NB 0532 3700) on the east side of the road about 1km south of Àird Uig. Head north-east across rough moorland for some 1.3km to the summit of Rubha Mòr (c160m). It is probably worth descending the cliff-top on the western side of the bay to get a good view of the face. Then descend the cliff-top on the eastern side of the bay to a slight flattening (where two iron stakes have been left in place). Abseil 75m directly to the grassy bay. Either belay on the abseil rope or on blocks set in the grassy terrain further right.

Sunset Boulevard   90m   E1 4c. Andrew Wielochowski, Noel Williams. 9 May 2017.

1. 30m 4c Make a rising leftwards traverse on suspect rock heading for the left-hand arete. Some 5m before the arete place a tape over a small stumpy spike. Move left again then step back right to stand on the spike. Step up and make a delicate move to gain a line of weakness leading left to the arete (excellent belay).

2. 30m 4a Climb a prominent groove and step out right near the top on good holds. Continue more easily up the arete. Eventually traverse left on grassy ground to reach a wide crack with a chockstone.

3. 30m 4b Step back right onto the face and climb slightly rightwards on good holds. Then traverse left to a ledge where the character of the rock changes. Climb blocky holds with care (no protection) and finish up a short corner.

Bernera, Crùlabhig:

All Hail King Silly   20m   E6 6c ***. Mark Garthwaite, Rab Anderson. 1 Jun 2017.
Start at the same point as *Lard of the Pies*, then go up and right to climb the obvious line to finish up *Mixed Blessing*.

Gneiss To See You, To See You Gneiss   20m   E6 6b ***. Mark Garthwaite, Rab Anderson. 3 Jun 2017.
Climb the centre of the wall right of *Crimpology*, up and right by a crack. Stand in the break and power through the bulge to finish up the groove of *Southern Breeze*.

The next two climbs are about 100m further right, just left of a grassy chimney-gully.

The Major's Reserve   20m   E1 5b *. Rab Anderson, Mark Garthwaite. 3 Jun 2017.
Start as for *Wild Orchid* and continue straight up by ledges to a higher ramp. Move up and right then swing out right and cross the headwall to finish up the recess of *Wild Orchid*.

Wild Orchid   20m   E1 5b **. Rab Anderson, Mark Garthwaite. 1 Jun 2017.
Just left of the grassy chimney-gully, gain a short ramp and climb this. Move up to the roof (micro cams) and climb the fine crack up the headwall to finish up a recess.

Dail Beag:

The following route is on the headland between Preacher's Geo and Big West Wall (NB 2257 4648). The rock is rotten at about two-thirds height and not recommended. Abseil from blocks at the western end of the headland overlooking the end of Big West Wall. Anchors are set back a few metres to west of abseil line, additional anchors just above lip of the wall. 35m to ledge around high-tide level.

Lewis Bites Back   35m   H.Severe 4a. Paul Drew, Pete Johnson. 12 Jun 2017.
Start at the foot of the abseil and climb an easy groove to good ledges at about 10m. Go directly up the steep wall on big jugs to a ledge below the overhanging headwall (abseil line). Step left and climb the crack and loose ground above. Belay from the abseil blocks.

Note: Further routes were done in the area of Black Geo,West Face/Cave Slab (Black Zawn p107 in 1996 SMC guide) but yet to be checked if they are new.

NORTH HARRIS, Creag Mo:

The Mighty Chondrion   60m   E7 6c **. Dave MacLeod, Masa Sakano. 6 Apr 2017.

The central fault at the back of the main crag amphitheatre gives two contrasting pitches, with strenuous but well protected horizontal roof climbing on the first.

1. 20m 6c Climb a flake-crack to the border with the roof. Pass a couple of dubious holds in the soft rock patch here to gain the roof crack. Arrange gear with difficulty and make hard moves to a resting position with a knee-bar in the wide crack (Camalot 3.5). Hard moves lead to improving holds rounding the lip to gain a short chimney and a small ledge over the lip.

2. 40m 5c A very traditional pitch up the wide fault, often climbing on the right wall or arete of the fault, but not if this is affected by drips from an overhead seep. Continue to the large grassy terrace and belay. Either escape right along this, or climb another short easy pitch to the top.

NORTH HARRIS, Sròn a' Sgaoth (NB 1461 0396):

Sron a' Sgaoth is the western top of Sgaoth Iosal. The crags lie on the west and south-west prow of the hill. Steep slabs with a prominent, brown waterworn streak lie on the right, facing south-west whilst a steeper nose lies above and left, facing west. The rock is good quality gneiss, mostly very clean but blocky higher up.

Park opposite the three turbines off the A859, 10mins drive north from Tarbert. The crags can be reached in 30mins of steep hillside. Descents for all the routes lie down a gully bounding the nose on the left (north-west) of the routes, where a grass terrace at the crag base is reached by taking the second grass niche leftwards from the scree-filled gully back left to the foot of the routes. It is possibly easiest in ascent or descent to or from the crag to keep right of the lower continuation of the gully and weave up or down grassy areas. A short, broken rock step is taken by a left-trending line to reach a grass terrace below the crags.

Hooded Corner (SMCJ 2016) starts at the nose on the left of the crag overlooking the descent gully.

The crag is split by two corners to the right of *Hooded Corner*, with a tier of rock below. The following climb and *Aon* (2009) take the corners.

Stonecrop Corner   40m   MVS 4b *. John Mackenzie, Andrew James. 20 Jun 2017.

This climbs the less obvious left-hand corner, starting from the lower tier at a big flake. A pleasant climb, easier than it looks.

1. 20m Climb twin cracks up a short steep step to the shelf above. Move right to the bollard on *Aon*, then back up left to an exposed stance.

2. 20m Climb the left wall of the corner to the capping bulge, step right, then over it to continue to a good thread.

Turbinator   35m   HVS 5a **. John Mackenzie, Andrew James. 20 Jun 2017.

To the right of the two corners the crag swings right and steepens. This climb takes the prominent crack-line left of the right-trending line of overhangs. Some very good, sustained crack climbing, adequately protected. A short step below the crack leads to the undercut crack, some good moves up the crack lead to a wide crack; continue up this past stable blocks to the top.

The slabs to the right of the nose are the lowest situated crags on the face, with a steep lower wall on the left, a grass shelf above, the brown water streak to the right and less continuous slabs right again. Improved descriptions were sent for *Da* and *Tri*.

To the left (looking up) of the grassy gully which is left of the nose of the hill are three buttresses. The smaller one adjacent to the gully provided the next route.

Mistaken Identity   40m   V.Diff. Andrew James, John Mackenzie. 20 Jun 2017.
The left-hand side overlooking the gully that separates this crag from the next one on the left, has a fine lower slab of perfect rock.
1. 15m Climb the perfect slab.
2. 25m A blocky scramble taken on the left.

Minor Crags:
For a quick drying solution to the Harris rain, there are some small crags to the north of the A859 south of Tarbert and quite close to the Losgaintir turn off. NB 1334 9479, Alt 170m.
Stalwarts' Bluff is just visible from the road. Park at the large clearing by the concrete fanks. 10mins easy walking reaches a 10m high crag with a steep left-facing sidewall. Routes by Andrew James & John Mackenzie on 22 Jun 2017.

Bluffer   12m   MVS 4b *.
The left-facing sidewall is bounded by a ramp. Climb the ramp to its top, move up to a girdling crack and step right onto the face to finish.

Puffer   12m   MVS 4b.
The sidewall has a slanting crack-line. Climb this to pull onto the front face and finish up the easier rib on the left.

Suffer   10m   V.Diff.
The front slabby face is climbed centrally finishing up a narrow crack.

AN CLISEAM, Coire Dubh Slabs:
An improved description was sent for *The Harris Jig* (SMCJ 2009).

MULLA, Loch Beag Crag:
(NB 220 028)   Alt 170m   South-West facing
This is a small roadside crag on the knoll of Mulla (220m) above Loch Beag, just south of Loch Mòr, on the minor road to Reinigeadal .These lochs lie beneath Tòdun (528m), the shapely hill seen from the high section of the A859 between Tarbert and Stornoway. The Scaladale Outdoor Centre use the crag. The Upper Tier is in the 2016 new routes section.

Lower Tier:
This contains five routes. Route 1 and Route 2 follow vague cracks and grooves at V.Diff and Severe; Route 3 goes straight up the right side of the capping boulder

at Severe; Route 4 is a diagonal line to the top bulge at H.Severe 4b and Route 5 is a direct to the top of the diagonal at VS 4c/5a.

NORTH UIST, Eaval:

Route of all Eaval   50m   Diff. Iain Thow. 28 Aug 2016.
A clean slabby rib just below and SW of the summit, best approached from above, with the easiest descent being on the south side. Climb the rib (30m), then move left to the next rib, finishing up a slab and wall left of a leaning nose.

ST KILDA, Ruabhal:

Making a Splash   75m   E7 6c ***. Dave MacLeod, Natalie Berry. Jun 2017.
Superb rock and climbing, snaking a line through the steep, black roofed walls on the right side of the main wall. Descend by abseil from the lowest ledge on the access ramp, as for *Boat Race*. Start from ledges above the sea.
1. 30m 5b Climb the lovely black wall on excellent rock, trending leftwards, before traversing 3m hard right to a belay in a short corner, underneath the huge roof.
2. 20m 6c Step up to the roof and follow the large break left, around the corner to where it dissipates. Arrange gear and continue traversing left with difficulty on edges and poor undercuts in the roof to gain a good undercut (crucial small cam on lip on the left). Reach side-pulls over the lip and make a hard rock-over (crux) to gain a distant finger lock in the slab above. Step right to a block and climb the short steep wall directly above this to a large ledge.
3. 25m 5c Climb the recess above the ledge and steep flakes above (taking care with a couple of holds) to gain the easier finishing slab.

Dave MacLeod on the FA of Making a Splash (E7 6c), Ruabhal, St Kilda.
Photo: Chris Prescott, Dark Sky Media.

Old Boy Racer 80m E8 7a **. Dave MacLeod, Natalie Berry. Jun 2017.
An excellent route on great rock, with a fingery crux roof. Descend by abseil from
the lowest ledge on the access ramp, as for *Boat Race*.
1. 30m 5c Climb good cracks trending leftwards for 20m, before traversing
leftwards and stepping slightly down to a hidden ledge below the right end of a
long roof system in the wall.
2. 15m 7a Climb up to the roof and traverse left along the break for 5m. Pull
through the roof on tiny crimps and make a desperate move left to a large flat
side-pull. Gain better holds and gear and move steeply up and back right slightly
to a break and a hanging belay (to avoid rope drag).
3. 35m 6b Step up and left into a triangular niche. Climb steeply rightwards to
gain a standing position above the overhang. Move back left on slopers to gain
good holds and a corner which leads to the easier corner leading up the left edge
of the large slab to the top.

INNER HEBRIDES AND ARRAN

RUM, Hallival, Sunny Crag:
(NM 403 966) Alt 320m South facing
This small crag is just north of Pineapple Crag and is guarded by an overhang.
Approach as for Pineapple Crag, 1hr 15mins from Kinloch.

Sunny Rib 14m Severe *. Colin Moody, Cynthia Grindley. 7 May 2017.
The rib at the right side of the crag. Start below and right of the rib. Climb up past
a bulge to a corner-crack, step left and climb the rib.

Sunny Wander 16m Severe. Colin Moody, Cynthia Grindley. 7 May 2017.
Go up to the bulge on *Sunny Rib*, then step left into the corner. Go up the corner,
then move left and finish easily.

Askival, Pineapple Crag:
(NM 407 963) Alt 280m
Pineapple Crag (Inner Hebrides & Arran p 51) is probably the easiest crag to
approach on Rum. The 'big blank slab' mentioned in the guide lies in the centre
of the crag.
　　Follow the Dibidil path and cross the burn east of Hallival (NM 409 968). From
here the crag is obvious up the hill to the south-west, 1hr 10mins from Kinloch.

Big Blank Slab:
This excellent east facing slab is the most obvious rock feature that can be seen
from the ferry when approaching Rum. There is a long overhang at the base of
the slab; *Blank Cheque* goes through this.

Wet Blanket 16m VS 4c. Colin Moody, Cynthia Grindley. 7 May 2017.
Climb the crack left of *Firing Blanks*, finish up ledges. Probably slow to dry.

Firing Blanks 18m VS 4c *. Colin Moody, Cynthia Grindley. 7 May 2017.
Climb the crack left of the long overhang, move right at a slight overlap and
continue up the next crack to heather.

Blank Cheque   32m   HVS 5b **. Colin Moody, Billy Hood, Steve Kennedy.
13 May 2017.
Two cracks go through the long overhang guarding the slab. This route starts from
the grass ledge below the overhang. Climb up the left-hand crack, which is
awkward and strenuous but very well protected. Continue up past a short wider
section, then step right and climb the prominent crack which bends slightly to the
left. The final 2m were avoided by moving right.

Blank Canvas   32m   E1 5b **. Steve Kennedy, Colin Moody, Billy Hood.
13 May 2017.
The rightmost disjointed crack-line. Start from the far right end of the grass ledge
at the base of the arete. Step up just right of the arete, climb a short wall, then pull
left onto the edge to reach the top of a pedestal. Traverse hard left along a sloping
ledge for 2m to reach a deep crack. Climb the crack which leads to tramlines close
to the arete. Traverse left along the tramlines for 3m to the base of a thin crack
which is followed to some blocks where the crack continues leftwards. Make thin
moves across the wall on the right under a small bulge, via a small flake, to reach
another thin crack (crux). Climb the crack and finish on the left.

Wart Crag:
(NM 401 947) Alt 360m
This crag lies below the south end of Clough's Crag and faces south.
Approach: Follow the Dibidil path, then head up, 2hrs from the ferry.

The Search   18m   Severe *. Steve Kennedy, Cynthia Grindley, Colin Moody.
6 May 2017.
Start up a wide crack just right of the left edge of the crag. This leads to a slab.
Continue by cracks close to the edge and finish by a short corner on the left.

Long Walk   20m   VS 4c *. Steve Kennedy, Cynthia Grindley, Colin Moody.
6 May 2017.
Climb the corner of *The Tracker* for 2m, then make awkward moves horizontally
left along a narrow ledge to the base of a left-facing corner. Continue up the corner,
step left and finish directly by the continuation crack.

The Tracker   18m   VS 4c **. Colin Moody, Cynthia Grindley, Steve Kennedy.
6 May 2017.
A corner-crack right of *The Search*.

Wart Way   18m   Severe. Colin Moody, Cynthia Grindley, Steve Kennedy. 6 May
2017.
On the right-hand wall is an overhang about 4m up; start below this. Move up,
then right onto the rib. Climb the rib, continue up a crack and over a bulge.

MULL, Aird Dearg:
Nice to be Back   8m   HVS 5b **. Pete Whillance, Colin Moody. 12 Apr 2017.
The twin inset cracks just right of *Dearg Ard* (Inner Hebrides p109). Harder than
it looks.

Ready to Go   7m   VS 4c. Pete Whillance, Colin Moody. 12 Apr 2017.
Takes the crack in the rib right of *Red Oak*. Move up into a corner below an overhang. Step up right and follow the crack in the exposed rib.

Red Tartan Army   7m   HVS 5a *. Pete Whillance, Colin Moody. 12 Apr 2017.
The last line on the south face, before it turns into a west facing Gully Wall, is a prominent groove. Move up carefully over a shale band to the foot of the groove. Pull over a bulge to enter and follow the groove to the top.

April Isn't Summer   8m   E1 5b *. Pete Whillance, Colin Moody. 12 Apr 2017.
Some 20m left of *Red Tartan Army* on the Gully Wall is a striking crack in a slight groove. Start just right of a small tree. Pull over a bulge to gain the jam crack and follow it steeply to the top.

Balmeanach:
The Wrist Business   16m   F5+ *. Colin Moody, Dot MacLean. 24 Aug 2016.
The first line right of *Otter Fridge* (SMCJ 2016).

Glueless Groove   16m   F6a+ *. Colin Moody, Cynthia Grindley. 27 Aug 2016.
Lies just right of *The Wrist Business*.

Creich (NM 322 235):
Two Severes were climbed by Colin Moody & Cynthia Grindley on 13 Aug 2016 on one of the lowest crags.

Fionnphort, Corner Crag:
This is round left of *Afflictions Rock* (Inner Hebrides p151). A main wall, vertical on the right to gently overhanging on the left, reaches a corner with a smaller steep wall at right angles to it, and facing Fionnphort. There's a large boulder underneath the crag with a smooth sloping top, surrounded by brambles.

Kill or Cure   8m   VS 4c. Lia Guest, Adam Russell. 16 Apr 2017.
Step off the boulder at the base of the crag and climb the obvious crack-line to the tusk-like roof, undercut this left and pull over to the top.

Snake Oil   10m   VS 5a. Adam Russell, Lia Guest. 16 Apr 2017.
Climbs the next crack down and left from *Kill or Cure* straight up then slightly left up to a spike hold above half-height, continuing more or less direct to the top.

Cod Liver Wall   10m   HVS 5a. Adam Russell, Lia Guest. 16 Apr 2017.
Takes the wall left of *Snake Oil* straight up via slanting breaks to gain the same spike-like hold from the other side. From this, climb up leftwards to the top, or direct.

School Crag (Inner Hebrides p158):
Nippy Sweetie   8m   E1/2 5b *. Ewan Lyons, Colin Moody. 19 Jul 2016.
Climb the faint crack left of the orange streak on the left wall of the crag.

Jigsaw   12m   E2 5c **. Ewan Lyons, Colin Moody. 19 Jul 2016.
The blunt rib left of *School's Out*.

ERRAID, Upper Tier, Right Side:

Immersion   10m   E4 6a/b *. Adam Russell. 17 Apr 2017.
The arete and crack to the right of the alcove, with good climbing and good but awkward-to-place gear. Pull on and make a move up to a good hold on the left of the arete. Gain a standing position on this hold using the crack and arete. Climb direct to the break, ledge and top. Tech grade depends on rockover flexibility/ability.

Midgey Crag:

(NM 298 191)   West facing
This is a minor crag near the top of the high point of the south end of Erraid, across a small inlet from the main upper tier.

Coconut Cracks   8m   H.Severe 4b. Corinne Bunton, Andrew Appleby. 27 Aug 2016.
Climb twin cracks up the wall to the highest point of the face.

Arete du Midgey   8m   H.Severe 4b *. Andrew Appleby, Corinne Bunton. 27 Aug 2016.
Start up the cracked left face of the arete, traverse left along the breaks then pull onto the slab.

KERRERA:

Adrian Macleod &Tom Adams in Jun 2016 climbed a route on a small crag at the north tip of Kerrera (NM 843 312) – map provided and photos. The crag is a lovely little suntrap accessible by the Oban marina boat or canoe (our choice). Tom & Rob Adams in Oct 2016 climbed a further 3 short (7–12m) lines on it from HVS– E3/E4. Rock is a ridge of basalt. The SW face is clean and overhanging. The routes follow crack-lines and are pumpy and well protected.

COLONSAY, Strand Boulder (NR 363 904):

Park at the Strand car park on the south end of Colonsay and follow the coast round to the west, past the headland, 15mins. The obvious outcrop sits in a small bay opposite the islet of Rubha nan Ron. A descent gully is on the right. There are more lines to do. Routes by Eilidh Bauchop, Stewart Bauchop, 6 July 2016.

Twin Cracks   15m   V.Diff.
Start left of the obvious corner and climb to a shelf, follow parallel twin cracks up the banded wall to finish. The direct start climbs the overhang on the left at VS. Good belay 5m back on wires.

The Corner   15m   V.Diff.
Climb the obvious right-angle corner with interest to the top.

The overhung nose right of the corner would be about HVS.

Easy Wall   12m   Diff.
Start at the bottom of the grassy descent gully (bounding the crag on its right) and climb slabs and ledges undercut on the left.

ARRAN, Cir Mhor Note:

Adam Russell climbed a more direct finish to *Hardlands* in May 2017, one which prolongs the superb climbing on pocks. Gain the huge pocket as per the normal route, then climb straight up following the line of pocks, slightly right then slightly left to gain the left arete at a point directly above the huge pocket. A bit more run out but the same grade (picture provided).

Goatfell, South Slabs:
Pochmahone Direct 415ft Scottish VS. John Mackenzie, K.Smith. 30 Sep 1972. Basically a more logical and direct route than Pochmahone following a natural line not avoiding the difficulties (seemed a bit bold at the time).
1. 45ft. As for *Pochmahone* or a little on the left, starting in the centre and exiting by a thin score on the slab.
2. 80ft. Climb directly up the slab above the flake belay to below an overlap.
3. 80ft. Straight up the overlap and friction to ledge and block.
4. 150ft. Straight up a steeper wall to a line of pocket holds right of a curved overlap. Friction up to the base of the long curved diedre. Follow this and over the crux scoop at the top.
5. 60ft. Climb directly up the easy slab to a steeper finish.

Cioch na h-Oighe, The Bastion:
Unnamed 90m E8 6c ***. Iain Small, Adam Russell. 10 May 2017. Takes the impressive sweeping slab and wall between *Armadillo* and *Great Escape*.
1. 45m 6c A big pitch. Start up a short hanging groove a few metres right of *Armadillo* with a small rectangular roof at about 5m. From the top of this, head up and right (some crumbly rock), then up left until hard underneath the first long roof. Undercut through the right side of this, then move up to an overlap below the huge roof. A hard move gains the right side of this. Follow the groove up until a break leads left onto a magnificent sweeping slab. Climb straight up this slab up to a thread and a diagonal break. Move slightly leftwards up this to pull right onto the steeper wall above where a line of pockets lead over right to the bolt belay on *Abraxas*.
2. 45m 6a Step left and move up to gain and follow the curving overlap leftwards to its termination near the corner. Layback up this corner until it peters out where a reach round left gains good holds. Rockover, then follow the easiest line to the top, either left up the ramp or go halfway up the ramp and pull right onto the wall via a juggy pocket and up to gain the *Tidemark* ledge.
Note: A third rope was used on the initial wall to limit drag. A few days dry sunny weather are required to dry out the seeps down the main wall from the *Abraxas* break – tactical use of super absorbent Plumb Pads on the day due to it being overcast.

Glen Sannox Slabs:
Slapstick Wall Right-Hand Finish 75m Severe. Colin Moody, Cynthia Grindley. 22 Apr 2017.
1. 50m From the belay after pitch 2, move right and climb the slab, then move right to a huge block.
2. 25m Climb the easy rib above.
Note: Two parties repeated *Slapstick Wall* and thought VS 4b because of the bold third pitch.

SKYE

A winter crossing, probably the first, of Black and Red Cuillin was made by Nigel 'Yorky' Robinson & John McKeever from 2 Apr 1988 to 5 Apr 1988.

SGÙRR A' BHASTEIR:
Formali Known As   100m   IV,4. Mike Lates, Pok Siwinski. 12 Jan 2017.
1. 50m Follow the broad rib left of *Mike The Bhasteird* and belay on the ledge below the left-rising chimney fault.
2. 30m Climb the fault, then break back rightwards above to a hanging belay below the steep groove.
3. 20m The groove was avoided on the right to finish on the broad rib above.

SGÙRR THUILM, North Face:
Giant's Gully   450m   III,6. Mike Lates, Lucy Spark. 13 Jan 2017.
The longest gully splitting the north face is hidden from the road but is very obvious after passing the Fairy Pools. Climbed in very thin cover, it gave a lot of fine, mixed chimneying pitches with fun climbing in great rock architecture. May bank out completely to give a far easier line. Top out 30m from the summit.

SGÙRR MHICCOINNICH, South Face:
The Silver Fox   235m   V,5 **. Mike Lates, Sophie Grace Chappell. 19 Nov 2017.
Climbs the obvious, long curving fault-line on the left side of the face. Start 100m west of *Jeffrey's Dyke*. Easy broad terrain leads to a steepening and narrowing in the dyke (125m). Climb mixed terrain with continuous interest for two pitches (80m). The dyke ends in an amphitheatre with a choice of steep finishes. Climb a right-trending crack-line centrally up the back wall on good gabbro on a (30m). Easy terrain leads to the crest of Sgurr MhicCoinnich.

West Buttress   335m   V,6. Will Rowland, Fran Thompson. Mar 2016.
Start as for the summer route, at the toe of the buttress.
1. 55m Climb an icy gully to the crest. Continue up the crest to a spike just to its right.
2. 70m Follow an easy stepped ramp just to the right of the crest to an obvious steepening.
3. 55m Climb the steepening and break out left rejoining the crest. Traverse left below a rock wall until an exposed ice ramp can be climbed. Follow the ramp to the right and then straight up over iced slabs and bulges.
4. 35m Continue up iced slabs to a snowfield which terminates at a rock wall.
5. 25m Climb the wall, then traverse up and left, then back right on steep exposed snow, leading to a pedestal on the crest below a short, steep rock wall.
6. 30m Pass the steep wall on the right to reach easy ground which then leads to Collie's Ledge.
7. 20m Climb the obvious corner, then break out onto the right wall. Alternatively, go straight up the corner.
8. 25m Climb the fine wall right of the chimney. Continue along the ridge to a steep wall with a slabby right side.
9. 20m Step right onto the slab and climb it to the summit.

SGÙRR THEARLAICH Note: *Curse of the Hobgoblin* confirmed as VI,6 and 3 stars.

SGÙRR ALASDAIR, Stone Shoot Face:

Chinatown Shuffle 25m V,6. Michael Barnard (unsec). 12 Feb 2017.
Climbs an obvious line of left-trending grooves/corners near the top of the Stone Shoot. Unfortunately a very nasty-looking block has to be passed low down which is almost impossible not to use, but it does feel mechanically sound!

SRÒN NA CÌCHE, Eastern Buttress:

Note: *Creag Dhu Grooves*. Peter Herd linked pitches 2, 3 and 4 in a single 40m pitch, which should at least be a recommended alternative.

COIRE A' GHRUNNDA, Sron na Ciche, South-East Face, South Crag, Lower Buttress:

Liberty 75m HVS 5a *. Steve Kennedy, Cynthia Grindley. 9 Oct 2016.
On the left side of lower slab, approximately 15m left of *Cuckoo Groove*, is a left-facing corner leading to a large overhang below a pale coloured wall and corner in the steep upper tier. Enter the corner by slabs from the left. Climb the corner, pulling out right at the top, then continue up slabs to belay below the undercut pale wall (35m). At the right end of the overhang (just right of the pale wall) is a steep corner with a slabby right wall leading rightwards. Pull steeply into the corner which is followed to slabs and a left-trending fault. Follow the fault to reach the left edge and finish up the edge (40m).

Right of *Rapid Progress* is a short deep chimney (mentioned in the guide) and an attractive slabby wall immediately right of the chimney. The wall is split by a number of crack-lines running diagonally right. The cracks diminish in length and width from the left, culminating in the thin crack of *Phantasma*.

Daydream 28m VS 4c *. Steve Kennedy, Cynthia Grindley. 9 Oct 2016.
The leftmost crack. Start almost at the lowest point of the wall and climb a short V-shaped groove to reach the crack. Climb the crack, gradually making use of the adjacent deep crack on the right as the two cracks converge.

Phantasma 28m VS 4c *. Steve Kennedy, Cynthia Grindley. 9 Oct 2016.
The two rightmost parallel cracks. Climb to a small alcove and follow a narrow ramp leading rightwards to the thin right-hand crack. Continue by using the left-hand crack mainly for hands.

South Crag:

Owl Buttress Left 120m IV,4. Pok Siwinski, Michael Barnard. 13 Jan 2017.
As for the summer route (to Pinnacle Rake). In good ice conditions a groove in the upper wall would give a fine finish.

Upper Coire a' Ghrunnda:

Two Bottles Later 160m III. Will Rowland, Fran Thompson. Mar 2016.
On a pyramid subsidiary peak between the TD Gap and Sgurr Dubh Mor. The route goes up the centre of the broken face directly up to an obvious cascade, starting at NG 453 204.
1. 55m Cross short icy steps and steep snow.
2. 50m Move up snow and ice trending left.
3. 55m Follow icy ramps and shallow groves to reach the left side of the cascade. Climb the cascade via to finish up short walls.

SGÙRR A' GHREADAIDH, Coir'-Uisg Buttress:

Skye Fall   45m   E6. James McHaffie, Dan Varian. 13 Oct 2016.
The nice groove about 10m right of *Skye Wall* has a blank looking entry wall.
1. 30m 6b/c Climb the easy ramp on the right for 15m and place some big cams.
A horizontal traverse line leftwards has some RPs near the start, a desperate move
in the middle and a bold ending to gain the groove above which itself is about
E1 with good gear leading to big ledges leading rightwards into the massive corner
where it overhangs.
2. 15m 5c Climb the strangely awkward corner to the top.

Moonrise Kingdom   130m   E9. Dan Varian, James McHaffie. 12 May 2017.
An amazing route picking the line of least resistance up the middle of the crag.
The climbing on the second pitch is immaculate but it is certainly one of the most
serious pitches in the UK, being comparable to *Indian Face*. Start at the toe of
the buttress, 20m down left of *Skye Wall*.
1. 30m 6b Climb up for 8m to gain the big horizontal running left onto ledges
and follow it for 5m before making a few moves up into the greeny white rock
leading to some good holds and disappointing gear. Strange and committing
moves up and left gain the groove which leads to the overhang.
2. 40m 6a/b The Indian Face pitch. Undercut the roof rightwards and make a
tricky pull into the groove to the next roof. Moves up the face leads to a thin roof
above and the last proper gear for a very long way. Step right around this roof to
a disappointing 'ledge' and hand-traverse this leftwards a little way. Make a nest
of skyhooks and extend them. A committing move leads leftwards and up off the
left-hand end of the ledge where technical and serious face climbing for much
longer than you'd like eventually gains a shallow wire in a flake (kneebar) and a
Cam on the right. Steep moves lead to some better holds which lead up rightwards
to a sloping ledge and thankful hands-off (crucial micro cam). The short and slim
groove above has a tricky move/jump for shorties to gain sinkers at the break and
a swing right to belay in the break on Cam 3.5 and 4. A dangerous and spectacular
pitch.
3. 60m 6b Climb above the belay for 2m to sinkers (good Cam 4). Stand
awkwardly on these and using sidepulls, make a couple of tricky moves up to gain
good holds and ledges leading leftwards to a long groove on the left which leads
more easily right to the top.

BLÀBHEINN , South Buttress:

Canopy   140m   VI,6 **. Michael Barnard, John MacLeod. 24 Feb 2017.
The great chimney-fault. A difficult route with a committing final section.
1. 25m The right-slanting groove leading to the foot of the chimney-fault.
2. 50m Climb the chimney-fault past numerous chockstones and a short squeeze
section. An excellent sustained pitch.
3. 15m Continue more easily to below the upper chimney of the summer route.
4. 15m Take the obvious slabby traverse left to ledges on the crest of the buttress.
5. 35m Continue left for 5m to below a slabby groove. Gain this (bold) and follow
it up and left to the left end of the top bulge. Traverse right to the right end of the
bulge. A tricky finish up the right arete leads to easier ground.

Note: *South Buttress Gully* on Blàbheinn South-east Face was climbed in
extremely thin conditions at about VI,6. Consensus is now that this great line is
grade III in 'normal' conditions, not II as in the guidebook.

Steve Kennedy on the FA of 21st Century Schizoid Man (E4 6a), Bornesketaig, Skye.
Photo: Colin Moody.

East Ridge:
A small buttress just below the base of the east ridge at NG 537 214. The buttress has two tiers and the climbs are on the upper tier.

Justine Time   20m   Severe 4a. Oliver Barr-Skeoch. 28 May 2017.
Start in an obvious inverted V-groove and climb the crack-line above.
Note: A steep rought slab 3m left of the above was climbed at H.Severe 4b.

FLODIGARRY:
Diamonds   35m   E2 5b **. Robert Durran, Lucy Spark. 14 Jul 2016.
From a belay at the foot of the span, move right as for *Sea Slaters Groove*, then step right again into the next groove. Climb straight up the wall passing a big spike and turning a bulge rightwards to reach the ledge. Finish up *Lucy in the Sky*. Good sustained technical climbing, though slightly eliminate.

BORNESKETAIG:
21st Century Schizoid Man   22m   E4 6a ***. Stephen Kennedy, Cynthia Grindley, Colin Moody. 16 Jul 2017.
This unique and stunning route is on the front of the pillar left of *Power to Believe*. Protected with small to medium Cams, several in shallow horizontal breaks.

EARLISH (south of Uig) (NG 381 612):
Turn off the Portree–Uig road and park at a footpath gate at the far end of the Earlish straight (NG 3845 6117). Follow the path to the beach at Camus Beag where the unmissable pale dyke juts out on the east side of the bay 300m ahead.

Prowler   50m   E1 5a **. Noel Williams, John Mackenzie, Simon Richardson. 13 Jun 2017.
A fine and unusual climb following the narrow arete of the prow-like dyke.
1. 30m 4c Climb the arete directly to below an overhung recess. Step right and climb the wall moving up left to reach a small ledge on the left side of the arete. Continue up the arete and mantelshelf onto a big flat platform. Belay at the back.
2. 20m 5a Climb the narrow arete initially, move onto the right wall and climb this close to the arete on scalloped holds. Reach a crack (first protection) and climb to the headwall, taken just right of a flared crack, crux, good small Cam above the flared section of the crack. The top is just above, a flat platform.

HUSABOST Note:
Andy Moles thought *The Hermit* was E3 5c **, not E2 5b ***. *Old Man's Cows* looked like a solo.

NEIST, Upper Cliffs, Seagulls Sector:
Flying Door and *The Physician* (SMCJ 2015) repeated by Ian Taylor. Both three stars but thought E3/4 5c rather than E2.

Financial Sector:
Bit-Coiner, *Bingo Wings* and *Daylight Robbery* (SMCJ 2015) all repeated and thought E3 5c **. *Seven Days* was E4 6a *** and a future classic.

Bingo Wings, Alternative Finish   10m   E1 5b *. Ian Taylor, Tess Fryer. 8 May 2017.

From the large boulder at the top of the *Brass Monkey's* chimney, climb up the rib on the left, then leftwards round the top bulge.

Gritstone Reminiscence Bay:
Note: *Seven Days* and *Braveheart* (SMCJ 2014) are the same route.

Poverty Point:
The Poverty Trap   30m   E3 5c *. Tess Fryer, Ian Taylor. 6 May 2014.
A crack-line up wall right of *Rhubarb Crumble*.

Mix and Match Area:
Dummheit   35m   E5 6a **. Ian Taylor, Tess Fryer. 7 May 2017.
The 'even fiercer crack' on the north facing wall mentioned in the introduction to the section. Excellent and very well-protected, but loses a star due to some loose blocks at ¾ height.

South of the Steps, Sonamara Area, Pinnacle Flake Area:
Approximately 100m south of *Don't Leave your Dad in the Rain* along steepening grassy slopes, a huge 20m light-brown flake leans against the crag. There is a fine unclimbed crack up the centre of the seaward side and a deep chimney behind. The top of the flake narrows to a pinnacle. The first route climbs up the left side of the pinnacle. All the climbs have had some cleaning but remain a little fragile and somewhat verdant in places. Although there are faint sheep tracks, this is not a good area for rock boots and an abseil approach is much more friendly. There is a selection of rock belays, some excavated, and the odd stake at the top.

Danegeld   30m   HVS 5a. Morten Hansen, Kathy Tighe. 22 Jun 2015.
Start in an alcove, capped by a big chockstone at approx 8m, on the left side of the pinnacle flake. Get into, and out of (crux) the alcove into a grassy bay. Climb inside, or outside, the flake chimney above to a left exit at the top.

Pancho   15m   HVS 5b *. Mick & Kathy Tighe, Paul Rosher, Morten Hansen. 18 Aug 2015.
A steep grassy rake runs steeply up left from the bottom of the chimney flake with a fine wall above, decreasing in height as you progress up the rake. This route takes the first cracked groove line a metre or so up the rake. A small wire protects the initial moves in from the left and a big cam is handy for the next section which leads to a short, tricky corner-crack and easier ground.

Returning to the light-brown pinnacle flake, the most obvious feature is the fine-looking, unclimbed crack straight up the middle. The following route climbs up behind the pinnacle flake, starting in a grassy bay.

Golden Flake   30m   HVS 5a/b **. Mick & Kathy Tighe, Morten Hansen. 14 Jun 2015.
Scramble up the grassy bay to the bottom of the chimney on the right side of the flake. Surmount the big jammed block at the bottom and power up the outer edge of the flake. Get on top of the pinnacle, step across onto the wall and tackle the wee overhang above.

Ivy Crack   30m   HVS 5a *. Kathy & Mick Tighe. May 2013.
A further 15 or 20m right (east), two sections of ivy climb the wall left of a grassy bay (bluebells in spring!). Climb the crack to the right of the ivy and the fine left-hand groove above.

Bluebell Groove   30m   HVS 5b **. Mick & Kathy Tighe. May 2013.
Scramble up onto the bluebell ledge into the excellent open groove a few metres right of *Ivy Crack*. A near perfect, unclimbed crack-line runs up the right edge of the groove.

Moonen Bay   30m   E1 5b *. Mick & Kathy Tighe, Morten Hansen. 22 Jun 2015.
A few metres right again is a narrow bay with a fine crack-line on the left and a more broken groove line to the right. Take the left-hand crack via a short wall from Bluebell Ledge.

60 Minute Cleaners   30m   VS 4b *. Mick Tighe, Simon Fraser. 14 Jul 2015.
Start to the right of Bluebell Ledge, but instead of heading up to *Bluebell Groove*, go up a cleaned recess to a diagonal groove line with a bulge at the top. Surmount the bulge (crux) to a grassy bay and climb the chimney above.

Juniper Groove   30m   Severe. Paul Rosher, Simon Fraser. 16 Jul 2015.
Approx 10m right of *60 Minute Cleaners* is a small bay with a slightly left-trending fault-line running up the full height of the crag, finishing up a short chimney. Extensively cleaned.

Tower Area:
A further 20m right (east) from *Juniper Groove* is a fine tower of rock around 40m high, with an overhang at two-thirds height which has a perfect hanging crack to the right.

The Tower   30m   HVS 5b. Mick & Kathy Tighe. May 2013.
Start in a little bay just up and left from the lowest point of the crag. Climb a short open groove to a platform on the right. Make a difficult move back left into a crack-line directly under the overhang, which is passed on the left by a short jam crack, and exit into the upper gallery.

Old Man & The Sea   18m   E2 ***. Mick & Kathy Tighe, Morten Hansen. 19 Aug 2015.
The fabulous overhanging crack to the right of the nose, starting up the fine crack directly below. Perfect protection on near perfect rock.

Hebridean Sharker   25m   HVS 5a/b **. Mick & Kathy Tighe. 15 Jun 2015.
A few metres right and slightly uphill there is a deep recessed groove. Go up over blocks and cracks to a big ledge. The excellent cracked groove above is hard to start.

Tex   20m   HVS 5a/b **. Mick & Kathy Tighe. 15 Jun 2015.
The next cracked fault a few metres right.

Top Notch   10m   VS 4c *. Kathy Tighe, Morten Hansen. 15 Jun 2015.
A jam crack at the top right end of the crag takes medium/large Cams.

ELGOL, Suidhe Biorach:

Mortal Panic 25m E5 6a. Edward Nind, Masa Sakano. 24 Oct 2016.
Between *Digitalis* and *Jamie Jampot*. Eliminate and contrived but with excellent climbing. Avoid straying onto *Digitalis* until the shared jug rest and avoid bridging or gear in *Jamie Jampot*. From the start of *Digitalis* climb directly up the wall (microcams essential) to a good undercut in a small obvious overlap. Move up and right (first crux), then back left to a big flake and rest. Continue straight up until level with the huge jug at the top of the flake on *Digitalis*, take this and rest. Traverse horizontally right (second crux) past a long flake (possible wires but would be hard to place), across *India* and to the arete. Climb the arete spectacularly but more easily and finish up the final crack of *Arc of the Covenant*. Harder for the short. Could be 6b. Without wires in the central flake, a fall for second or leader is serious.

Pretty In Pink 20m E6 6b *. Edward Nind. 23 May 2017.
Start as for *Mortal Panic* but after the first crux, move up and right, crossing *Digitalis*, to arrive at a mossy ledge. Make a hard move up to a flake rail, climb this then move directly up to a thin break and better holds. Move slightly left to two flat holds in the break and then finish directly.

Super Ego variation 30m E2 5c. Edward Nind, Masa Sakano. 24 Oct 2016.
A variant of *Altar Ego*. Climb *Altar Ego* pitch 1. Take the wall right of the corner of *Altar Ego* pitch 2, traverse right and across this to the arete, climb this on its left side (common with *Revenge of an Angry Cosmos*) and finish easily.
Note: *Altar Ego* was thought to be E2 5c by the same team.

Revenge of an Angry Cosmos 30m E3 6a. Edward Nind, Masa Sakano. 23 Oct 2016.
A classic line with excellent climbing and good protection. Start up the wall just left of *Arc of the Covenant*. Climb up and right to cross *Arc* at the large ledge and continue up and right into a huge niche under a wide roof. Traverse right through the roof and move up to a large sloping ledge. Climb the thin crack directly above (crux) then avoid the huge roofs and guano ledges above by moving diagonally up and right (passing a slightly dubious block under a roof) until it is possible to climb steeply up and left breaking through lesser overhangs. From the ledge under the final overhang move left to the arete, climb this on its left side and finish easily. Top of the grade. E5 6b for the short.

POINT (AIRD) OF SLEAT, Creag Mhor:

Mentioned only briefly in the current guide (p254), but a worthwhile south facing venue in a beautiful setting with a nice sandy beach nearby. The UKC website has descriptions of previously recorded routes.

On the Edge Severe 4a *. Steve Kennedy, Cynthia Grindley. 25 Mar 2017.
Instead of starting up the crack of *Leftward Leaning*, climb the left arete directly to a large roof (joining *LL* which comes in from the right). Step left above the roof and finish up the arete as for *LL*.

Well right of the main buttress and at a lower level, are two narrow clean buttresses separated by a shallow heather filled gully.

Blue Wind   25m   VS 4b **. Steve Kennedy, Cynthia Grindley. 25 Mar 2017.
The left-hand buttress which has a clean broad base, contains a number of cracks which gradually narrows with height. Start up the most pronounced crack approximately in the middle to reach a horizontal break. Finish by cracks on the left side of the narrow upper rib.

RONA:
Many new routes have been climbed by Mark Hudson and friends. A complete write-up for Rona is in the New Routes section on the SMC website.

NORTHERN HIGHLANDS NORTH

ARDMAIR:
Many new routes have not been sent to the SMC but are recorded here: <http://www.northwestoutdoors.co.uk/northwestoutdoorsullapool/2014/11/ardmai r-update.html>

The Ignoble Aesthete   35m   E4 6a *. Ian Taylor, Tess Fryer. 10 Oct 2016.
Start as for *Gravity's Rainbow* to the first good ledge. Climb the right-hand groove then go right onto a ledge and a junction with *Noble Savage*. Attack the thin crack directly above, pulling over onto a sloping ramp. Finish up the corner above.

Fantasy Wall:
About 1km north of the Ardmair Crag parking, turn left down a rough road and park on the bend after 50m (signposted Dun Canna parking). Continue along the road to the bungalow then go left across a stream, head over to a line of trees and follow them rightwards to find a small hidden wall (NH 122 991).

Beware of the Bull   8m   E5/6 6b *. Ian Taylor. 28 Apr 2016.
A line up the left side of the wall. Headpointed above mats.

CUL BEAG, Lurgainn Slabs, West Face:
(NC 1371 0769)   Alt 300m   South-West facing
See SMCJ 2010. Above the gully exit is a tiered series of slabs that start lower than the Lower Slabs that lie further left. Boulders on the skyline lie near the finish of the following routes.

Pebbledash   95m   Severe 4b *. Andrew James, John Mackenzie. 17 May 2017.
1. 30m 4b A short introductory slab with a turfy groove leads easily to a ledge. Above lies a clean red slab, taken centrally, giving a fine delicate pitch. Belays near a turf filled crack on the left above the ledge.
2. 30m 4b Climb the rippled and pebble-dashed slab delicately to the right of the crack to an easing. Step left and finish more easily to a big ledge and chockstone.
3. 35m Move right up broken ground to a rib overlooking an edge and climb this pleasantly to the top.

Lower Slabs:
These lie up left from the foot of Pebbledash, reached by a turfy scramble and a traverse along ledges. A prominent corner on the right, taken by *Forgotten Groove*

Nicola Bassnett on Cryoconnect (E2 5c), Rona. Photo: Roger Brown.

Mike Hutton on Orbit (E3 6a), Rona. Photo: Roger Brown.

(SMCJ 2010), a big square-cut recess taken by *Edge Clipper* left again and finally a big roof-topped alcove identifies the steeper base of these slabs.

Edge Clipper 40m HVS 4c **. Andrew James, John Mackenzie. 26 May 2017.
Probably the best route here, bold in places but fine clean climbing. Start in the square-cut recess and climb the left edge of the lower slab to reach the corner on the right. Move up to a thin crack and step right on onto the edge above the crack. Climb delicately up left along a narrow ramp to finish up the central corner.

Jammy Dodger 35m HVS 5b *. John Mackenzie, Andrew James. 26 May 2017.
The overhanging right wall of the roofed recess on the left of the slabs has a right-slanting crack. Climb this to reach the slab above. The slab is much easier and though several lines are possible, the route took a pleasant amble to the right of a heathery crack via a big flake and finished by a shallow corner.

Middle Tier:
This short tier lies directly above the Lower Tier and is of good pink rock save for a heathery central corner and a few turfy cracks. *Precambrian Doddle* (SMCJ 2010) lies to the left of the corner.

Archean Pleasures 20m Severe *. Andrew James, John Mackenzie. 26 May 2017.
To the right of the corner between two turfy cracks is a clean slab. Climb the slab just left of the straight right-hand crack, using the crack for spaced protection. Pleasant and quite delicate climbing.

WICKET GATE CRAG:
Buffalo Girls 20m E4 6a **. Tess Fryer, Ian Taylor. 9 Oct 2016.
Start a few metres left of the big imbedded flake at a narrow clean wall. Climb to some square roofs and make a long reach up and left to a good flat hold. Move left to a thin crack and follow this until a move rightwards gains a ledge. Finish more easily.

Stags With Horns 12m E3 5c *. Ian Taylor, Tess Fryer. 9 Oct 2016.
Start 10m right of the imbedded flake below a small roof at 5m. Bold moves gain the roof, then easier climbing leads to the top.

REIFF, Bouldering Cliff:
Lutra Lutra Go Go Go 20m E5 6a *. Ian Taylor, Tess Fryer. 3 Jun 2017.
A committing right-hand finish to *An Dobhran Mara*. Climb *An Dobhran Mara* for 10m, then traverse right on edges and make a hard move up to better holds. Keep going right to gain a hanging corner and finish up this.

Black Rocks:
The Return of the Herring 20m E5 6a ***. Ian Taylor, Tess Fryer. 9 Oct 2016.
The prominent arete left of *Hourglass Groove*. Start at a sea-level ledge directly below the arete. Climb a black wall to a shelf and continue up the arete to a foot ledge and poor RPs. The bold crux above leads to breaks and a jammed block. Finish up a fine finger-crack.

Microbuckets   25m   E1 5b. Tess Fryer, Ian Taylor. 9 Oct 2016.
Start left of *Nameless Route* at a big triangular niche. Climb directly via a square niche and a thin crack to a junction with *Nameless Route* at its steepening. Move right and make a long move through a bulge. Continue direct to the top.

Pink Bay:
The following three routes are on the first obvious prow (*Gabhagan* lies on the second one). A deep cleft on the north-west side with a huge jammed boulder is a useful identifying feature.

Orange Cemetery   12m   E1 5b. Michael Barnard, Alan Hill. 29 Apr 2017.
Starting just left of the cleft, climb a steep vertical crack.

Amused to Death   15m   VS 4c. Michael Barnard, Alan Hill. 29 Apr 2017.
The slabby right-slanting corner-line just left of the above.

The End is Nigh   15m   VS 4b *. Alan Hill, Michael Barnard. 29 Apr 2017.
The fine slabby wall further left. Start on the right and climb directly to a ledge. Step right and continue to the top.

The following four routes lie on the north-west wall of the *Gabhagan* prow. Note the description for that route should read 'Climb the line of corners on the LEFT side of the arete which lead LEFTWARDS to under a huge roof.'

Space Dementia   20m   E2 5b **. Michael Barnard, Alan Hill. 29 Apr 2017.
Climbs the line of steep cracks just right of the arete. Start on the left side of the arete (as for *Gabhagan*) and move up to take the obvious break leading around the arete. Continue up the line then break out diagonally right below roofs to reach a ledge. Step left and finish up the short top wall.

Dark Shines   20m   HVS 5b **. Michael Barnard, Alan Hill. 29 Apr 2017.
Start 2m right of the arete and move up rightwards to the large niche. Exit this on the right and continue up to a ledge. Step left and finish up the short top wall (as for *Space Dementia*).

Bliss   25m   HVS 5a **. Michael Barnard, Alan Hill. 29 Apr 2017.
A few metres right of the above is a small left-facing corner. Start just right of this and climb via breaks up the initial wall, then the leaning wall above to reach the upper ledges. Finish up the slab above.

Micro Cuts   25m   VS 5a *. Michael Barnard, Alan Hill. 29 Apr 2017.
A few metres right again, take the obvious line up left to ledges. Ascend the leaning wall just right of where *Bliss* goes (crux), then continue more easily to the top.

Megalomania   25m   E3 5c **. Michael Barnard, Alan Hill. 30 Apr 2017.
A line up the right side of the big wall left of *Gabhagan*. Take a full set of cams from micros to Camalot 4 (plus another large Cam for the belay). Climb via breaks up the far right side of the wall to level with the niche of *Gabhagan*. Now make a long move to the next break and a further tricky move to gain the upper ledge system. Step right and continue more easily to the top.

ASSYNT, Creag Rodha Mor (Super Crag):
Captain Beanheart 25m E2 *. Michael Barnard, Alan Hill. 9 Oct 2016.
Lies where the Burnished Walls meets the Main Cliff, though is approached as for the former. Pitch two would make a good upper pitch to *Crystal Shell*. Scramble up left from the base of that route to a raised platform below the right end of the Main Cliff.
1. 15m 4c Move left and climb a corner-crack to gain the low angled slab above. Go up and right to belay below an overhanging wall.
2. 10m 5b Climb the line of weakness up the wall to reach the prominent undercling at the top bulge. Finish up and right.

OLD MAN OF STOER:
Direct Start 10m HVS 5a. Stewart Anderson, Maciej Brzeski. 22 Jul 2016.
A direct on pitch 1 (possibly E1 5b). Climb directly above the tyrolean anchor for about 4m, then go diagonally left and finally traverse left to join the original route.

BEINN AN FHURAIN:
Headstone Rib 200m III,4. John Higham,Iain Young. 11 Feb 2017.
Na Tuadhan throws down a long but relatively easy angled, rocky rib down towards Coire a' Mhadaidh, well seen in profile from the Conival – Beinn an Fhurain col. *Headstone Rib* follows this rib. Start at the lowest rocks and follow easy mixed ground, following the crest until the rib merges with the headwall. Move slightly left and follow a right-curving groove to the summit over ice, rock and rock.

CONIVAL:
As noted in SMCJ 2008, the first recorded ascent of the South-East Ridge of Conival was on 28 Dec 1968 by Alan & David Brook, David Leonard & David Weston. A detailed story of the day was provided.

SCOURIE CRAGS, Telegraph Crag:
Gunning for Nothing 15m E1 5a. Michael Barnard, Alan Hill. 23 Oct 2016.
Climbs steep cracks up the shorter wall immediately left of the main crag, passing a dodgy flake (not necessary to use).
Note: *Alice Cooper* is possibly E4 6a **.

FAR NORTH-WEST CRAGS, Upstream Crag:
(NC 259 462) West facing
This steep outcrop of reddish gneiss can be glimpsed on the drive east from Laxford Bridge and is just visible from near the parking spot (NC 250 466). Cross the nearby bridge and take the path near the river to the bend, then up to the crag, 20mins.

Caravanserai 15m VS 4c. Michael Barnard. 28 May 2016.
The obvious left-trending grooves/corners splitting the right-hand side of the crag. Start direct up diagonal cracks.

Down the Rapids 15m H.Severe 4c. Michael Barnard. 28 May 2016.
In the centre of the crag is an open corner. Start up the groove below this (a bit dirty, crux) then up the corner, passing a small holly. The prominent 'guillotine flake' feels keyed in but doesn't inspire confidence!

In the Land of Grey and Pink   15m   HVS 5a. Michael Barnard. 28 May 2016.
Climbs the fine red wall. Start up a cracked groove immediately left of the initial groove of *Down the Rapids*. Now climb the wall (making use of a flake-crack on the left) to gain a line of excellent flakes leading to the top.

Future Primitive   15m   E2 5c **. Michael Barnard, Alan Hill. 13 Oct 2016.
Start as for the above but step left from the flake-crack to gain slanting cracks leading up leftwards under a bulge. Climb these with difficulty (crux) before stepping back right and up to finish.

Gritty Wall:
(NC 254 533)   West facing.
This wall lies on the side of a gully and is seen from the road while driving towards Rhiconich from Kinlochbervie. It offers some worthwhile short routes and the rock is actually quite reliable (provided one doesn't try pulling on small crystals). Park at the next bend in the road, 5mins.

Red Wing Special   25m   VS 4c. Michael Barnard. 16 Oct 2016.
Start by a large spike at the left end of the wall. Step on this and climb the wall, staying just left of the flared crack. Finish up the crack just left of the top corner.

Drawing the Line   25m   E2 5b *. Michael Barnard, Alan Hill. 22 Oct 2016.
Start 2m right of the above and move up to tackle the bold and slightly concave wall. Continue up the top arete (crux).

Kaleidoscope   25m   VS 4b. Michael Barnard. 16 Oct 2016.
Start right of the above, below a slight rib. Move up this, then step right and go up to the main bulge. Climb through this (crux), then continue up and slightly leftwards to finish up a crack.

Occam's Razor   25m   H.Severe 4b *. Michael Barnard. 16 Oct 2016.
The line of the crag. Climb the flake-crack past the bulge (crux) and to its very top, then up to finish.

Carousel   25m   VS 4b. Michael Barnard. 16 Oct 2016.
Start just right of *Occam's Razor* and move up to climb thin cracks, then a bold slabby section to gain the top of the wafer-thin flake. Continue up to the top.

The following routes lie on a shorter wall up and right.

And Now for Something Completely Different   15m   HVS 4c. Michael Barnard. 16 Oct 2016.
Climbs the slabby left side of the wall, continuing directly through the bulge above.

Subject to Change Without Notice   15m   H.Severe 4a. Michael Barnard. 16 Oct 2016.
On the right side of the wall are two knobbly grooves. Climb the left one (crux at the top).

Time Flies 15m Severe. Michael Barnard. 16 Oct 2016.
The right-hand knobbly groove with a fine steep finish (crux).

Stag's Head Crag (NHN p259):
The approach track is signposted 'Badcall Peat Road'.
Triumph Cracks was thought HS 4b * (perhaps the best route here) and lies 5m right of *Hind Wall*, not 10m. Suggested description: 'Climb up leftwards, then back up a right-slanting crack, and up to finish.'

Peat Cutter's Wall 15m HVS 4c. Michael Barnard, Alan Hill. 23 Oct 2016.
This, the furthest right wall above the terrace, lies about 10m right of *Hind Wall* and was thought unlikely to be *Triumph Cracks*. Climb the wall using the left arete and continue to the top.

The Roaring Silence 20m VS 4c. Alan Hill, Michael Barnard. 10 Oct 2016.
Right of *Antlers Away*, a left-slanting crack leads to a heather clump. Continue up grooves above.
Note: Unsure how this route relates to *Aspen Crack*. Michael Barnard guesses the lower section may be the same but with a different finish (they wouldn't have given this E1). The above still seems worth recording as a VS line.

Creag Mhic Ghriogair:
(NC 239 560) South-West facing.
A fine steep crag with an easy approach from the road through Badcall Inchard (3mins). The crag's main features are a left-facing corner leading to a large horizontal roof, and a left-slanting crack up the wall to its left.

Fate's Warning 25m E2 5b *. Michael Barnard, Alan Hill. 11 Oct 2016.
Climbs twin vertical cracks left of the left-slanting crack.

Crack of Destiny 25m E1 5b ***. Michael Barnard, Alan Hill. 11 Oct 2016.
The superb left-slanting crack, gained via the corner below past a couple of saplings.

Brush and Mopsy 30m HVS 5a *. Michael Barnard, Alan Hill. 13 Oct 2016.
Climb the large left-facing corner to a big ledge (tree). Make a couple of moves higher, then take a line of holds up and right to the arete. Continue up a cracked groove just right of the arete to finish up a groove right of the top headwall. Take care with rope drag!

Mr McGregor's Gardeners 30m E1 5b **. Michael Barnard, Alan Hill. 22 Oct 2016.
Just right of the crag's main left-facing corner is a line of steep cracks leading to a smaller corner set below an arete. Climb the cracks past well keyed-in blocks, then up the corner to pass the roof with difficulty. Continue up a cracked groove just right of the arete to finish up the headwall above.

Lark's Foot and Cotton-tail 30m E2 5c *. Michael Barnard, Alan Hill. 22 Oct 2016.
The central line on Gardner's Wall. Start just right of the previous route and climb up into a niche (sapling). Move up through the bulging wall above (crux), then

Michael Barnard on the FA of Crack of Destiny (E1 5b), Creag Mhic Ghriogair, Badcall Inchard. Photo: Alan Hill.

continue more easily to the headwall. Step left to finish up this as for the previous route.

Rabbit Pie 25m E3 5c **. Michael Barnard, Alan Hill. 22 Oct 2016.
Slightly eliminate but excellent climbing up the thin right-hand crack in the wall. Move up past a large, well keyed-in spike and climb the line with hard-won protection to a semi-rest with a hand in *Lark's Foot and Cotton-tail* where that route moves right. Continue up the thin crack (crux) and gain the ledge via a small corner/crack on the left. Go up a short crack, then easily to the top.

The other routes lie further right on the hillside. The best feature (and visible from the road) is a slabby pillar with a thin crack up its middle and an undercut start; this is the line of *Call of the Mild*. The first route lies down and left of this, on a clean wall just left of a vegetated chimney.

Good Call or Bad Call? 25m HVS 5a *. Michael Barnard, Alan Hill. 22 Oct 2016.
Start 2m left of the chimney and climb to a disappointing ledge (crux). Continue directly to the top.

Bad to the Stone 25m HVS 5a. Michael Barnard, Alan Hill. 22 Oct 2016.
Start as for the above but take a low handrail out left. Continue up past a short crack, then move right to finish as for the above.

The next three routes lie up and right (or horizontally right from the top of *Good Call or Bad Call?*). 35m of rope is needed to reach the belays.

Call of the Mild 20m Severe **. Alan Hill, Michael Barnard. 22 Oct 2016.
The crack up the slabby pillar. A fine route and is much easier than it looks from the road.

Roger That 20m V.Diff. Alan Hill, Michael Barnard. 22 Oct 2016.
A line squeezed in just right of the above.

Over and Out 20m Severe 4c *. Alan Hill, Michael Barnard. 22 Oct 2016.
Start at the left end of the wall, just left of a large block. Climb intermittent cracks up a series of steps; a perfect overhead nut protects the crux move.

Wrinkled Wall:
(NC 214 563) West facing
This wall, which may be passed on the way to Rubha na Leacaig, offers some pleasant routes but some of the rock is suspect and it does not compare to the peninsula crags, 15mins from near the pier at Kinlochbervie.

Kea Crack 20m Severe 4c. Alan Hill, Michael Barnard. 12 Oct 2016.
The wide crack near the left end of the crag (crux at the start).

Krakapo 20m H.Severe 4b *. Alan Hill, Michael Barnard. 12 Oct 2016.
Climb the right side of the wall right of *Kea Crack*, then step right and follow the snaking crack up and leftwards to the top.

Hit the Deck!   15m   VS 4c. Michael Barnard, Alan Hill. 12 Oct 2016.
Climbs the left edge of the wall right of the heather gully, with a bold start up the initial wall (crux).

Bombing Runnel   15m   VS 5a. Michael Barnard, Alan Hill. 12 Oct 2016.
The pink right-trending runnel.

MODs and Rockers   15m   VS 5a *. Michael Barnard, Alan Hill. 12 Oct 2016.
Start 3m right of *Bombing Runnel* and climb the wall to the break, then step right to take the obvious black crack.

Target Practice   15m   VS 4c. Alan Hill, Michael Barnard. 12 Oct 2016.
The cracked fault right of *MODs and Rockers*, leading to a heather ledge. Step left and up to finish.

Tail Gunner   15m   HVS 5a. Michael Barnard, Alan Hill. 12 Oct 2016.
Start 5m right of the above and climb a thin crack to a horizontal break left of heather. Swing left and up to the top.

Aces High   15m   VS 4c *. Michael Barnard, Alan Hill. 12 Oct 2016.
Start at the right-hand edge of the face and follow cracks up and right, before traversing left above the overlap to gain the arete. Finish up this.

Rubha na Leacaig (NC 206 562):
Lying near the end of the small peninsula west of Kinlochbervie, these non-tidal crags give some good climbing in the low to mid grades. Park near the pier and head diagonally right up the hillside before moving left to cross the small hill then along to the crags, 25mins.

The Prow:
The first crag reached after the peninsula narrows, this short wall is easy of access and has a large platform at the base. The 'prow' itself is unmistakable.

New Moon   8m   V.Diff. Michael Barnard. 15 Jun 2013.
The crack at the right end of the crag.

Lifeboat Serenade   12m   VS 4b *. Michael Barnard. 15 Jun 2013.
Left of the above, climb leftwards up the shallow grooves.

Lost   6m   HVS 4c *. Michael Barnard. 15 Jun 2013.
A few metres left again, start at a crack and climb steeply into the groove above.

Transients   6m   Severe 4b. Michael Barnard. 15 Jun 2013.
Left again, an easy corner-groove goes up to below a roof. Climb the crack left of this, continuing direct up the top crack.

Left of this the crag becomes more broken before steepening again. The following two routes climb the wall right of the prow:

Gray Day   8m   H.Severe 4b *. Michael Barnard. 15 Jun 2013.
Move up to gain and climb the vertical crack on the right.

Back from the Edge   10m   H.Severe 4b *. Michael Barnard. 15 Jun 2013.
Starting left of the above, move up then step left and up leftwards to the top.

Gully Wall:
The next three routes lie on the steep dark wall facing the prow, and are not as difficult as their appearance would suggest!

The Trip   15m   VS 4b **. Michael Barnard. 15 Jun 2013.
Start 5m right of the boulder/chockstone ledge. Step onto the wall and climb boldly up to gain a slabby groove. Move up this then climb the steep groove above.

Thoughts   15m   Severe **. Michael Barnard. 15 Jun 2013.
The line of least resistance up the wall, aiming for the obvious shallow right-facing corners. From the boulder/chockstone ledge, go up to climb diagonally right to gain the slabby groove of *The Trip*. Move up this, then step left to follow the corners to the top.

Reflections   12m   H.Severe 4b *. Michael Barnard. 15 Jun 2013.
Start as for the above, but climb straight up the initial wall. Step left and move up the groove left of the *Thoughts* corners to finish up the top one.

In the upper part of the wall left of the previous routes is a short black V-groove, taken by the next route. To access this, scramble down the next rib further left and traverse across and down and continue along to below the V-groove.

Streams of Consciousness   15m   VS 5a *. Michael Barnard, Alan Hill. 11 Oct 2016.
Easier climbing up the lower crack and wall leads to the smooth V-groove. Move up this (crux, harder for the short) to gain better finishing holds. Well protected with small wires and RPs.

Looking leftwards along the crags from below The Prow, while the rock is extensive the lines are disappointing as the steeper sections are shorter than they appear from a distance. The next route takes a better defined buttress near the western end, gained by scrambling down from above and stepping in left (looking down). This buttress is characterised by a steeper side wall on its left. If however, the appearance is more that of a gaping cleft, then one is looking at The Roost!

Splash   15m   H.Severe 4a *. Michael Barnard. 15 Jun 2013.
Start below a blunt arete. Move up this, then leftwards through an overlap to finish up the obvious central groove.

The Roost:
This cliff, the most impressive feature here, lies just before the end of the peninsula (the top of the crag is on one's left immediately before the signalling light is reached). Scramble down and traverse in right (looking down). On the right-hand part of the cliff is an obvious smooth right-facing corner; left of this is a shallow vertical groove.

Shagged Out   15m   E1 5a *. Michael Barnard, Alan Hill. 24 May 2014.
The vertical groove is slightly bold but low in the grade.

Gulls Just Wanna Have Fun　20m　E1 5b ***. Michael Barnard, Alan Hill. 11 Oct 2016.
Further left the wall overhangs considerably as it overlooks the cleft at the back. This excellent route takes the obvious left-slanting line of weakness above the overhangs and below the headwall, with the crux gaining the final groove. Must be climbed outside the nesting season.

Bird Brain　12m　H.Severe 4b *. Michael Barnard. 15 Jun 2013.
Climbs the slabby wall left of the cleft. Step off the huge boulder, move up a slight arete, then step left to continue more easily up the shallow groove above.

Minister's Crag:
Looks out west from the end of the peninsula. Approach by scrambling down an easy V-groove near the left end of the crag (looking up).

Point of Order　8m　Severe 4b *. Michael Barnard. 15 Jun 2013.
Climbs a steep crack right of the descent.

Cornelius Fudge　8m　Severe *. Michael Barnard. 15 Jun 2013.
The next line right, a vertical groove.

Right of this is a steep wall with a fine right-left diagonal crack.

The Minister　15m　H.Severe 4b **. Michael Barnard. 15 Jun 2013.
The diagonal crack is sustained but with good holds the whole way.

Something Sinister　10m　H.Severe 4b *. Michael Barnard. 15 Jun 2013.
Start as for *The Minister* but then climb the groove above.

Down and right from here is an obvious easy angled V-groove.

Defence Against the Dark Arts　12m　H.Severe 4a *. Michael Barnard. 15 Jun 2013.
Move up towards the V-groove, then hand-traverse right to finish near the lip of the steep wall.

Severus　8m　H.Severe 4b *. Michael Barnard. 15 Jun 2013.
Climb the left-slanting crack at the right end of the crag.

Seal Island (NC 1758):
Eilean an Roin Mor (big island of the seals) lies between Oldshoremore bay and Sheigra. It is largely disappointing from a climbing point of view, but a short WNW facing wall (NC 180 588) gives some worthwhile routes on fine rock. It lies near the left end of the short line of crags seen from the Sheigra direction and is the first decent rock feature seen while kayaking west along the north shore of the island.

Big Seals, You are Beautiful　12m　Severe. Alan Hill, Michael Barnard. 8 Oct 2016.
The stepped rib marking the right end of the wall.

Sealing Time   12m   VS 4c *. Michael Barnard, Alan Hill. 8 Oct 2016.
Climbs cracks up the right side of the wall.

Genocide   12m   E2 5b *. Michael Barnard, Alan Hill. 8 Oct 2016.
The central line on the wall. Climb the crack to the break, move up to hairline cracks above and continue to the top with a solitary RP for protection (if you find it!).

Having a Good Time   12m   HVS 5a. Michael Barnard, Alan Hill. 8 Oct 2016.
The left-hand line. Move up to the break, then continue past a short vertical crack to reach the ramp-line above. Go up this, finishing up right on the ledge shared by the previous routes.

Let's Go Clubbing   12m   HVS 5a. Michael Barnard, Alan Hill. 8 Oct 2016.
Start just left of the above. Move up a short ramp to both gain and get established on the ledge up and left (crux, bold). Continue more easily to the top.

Cosmic Crag:
(NC 183 594)   Partially Tidal   South to West facing
The majestic sandstone cliff looking out towards Seal Island. A great approach (5mins from Droman pier) but can be birdy in the summer. The base is best accessed by an abseil from the fence down the big central corner of the crag; from here a scramble round to the left (looking in) takes one to the dramatic main amphitheatre with its huge roofed section. The following route is affected at high tide.

Exploring the Cosmos   35m   E2 5b ***. Michael Barnard, Alan Hill. 13 Oct 2016.
On the far left-hand side of the amphitheatre is an obvious steep right-facing corner-crack. Gain and climb this to its top, stepping left onto a ledge. Now move boldly up and right past wide breaks (huge Cam?) to gain the upper ledge system with interest. Go right to good gear then make a tricky move up to below a roof (small Cams). Pull out left to finish easily.

The big central corner is actually comprised of two smaller corners which meet near the top:

Night of a Thousand Stars   30m   E1 5b **. Michael Barnard, Alan Hill. 11 Oct 2016.
The harder left-hand corner. A sustained pitch with the direct finish up the top crack providing a fitting finale.

Fool's Moon   30m   E1 5b **. Michael Barnard, Alan Hill. 10 Oct 2016.
The right-hand corner has a nasty start up a short slanting crack. Starting from the ledge just above this gives a good HVS 5a.

The Cracked Block:
(NC 182 596)   Non-tidal   South-West to North-West facing.
The following routes lie on a huge block on the coast south of Sheigra (the line of *Rage Before Beauty* is actually visible from the campsite) and can be reached in a similar time from there or from Droman pier, 10mins.

Rage Before Beauty   15m   HVS 5a **. Michael Barnard, Alan Hill. 10 Oct 2016.
The big crack. The grade assumes the use of large Cams.

Pretty Thing   10m   VS 4c. Michael Barnard, Alan Hill. 10 Oct 2016.
A traditional test up the wide cleft right of the above.

Back 'n' Foot   10m   V.Diff. Michael Barnard, Alan Hill. 10 Oct 2016.
Bold climbing up the outside of the wide chimney on the SW face.

Local Delicacy   10m   HVS 5b **. Michael Barnard, Alan Hill. 10 Oct 2016.
A narrow alleyway has been formed between the block and the wall behind. This
route climbs the widening corner-crack next to the north entrance to the alley.

Alley Cat   10m   VS 4c. Michael Barnard, Alan Hill. 10 Oct 2016.
Climbs the crack up the block from the middle of the alley.

Creag an Dubh Loch:
Updraught pitches are 30m and 20m. The descent gully is wet, loose and
unpleasant even in a week of dry weather.

Ridgeway View Crag:
Rowlocks   10m   H.Severe 4b *. Ewan Lyons. 1 Aug 2016.
On a slab to the left of the *Oars Aft* slab, climb a small, curving right-facing corner
and finish up a wall.

Nagged   15m   Severe 4a. Mike Watson, Fiona Reid. 1 May 2012.
The crack system just right of the big heather choked groove to the left of *Classic
Crack*. Ascend this to a ledge at two-thirds height and then easily to the top.

Note: *Michael* (SMCJ 2012) and *Nagging* (SMCJ 2013) are the same.

BEN HOPE:
Notos   400m   III,4. Andy Nisbet, Steve Perry. 29 Jan 2017.
The next ridge right of *Viking Ridge* (ignoring a minor one immediately right of
Viking Ridge). It has a wide triangular base leading to a steep buttress above which
the crest becomes defined. Easy ground leads up right of the steep buttress; the
length starts from here. Traverse left immediately above the steep buttress and
follow the crest as closely as is sensible at the grade. A zigzag line was taken up
the highest steep section.

Scandi High   600m   IV,4. Andy Nisbet, Steve Perry. 8 Feb 2017.
A thinner snaking ridge which is the ridge right of *Valhalla*. The first steepening
was taken on the right leading to where the narrow crest starts. Follow this to a
steep section at the second bend. This was climbed by a hidden ramp leading left.
Follow the crest to a bigger steepening. This was passed by moving diagonally
right across turfy ledges followed by a short steep wall (crux), followed by a
groove leading back right. A bigger left-slanting fault was then followed until a
capped fault led back right. Continue up to a right-slanting fault through the last
steep tier.

Thor's Gully 300m II. Tom Bell, Tim Elson. 6 Mar 2016.
This is the right branch of *Valkyrie*, but the lower pitches were passed on the left to give this overall grade.

Ketosis 500m III. Sandy Allan, Andy Nisbet, Steve Perry, Sarah Sigley. 23 Mar 2017.
The next ridge right of *South Tower Ridge*. *Freya* is between them; the two recessed ridges mentioned in its original description are barely significant. The lowest tier was climbed at its left end and the next tier in the centre, after which the ground steepened. Trend left and up a short gully to pass on to the NW facing side of the ridge. Climb a long groove to the crest. Pass the first tower on the right, then follow the crest to the top.

Polar Express 500m IV,4. Andy Nisbet, Steve Perry. 14 Jan 2017.
The last big gully on the face, left of *Valentine's Ridge*, gave an outstanding climb in icy conditions without much snow. The watercourse starts in a recess and the ice pitch out of it was wet and soft. After easy snow was the crux pitch, 30m of steep ice of variable quality. The grade assumes this is solid and takes ice screws, otherwise V,4. After an easy section is the big upper gully left of the triangular buttress of *Valentine's Ridge*. It held several ice pitches and would be 250m Grade III on its own (could be reached from the left).

Ballot Buttress:
(NC 472 490) West facing
A buttress can be clearly seen from the car park at NC 461 476. A clean buttress of rock at the right end of the main face and with a large X that runs the height of the left side of the buttress. An old peg of unknown origin was found between the first two routes about 10m below the first belay ledge. A topo was provided for the routes.
Approach: Follow the walking path up on to the ridge and continue for 300m. Follow a terrace off to the left for easy access to the bottom of the crag, 50mins.

Creideamh 90m VS. Ross Jones, Helen Stocks. 5 Apr 2007.
1. 25m 4b Climb the slabby corner that forms the bottom left arm of the X to a small roof. Pull up and right round the roof and up to a ledge.
2. 25m 4a Climb a short crack and the corner above on the left to reach a small terrace. Climb a short wall to beneath the final headwall.
3. 30m 4c Climb the left side of the wall to the top.

Right of Passage 90m HVS *. Ross Jones, Matt Dent. 5 May 2017.
1. 35m 4b Climb the crack that forms the right arm of the X, leaving this to climb directly up the wall for 15m.
2. 20m 5a Climb the steep crack to the right and the wall above to a large ledge to belay below a blunt arete.
3. 35m 4c Climb up the side of the wall through blocks and then left to pull back on to the wall and a fine finish.

Daonfhlaitheas 50m E2 5b **. Ross Jones, Clare Jones. 30 Jul 2011.
Climb a right-facing wall some 30m to the right to a capping overhang. Take this on the left and follow cracks to the top.

Dòchas 30m E1 5b *. Ross Jones, Clare Jones. 30 Jul 2011.
Start from a raised ledge some 15m further right. From the top of a detached block pull up onto the wall above. Climb up and rightward to the rib above. Climb this and the wall above to finish.

Fios 25m VS 4b. Ross Jones, Helen Stocks. 5 Apr 2007.
A line on the right of the crag. Climb the centre of a small wall for 5m. Pull up onto the hanging wall above, then traverse right and up and leftwards before climbing the wall above.

CREAG NA FAOILINN:
Parental Approval 120m Severe 3c. Grant Cornwallis. 20 Jun 1987.
On the craggy west face of this grim little hill. Go up loose rock and vertical heather to below a big loose chimney (left, below first big roof/overhang). Thrutch up this then climb straight up sound but easy rock to a smooth section. Follow obvious twin cracks, trending left, then more ground to below a big oblong roof (obvious from the track). Trend left again (or up a bulging slab on cracks) to a loose pillar, then right. Continue to a final wall. On right is a loose flake with a deep fissure behind. On left is a pale corner (an obvious nick on skyline from track). Descent is by leftwards over slabs of sorts then down when an overhanging band is reached.
Note: A 20m Severe was climbed by Grant Cornwallis on a crag on the Bealach na h-Imrich's lower slopes (opposite Creag Shomhairle).

PORT VASGO:
Between the Prow area and Skull Island is a north facing wall above a sloping ledge that drops down into the sea. The next two routes are on this wall and left of *Bronxie*.

Cloud Games 20m H.Severe 4b. Ross Jones, Matt Dent. 6 May 2017.
Climb the crack-line up the wall to the left of the blunt prow and then the broken wall above.

The Navigator 25m E1 5a *. Ross Jones, Matt Dent. 6 May 2017.
Start immediate left of the blunt prow and pull up and onto hanging cracks that cut up the side prow pulling round onto the wall and up to the top.

Dallas Dreams 20m Severe *. Matt Dent, Ross Jones. 6 May 2017.
A route at the left end of the Skull Island face, left of *Skull Island* itself. Climb to a roof and hanging corner. Pull through this and then up in to a niche and then to easier ground above.

Midfield Beach (NC 581 653):
This is south of the crag at Port Vasgo, by the same approach but on reaching the shore, turn left and at mid to low tide, boulder hop round the corner to the beautiful sandy beach. This is the highest crag and without birds. Descend off the grass slope behind.

King of Cramp 15m HVS 5b *. Nick Taylor. 18 Aug 2016.
A crack-line on the left side of the buttress is well protected but steep towards the top. Finish up the arete.

Dimples McFringy   15m   VS 5a *. Nick Taylor. 18 Aug 2016.
Follow a groove and crack on the front face of the buttress to the obvious overlap.
A difficult pull through leads to easier climbing on the final upper wall.

AUCKENGILL, The Quarry, Orange Wall:
Fast Fuse   12m   HVS 5a **. Steve Perry, Grace Peach-Perry. 12 Aug 2016.
A parallel crack-line lies 4m right of *Nybster Groove*. Sustained with good
protection.

Force of Nature   12m   HVS 5b *. Andy Nisbet, Steve Perry, Jonathan Preston.
17 May 2017.
Right of *Fast Fuse* is a slightly thinner crack which doesn't reach the ground. Start
directly beneath.

Miss Dynamite   12m   HVS 5a *. Andy Nisbet, Steve Perry, Jonathan Preston. 17
May 2017.
Right again is another full-height crack, left of a grotty one.

ULBSTER, Salad Wall (ND 3405 4175):
An impressive wall bounded by a deep cave on its left and an obvious corner on
the right with a slabby right wall. The map reference needs checking. The obvious
corner is *Salad Wall* (SMCJ 2014).

Seeing the White   30m   E2 5c **. Simon Nadin, Rob Christie. Jun 2015.
Start as for *Salad Wall*. Climb directly into a hanging corner above which leads
to the roof. This is climbed leftwards into the final corner.

Unnamed   E1? Rob Christie, Charlie Macleod.
The wall to the left.

Unnamed   35m   E1 5b *. Simon Nadin, Charlie Macleod. Jun 2015.
Starts from the belay of *Hats off to the Catman*. Start up this until it is possible to
step left and make tricky moves around a bulge to enter the groove above. Take a
direct line to the top.

SARCLET:
Note: *A Paddlers Tale* is solid E4 5c.

Surfer Buttress:
Saga Saga   35m   E4 6a **. Simon & Louise Nadin. Jun 2015.
The impressive wall to the left of *Silver Surfer* has an overhang which runs the
length of the wall. The middle of the wall has an obvious corner.
Start just right of the corner and climb up into a groove line. Follow this for 5m
until moves right exit this onto the wall. Climb the wall directly to the roof above.
Gain a weakness in the roof by moving up rightwards to a Friend placement just
below the lip. A traverse left for 3m gains some positive edges where it is possible
to pull around the roof and onto the wall above. Climb this finishing rightwards.

Hidden Buttress:
An obvious reef lies 100m north of *Silver Surfer*. The first routes are on the
buttress just in front of this. At low tide it is possible to belay on the reef, otherwise

it may be necessary to take a hanging belay on the slab at the bottom of the route.

Line of Sight   20m   E4 6a **. Simon Nadin, Charlie Macleod. Jun 2016.
A black corner sits 4m to the right of the left arete of the buttress. Climb easily up the corner to the roof. From an undercut in the roof, it is possible to place good small wires in cracks above. A difficult sequence of moves around the roof gains a good hold and large Cams for protection. Another awkward move gains the black groove above. Follow this more easily to the top.

Stitch in Time   20m   E2 5c ***. Simon Nadin, Ed Nind. 22 May 2017.
From the same belay as *Line of Sight*, climb cracks and a shallow corner leading to the corner at the right edge of the roof on the previous route. Pull around the roof into the continuation corner. Moves right across the bulge to gain another crack (often wet). Follow the crack until forced right to tackle a final bulge and crack. Fantastic climbing with good protection but can be slow to dry.

Unnamed   20m   E5 6b ***. Simon Nadin, Murdoch Jamieson. 31 May 2017.
The right edge of the buttress has a series of stepped hanging corners. Starting off the right side of the slab, climb rightwards into the first of these corners. Climb this awkwardly until a resting position is gained below the main roof. A Camalot 6 protects the roof and the difficult crux moves to enter the next corner above. Climb the corner to just below the roof and then move right to the shallow corner above. This is followed until moves right lead to the arete. Climb this for a few feet before finishing up the wall on the left.

The next route is in the north facing recess around the arete from the last route. Needs good conditions.

Unnamed   22m   E4 5c **. Murdoch Jamieson, Simon Nadin. 31 May 2017.
Climbs the obvious corner until it peters out below an overhanging wall. A series of daunting moves on good holds lead steeply past adequate protection towards the final exit crack. Intimidating and spectacular climbing that passes through some very unlikely terrain.

Across the recess is a slim buttress with an overhanging prow above it.

Seal of Disapproval   25m   E2 5b *. Simon Nadin, Rob Christie. 14 May 2017.
From a hanging belay, climb the cracks in the centre of the buttress to a ledge below the left-hand sidewall. Gain a hand rail above and move right before making tricky moves to the obvious flake-crack above. Move up and then leftwards to the hanging ramp. This is climbed to a finish above its left edge.

Man or Mouse   25m   E4 6a ***. Simon Nadin, Charlie Macleod. 26 May 2017.
Fantastic climbing with amazing positions and good gear. Needs a good dry spell. Four metres to the right of *Seal of Disapproval* is a north facing corner with a good ledge at its base. Climb the black corner with increasing difficulty to a point 2m below the roof where a traverse left can be made to an obvious good hold and another hanging corner. Climb this passing the next bulge with difficulty (crux, can seep) to some better holds and a rest on the arete. Continue up the overhanging crack on the right side of the arete.

Across the bay from here is a prominent yellow arete with a bird infested left wall. This lies 5m to the south of the gloup at the top of the cliff. The next route starts from a ledge 2m left of the arete.

Paranormal   30m   E3 5a. Simon Nadin, Allan Sinclair. 9 Apr 2017.
From the ledge, climb the wall on the right via cracks to a good ledge. Follow a shallow groove above for 3m until a step right onto the wall 1m left of the arete. Climb the wall and then the arete itself to reach a shoulder below a final steep wall. The wall is tackled slightly to the right with numerous detachable holds. You have been warned!

Above the Gloup is an abseil stake. The next route is accessed from here and tackles the obvious central corner two-thirds up the wall.

Gloup Issues   30m   E1 5c **. Simon Nadin, Rob Christie, Allan Sinclair. Jun 2016.
Start from a good ledge at the bottom of the groove. Climb this to the first roof. Pass this on the right with tricky moves moving back left beneath another roof and into the main corner. Follow this to the next roof and crux moves into a slim final corner. This is climbed until it peters out where moves right gain the rib, groove and top.

Peekabo   VS. Rob Christie, Charlie Macleod. 9 Apr 2017.
The next groove to the right.

Djapana Buttress:
Unnamed   25m   E3 6a **. Simon Nadin, Ed Nind. 22 May 2017.
To the right of *Djapana* is an obvious corner set in the right arete. Belay from an obvious ledge near the bottom. It may be possible to start from a lower position with a low tide and calm sea! Climb the corner with awkward moves passing the obvious roof. Great climbing but can be very greasy so does need a dry spell.

ELLENS GEO (ND 327 407):
From Whaligoe Steps, walk north along the coastline for about 15mins until the pink sandstone and conglomerate walls are visible. An unusual cliff, with climbing that alternates between both sandstone and conglomerate bedding planes. On the whole these routes are well protected by Cams. They are however big lines, especially the right wall and generally require a full rack from micro Cams up to a size 4.
    The cliff is in two sections split by the obvious corner taken by *Where the Taught Wave Hangs*. The first route starts on a smaller buttress which juts out at right-angles to the main wall.

Ham it Up   15m   HVS 5b **. Rob Christie, Louise Nadin. 8 Oct 2016.
Climbs the obvious crack with a steep start.

The Draining Board   25m   E4 6a ***. Simon Nadin, Jacob Crisp. 6 Oct 2016.
Follows the line of the waterfall! Start at the base of a large corner leading to the left-hand side of the roof. Climb the corner and then the blunt rib on the right to good Cams in a break. Move right for 2m. Climb the wall directly followed by a black corner to the top.

ELLENS GEO

1. Gagging Clause E5 6a
2. Guest Pass Violation E3 5c
3. Stratagem E3 5c
4. Brains as well as Brawn . . . E4 6a
5. Hundreds and Thousands . . . E2 5c
6. So this is Summer E1 5b
7. Treading Water E4 5c

8. Where the Taught Wave Hangs . . . HVS 5a
9. Towed in the Hole E4 6a
10. Pig's Ear E4 5c
11. The Fracture Clinic E4 5c
12. Kathleen E3 5c
13. Non Stop Nitty Gritty E3 5c
14. Layer Cake . . . . HVS 5b

Gagging Clause 25m E5 6a ***. Murdoch Jamieson, Simon Nadin. 22 Jul 2015.
Seven metres to the right a steep crack leads directly to the right side of the roof.
Climb the crack with good but awkward gear. Pull through the roof and continue
steeply and spectacularly up the wall on good holds towards a blunt rib to the
right of the final corner on *The Draining Board*. Climb the rib finishing on its
right side.

Guest Pass Violation 26m E3 5c **. Ian Taylor, Tess Fryer. 8 Aug 2015.
Start up the shallow groove to the left of *Gagging Clause*. Climb the groove and
traverse right beneath the roof to finish up easier rock above.

Right again an obvious crack splits the yellow wall (project).

Stratagem 26m E3 5c ***. Simon Nadin, Rob Christie. 30 Jun 2015.
Two metres right of the yellow crack, an easy start up a sandstone corner leads to
a conglomerate corner and ledge. Above this another band of sandstone below a
curving flake-crack in a shallow groove leads to a step right onto a rib which is
climbed until a rest can be found beneath the headwall. Climb slightly rightwards
before committing to a reach back left into the crack which is followed with
difficulty to the top.

The next features to the right are an unclimbed conglomerate corner followed by
an undercut crack and roof in the arete.

Brains as well as Brawn 28m E4 6a ***. Simon Nadin, Murdoch Jamieson. 22
Jul 2015.
Start in the big sandstone corner below the hanging undercut crack. Climb the
corner and traverse right along the break to below the right-hand side of the
undercut crack. Climb steeply up into the crack and undercut leftwards out onto
the arete. Climb this for a few feet before swinging right onto the slabbier face.
Climb this to the left side of the large roof. An awkward and exposed move gains
the hanging corner above. Follow this steeply to the top. Originally graded E5.

Below the top of the cliff there is a grassy ledge near to the central corner line. It
is possible to reach ledges at the bottom of the cliff by a free abseil from here.
The next three routes start from approximately the same point.

Hundreds and Thousands 30m E2 5c ***. Simon Nadin, Rob Christie. May
2015.
Start from the ledges beneath the large corner and roof. Traverse leftwards for 2m
to gain another ledge. Climb steeply up the sandstone, passing lots of breaks to
gain the hanging conglomerate corner above. Follow this until it is possible to
move leftwards across the left wall just below the next sandstone band. Climb
this steeply to finish up a shallow conglomerate corner.

So this is Summer 30m E2 5b ***. Simon Nadin, Rob Christie. May 2015.
Climb the corner above the ledges to the left side of the roof. Pull around this on
its left before making steep moves back right across the wall to gain the crack.
Follow this to the grassy ledge below the top.

Tess Fryer leads Towed in the Hole (E4 6a), Ellens Geo. Photo: Simon Nadin.

Treading Water   30m   E4 5c ***. Simon & Louise Nadin. Jun 2015.
The next shallower corner leads to the centre of the roof. Commit to a traverse right and gain the shallow groove at the side of the roof. Pull through here to a rest. Move up a slightly leftwards to get gear before traversing back rightwards to climb the centre of the wall and small roof at the top.

The next route is the large central corner bounding the left side of the sheer, mostly sandstone wall.

Where the Taught Wave Hangs   HVS 5b ** (SMCJ 2006)
The obvious central corner. A direct finish makes it E1.

The first route on the right wall starts below the wide chimney-crack and prominent hanging arete.

Towed in the Hole   32m   E4 6a ***. Simon Nadin, Rob Christie, Louise Nadin. 8 Oct 2016.
Spectacular and varied climbing. Climb and bridge the deep cleft until it is possible to step left (good cams on the right) onto the hanging nose. Move leftwards across the slab to the arete. Pull up through the bulge in a very exposed position to gain better holds on the left. Steep fingery wall climbing follows a vague crack-line above.

Pig's Ear   32m   E4 5c ***. Simon & Louise Nadin. Sep 2015.
Low down and 3m to the right is an obvious white streak. Climb up to this and follow a vague weakness rightwards for 2m (cams in slightly flared pockets). Move diagonally left across the wall until a crack can be reached. Follow this to the roof above (3.5 & 4 Friend). A long reach gains a good hold in the middle of the roof and powerful moves attain a standing position on the lip. Finish more easily up the corner above.

Ian Taylor on The Fracture Clinic (E4 5c), Ellens Geo. Photo: Simon Nadin.

The Fracture Clinic 32m E4 5c ***. Simon & Louise Nadin. 27 Sep 2015.
Start from the same belay as *Pig's Ear*. Traverse right from the top of the white streak for 2m. Steep moves through the bulge above gain a crack-line. Move up this for 2m before climbing rightwards across the wall to the next crack system. Climb this before moving right again into yet another crack. Follow this to a bulge which is passed with difficulty to gain the final corner. Follow this to the top.

The next two routes start from the same belay below a large corner and roof which has a crack running the length of it.

Kathleen 32m E3 5c ***. Simon & Louise Nadin. 2 Oct 2016.
Climb the corner on the left of the belay to another roof. Move left beneath this to reach a crack shared with *The Fracture Clinic*. Climb this for 2m before moving right across the wall to reach a crack. Follow this to the conglomerate bulge with a deep crack on its right. Pull through the bulge above the crack to gain the wall above. Fingery climbing leads slightly leftwards up a vague crack and hidden pockets to gain sanctuary of good holds below the top. Finish up the short wall to the right of the arete.

Non Stop Nitty Gritty 32m E3 5c ***. Rob Christie, Allan Sinclair. Sep 2016.
Cracks above the belay lead to the looming corner and roof. Difficult moves gain entry into the bottomless corner-crack. Once beneath the roof, a thank god foot-ledge helps progress rightwards to the end of the roof. More sustained climbing leads rightwards to the final corner-crack. Intimidating and requiring careful rope management.

Layer Cake HVS 5b ** (SMCJ 2006)
Follow the corner-line running the full height of the cliff with the crux at the top.

MID CLYTH, Inset Wall:
Amateur Operatics 15m E3 5c **. Peter Herd, Liam Malone. 14 Jul 2016.
A line straight through the steepest section of the wall between *Susan* and *Theatre of Cruelty*. Start as for *T of C* but move right from the starting flake to follow a thin crack up to an obvious steepening. Climb directly through this to a ledge near the top and finish directly by the shallow groove.

Stack Area (Skerry Mor):
Note: *Simon Says* is solid E3 5c. *Simon Says* and *First Passed the Post* are well worth **, as are the *** routes on the Inset Wall.

LATHERONWHEEL, Big Flat Wall:
Macallan's Choice, Direct Start E2 5b **. Simon & Louise Nadin. Jun 2015.
Hand-jam up the well protected, overhanging crack leading out of the roof of the niche to join the original route.

DWS:
A deep water soloing venue at Latheronwheel. This is the most southerly buttress so far. Seen from the top of *Shearwater*, a rocky ridge descends to the sea. An obvious slanting crack splits the left side of this overhanging wall. Scramble down to the edge of the buttress from where it is possible to access a 5c traverse which can be climbed to the obvious niche and crack by the right arete. The arete

can be climbed at 5a as an escape but the top section isn't of the best quality. The smaller crack-line that leads directly to the top of the slanting crack is 5b.

Deep South:

A new buttress between DWS and *Shearwater*. There is a rocky platform at the bottom which is mostly unaffected by the tide. It is possible to scramble down the gully to the north.

Deep South 15m E1 5a **. Rob Christie, Charlie Macleod, Allan Sinclair, Simon Nadin. 2017.
An obvious corner capped by a roof.

Unnamed 15m Severe *. Rob Christie, Charlie Macleod, Allan Sinclair, Simon Nadin. 2017.
The wall and cracks just to the left of the right arete of the buttress.

It is possible to walk along the bottom of the ledge system until a chasm is reached. The buttress to the left of this has been climbed at about VS, as well as some other lines.

Shearwater Wall:

The left side of this wall is very undercut and above deep water with an obvious steep crack.

Ma Cloud of Cordite 5c DWS *. Simon Nadin. 26 Mar 2017.
Traverse out just above the water line to climb past the bottom of the crack and onto the left arete. Follow this passing the left edge of a roof. Finish easily rightwards.

Walnut Whipper 5c DWS *. Simon Nadin. 26 Mar 2017.
Traverse out to the crack and climb this, sometimes damp.

Mindfall 8m HVS 5a *. Simon Nadin, Rob Christie. 5 Feb 2017.
Start 2m left of *Shearwater* at a large flake and climb directly to a shallow corner near the top of the crag.

Deep Blue 8m HVS 5a *. Simon Nadin, Rob Christie. 5 Feb 2017.
Climb the wall and breaks 2m right of *Shearwater* leading to a right-facing corner. Finish up this.

Unnamed 8m Severe *. Simon Nadin, Rob Christie. 5 Feb 2017.
Climb the wall and corners 2m right again.

South Corner:

The following two routes were climbed as DWS. Access is by scrambling down the south side of the buttress and traversing to the base of the routes. Needs high tide.

Marjoram Habit 13m HVS 4c **. Simon Nadin. 29 Jan 2017.
A steep wall leads to a shallow scoop 2m right of dream.

Dill the Weed   14m   HVS 5a. Simon Nadin. 29 Jan 2017.
Starts up the corner just left of the right arete of the buttress. Follow this until the corner steepens and it is possible to step out right. Climb under the roof and around its right side before stepping back left to finish up the front of the buttress.

ORKNEY, Old Man of Hoy:
East Face Chimney Variation   145m   E1 5a *. Richard Ive, Robert Moorcroft. 13 Sep 2016.
An exciting and memorable alternative to pitch 4 of the original route. Due to the traversing nature of the fifth pitch, the route requires a confident approach from both leader and second.
1. to 3. Climb the first three pitches of the original route to the large ledge.
4. 45m 5a Climb up the left-hand chimney. Continue up the corner above to reach an imposing overhang. Belay at the right edge of the overhang.
5. 10m 4c Embark on a delicate rightwards traverse across the impending left wall of the original route's final corner pitch. This gains a belay on the original route. An exciting pitch.
6. 20m 4c As for the original route to the summit.

North Gaulton Castle:
Solitude   45m   E2 5b *. Kevin Woods, David Macmorris. 23 Jul 2016.
Start at a ledge at the base of the north-west arete, accessed by boat at high tide.
1. 25m 5b Climb up and slightly right on good rock to a recess. Pull through a blocky overhang to a large pale coloured break, wriggle leftward and surmount a further step to the base of the green steps.
2. 20m 5b Climb up the blocky staircase before making bold and committing moves up the face left of a thin groove to a ledge. Finish up a short crack.
Note: Kevin Woods thinks the *Original Line* and *Out of the Blue* are different, although starting at the same place, and has sent a topo.

South Ronaldsay, Grimness:
Heading south on the 4th Barrier, take the first exit (signposted Honeysgeo) and drive to the beach where you can park at its north end (ND 487 935). Walk south along the road, then first left and through a gate. Follow cliff around until ND 493 927, marked Out Hillock on the 1: 25000 map, 15 to 20mins.
   The crag is a south-east facing sea-cliff maximum height 15m. Descent is possible via a scramble at the very north end but better is to abseil from a large attached block down *Well that's not what I Expected* (240cm sling). Routes are listed south to north.

Main Crag:
Cheese Louise   15m   V.Diff. Iain Spence, Linda Somerville. Apr 2017.
Start at the bottom of the dyke close to the sea or step across the gap. Climb just to the right of the roof up easy slabs and finish up a corner-crack.

Brum   15m   V.Diff. Linda Somerville, Iain Spence. Apr 2017.
Start in the middle of where the dyke slopes up steeply. Follow easy angled slabs, finishing up through the small roof.

Cleopatra the Chiropractor 15m Diff. Iain Spence, Donna Stephenson. Mar 2017.
Start just before the basalt dyke drops away. Go up and left, following easy slabs until underneath small roof. Move to the left of this and finish up a corner-crack.

Mulher de Guerra Portuguesa 15m V.Diff. Iain Spence, Beta Rodrigues. Oct 2016.
A gentle slab onto a ledge, then climb a corner-crack on a steeper slab.

Assipattle 15m Severe. Iain Spence, Antony Mottershead. Aug 2016.
Go straight up left of a crack to an easy slab traverse below small roof. Go between two roofs and up a thin crack, then finish straight up or head right onto a slab.

Ken Made Us Fat 12m Diff. Ross Mackie, Ken Shuto. Sep 2016.
The left edge of the large slab changes into an arete, then back into a slab.

Well that's not what I Expected 12m V.Diff. Ken Shuto, Ross Mackie. Sep 2015.
Straight up right of the large wide slab.

Suomi 15m Diff. Iain Spence, Laura Hackman. Jul 2015.
Same start as *Ken Made us Fat*, but head right to a flake. Go to the left of a small roof, then finish up through an open corner to the highest point.

The Hup Step 15m Severe. Gareth Squire, Iain Spence. Sep 2016.
Straight up the slab then up through the first roof to the right of the large slab.

Arabella the Killer Whale 15m VS. Linda Somerville, Iain Spence. Sep 2016.
Straight up easy ground onto the small slab, then through the second roof.

Mjolnir 14m Severe. Gareth Squire, Iain Spence. Aug 2016.
Start left and head towards the large flake. Squeeze underneath this to the right, then finish to the right of the double roof.

Rumpelstilskin 14m H.Severe. Antony Mottorshead, Iain Spence. Aug 2016.
A direct steep route through gaps between roofs.

Pineapple Socks 14m Severe. Linda Somerville, Iain Spence. Sep 2016.
Go up a slab to the right of the flake to the large roof. Traverse underneath then to its left.

Mutant Gabloos 13m H.Severe. Linda Somerville, Iain Spence. Aug 2015.
Go up a steep wall onto an awkward slab, then straight up through the largest part of the roof, easier than it looks.

Neil the Seal 13m V.Diff. Linda Somerville, Keith Dampney. Jul 2015.
Start at an inconspicuous thread up through two large horizontal cracks, then finish in a corner to the right of a roof.

Frank the Blind Sheep 10m V.Diff. Iain Spence, Linda Somerville. Aug 2015.
To the right of *Neil the Seal*. Finish up a thin crack in the blank looking wall.

Mike Soldner on Motion Suspended (E2 5c), Mirki Wall, Shetland. Photo: Ross Jones.

Jormungandr   10m   Severe. Iain Spence, Beta Rodrigues. Apr 2016.
Climb a very open corner and thin groove to a hole, then up a steep wall and a very small roof.

Remote Control   9m   VS. Scott Johnstone, Iain Spence. Mar 2017.
Go straight up through the large square hole and finish left.

NORTHERN HIGHLANDS CENTRAL

STONE VALLEY CRAGS, Flowerdale Wall:
Just right of the extreme left end of the buttress is a shallow heathery bay.

Extra Thyme   25m   VS 4c. Jonathan Preston, Chris Robinson, Sarah Atkinson. 8 Oct 2016.
Start just right of the bay where the rock is undercut. Climb through to a good spike on the left. Follow the white coloured groove above. Step left at heather and continue up to a short corner. Finish up this and easier ground above.

Asphodel   25m   E2 5c. Jonathan Preston; Chris Robinson. 8 Oct 2016.
The impending wall between *Heather Mourning* and *Rock Around the Block*. Climb stepped rock to a steepening. Fingery moves through the bulge lead to better holds. Continue more easily via some blocky rock to the top.

STONE VALLEY CRAGS AREA, Meall an Triubhais Dhuibh, Main Wall:
Militant Tendency   20m   E2 5b *. John Mackenzie, Andrew James. 9 Oct 2016.
A route with a strong bias to the left, taking the slanting crack in the lower tier. The innocuous look is a deception; it is well protected but sustained and leads to the heather and the larch belay above. It forms a more direct start to either of the other two routes described in the SMCJ 2014.

PORT ERRADALE, North Stack, Seaward Face:
Tenks Tours   13m   H.Severe 4b. Richard Harrison, Ben Noble. 17 Apr 2017.
Climb the crack starting with the hardest move, then follow a left-trending curving crack to the top on good holds and good rock. The rock on the other routes on the stack is less good.

LOCH TOLLAIDH, Ewe Walls:
Ewebiquitous   25m   HVS 5a. Jonathan Preston, Andy Nisbet. 8 May 2016.
Start 5m right of the heathery break which is just left of *Ewe Tree Slab*. Climb up into a shallow groove, gain a ledge on the right, then traverse 3m right to cleaner rock leading first up, then slightly right to join the top of *Foot in Mouth* up the final arete.

LOCH MAREE CRAG:
The Circus   45m   8a+ ***. Dave MacLeod. Jun 2017.
The extension to *Hafgufa*, originally bolted by Ian Taylor, finishing up the soaring prow at the top of the crag. The upper part is only about 7b+ in itself but makes the whole pitch a superb trip with sustained interest.

GRUINARD BAY CRAGS:
More Cowbell 10m E5 6a **. Ian Taylor. 9 Mar 2017.
At a lower level and left of Post Crag is an area of small walls and aretes. This route climbs the wall just left of the tallest and most obvious leaning arete. Headpointed above a bouldering mat.

Jetty Buttress, Short West Wall:
Hissy 15m HVS 5b. Jonathan Preston, Andy Nisbet. 9 May 2017.
Start just right of the gully. Move up, then swing left (to avoid a wet step). Climb a left-facing corner and step right until under an overhanging crack through the overhang above. Climb the crack.

Goat Crag: New routes here at:
<http://www.northwestoutdoors.co.uk/northwestoutdoorsullapool/2016/6/14/goat-crag-top-deck>

CARN NAM BUAILTEAN, Sylph Buttress:
Sylph, Left-Hand Finish 30m VS 4b *. Sarah Atkinson, Jonathan Preston. 11 May 2017.
1. Instead of moving right (the guidebook says left but this is wrong) to the blunt arete, carry on straight up to belay below a steep crack.
2. Climb the crack with an awkward move at mid-height.

Gossamer Right-Hand Finish 30m VS 4c **. Sarah Atkinson, Jonathan Preston. 11 May 2017.
From the belay at the top of pitch 1 of *Sylph* and *Gossamer*, go right for 5m and climb the obvious twin cracks to a ledge in a niche. Step up and climb the continuation crack and slab to the top. A great pitch on excellent rock.

CARN NAM BUAILTEAN, Golden Buttress:
Note: Jonathan Preston notes that all three routes can be done in one pitch; 45, 50 and 40m respectively. The perched blocks on pitch 1 of *Heart of Gold* have been trundled.

FANNAICHS, Icicle Works Crag:
Love is a Wonderful Colour 25m III. Ewan Lyons. 5 Mar 2017.
A line of least resistance up the ice sheet on the right of the crag.

STRATHFARRAR, Sgurr na Muice, North-East Face:
Globetrotter 280m III,4 *. John Mackenzie, Andrew James. 29 Jan 2017.
To the left of *Trotters Gully* (p344 of NH Central) is a broad turfy buttress forming its left wall. Left of centre on this buttress is a turfy runnel which lies left of a shallow gully.
1. 35m Start up the steepening turfy runnel to belays on the right.
2. 30m The runnel steepens and narrows and is climbed to a hidden rock recess on the right.
3. 40m Traverse horizontally left into a hidden narrow gully which is climbed to its exit.
4. 40m Continue in the same line heading for a closed continuation of the gully, but move right to a good flake below a rock wall.
5. 45m Continue up to easier ground which steepens to another rock wall.

6. 35m Step above the stance and climb to an iced slab above which good ice leads directly to a narrow prominent chimney. Climb this steeply; a fine pitch.
7. 50m Move left from the stance to follow a turfy runnel to the top.

STRATHCONON, Creag Ghlas, West Buttress:
Glitterati 20m VS 5a. Sarah Atkinson, John Lyall. 11 May 2016.
Start just left of the heathery crack, left of *Gloaming Wall*, and go up by flakes to join the upper part of the crack for a short way. Make thin moves left to a left-slanting ramp near the top and step back right to the finish of the crack.

BEN WYVIS AREA, STRUIE HILL CRAG:
Old Kids on the Block 25m Diff.
Right of *Pink Slab* and 2m right of a pine tree, climb the left side of an arete for 4m, then step right and continue to the block finishing behind it by 8m of heather.

Achilles Left-Hand 20m VS 4c **. Dave Allan, Davy Moy. 25 May 2017.
Starts as for *Achilles Chiel* but finishes left. Climb a left-slanting rib then a short arete to a slab. Trend left to a small slanting overlap and follow the thin crack leading from it.

Le Cadeau 20m HVS 5a *. Dave Allan, Davy Moy. 9 May 2017.
Climb the recessed corner behind the slanting rib of *Achilles Chiel* to an overhang. Follow cracks above to the slab and finish midway between the miniature corner on the left and the wide crack on the right.

The Whip 25m Severe. Dave Allan, Davy Moy. 25 May 2017.
This pleasant climb, right of *Hairy Eyrie*, follows the big, open, slightly dirty corner and wide crack with a small tree near the top. Start up the wall just right of the corner.

Grey Slab is renamed *Pocket Slab*.

MOY ROCK:
Little Squeezer 6c+. Andy Tibbs. Jun 2016.
Between *Little Teaser* and *Pulling on Pebbles*.

Cobbledegook 25m 7a *. Ian Taylor. Feb 2017.
Climb *Pulling on Pebbles* to half-height, then follow the right-hand line of bolts to finish at the chain of *Ticks Ate all the Midges*.

NORTHERN HIGHLANDS SOUTH

KNOYDART, Monny Crag (NM 733 995):
Approach: From Inverie, follow the Airor road for 1 mile to parking on the right before a fork in the road. Walk along the low left fork, then follow the rocky beach to cross a tidal inlet to the south. Follow the coast line back south-east to the monument. The south facing crag is now well seen.
Descent: Easy grassy ground between the two main crags.

Left Buttress:

Gripping Doune   45m   V.Diff 4a. Peter Abernethy, George Crossley. 11 May 2017.

On the far left of the left-hand buttress, climb a couple of steep moves to a long right to left ramp. Ascend the ramp to a final airy move to a grassy ledge and then a slab to the top.

Main Buttress:

Illuminati Confirmed   80m   Severe **. Ben Norris, Kirsty Tulloch. 10 Apr 2017.

Takes the obvious line from the lowest point of the crag, left of centre when viewed from the monument.

1. Start from a tall boulder below a prominent triangular feature. Climb to this, then step up and right (or take the bulge direct) to the first wide ledge.

2. From a band of orange rock, climb the wall, stepping right and up to another wide ledge.

3. Climb the faint crack to a small bulge above another ledge. Surmount this (crux), then continue up to the summit.

Main Buttress, Right Wall:

Approaching from the lowest buttress, walk up a steep grass slope to the bottom of a diamond shaped wall.

Plastic Madonna   20m   V.Diff 4a *. Peter Abernethy, George Crossley. 13 May 2017.

Climb the slab to a left-slanting bulge and follow this 8m to a weakness and a prominent quartz vein. Gain the slab and easier ground above to the top.

Monumental   20m   Diff. George Crossley, Peter Abernethy. 11 May 2017.

Start right of *Plastic Madonna*. Climb the furthest left of right-slanting cracks to gain the rib and use this to pass the steep bulge on its right side to reach the top.

DRUIM SHIONNACH, West Face:

Children of the Grave   90m   IV,4 *. Steve Kennedy, Andy MacDonald. 5 Mar 2017.

Start below two parallel grooves about 10m left of the wide capped chimney which is just left of the start of *Hurting II*. Climb the left-hand groove which ends at a small roof at 15m. Surmount the roof by a slab on the left and continue directly up mixed ground to belay on the main ramp just right of the upper chimney of *Poems* (50m). Finish either by the chimney or by moving right and finishing by the upper part of the ramp (40m).

THE SADDLE, Forcan Ridge South Side:

Travelsick Ptarmigan   120m   III. John Lyall, Pauline Dix, Jan Roberts. Feb 2011.

The crest of the rib left of *Millenium Chimney*. The route was gained from a short way up *Millenium Chimney* but could be started more directly. A delicate traverse left gained a turfy line up the rib, which gave bold but good climbing, with a steep section round a block.

A' CHRALAIG, Lochan na Cralaig:

Dream of White Ledges   140m   II. Andy Nisbet, Steve Perry. 25 Nov 2016.

A diagonal line up the right face of *Curled Buttress*. Start down right of its crest (well below *Curled Buttress*) and climb an easy ramp to a spike (10m). Continue up the ramp to its top, then traverse an exposed ledge round an arete before moving up on turf to a rock outcrop (60m). Go diagonally right and up a turf ramp, continuing right to a slabby corner leading up to the cliff-top (70m).

MULLACH FRAOCH-CHOIRE:

Carry on Nurse 150m II. Sandy Allan, Andy Nisbet, Sarah Sigley. 5 Mar 2017.
A fault-line between the central and north buttresses. Low in the grade. Climb via a wide slot to an easy right-slanting snow ramp which leads to the highest crest. A finish back south along the crest improved the route.

Meshuga 180m III. Andy Nisbet, Steve Perry. 9 Mar 2017.
The left side of the north buttress forms a separate crest. Start centrally via a groove until forced out right to an edge, then climb this and move back left to easier slope (45m). Climb the slope to a steepening and go up its right side to a wall (45m). Climb a ramp leading right, then return left to the crest (45m). Follow this to the summit of the left-hand of a pair of ridges (45m). *Frayed at the Edges* climbs the right-hand ridge to its tower and col.

Note: The gully between the south and central buttresses was used for descent, Grade I. The central buttress was climbed by Andy Nisbet in Jan 2017 at Grade II by a right-slanting ramp, then a return left to the easy upper slopes. Andy Nisbet also climbed a better finish to *Frayed at the Edges* on 23 Feb 2017. From the col, descend 10m back towards the corrie, then climb a corner to the highest ridge crest, 30m Grade III.

MEALL GORM:

Colorado Grooves 160m V,6. Simon Richardson, Tom Bohanon. 13 Feb 2017.
Start between *Gormless Grooves* and *Gorm Gully* below an inverted triangle of rock.
1. 50m Step right from the belay and climb turfy steps up a right-facing corner, then move easily up to a second right-facing corner that leads to the first terrace below a distinctive black wall.
2. 25m Climb a shallow right-facing groove in the black wall via prominent bosses of turf to a small pedestal. Continue up the steep right-facing corner above to the second terrace.
3. 30m Traverse 10m left along the terrace around an edge and climb the line of weakness in the wall above to the third terrace.
4. 30m Continue straight up above terrace to a right-trending ramp that leads to easy ground.
5. 25m Continue straight up and finish up a short left-facing gully.

SGÙRR A' CHAORACHAIN, Patey's Wall:

Wrathchild 35m E2 5c *. Michael Barnard, Alan Hill. 27 May 2017.
Climbs the next break in the wall left of *Gideon's Wrath* (through the 'white patch' mentioned in the description for that route). Continue through the overhang as for *Gideon's Wrath* but then finish directly instead of trending right.

No. 5 Buttress:

Bungalow Bill 20m E1 5a. Michael Barnard, Alan Hill. 9 Jun 2017.
Just above the road. Climb cracks up the left side of the steeper right-hand buttress

(the left-hand buttress is the start of *Vine Street*). Start up and right of the central rib, below a short right-facing groove. Move up this until forced out left onto ledges, then go back up right and follow a thin crack to below its vegetated upper section. Step right and follow another crack to the top.

SGÙRR A' CHAORACHAIN, Far North Buttresses:
Note: Andy Nisbet climbed the right branch of *The Gully in 3D* at Grade III on 14 Feb 2017.

LOCH DUGHAILL CRAGS (SMCJ 2016, p178):
The Archivist – a direct finish was climbed up the obvious thin crack (E1 5b *). This makes a better route, so the original way (regraded HVS 5b) is now a variation. *Dughaill and Dillon* and *The Magic Roundabout* have both been regraded Severe.

Father Maguire   12m   VS 4c *. Michael Barnard, Alan Hill. 7 Jun 2017.
The right-hand line on Dughaill's Wall. Start just right of a slanting crack in the lower wall. Move up, then step left and climb the upper part of the crack to gain the ledge below the headwall. Continue directly up this (good Cam protection).

Alternative Facts   10m   H.Severe 4a. Alan Hill, Michael Barnard. 7 Jun 2017.
Climbs the crack up the wall on the right (some loose rock and vegetation).

Craggy Island   12m   VS 4c. Michael Barnard, Alan Hill. 7 Jun 2017.
Climb mid-way between the crack and the arete to its right, finishing up the arete.

Hanging Chad   15m   H.Severe 4b. Alan Hill, Michael Barnard. 7 Jun 2017.
Around the corner from the previous routes is a wide crack leading to a roof. Climb the crack and move right to gain a ledge. Continue up the hanging groove above, stepping right and up to finish.

Upper Tier:
Home Economics   12m   VS 4c *. Michael Barnard, Alan Hill. 7 Jun 2017.
Lies on the *Quiz Kid* pillar. Gain the pillar directly and continue via horizontal breaks; where these become rounded, step left and up to finish as for *Quiz Kid*.

Sewing Practice   12m   Severe 4b. Alan Hill, Michael Barnard. 8 Jun 2017.
Climbs the most prominent crack in the wall right of *Quiz Kid* (just left of an easier groove).

Extra Revision   12m   H.Severe 4b *. Michael Barnard, Alan Hill. 7 Jun 2017.
The left-hand line on the *Swot Team* prow. Climb a thin crack leading to a wide break (large Cams). Traverse right to gain the arete, then finish as for *Swot Team*.

Punishment Exercise   12m   E2 5b *. Michael Barnard, Alan Hill. 8 Jun 2017.
Start as for the above, but step left below the break to climb the thin vertical crack.

Suspect Detention   10m   VS 5a. Michael Barnard, Alan Hill. 8 Jun 2017.
Lies on the NW face of the pinnacle. Climb the vertical cracks up the wall (hard to start and steep at the top).

Stoats 'n' Pollcats   20m   VS 4c *. Alan Hill, Michael Barnard. 8 Jun 2017.
Behind and just past the pinnacle is a cracked rib leading to a lower angled rounded arete. A crack starts up the crest of the rib; climb the next crack just right of this, leading through a bulge (crux). Continue up the fine upper arete.

CREAG AN FHITHICH EAST:
(NG 894 538)   North-North-West facing
These routes lie further left on the hillside from the existing Creag an Fhithich climbs, again on the top tier below the skyline. The crag is seen ahead when driving south towards Annat from Torridon village, with the routes being on a larger wall on the far right side of the visible face. Park in Annat (NG 894 544) and follow the hill path until just past the trees, then go rightwards up the hillside to reach the crag (20mins). Alternatively take a left-slanting approach from near the pub (park at the road bridge), or combine with Creag an Fhithich and contour round. Note that 50m ropes are needed for some of the routes in order to reach the belays.

The highest part of the crag is an impressive dome of rock on the right. Routes are described right to left from here.

Can Salmond   25m   HVS 5a . Michael Barnard, Alan Hill. 9 Jun 2017.
Start below the right side of the dome, at a short vertical crack. Go up this until possible to gain ledges on the right (stepping right higher is E1 5a), then move up to a short left-facing groove. Thrutch up this to gain the ledge above, then step left to climb the upper wall past a small larch.

Sturgeon's Supper   25m   VS 5a *. Michael Barnard, Alan Hill. 9 Jun 2017.
Good climbing up the crack and corner on the left side of the dome.

Moving left, the ground becomes more slabby and low angled; the next route lies on the left side of this section:

Orange Roughy   20m   Severe *. Alan Hill, Michael Barnard. 9 Jun 2017.
Easy climbing leads to a fine crack in the slabby upper wall.

Left of the above is a shorter steeper section of crag with two obvious parallel crack-lines.

Great White Shark   15m   E2 5b **. Michael Barnard, Alan Hill. 9 Jun 2017.
A direct and serious line up the centre of the wall right of the right-hand crack. Climb easily up to the break below the wall, then move up to a higher break (good Cams, last protection). Continue with sustained interest, finishing left up the final slanting break.

Salmond's Leap   15m   VS 4c *. Michael Barnard, Alan Hill. 9 Jun 2017.
The right-hand crack.

SGÙRR DUBH, Larch Tree Crag (SMCJ 2015, p488):
Sadly, the larch tree which gave the crag its name is no more. It was found lying on the ground stripped of most of its bark – looked like a stag attack.

Stag Attack   20m   VS 4b *. Steve Kennedy. 1 May 2017.
The thin crack on the wall left of the jamming crack of *Larch Tree Crack*, joining that route near the top.

Stripper   25m   V.Diff *. Steve Kennedy. 1 May 2017.
Start about 5m right of and above the start of *Larch Tree Slab* and climb a crack-line leading over a small bulge to the headwall. Finish up the slab on the left beneath the headwall.

HAIRPIN CRAG:

Hair-Trigger Hanging   30m   E2 5c *. Michael Barnard, Alan Hill. 8 Jun 2017.
Start just left of *The Text Book*. Climb just left of that route until possible to gain a ledge on the left. Step left and move up to below the roof, then traverse right to gain a ledge below the right side of a slabby wall leading out left to the arete. Traverse the wall (crux) to finish up the arete and easier grooves above.

Trumpets of Jericho   30m   E2 5b *. Michael Barnard, Alan Hill. 8 Jun 2017.
Start as for *The Text Book*. Climb up into the corner, but then take the steep crack up the left wall, finishing up the arete.

INVERALLIGIN TO DIABAIG, Inveralligin Sea-Cliffs, Boomerang Crag (NG 811 571):

A small south facing crag of impeccable gneiss situated below the main path on the Rubha na h-Airde Glaise peninsula on the hillside above Discovery Rock.

Down Under   9m   VS 4c *. Cynthia Grindley, Steve Kennedy, Colin Moody. 16 Oct 2016.
Start just right of the left edge and climb a short slab to gain a left-facing corner. From the top of the corner, move right onto a shelf and finish up slabs.

Aussie Round   9m   Severe 4a *. Colin Moody, Cynthia Grindley, Steve Kennedy. 16 Oct 2016.
The central crack system.

Kylie   9m   VS 5b *. Steve Kennedy, Cynthia Grindley, Colin Moody. 16 Oct 2016.
The wall 2m right of *Aussie Round*. A few initial, thin technical moves lead past a couple of horizontal breaks to the easy upper slab.

Rubha na-h Airde Glaise:

Headland of the grey or hoary height.
Approach: Park at Wester Alligin and approach as for Creag Alligin to a bifurcation at NG 813 572 where the Diabaig path heads off west over the moor. Continue south-west 60m above the shoreline on a faint path to a flat boggy area 500m before the tip of the peninsula. The outline of Discovery Rock is seen on the hillside to the right. For Big Bill's Crag turn down left to the shore at a ruined shieling a little further towards the headland. For Peninsula Crag head down a slight hollow running south-west (thick bracken) to the shore and the crag is immediately on the right.

Peninsula Crag:

(NG 808 607) Alt 10m South facing

This impending cliff of red gneiss lies on the left side of the promontory shoreline directly opposite the Shieldaig narrows and gives some excellent climbing. The sloping stratification provides added interest. The harder routes were briefly inspected and cleaned before lead. Routes are described from right to left, starting with a smooth reset wall just above and right of the main wall.

Penny for your Thoughts 10m E2 5c *. Martin Moran, Robin Thomas. 25 Mar 2016.
Start in the centre, climb to a detached flake, then go left to a thin break and steeply up to a finishing flake.

The main wall is gently overhanging apart from an easement at two-thirds height.

Lines on my Face 16m E3 6a **. Martin Moran, Robin Thomas. 22 Jul 2016.
On the right edge of the wall climb into a niche, exit left on a handrail and move up with difficulty to gain big holds in the glacis. Climb the upper wall on positive holds to a sloping finish.

It's a Plain Shame 16m E4 6a **. Martin Moran, Robin Thomas. 22 Jul 2016.
Move up left from the start of *Lines on my Face* under a bulge. Surmount this by a bold move to good holds and runners in a ramp, and pull on to the resting break. Fix a runner up right in *Lines on my Face* then climb the wall just left by some stretchy moves to a short, obvious finishing flake.

Wind of Change 18m E5 6a ***. Martin Moran, Robin Thomas. 25 Mar 2016.
The original route of the crag starts down left at the base of the wall. Climb a steep flake-crack, then move strenuously out left for 2m along a sloping break, make a difficult move left at its end to a vertical weakness and pull up to a break (crux). Move right along this to a good resting position. Move awkwardly out left on a finger break and pull straight up to a finishing flake.

Do You Feel Like We Do? 18m E5/6 6a ***. Martin Moran, Robin Thomas. 22 Jul 2016.
The impending wall 3m to the left provides an arm-wilting direct version of *Wind of Change* with just adequate protection. Pull over the first bulge using a thin crack to gain holds in a niche and continue straight up to join *Wind of Change* just below the break (beware loose rock). Continue up this to finish.

A vertical vegetated gully bounds the main wall on the left. The walls to the left are more primitive in appearance. A ledge at two-thirds height is thickly-covered in heather and saplings.

Reawakening 10m E1 5b *. Martin Moran, Robin Thomas. 22 Jul 2016.
Gain the huge flake in the middle of the wall by some sharp fingery cracks and climb it to a lower-off from the crowning spike (in-situ sling). After intensive gardening the route might be extended to the upper wall.

COIRE DUBH CRAGS, Creag Coire Dubh:

Salute the Sun　30m　H.Severe *. Sarah Atkinson, John Lyall. 14 Jun 2016.
Just right of the large block/pillar on *Sandcastle* is a dirty looking groove running
the full height of the crag. Follow this to the top.

DIABAIG:

Dire Arete　25m　E1 5b. Michael Barnard (unsec). 2 Oct 2016.
The fine hanging arete marking the crag's change in aspect. Start as for *Apprentice
Bhoys*, then traverse left above the roof to good gear below the blunt arete. Make
a tricky move to start and continue boldly to the top.

Note: Michael Barnard did *Brimstone* with an *Afterglow* variation. Via pitch 2
of Afterglow but without the hard finish, instead stepping back into *Brimstone*.
He thought the route even better, same grade.

BEINN ALLIGIN:

Salvation Ribs　300m　IV,3. John Jackson, Joanne McCandless, Graeme Crowder,
Martin Holland, Doug Spencer, Neil Hamlett. 4 Mar 2017.
Climb the buttress left of *West Coast Boomer* starting up a turfy groove through
the lower tier, 10m left of the start of the gully. Above much variation is possible
with easier lines generally being out left until moving back right after four pitches
to overlook *West Coast Boomer* where the angle eases. Best with well frozen turf,
but could save the day if the ice lines aren't in condition.

LIATHACH, Coire na Caime:

Equilateral　250m　IV,5. Andy Nisbet, Steve Perry. 5 Feb 2017.
The right edge of the squat triangular buttress left of *Fat Man's Folly*. Start at the
right edge of the base and climb a two-stepped fault. Pass right of a long wall and
go up left to a terrace (50m). Continue above, then go left and back right to gain
and climb a wide slot leading to another terrace (60m). A steep final tier was
avoided by going right into *Fat Man's Folly* for a short way, then back left to its
top. Follow the easy crest above until it merges with snow slopes leading to the
top.

Redcloak Rib　120m　II. Neil Wilson, Simon Richardson, Roger Webb. 1 Mar
2017.
The well-defined rib right of Bell's Buttress.

Northern Pinnacles:

Hell Side　150m　III. Andy Nisbet. 13 Feb 2017.
On the NW face of the Northern Pinnacles ridge (the opposite side from the
existing routes) are several ridges. Many are broken but this one is continuous
and leads to the top of the second last pinnacle, climbed by the route *Holy Ghost*
on the Coire na Caime side. Its distinctive feature is a steep smooth section of
crest at mid-height. Start in the centre and trend left to gain the base of the smooth
section. Traverse right under this, climb the first sensible groove and traverse back
left above it. Follow a sharp crest with one deviation right to gain the top of the
pinnacle.

Sgorr a' Chadail:

The Path and the Way Direct　40m　E1 5b *. Rory Brown, Thomas Shaw. 8 May
2017.

A direct start to *The Path and the Way* (SMCJ 2016) which takes the obvious crack-line through a small roof. The crack then continues straight up, to join the cracks and grooves in the upper half of the original route.

Stuc a' Choire Dhuibh Bhig:

The following routes lie on the upper tier of rock immediately left of *Stringless Gully*. The crag is best approached by ascending ground left of the lower tier (steeper on the right).

The Stringman 25m VS 5a **. Michael Barnard, Alan Hill. 6 May 2017.
The best line on the crag is a prominent, widening vertical crack just left of an arete. Go up a short wide crack to a ledge then step right and up a thin crack. Move left to climb the vertical crack (crux).

The other two routes lie on a clean slabby wall further left.

String 'Em Up 25m HVS 5a *. Michael Barnard, Alan Hill. 6 May 2017.
A shallow groove leading to a right-slanting flake in the upper slab.

Slender Threads 25m E2 5b **. Michael Barnard, Alan Hill. 6 May 2017.
Slightly eliminate but very good climbing right of *String 'Em Up*. Move up the blunt rib right of that route to reach a ledge, then a higher ledge. Place a Cam in *String 'Em Up*, then continue up the rib to below the upper slab. Finish up the thin snaking crack right of the right-slanting flake.

The following route climbs vertical cracks up a fine clean wall in the upper tier right of *Triceratops* (well seen from below). This tier is best gained from the right.

Velociraptor 15m E1 5b **. Michael Barnard, Alan Hill. 6 May 2017.
The vertical cracks, with the crux moving left to gain the upper crack.

Bottleneck Slide 15m HVS 5a. Alan Hill, Michael Barnard. 6 May 2017.
The wide corner-crack immediately to the right (Friend 6 useful).

BEINN EIGHE, Far East Wall:

Groovin' High, Variation Start 30m 5a. Michael Barnard, Alan Hill. May 2017.
Two metres left of the normal start is a thin crack. Climb this and move up and left to blocks, then back up rightwards via a series of ramp-lines. Step right below the final wall to gain the belay ledge as for the normal way.

Eastern Ramparts Note: After pitch 2 of the *Eastwood Variation*, moving left along a flake-crack to regain *Pale Rider* (5b) allows this to be climbed at E2.

Sail Mhor:

West Ridge of Morrison's Gully 300m II. Mark Robson, Gavin Mackenzie. 11 Feb 2017.
A mountaineering wander with fine positions, but a little unbalanced by a short steep step of tech 4 one-third of the way up. Likely to have been climbed before. Climb a little way up into the base of *Morrison's Gully* (No.1 Gully) to where it narrows and it's possible to traverse easily out of the gully onto the right (west) flank. Continue rightwards and upwards over small rock steps and easy ground

to a short wall. Surmount this with difficulty and then straight up over more easy ground to a spectacular flat rock platform. Continue up the ridge to the summit of Sail Mhor.

Sgùrr Ban:
Bandersnatch   200m   II. Ewan Lyons. 10 Feb 2017.
A line of least resistance up the right side of the crag. Start in the centre of the crag below the large steep wall (right of *The Ramp*). Trend up left to the bottom of a ramp underneath small overhangs. Follow the ramp up right to gain a rib to the left of a cul-de-sac gully. Go up the rib and step right into the shallow continuation gully which is followed to the top.

CAIRNGORMS

COIRE AN T-SNEACHDA, Aladdin's Buttress:
Torment   100m   E2 5b. Brian Davison, Andy Nisbet. 18 Sep 2016.
The highlight was the arete overlooking *Damnation* corner. Start just left of the toe of the buttress.
1. 35m 4c Climb a wide groove, often wet, and go up to a nose. Step left on to its top, then climb slabs up and right to a crack in the right wall of a grassy ramp on *Genie*.
2. 20m 4b Pull into the crack and climb slabs to the belay of *Damnation* below its corner system.
2. 30m 5b Climb the corner to a flake and step right. Go up slab to the point where *Salvation* crosses the overlap. Cross the overlap just left of this (or as for *Salvation*, easier), then move diagonally left to near the arete. Move up, then gain the arete. Continue just right of it to the belay of *Damnation*.
3. 15m 5b Climb a crack leading right through a steep section, then easier to the top.

COIRE AN LOCHAIN, No.1 Buttress:
Intravenous Fly Trap   70m   X,10. Greg Boswell, Scott Grosdanoff. 8 Feb 2017.
1. 35m Climb the stepped wall 2m to the left of the *Big Daddy* corner. Climb the left side of the wall passing a small overlap, then direct up a crack to reach a hanging pod on the arete. Climb this, then trend right to reach the terrace.
2. 35m Finish up any of the upper pitches from the terrace.

No. 3 Buttress:
Ewen Crest   90m   IV,5. Susan Jensen, Andy Nisbet, Jonathan Preston. 28 Dec 2016.
Start just inside *The Couloir* and traverse right on to the crest. Climb grooves to where *Ewen Buttress* reaches the crest (30m). Cross that route and continue up the crest to a pinnacle (30m). *Rear Entry* joins near here. Continue up slabby ground just left of the crest to the top of the buttress (30m).

No.4 Buttress:
Bulgy, Direct Finish   HVS 5a ***. Michael Barnard, John MacLeod. 27 Aug 2016.
Where the normal route goes left through the twin roofs, instead climb steeply up

*Brian Davison on the FA of Torment (E2 5b), Aladdin's Buttress, Coire an t-Sneachda.
Photo: Andy Nisbet.*

the top wall, moving left to use the left edge. A finely positioned pitch and generally well protected (take a full set of Cams up to 4).

SHELTER STONE CRAG:
Note: Ken Crocket & Ian Fulton climbed *Consolation Groove* free in Sep 1971, the first recorded free ascent.

HELL'S LUM CRAG:
Kiwi Slab, Direct Start 70m IV,4. John Lyall. 5 Jan 2017.
Start up a narrow chimney slot about 5m left of the deep right-facing corner of *Big De'il*. Follow this fault and steep ice just right of an icicle fringed boss, to gain the foot of the left-facing corner of the original route, at the end of the traverse.
Note: JL had climbed a line close to this in the mid-eighties, but it seems worth a new description as it gave a superb natural line.

Thin White Duke 150m V,4. John Lyall. 5 Jan 2017.
Start just left of the narrow chimney slot, and climb ice up a slight rib, then slabs, and follow a shallow, left-slanting corner to the left of the icicle fringed boss to reach the traverse of *Kiwi Slab*. Follow the ice sheet above; between *Kiwi Gully* and the corner of *Kiwi Slab*, make a thin move left, then follow a slim, right-slanting corner/groove, then easier slopes to the top. Climbed on perfect ice.

STAG ROCKS:
Last Gasp 70m III/IV,5. John Lyall. 5 Feb 2017.
Starts about 10m left of *Final Groove* and follows a groove! Gain the hanging,

icy groove line by a steep initial wall, and follow this until possible to gain the parallel fault on the left, which leads to a steep wall. Move up left by a crack to gain a big ledge. Move right and onto a block, then up the right edge of the recessed area, passing the roof and finishing by a turfy crack. A surprising route.

Notes:
Andy Nisbet & Masa Sakano started *Triple Towers* by a 60m pitch out left from *CM Gully* (the crest had no snow) at Grade III to reach the bay above the ice on Stag Route. *CM Gully* looked Grade IV and certainly not II/III. John Lyall climbed *Serrated Rib* and thought it tricky for Grade II, but all the routes climbed by Bill March in Nov 1969 were undergraded.

MAM SUIM, Creag na h-Iolaire:
Operation Grouse 40m III. Simon Richardson, Roger Webb. 24 Feb 2017.
The left-facing corner continuing straight up from the initial short gully of *Storms of Life*.

The Heroes of Telemark 40m III,4. Simon Richardson, Roger Webb. 24 Feb 2017.
A line between *Storms of Life* and *Fate is not an Eagle*. Start up the initial ramp of *Fate is not an Eagle*, then break left up an awkward wall just before the steep corner. Continue up, traverse right, then take a parallel line right of *Storms of Life* up a steep fault in an exposed position to reach easier ground.

CREAGAN COIRE A' CHA-NO:
Plasma Gully, Asthma Finish 20m III,4. Jon Foden, Ivor McCourt. 5 Jan 2017.
Follow *Plasma Gully* for most of its length to just before it turns right and steepens. Follow a groove up the steep left wall for 15m to a ledge running right (easy escape). Finish directly up the left wall via a niche and overhanging blocks, well protected fun!

Big Boy Made Me 60m II. Euan Whittaker, Martin Holland. 5 Jan 2017.
The gully immediately left of *Once Were Alpinists*.
1. 35m Climb the gully to where the angle eases.
2. 25m Continue up easier ground to the top.

Cosmopolitan Chimney 60m IV,6. Roger Webb, Simon Richardson. 25 Nov 2016.
To the right of the broken right flank of *International Rib* is a gully topped by a steep narrow chimney. Climb the gully (35m) and continue up the chimney above to a difficult exit on the right.

Half Blood 50m III. Roger Webb, Simon Richardson. 25 Nov 2016.
The line of grooves to the right of *True Blood Direct*.

CNAP COIRE NA SPREIDHE:
Rampe Exposé 300m II. Roger Webb, Simon Richardson. 28 Nov 2016.
Start 50m left of *Goulotte Cachee* and follow a ramp-line into the amphitheatre. Continue along the ramp then break left up a steep wall to the upper snowfield. Climb left of the ridge defining the right edge of the snowfield and exit right up a well-defined wide gully to broken rocks (normally snow) and the top.

Rampline 300m II. Ron Walker, Fi Chappell. 5 Dec 2017.
Just right and parallel to the above route to about halfway, then shares the wide gully, but continues up on the right side of the ridge to the top, zigzagging and breaking through a series of walls, chimneys, ramps and a short steep icy wall before finishing up a wall of big jammed blocks close to the right side of the central ridge.
Note: Ron Walker thinks he has probably climbed and skied the left side of the ridge with a much bigger build-up.

The following four routes lie on another crag which is passed just before reaching the main rock climbing crag. The main feature is an obvious wide flake-crack.

Cheap Day Return 12m VS 5a **. Michael Barnard, Alan Hill. 10 Sep 2016.
Climb another crack just right of the main flake-crack (crux) and continue up the slab above to finish as for the next route.

Kick out the Jams 12m E1 5c **. Michael Barnard, Alan Hill. 3 Sep 2016.
A struggle up the wide flake-crack (crux). Continue up the equally good upper flake-line.

Further left and up are two parallel corners and a rockfall scar.

Slipstream 15m H.Severe 4b. Alan Hill, Michael Barnard. 3 Sep 2016.
The right-hand corner above two large blocks. Good solid rock.

Savage Slut 15m HVS 4c. Alan Hill, Michael Barnard. 3 Sep 2016.
The left-hand corner has more than its fair share of loose/rotten rock, passes near a 'death block' and is not recommended.

The next routes lie on the main wall of the crag (right of *Beyond Superstition*) which bears a strong resemblance to some parts of Clach na Beinn.

Acolytes of Gloom 15m E2 5b **. Michael Barnard, Alan Hill. 10 Sep 2016.
A fine line up the wall right of *Beyond Superstition*, but forced out right near the top. Start up *Prologue Groove* for a couple of moves, before undercutting left below the roof and pulling through to gain the line of flakes. Continue more easily to a large hold and good nut, then move up and make a delicate move to the obvious thin flake. Step right to finish as for *Prologue Groove*.

Prologue Groove 15m Severe *. Alan Hill, Michael Barnard. 3 Sep 2016.
The groove in the centre of the crag.

Five metres right of the groove is a vertical chimney; immediately left of this is a blunt rib with a thin flake-crack either side of the crest.

Baron Von Tollbooth 15m E2 5b **. Michael Barnard, Alan Hill. 3 Sep 2016.
Start just up from the base of the rib and gain a hold on the left. Climb the rib using both flake-cracks (little or no protection) to reach respite at a horizontal foot ledge. Continue up then step left to finish up the fine upper crack.
Variation: Chrome Nun Finish E2 5b **. Michael Barnard, Alan Hill. 10 Sep 2016.

From the base of the upper crack, step left to climb the upper tower, finishing directly. A good finish and better in keeping with the main route.

Afterburn   15m   Severe. Alan Hill, Michael Barnard. 3 Sep 2016.
The vertical chimney.

One Year 'til the Bus Pass   15m   HVS 5a *. Michael Barnard, Alan Hill. 3 Sep 2016.
The obvious left-slanting line in the crest right of the chimney. A bold start (crux) leads to easier climbing up the crack, with the twin flakes on the left providing a good finish.

Blaeberry Jam   40m   HVS 5a. Michael Barnard, Alan Hill. 10 Sep 2016.
Just past the main crag a fine steep tower is visible with some lighter coloured rock to the right. This route climbs cracks to the left of the crest, then up the main crack above to finish directly. A bit vegetated lower down, but improves with height.

The Pinnacles:
The 'finger of rock' seen on the approach is actually the first of a group of three.

Supersonic Scientist   10m   HVS 5a ***. Michael Barnard, Alan Hill. 10 Sep 2016.
The left-slanting chimney-crack on the underside of the first pinnacle gives a brilliant wee climb.

Methodist Missionary   15m   E1 5a *. Michael Barnard, Alan Hill. 10 Sep 2016.
Facing the above is the large slabby face of the smaller second pinnacle. This route climbs a ramp near the left edge to a small roof (RPs) before finishing up the slab above.

CRAIG RAIBEIRT:
Firefly Corner   30m   V,6. Iain Small, Simon Richardson. 23 Nov 2016.
The prominent corner right of *Typhoon Corners*. Climb *Typhoon Corners* for 10m, then continue up to the roof. Step right below it and pull up on helpful holds onto wall above. Finish up this to the top.

LURCHER'S CRAG, South of South Gully:
Boules   100m   II. Sandy Allan, Susan Jensen, Andy Nisbet. 27 Dec 2016.
Start left of the ridge of *Skittles*. Climb a fault-line up right towards *Skittles* but take another line leading left after 10m. Follow this to a subsidiary crest and take this back right to finish at the same place as *Skittles*.

Receding Hare   100m   II. Sandy Allan, Susan Jensen, Andy Nisbet. 27 Dec 2016.
The shallow gully between *Skittles* and *Ten Pins*.

The Alley   100m   I. Andy Nisbet. 5 Dec 2016.
A narrow gully between *Ten Pins* and the *Punchdrunk* buttress.

The Seeker   110m   II. Andy Nisbet. 2 Jan 2017.
A ramp-line left of the *Punchdrunk* buttress crest. Start just inside *The Alley* and

go out right to gain the base of the ramp which is formed left of a vertical wall near the crest. Follow the ramp to its end, then go up right to the crest (60m). Move out left and climb left of the crest until forced to join it and the other routes to the top (50m).

Storm Barbara   110m   III. Andy Nisbet, Jonathan Preston. 22 Dec 2016.
The depression between *Pug Face* and *Drystane Ridge*. Climb the depression to a bay below a steep wall. Traverse right with a step down until about 10m left of the crest of *Drystane Ridge* (30m). Climb up slightly leftwards to a left traverse below a steep wall and reach a chimney-crack (30m). Climb this and move left to reach the easier upper depression (10m). Climb this to the top (40m).

Far South End:
Theory of Relativity   45m   VII,9. Steve Perry, Andy Nisbet, Jonathan Preston. 7 Nov 2016.
A groove and crack-line just right of the crest which forms the left edge of the front face of the buttress with the Canis routes. Very strenuous but good protection. Start at the base of the crest.
1. 15m Climb steeply into a ramp which leads to an overhanging groove. Climb this with difficulty to ledges where the angle eases.
2. 15m Continue to a small pinnacle and the crack-line directly above.
3. 15m An easier continuation leads to easy ground.

Wolfpack   40m   VI,7. Andy Nisbet, Steve Perry, Sarah Sigley. 23 Nov 2016.
A groove just left of the right crest of the Canis buttress.
1. 20m Make steep moves leftwards to enter the main groove and climb it to the right crest. Go up just right of the crest to a narrow chimney behind a pinnacle on the crest.
2. 20m Climb the chimney to the top of the pinnacle. Follow the crest to easy ground, joining *Canis Major* high up.

SRÒN NA LAIRIGE:
East of the summit is a small cliff comprised of a rib and buttress.

Stickleback Rib   70m   II. Roger Webb, Simon Richardson. 2 Jan 2017.
Climb the well defined left-hand rib in two pitches.

Shark   70m   V,7. Simon Richardson, Roger Webb. 2 Jan 2017.
The buttress to the right of *Stickleback Rib* is characterised by a huge down-sloping flake at its base.
1. 30m Start in the corner left of the flake and climb steeply up to a vertical wall. Climb first left, then right to exit on the right edge.
2. 40m Bear left up steep blocky ground to gain an easier finishing ridge that finishes at the same point as *Stickleback Rib*.

BRAERIACH, Garbh Choire Mor:
West Gully, Left-Hand Finish   70m   II. Simon Richardson. 20 Jan 2017.
From near the top of *West Gully*, take the narrow left exit that cuts into the right flank of *West Buttress*.

Tewnion Slabs   100m   III. Simon Richardson. 20 Jan 2017.

In lean conditions an ice streak forms down the slabby wall between *Sphinx Gully* and *Pinnacle Gully*. This leads to a right-trending ramp and provides a short climb approximating to the summer line climbed by Sandy Tewnion in Jul 1940.

Coire an Lochain:

Sinister Dredge   100m   III,4. Roger Webb, Simon Richardson. 5 Jan 2017.
The right-facing corner left of *Ice Elation*. Icy slabs lead to the main corner, which bears left at half-height and contains a couple of steep bulges in its upper half.

Einich Cairn, Coire nan Clach:

Forgotten Face   70m   V,7. Roger Webb, Simon Richardson. 29 Jan 2017.
The front face of *The Forgotten Pinnacle*.
1. 30m Climb deceptively awkward slabs (which bank out later in the season) to the base of the steep front face.
2. 20m Continue up the gully on the left, then move back immediately right onto a flake-platform on the front face. Climb the steep cracked wall above to the top of the pinnacle.
3. 20m Descend to the col behind and finish up the easy connecting ridge to the plateau (as for *The Forgotten Pinnacle*).

BEINN A' BHUIRD, Coire nan Clach:

Stonewall Ramp   180m   III. Simon Richardson. 15 Mar 2017.
The right wall of The Promontory is cut by an ice-smeared ramp. Move easily up snow to the ramp, climb a short ice smear and continue up the shallow gully above to the broad front crest of The Promontory. Finish up easy ground to the top.

Cleirich Couloir   120m   II. Simon Richardson. 27 Jan 2017.
The open icy gully immediately north of the small lochan in the right lobe of the corrie starting at NJ 099 003 is fed by a spring and provides a worthwhile climb in lean conditions mid-winter.

LOCHNAGAR, Southern Sector, The Sentinel:

Paladin   130m   V,6. Simon Richardson, Sophie Grace Chappell. 22 Dec 2016.
Start 70m left of the toe of the buttress and climb easy mixed ground to the start of the summer route. Follow the summer line to the top.

Perseverance Wall:

Columbus Rib   70m   IV,4. Simon Richardson, Ben Richardson. 28 Dec 2016.
The well-defined rib between *Resolution Gully* and *Lunar Eclipse*.
1. 40m Start just right of *Resolution Gully* and climb through a steep bulge on the right wall. Continue up a turfy V-groove to a tower and climb the right flank of this via good cracks to a ledge.
2. 30m Step left and climb the right-trending groove to the top of the buttress. Scramble along a short horizontal section to reach easy snow and the cornice.

The Cathedral:

Fat Daddy   70m   VI,7. Guy Robertson, Pete Benson. 25 Nov 2016.
A good short route between *Cracker* and *Cathedral Chimney*. Start up on the left wall of *Cathedral Chimney*, immediately opposite the start of the difficulties on *Magic Pillar* at a rockfall scar.
1. 20m Gain the obvious steep groove from the right and follow this to ledges.

2. 20m Climb short walls and ledges up right towards the edge, then go straight up a steep right-facing flake-crack with a hard exit onto a ledge. Follow wide cracks back up trending left onto an airy perch on the ridge.
3. 30m Climb directly up short turfy steps.

CREAG AN DUBH LOCH:

Spitfire 75m E2 *. Michael Barnard, Susan Jensen. 17 Jun 2017.
A good main pitch up the area of wall between *The Fox Moth* and *Bare*. Start 5m left of the latter, at an easy right-facing groove leading to a higher grassy ledge.
1. 45m 5b Go up to the higher ledge, then boldly via thin cracks to reach gear below a bulge. Climb through the bulge, then make a long traverse left across a slab to an obvious, short right-facing corner. Climb the corner and move up before stepping back right on a slab towards a shallow left-trending fault. Climb the fault, then step right and up via thin flakes to level with the 5a corner on *Dragonfly*. Step left into this and continue up to a short right-facing corner.
2. 30m 4b Climb up to gain the ledge above, step left, then continue up past ledges to reach *The Caterpillar*.

False Gully Wall:

Anaemia 70m E5 ***. Jules Lines (rope solo). 31 May 2017.
This excellent varied climb takes the most natural line and is essentially a combination of *An Spearag* and *Sans Fer* with a new third pitch. It is the twin line to the *Sans Fer / Iron in the Soul (Sans Soul)* combination and is a small step up in standard. It should be nice and clean. Start at the right side of the abseil block.
1. 15m 6b Climb the thin crack by mainly using good holds on the left wall. At 6m the holds run out. Stretch in a good nut, then make some tenuous moves right on sidepulls (crux with overhead protection) to gain a partial rest at the base of the flake. Climb the flake past an undercut flange with a bold finish onto a smooth shelf. Belay immediately on the right, small nut and Cams. This is a less sustained method than the original, *An Spearag* which traversed the horizontal break a little higher to gain the flake.
2. 25m 6a Climb the dwindling groove above and continue through the roofed alcove to gain a crack that leads up to a block and crevasse belay.
3. 30m 6a Above is a bulging crack. Go right along a shelf on undercuts and using a high pinch, pull back left into the top of the crack. Follow the line into an open V-groove, step left and continue up the easy rib to the top.

Magrathea 70m E9 ***. Jules Lines, Steve Perry. 5 Aug 2016.
A stunningly minimalistic line up the blank wall to the right of *Slartibartfast*. Start at left side of the abseil block at the base of the wall.
1. 20m 7a Climb in the line of the hairline crack (IMP's) to a poor shakeout where a cluster of uninspiring, but 'potentially' adequate micro-wires can be placed. Continue via a desperate sequence of moves to reach a jug atop the wall. Move up onto a shelf on the right; small wires in a slot above provide the belay.
2. 20m 6a Climb the beautiful leaning groove above to a large flake block.
3. 30m 6a Take the short right-facing corner above and follow the line to a niche. Pull left onto a rib and continue up this to the top.

Mostly Harmless 70m E5 ***. Pitch 1 by Jules Lines, 1 Aug 2016 rope solo; Pitches 2&3 by Jules Lines, Danny Laing jnr, 12 Jun 2015.

This superb climb is as good as *Slartibartfast*, but will need a few days of good weather to dry it out on the upper pitches. Pitches 2 and 3 were cleaned as the proposed finish to the main pitch of *Magrathea*, but it was later decided that it would make a great, wholly independent route with the addition of a new first pitch at a more amenable standard. Start to the left of *Slartibartfast* at a rectangular hole directly beneath the central crack on the wall.

1. 20m 6b   Boulder up the wall for 5m to gain the first good layback hold at the start of the crack proper; place a crucial IMP4 with difficulty in the base of the seam just to the right (crux). Continue laybacking up the crack to join *Slartibartfast* and belay on the shelf.

2. 20m 6a   Pull onto the rib on the right and follow the overhanging crack to a rest at the base of the acutely leaning corner. Climb the corner (large Cam) by wide bridging, which is also required to negotiate the 'permanent' weep here. Near the top of the corner, place a high nut, step left onto the rib and climb delicately up to a shelf and flake belay. A short and tough, well protected pitch that is one of the best on the mountain.

3. 30m 5c   Climb directly behind the flake and move awkwardly rightwards onto the base of the large slabby ramp. Climb straight up a series of tiny left-facing grooves and a layback to land on a large ledge. Step right and finish up the rib.

NORTH-EAST OUTCROPS

COVESEA:

Tusken Raider   30m   E3 5c *. Peter Herd, Russell Birkett. 1 May 2017.
A mid-height girdle of the main wall in Boulders Bay. Start up *Sandanista* and follow obvious flat holds across the wall, climbing above the roof and joining the following route. The middle section is bold and care should be taken to protect the second.

Fascist Republic   15m   E2 5b **. Steve Perry, Julian Lines. 19 Apr 2017.
Climb up *Banana Republic* past the roof. Now make an exhilarating traverse above the roof, all the way to the corner of *Fascist Octopus* using an obvious handrail and placing a good Cam in the crack of *Banana Republic – Corbyn Variation*. Once at the corner, make a couple of bold mantels to reach good protection in the upper corner.

Anchuria   15m   E6 6c **. Jules Lines. 26 Mar 2017.
The roof and wall to the left of *Banana Republic*. Start off a boulder and climb the wall to the roof just right of a black weep. Make athletic moves through the roof and continue up the hairline in the wall above, shifting to its right side just below the top.

Prisoner of Conscience   15m   E7 6b **. Jules Lines. 30 Apr 2017.
A direct line through the overhanging face to the right of *Bottle Dungeon*. Boulder up on crimps to a flat jug at 3m in the faint right-hand groove system. Follow the flying groove up and left to a hands-off rest at half-height. Launch up and right into a sequence of blind right-facing corners and pull wildly through the roof to get established on the leaning headwall. Finish up this more easily.

The Bear   15m   E1 5a. Steve Perry. Michael Barnard. 24 Jun 2017.
Climb the corner beside *Honey Barrel*.

Typhoon   15m   VS 5a. Steve Perry, Sarah Sigley. 21 Mar 2017.
An easier route on the wall (and easier still using a bunk-up at the start). Start as for *Celebrate the Bullet*, then step right and climb up to the roof directly beneath the upper crack of *Protection Racket*. Traverse rightwards under the roof to the base of a crack on the west face. Climb this on jugs to the top.
Note: A direct start from below has been climbed but only as a boulder problem. Doing this and the top would probably drop the grade.

I Live, I Die, I Live Again   15m   E4 6a *. Steve Perry. 18 Apr 2017.
Starts in the corner left of *Creepie Crawlie* where a small seep in the bottom can be avoided. Make a boulder problem start and arrange gear in a thin vertical crack before a bold but easier traverse right along a rail. Welcome gear in another thin vertical crack and steady wall climbing leads to a second roof. Finish as for *Creepie Crawlie*.

PASS OF BALLATER:
Odorono   10m   E1 5c. Michael Barnard (unsec). 13 Jun 2017.
Eliminate, but a good move. Climb *Stinker* to place gear under the overlap, then step down and left to join *Brut*. Now move up and pull directly through the overlap to finish easily.

Zapata   8m   HVS 5a. Greg Strange, Rob Archbold. 14 Jul 2016.
Start 1m right of *Fungus Face* and climb the wall left of *Lime Chimney*, finishing at a small right-facing corner.

Poker's Rib   E6 6b *. Jules Lines. Mar 2017.
Start on the boulder as for *Peel's Wall* and pull on at undercuts, then move left to gain a good pinch on the rib. Follow the rib to the horizontal. Using a mono, rock up to gain a set of tiny crimps that veer right, then slap for a very smooth pinch on the rib. Use this go for the top.

Slope Shoulders   E4 6b *. Jules Lines, Richard Biggar. Summer 2016.
The direct finish to *Slope Arms* gives a fine and fierce micro pitch. Start up *Slope Arms* and at the break (small cam), gain a pinch in the seam up and right. Finish direct.

Morphine Drip   E7 6c **. Jules Lines. 26 Oct 2017.
The central line following a hairline seam 2m to the right of *Private Parts*. Start at the diamond shaped block and gain a slot in the wall. Make a desperate move to gain a niche hold before sprinting up to a superb finishing sequence in the scoop at the highest part of the wall. Probably F7c and graded for gear placed on the lead as per FA.

IVF   E5 6b. Jules Lines. 2016.
Pull through the roof as per *Copulation* and then improvise right to a good hold on the arete. Finish up it in a fine position.

Sobriety   E5 6b **. Jules Lines. Jan 2017.
The parallel line to the left of *Larup Head* gives a good pitch at the upper limit of
the grade. Make bouldery moves via an undercut and blind flake to reach a break.
Continue direct via a sustained sequence to gain a narrow ledge. Continue on up
the crack in the upper wall veering slightly left to finish on jugs.

GLEN CLOVA, Lower North-West Crag:
For a Handful of Beans   30m   HVS 5a **.
The route as described in SMCJ 2015 Journal was repeated. Following cleaning
and removal of several large loose blocks, the undernoted description provides a
more direct independent line.
   Good climbing up the centre of the wall. Climb direct up a cracked wall to a
niche and arrange protection in the wide left-curving crack above. Step back right
and climb the wall above on good positive holds, trending left to a large rowan.
Finish up a crack above past a further rowan.

HIGHLAND OUTCROPS

CALLENDER SPORT CRAG (NN 6298 0879):
A conglomerate sport crag developed by Ian McCabe, Peter Nellist and others.
The latest info is on <http://callandercrags.weebly.com/>
Approach: From the A84 that runs through Callander. Where the A84 changes
from Stirling Road to Main Street, turn north up Bracklinn Road, a minor road
signed for 'Bracklinn Falls, The Crags' and 'Golf Course'. After 500m turn into
the parking on the left signposted 'Callander Crags'. Walk 200m west past a
barrier along the forestry road, then turn right uphill on the big path marked with
a red waymarker. Follow this uphill round several bends for 15-20mins until below
the crag where a clear path goes off horizontally left beneath the cliffs. 50m along
this path, opposite a large tree, and with a fallen log pointing the direction, a
smaller path leads off rightwards through birch saplings and undergrowth to the
foot of the crag. The cleaned section is clearly visible from here. Routes described
right to left.

Cobbled Path   20m   5b (8 bolts)
The first line of bolts. Climb the left side of the vague rib to the rightmost lower-
off below a tree.

Conglomerate Pickpocket   20m   5c (8 bolts)
Climb the second line of bolts to a section of juggy pockets, then up an incipient
rib. At the sixth bolt tread delicately rightwards to move up to the rightmost lower-
off below the tree.

Pebble Dash   20m   6a (8 bolts)
Climb as for *Conglomerate Pickpocket* to the 6th bolt, then trend slightly left onto
the steeper thin headwall to the second lower-off from the right.

Original Mossy Crack   20m   5b (8 bolts)
Climb the third line of bolts, following an intermittent crack-line. At the top the
bolts are first left then right of the crack. Particularly enjoyable climbing.

House of Marbles   20m   5c (9 bolts)
Climb the fourth line of bolts. There is a bit of a stretch to clip the lower-off from the ledge just below the top.

Jacket Off   21m   5c (9 bolts)
The leftmost bolt line to date. Still mossy but climbable.

BALQUHIDDER, Creagan Nam Putan:
Even Mhor Temptation   E2 5b. Andrew Woolston, Mike Wilson. 8 Jul 2016.
A direct finish to *Mhor Temptation*. The route goes left at an overlap at half-height. The direct finish goes straight over the overlap and direct to the top. Slightly harder than the original.
Note: *Monachyle Munchies* was thought only worth one star; the start is unprotected and contains the hardest climbing with the crack petering out to an easy finish.

ARGYLL, Creag Nam Fhitheach:
America, Direct Start   25m   HVS 5a *. Gary & Karen Latter. 6 Nov 2016.
Start beneath the short left-facing groove just right of *Metamorphosis*. Climb the groove and direct above to gain the crack leading to the normal route.

GLEN GOUR, Indian Slab:
Cherokee   90m   HVS 4c *. Jonathan Preston, Andy Nisbet. 5 Jul 2017.
1. 25m 4b   Start up *Outrider* and move right to below the hanging slab (as for *Ambush*).
2. 40m 4c   Climb the hanging slab direct, starting up 2m left of its right corner, later trending slightly left.
3. 25m   Finish rightwards up a broken rib.

ARDNAMURCHAN:
The Mighty Fin   80m   HVS 4b. Mike & Paul Brian. 28 Aug 2016.
South-West of Kilchoan at NM 461 623, an impressive blade of rock rises from near sea-level to a height of about 120m. Although the crag is difficult to spot from the land, it makes a spectacular sight from the Oban to Barra ferry. From Kilchoan, take the road to its end past Ormsaigbeg and park in a small quarry. Follow a sheep track to the top of the crag, 20mins. The west face yields some pleasant climbing on good rock but protection is poor, so routes have only been top-roped apart from a short chimney-crack towards the landward end of the cliff (V.Diff). The most obvious line follows the crest of the fin, which gives three exhilarating but poorly protected pitches. Approach by abseil down the gully on the east of the fin.

Wedge Buttress:
Nymph   35m   V.Diff *. Cynthia Grindley, Steve Kennedy. 6 Nov 2016.
Climbs a line close to the left edge (left of *Pixie*). Start up a corner-crack close to the left side of the base to reach a wide ledge below a steep wall. Move left and climb cracks to reach a prominent left-facing flaky corner (about 3m from the edge) which leads to the upper slabs.

Meall an Fhir-eoin:
Happy Cow   30m   VS 4c. Alan Halewood, Nathan Adam. 17 Apr 2017.

Start at the toe of the rib forming the left side of the heather corner left of *Raging Bull*. Follow the crack up onto the slab and to the base of the undercut wall on the left. Climb this by thin flakes on the left.

Linear Zone   40m   VS 4c *. Steve Kennedy, Cynthia Grindley, Colin Moody. 2 Apr 2017.
Climbs the right side of the whaleback joining *Ring of Fire* near the left end of the hand-traverse. Make a move or two up the corner left of the whaleback, step right and climb a pock marked wall to a small roof. A crack on the right side of the roof leads the top of the whaleback (joining *Ring of Fire*). Finish up the crack in the final short wall as for *Ring of Fire*.

LOCHAILORT CRAGS, Quadruple Crack Buttress (NM 799 831):
This small crag is situated about 80m left of Boathouse Crag at a similar level. South facing and characterised by four crack-lines, the middle two being wide and chimney like. Approach by walking about 300m west along the A830 road from the Boathouse parking spot before heading almost directly up to the crag, just before some small trees, passing a telegraph pole on the way uphill (15mins). Good block belay at the top situated well back. The routes are described from right to left.

Line Dance   12m   VS 5a *. Steve Kennedy, Eileen Blair, Cynthia Grindley. 2 Jun 2017.
The rightmost finger-crack starting at the lowest point which initially forms a right-facing corner leading to a roof. A tricky move leads around the roof to a small corner breaching another small roof. Climb the corner and slab above, joining the previous routes at the final short slab.

Triple Step   12m   V.Diff *. Cynthia Grindley, Steve Kennedy. 3 May 2017.
The wide chimney-crack left of *Line Dance* containing some large chockstones in the upper part and finishing by a short cracked slab.

Jazz Square   12m   V.Diff *. Steve Kennedy, Cynthia Grindley. 3 May 2017.
The next chimney-crack immediately left of *Triple Step*, finishing up the cracked slab.

Charleston   10m   E1 5b **. Steve Kennedy, Cynthia Grindley. 7 Jun 2017.
The thin crack on the left wall, starting about 5m left of and slightly higher than *Jazz Square*. Sustained with little protection in the lower part. Follow the crack, with the assistance of sidepulls and flakes on the right, finishing up a short slab.

Ten Step   8m   Severe. Steve Kennedy, Cynthia Grindley. 7 Jun 2017.
Start 3m left of *Charleston* at a quartz vein. Climb the initial vein, move left onto a ledge, continue up the inset slab above and finish out right.

Boathouse Crag:
T.R.E.   15m   E2 5b. Ali Rose. 20 Jun 2017.
The wall left of *Das Boot*. Start 2m left of that route and go up a steep wall (under the tree's branches) towards the right edge of a perched block. No protection for 8m.

Beinn Bheag Slab:
The 45 14m E4 6a. Kev Shields. 25 Mar 2017.
Climb the slab trending leftwards from the obvious thin crack to the left of *Jacobite Rising*. Thin, smeary and bold.

Ardnish, Gecko Crag:
Frog Eyed 8m Severe 4b *. Carol Goodall, Elsie Riley. 21 Aug 2015.
Climb the back of the cave on good holds, exiting right.

Reptile Roof 8m HVS 5a *. Elsie Riley, Carol Goodall. 21 Aug 2015.
Climb the obvious roof at the far west of the crag, moving slightly rightwards over the roof.

Chocaholic's Buttress (Loch nan Uamh):
Du Teillay 12m HVS 5a. Kevin Woods, Alasdair MacLennan. 14 Oct 2016.
The left-hand face with the prominent overlap at half-height. Start several metres left of *Cadbury Flake* at a rib left of a groove. Climb the rib, traverse out right across a hanging slab, and pull over a bulge and block to a slabby top out and tree.

European Union Crag:
(NM 713 843) South facing.
This crag is just west of Chocaholic's Buttress (p310), near an EU road sign. Probably safest to drive beyond the sign, turn and park near the sign facing east. Walk up left (west) to the crag, 2-3mins.

European Court of Human Rights 7m Severe *. Colin Moody, Cynthia Grindley, Steve Kennedy. 24 Apr 2016.
At the left end of the crag (behind trees) is a slab with an undercut base. Climb this to the grass ramp where there is a large block belay up and left.

Eurocrat 12m E1 5b *. Steve Kennedy, Cynthia Grindley, Colin Moody. 24 Apr 2016.
Climb the arete (protection is awkward) and continue up to the grass ramp. Finish up the short steep slab.

Green Paper 12m VS 4b *. Steve Kennedy. 24 Apr 2016.
Climb the unprotected slab left of *Maastricht Treaty* to the grass ramp; finish as for *Eurocrat*.

Maastricht Treaty 10m Severe *. Colin Moody, Cynthia Grindley, Steve Kennedy. 24 Apr 2016.
Follow the obvious crack-line.

Brussels 8m VS 5a *. Colin Moody, Steve Kennedy, Cynthia Grindley. 24 Apr 2016.
The corner-crack at the right-hand side. Gain the ledge, then climb the corner-crack.

Euro Sceptic   12m   V.Diff *. Steve Kennedy, Cynthia Grindley, Colin Moody. 24 Apr 2016.
The rib at the right end of the crag, trending right at about mid-height. The finish is 4b but is easily avoided.

Crimson Crag, Loch nam Uamh (NM 713 843):

A small south-west facing sea-cliff is situated about 3 miles east of Beasdale on the north shore of Loch nam Uamh, a short distance south of the A830 close to a wide bend in the road opposite the European Union Crag (SMCJ 2016 p208). The routes are short but on impeccable rock and ideal for an evening or passing visit. Accessible at low to mid tide. About 3mins approach from the road verge!

Approaching from the road, the crag runs southwards below a grassy knoll. The first rocks reached comprise a 5m cracked bulging wall, and thereafter a series of short slabby walls and corners, a prominent overhanging wall and a final slabby area.

The initial wall is undercut with two boulders at the base and offers three good boulder problems (Steve Kennedy, 6 Oct 2016).

Hulk   f5+
Start just left of the leftmost boulder and follow a line of flakes trending left to a large hold then pull right.

Ape   f5
The central line. Sitting start from the leftmost boulder, climbing directly then finishing rightwards.

Tomboy   f4
The right edge from the rightmost boulder.

The slabby walls to the right can be climbed almost anywhere. Beyond, the crag steepens and the more defined routes are described from a prominent arete forming a prow on the left of the main overhanging wall.

The Nose   9m   VS 4c *. Steve Kennedy, Cynthia Grindley, Colin Moody. 9 Sep 2016.
The arete is climbed directly passing a prominent pointed flake, finishing up a crack just left of the edge and a short slab above.

Shelf Route   10m   VS 5a *. Steve Kennedy, Cynthia Grindley. 4 Sep 2016.
Start as per *The Nose* up to the pointed flake. Pull strenuously out right along a shelf for a couple of moves, then move up onto a slightly higher shelf and finish up a corner and slab on the right.

Animal, Left Finish   9m   VS 4c **. Steve Kennedy, Cynthia Grindley. 4 Sep 2016.
A crack runs up the overhanging wall right of *Shelf Route*. Make steep juggy moves up the crack, pull left into a corner at a bulge below the headwall and finish up *Shelf Route*.

Animal, Right Finish   9m   VS 5a **. Steve Kennedy, Cynthia Grindley. 4 Sep 2016.
Pull out right from the top of the crack at the bulge and make a thin move on small quartz holds directly up the headwall to finish.

Tears   8m   VS 4b *. Cynthia Grindley, Steve Kennedy. 4 Sep 2016.
Start at a small corner next to a flat foothold 2m right of *Animal*. The wall is climbed slightly rightwards into a corner. Continue directly up a crack and steep finishing wall (crux), ignoring the exit on the right.

Sweat   8m   Severe 4a *. Steve Kennedy. 4 Sep 2016.
Start below a small overhang 2m right of *Tears* and pull over onto a quartz studded wall. Move up rightwards to a ramp and finish by a rib on the right.

The following routes are located to the left of the overhanging wall.

Book End   8m   V.Diff *. Cynthia Grindley, Steve Kennedy. 4 Sep 2016.
The corner immediately left of the overhanging prow (*The Nose*) with a steep start but on generous holds (sometimes damp), finishing up a short slab on the right.

Mini Nose   7m   VS 4c *. Steve Kennedy, Cynthia Grindley. 4 Sep 2016.
Left of *Book End* is a narrow slabby buttress forming a small prow on the left side. Steep initial moves over a small roof lead to a slab which is climbed near the left edge via a small finger pod in a crack (without using the corner on the left at any point!).

Wee Corner   7m   Mod. Steve Kennedy. 28 Aug 2016.
The wee corner immediately left of *Mini Nose*.

On the opposite (east) side of the grassy knoll is a short, clean slabby wall with a rounded arete. It is even closer to the road than the main wall.

Thirty Seven Steps   7m   VS 4b *. Steve Kennedy, Cynthia Grindley. 6 Sep 2016.
The name refers to the distance from the road verge! Climb the system of flake-cracks immediately right of the rounded arete.

Forty One Steps   7m   Severe *. Cynthia Grindley, Steve Kennedy. 6 Sep 2016.
Follows the slim right-facing corner on the slab just left of the arete.

CREAG MHOR BHRINICOIRE:
Note: Kevin Woods thinks that that the initial slab of *Penguin Monster*, as marked on the topo in Highland Outcrops South, may be the location of *A Reflection* and that *Penguin Monster* would then start to the left or right. *Morar Magic* and perhaps also *Election Mania* may also describe this same slab.

GLEN NEVIS, Repton Buttress:
Bullet Variation Start   6m. Nathan Adam. 2017.
Follow an undercut flake-crack leftwards to join the little sapling on *Bullet*.

Pandora's Buttress:
Dave MacLeod re-climbed *Move it or Park it* (E5 6c) without its in-situ pegs at

the crux, which have now rotted away. It is still a well-protected route overall, but could be worth E6 6c.

Secretaries' Buttress:

Pablo   25m   E6 6b **. Gary Latter. 23 Oct 2016.
A line up the right side of the top tier. Start up the fault of *Secretaries' Crack* for 5m to a projecting boss on the left. Pull round this leftwards into the hanging left-slanting groove and peg runner. Move left and up to a good hold in a quartz recess, then leftwards to join *Ring of Fire Right-Hand*. Pull out rightwards and over a bulge to rejoin that route and climb directly above to join *Vincent*. Pull straight up the wall above and continue directly up rightmost of parallel cracks to finish at a good flake.

Verbatim   18m   V.Diff *. Gary Latter. 11 Oct 2016.
The right edge of the wide dyke of *Secretaries' Crack*. Move up rightwards to good holds and continue up the rib.

Autumn Leaves   20m   VS 4c *. Gary Latter. 11 Oct 2016.
Start at the same point as *Verbatim*, but step down right to follow a line of good holds rightwards to gain a diagonal crack. Move up leftwards and trend left to finish up the right side of the rib.

Tilted   25m   HVS 5a *. Gary & Karen Latter. 23 Oct 2016.
Start as for *Verbatim*, but step down and follow the diagonal crack rightwards to finish at a tiny rowan.

Plagiarists   20m   E4 6a **. Gary Latter, Ewan Lyons. 11 Oct 2016.
The diagonal fault that splits the first and second tiers originates as a jam crack splitting the initial roof. Climb this through the roof and step right and up to ledge. Move up onto the wall and climb directly, then move leftwards to a good jug just before a prominent diagonal crack. Finish quite boldly with difficulty to the apex of the wall.

Crown Buttress:

Cool Beans   15m   E2 5b. Steve Holmes, Tom Lawfield. 27 Mar 2017.
Climb steeply to gain the slab passing a foot long wobbly block on the right. Climb straight up the slab to the niche just right of the final moves of *Palpitation*.

Bistro Buttress:

Tupilaq   17m   E5 6a **. Steve Holmes. 2 May 2017.
At the left end of the buttress. Fierce moves through the roof to get established on the wall, then climb the thin crack with difficulty straight to the prominent pine.

Whale Rock (Gorge) Area:

Brownlee Diagonal   8m   HVS 5a *. Mark Roe (DWS). 5 Oct 2016.
The right to left diagonal crack on the wall to the left of *Calladine Prow* (SMCJ 2016). Abseil or down-climb to the very bottom of *Escape Corner*, and make difficult moves left to gain the face. Once established, follow the main crack-line with progressive ease to a tricky final move on the wall's left arete.

Murdoch Jamieson on the 2nd ascent of Isinglas (E8), Binnein Shuas. Photo: Iain Small.

BINNEIN SHUAS:
Stronghold   50m   E8 6c **. Dave MacLeod. May 2017.
Exciting and technical climbing through the barrel shaped roof right of *Storming the Bastille*, following the line of a thin seam. Climb *Greatness and Perfection* to the break at the back of the roof. Traverse right for 2m as for that route to a knee-bar rest. Make a couple of moves into the roof, past a good hold and arrange cams in a small slot. Make a hard move and place a crucial 0.5 Camalot in a pocket. Continue with hard layback moves to good holds and gear over the lip. Step right and follow a quartz crack to gain the easy top slab. Continue easily up this to the terrace. F8a climbing.

Siege Engine   60m   E7 6c***. Iain Small (unsec). 12 Oct 2016.
A mega endurance trip taking the huge diagonal fault in the left side of The Fortress. Well protected but sustained with the crux near the top. Start below the left wall of the amphitheatre.
1. 30m 6c Climb easily up the short slab to gain the diagonal undercut feature leading out left to *The Rubyiat* and a good rest on the arete. Arrange gear and launch rightwards along the diagonal ramp/flake. Continue to a stopping place below a roof and an in-situ thread runner. Step right and climb the steep groove (crux) to eventually gain a welcome jug just before the lip. A further sting in the tail leads to a belay on the slab above.
2. 30m 4b Climb easily up the slab above.

Wallachian Prince, Independent Start   6a. Iain Small, Adam Russell. May 2016.
A direct and independent start, but with no gear.

Pre-Emptive Strike   40m   E6 6b. Iain Small (unsec). 3 Jun 2016.
Start up *Delayed Attack* to the crux roof, pull around its left side and climb a slim hanging corner and its right arete. From a small flake atop the arete, launch up an overhanging wall leftwards to flanges, then pull out tirhg ton to less steep ground. Finish up a featured wall.
Note: Iain Small has made an independent start to this route at E8 named *Isinglas*.

CREAG BHUIDHE:
The following routes lie on a smooth-looking wall down and left from *Low Impact* (p340 Highland Outcrops South). The wall features two obvious crack-lines; left of these is a left-trending ramp-line.

Yellow Fever   30m   VS 4c *. Michael Barnard, Alan Hill, Paul Torode. 2 Apr 2017.
Climb the ramp to its top, then move up to ledges (bold). Continue up a crack (crux) to the prominent tree. Either abseil off from here or continue to the top of the crag.

Midriff Crisis   15m   H.Severe 4b *. Alan Hill, Michael Barnard, Paul Torode. 2 Apr 2017.
The left-hand crack, leading to a V-groove.

Lag Time   15m   VS 5a. Michael Barnard, Alan Hill, Paul Torode . 2 Apr 2017.
The right-hand crack has a tricky start but soon eases off.

The Irn Bru Lady 15m VS 4b. Alan Hill, Michael Barnard, Paul Torode. 2 Apr 2017.
The rib marking the right end of the wall.

CRUBENBEG CRAG:
This lies 700m west of Crubenbeg holiday cottages and is seen clearly from the A9.

Crubenbeg Twin Cracks 70m VS 4c. Mike & Paul Brian. 29 Aug 2016.
On the upper part of the crag, two parallel cracks about 1m apart lead to a small roof. The line can be studied from the cairn on the nearby tor. Start directly below a large rowan tree.
    Climb either to its left on a pillar of blocks, or more easily and cleanly to its right. A thin rising traverse then leads to a belay. Traverse left below an overhang and gain a chimney-crack at its left end. Traverse back right above the lip of the overhang (crux) until established below the twin cracks. Climb the cracks and escape a roof to its left. Finish directly below a TV aerial.

CREAG DUBH, Little Rock:
All the routes on the steep wall were cleaned Sep 2016. There is a rope sling and maillon on a thread up the slope (25m abseil). Both *Heather Wall* and *This One* were repeated by Gary Latter, and thought to be E4, (not E5), both very well-protected. The plaque on *This One* protrudes (not 'incut'), and the route only comes close to *Heather Wall* at the overlap near the top. It is marked incorrectly on the topo in the new Highland Outcrops South guide. The line marked approximates to the following route.

Ling 15m E5 6a **. Gary Latter. 20 Sep 2016.
Start midway between *This One* and *Un Petit Mort*, directly beneath a prominent wide vertical slot. Climb directly to the slot, then right to another V-slot and good holds above. Move back left and up into a tiny left-facing corner. Move left to a good quartz undercling beneath overlap, then direct on good holds to finish leftwards at the same point as *This One*. Very well protected.

Great Wall:
Under the Skin 40m E3 5c **. Gary & Karen Latter. 11 Sep 2016.
Bold climbing leading to a well protected crux, taking the obvious line between *The Hill* and *Inbred*. Start midway between the two. Go directly past incut flakes to a Cam slot at 5m. Move left, up, then back right, then direct up the wall, crossing the small roof in its centre to good holds. Make a hard move from good horizontal break (Cam slot), then slightly rightwards. Pull through the right end of the roof above the ledge on good holds and follow the fault diagonally leftwards, then direct up the wall to a thread.

Inbred Super Direct 40m E1 5b ***. Gary & Karen Latter. Aug 2016.
A superb direct pitch, well protected after the niche. Follow Inbred as far as the triangular niche. Climb the crack above steeply on good holds then trend slightly leftwards to gain the right end of a large ledge above. Pull through a crack at the right end of the roof on good holds, then follow a diagonal fault leftwards, then direct up the wall past good horizontal breaks to the thread belay.

Lower Central Wall:

Scampi Fries   30m   E1 5a *. Ewan Lyons, Colin Morrison. 11 Sep 2016.
A direct line left of *Phellatio*, finishing up that route. Take a parallel line left of *Phellatio*, initially poorly protected, to reach a ledge on *Phellatio* below overhangs. Climb direct through them to finish up the final crack of *Phellatio*.

DUNTELCHAIG, Seventy Foot Wall:

Cartostrophe   15m   E2 5c. Michael Barnard, Steve Perry. 25 Jun 2017.
Some good climbing up the wall between *Razor Flake* and *Seventy Foot Wall*. Start as for the former, going left along the flake but then standing up on it (gear in the break above). Move up to a good hold on the right (crux), then resisting the temptation to use the *Seventy Foot Wall* edge, gain the main break. Traverse left to finish up *Razor Flake*.

Insomnia, Sleepless Start   E2 5b. Michael Barnard, Steve Perry. 25 Jun 2017.
A worthwhile alternate start, giving a fully independent route. Climb the obvious right-trending line of flakes between *Seventy Foot Wall* and *Ann Boleyn's Crack* (possible to reach across and place a nut in the former before the crack widens).
Note: Michael Barnard notes that for *Insomnia* original, the description should say 'gain the right side of the arete directly'. Even then, the grade should be E4 6a.

ASHIE FORT:

Mayday Mayday   10m   E3 5c *. Davy Moy. 1 May 2017.
Between *The Wall* and *Fat Bird*. Go up to a shallow right-facing corner, climb nearly to its top, then go left on small crimps to the left edge of the slab, finishing straight up. Small finishing holds and poor gear throughout.

BEN NEVIS, AONACHS & CREAG MEAGAIDH

BEN NEVIS, Gardyloo Buttress:

Tower Face Crack   80m   VI,6. Iain Small, Simon Richardson. 27 Mar 2017.
A winter ascent of the summer line. Excellent climbing in an exposed position and a good choice in lean conditions. Start in *Tower Gully* approximately level with the top of the first pitch of *Smith's Route*.
1. 20m Step left onto the right flank of Gardyloo Buttress and climb the left-hand of twin grooves (*Right Edge* takes the right-hand groove) to belay on a small terrace below the main icefall of *Right Edge*.
2. 50m Traverse left and climb the striking crack that runs up just right of the arete to where the angle eases.
3. 10m Easy ground leads to the top.

Tower Ridge, East Flank:

Grand Central   80m   VI,6. Simon Richardson, Robin Clothier. 22 Jan 2017.
A mixed route up the buttress between *Upper Tower Cascade Left* and *Upper Tower Cascade Central*. A useful option when conditions are very lean.
1. 20m Start at the toe of the buttress and follow the groove-crack that slices left below steep walls. Climb over several bulges and belay below a steep step.
2. 30m Climb a steep crack through the step, them bear right up another crack

system that leads to a steep open corner topped by a snow slope.
3. 30m Snow and mixed ground lead to the final few metres of *Tower Ridge*.

Cloudjumper 60m VIII,9. Dave MacLeod, Helen Rennard. 5 Mar 2017.
1. 30m Start at the foot of a left-slanting ramp, about 10m left of *Urchin*. Ascend the technical ramp to a cracked overhang. Climb this direct (crux) to a good ledge. Trend right and mantelshelf onto a large ledge below a short very steep wall.
2. 30m Traverse right beneath the steep wall (deceptively delicate) until possible to move upwards. Make a few tenuous moves upwards before reaching more straightforward ground and the top pitch of *Red Dragon*, trending left at the top to reach *Tower Ridge*.

Creag Coire na Ciste:
Swift Runner 180m VII,7. Simon Richardson, Iain Small. 23 Mar 2017.
A good mixed climb taking a direct line cutting through the upper traverse of *Wendigo*.
1 and 2. 70m The route starts up the lower tier that is often avoided when climbing on this part of the mountain. Start 15m left of *North Gully* and climb the narrow gully-ramp that curls around the right side of the lower tier and overlooks *North Gully* in its upper half.
3. 30m Continue up the snow slope above to belay 10m below the left-trending gully-ramp of *Tick Tock Croc*.
3. 30m Climb the imposing tower above by following a hidden line of flakes that cut diagonally across its front face. Finish directly and belay just below the summit.
4. 50m Move up to a ledge, cross *Wendigo* and continue up the steep groove above on thin ice (crux and no protection for 25m on the first ascent) to reach the terrace below the final headwall. Traverse right 5m and finish up the steep, left-leaning narrow corner to the top.

Tick Tock Direct 180m VII,7. Iain Small, Simon Richardson. 24 Mar 2017.
A direct version of *Tick Tock Croc*. Start 10m left of *Swift Runner* below an icefall in the lower tier that is defended by a hanging icicle fringe.
1. 50m Climb up to the icicle fringe and climb it (strenuous but will often form thicker ice) and continue up the icefall above.
2. 55m Continue up snow to the gully-ramp of *Tick Tock Croc*.
3. 25m Climb the gully-ramp of *Tock Tock Croc* and belay 5m below its top.
4. 40m Traverse 3m right to enter a thinly-iced bottomless groove. Climb this to the terrace below the final headwall.
5. 20m Finish up the steep groove just right of the steep left-leaning corner of *Swift Runner*.

North Wall of Carn Dearg:
Failure is not an Option 240m VIII,9. Iain Small, Simon Richardson. 22 Mar 2017.
A challenging mixed climb starting up the steep triangle of overlapping slabs between *Staircase Climb* and *Macphee's Route* and finishing up the deep striking corner in the headwall right of *Waterfall Gully*.
1. 40m Start 5m left of *Macphee's Route* and climb thin icy slabs for 15m to gain a narrow turfy break that leads diagonally up and left to an awkward belay below a vertical wall that defines the left side of the triangle. A bold pitch.

2. 55m Ignore the continuation up and right. Instead, step left and climb the narrow hanging ramp in the vertical wall above which leads to an easier ramp that runs up to the apex of the triangle of overlapping slabs.

3. 80m Continue up the central depression (snow and easy mixed) to below the impressive triangular headwall.

4. 30m From a point 5m up and left of the right toe of the headwall, move up and right across a short slab and climb a steep vertical crack to easier ground (as for *From the Jaws of Defeat*). Move up, then right, to gain a small sloping stance below the imposing right groove line that slices through the right side of the headwall.

5. 35m Climb the groove over three steps to gain the top of the headwall. An extremely steep and sustained pitch. The route finishes here. Three ropelengths lead up and left to the upper crest of *Ledge Route*.

The Shape of Things to Come   110m   IX,9. Iain Small, Simon Richardson. 2 Mar 2017.
A technical mixed climb taking a direct line up the centre of the wall. A combination with the third pitch of *Brave New World* would result in an even more sustained and direct outing – potentially one of the finest modern mixed lines on Ben Nevis.

1. 35m Start as for *Brave New World* and climb the first 5m up the initial wall to the large spike. Instead of following the left-trending ramp of *Brave New World*, continue directly up the vertical cracked wall above with increasing difficulty to gain Broad Terrace. Belay directly below an imposing right-facing corner.

2. 35m Gain the base of the corner and climb it with increasing difficulty until 2m below the capping roof where an exposed step left can be made to a foot ledge. Gain turfy grooves above and climb directly up to Diagonal Terrace and a large flake.

3. 40m Move left along the terrace for 5m and from the top of a large flake, climb a weakness in the vertical barrier wall above and continue up less steep ground above to gain a steep shallow vegetated bay. Move right, climb past two diagonal faults, then make exposed moves back left above the bay to below a barrier bulge guarding access to the slim left-facing corner above. Gain the corner strenuously and climb it to the girdling terrace. From here the first ascent team moved up and right for 15m to gain the finishing abseil of *Brave New World*.

AONACH MOR, Coire an Lochain:
Merlin   80m   III. John Stewart & partner. 31 Jan 2006.
This is a good icy line when conditions are lean. Start 10m right of Homo Buttress. Follow a line of ice in a shallow gully (45m). Ascend ice and snow left to the top (35m).

Big Gully   80m   II. Andy Nisbet, Jonathan Preston. 25 Apr 2017.
The big gully between Homo Buttress and The Prow has never previously had a recorded ascent, mostly due to big cornices. The Ben Nevis guide mentions it as a possible descent, but one can only presume it means by abseil.

An Cul Choire:
Sprinter Service   150m   II. Alan Halewood, Jamie Bankhead. 10 Nov, 2016.
Just right of the base of *Aonach Seang* is a broad gully that narrows obviously at its top. In early season this can give an icy step that would bank out later. The

gully peters out onto the headwall above but a traverse left takes you onto the top of *Aonach Seang* for an easy finish.

AONACH BEAG, Lower West Face, Skyline Buttress:

Parasol   120m   II. Sandy Allan, Andy Nisbet. 3 Mar 2017.
A groove line which is shaded from the sun. Start at the left side of a bay some 30m right of *Bottleneck Gully*. Climb the left of two faults to reach and climb a right-slanting recessed ramp to a big snow patch. Go to its top and climb a deep groove and its left branch to another snow patch. Taking left-hand options, climb two tricky grooves to the top (hard when lean but bank up).

Skyline Ridge   150m   II. Andy Nisbet. 27 Feb 2017.
A vague ridge which forms the right edge of this section of buttress with *Bottleneck Gully*. Start in the bay some 50m right of *Bottleneck Gully*. Follow a low-angled ramp out right to the crest. Follow the left side of the crest (the right being very escapable), open to variation, to a final optional tier with some fine flakes on its left.

STOB COIRE AN LAOIGH:

Note: Erick Baillot & Dave Kerr climbed the hanging corner/ramp right of *Centrepoint* on 5 Mar 2017 at VI,6. Climb a short groove to a low ledge then a steeper wall, trending right at its top to gain the corner/ramp. Climb this to the ledge below the upper tier.

CREAG MEAGAIDH:

These routes are on the right as you enter the Inner Corrie, starting right of the lowest wall at a big gully, which may be *The Soldier's Song*, but uncertain. The first route climbs the rib on the left of the gully.

Ardairnuff   160m   V,6. John Lyall, Pete MacPherson. 19 Nov 2016.
Gain the route by the big gully and follow the left fork to where it turns up the fall line, then gain the vague rib on the right. Follow this escapable lower section, with one awkward wall, to an easing in the angle. The steep tower above is split by a widening crack (crux), then a slab is climbed, followed by a superbly helpful pillar to the top.

Softairnuff   140m   III/IV,4. Graeme Ettle, Justin Finlay, John Lyall . 21 Nov 2016.
Climbs up the buttress to the right of the big gully. Start by following a ramp rightwards under the broken lower wall, and go up easy ground to gain parallel grooves about 15m left of the left-hand of two icefalls. Take the left-hand of the grooves and continuation up a chimney on the left, to gain a big terrace. Go up the rib above and over a short wall to a belay ledge in a corner. Move to the right side of the blocks above and go up by brilliant cracks and edges. A short final wall is taken on the left.

GLEN COE

BUACHAILLE ETIVE MOR, The Chasm to Crowberry Traverse:

A clean buttress on this traverse. The rock is good quality and naturally quite clean, technical, and the angle is just off vertical. The buttress is just to the right of the start of *Neolith* (Glen Coe p51).

Endolith   25m   E5 6a *. Iain Small, Blair Fyffe. Jul 2017.
A shallow groove up the left-hand side of the buttress. Start just right of a down-pointing flake. Make tricky moves up into the shallow groove. Follow this to its top. Step right to climb a very thin intermittent crack directly to the top.

Megalith   25m   E6 6a *. Iain Small, Blair Fyffe. Jul 2017.
Start at a diagonal groove just right of the start of *Endolith*. Make hard moves up the groove to easier ground. Climb up and right to the left end of an area of overlaps and a small rock scar. Step left and make hard and blind moves directly up. Continue straight up the wall (sustained), stepping right just below the top of the crag.

The Chasm note: Ewan Lyons has sent a pitch by pitch description of *The Chasm* with photos of each pitch. On the SMC website.

Creag a' Bhancair:
Constant Gardener   100m   E6 6b **. Iain Small, Blair Fyffe. 19 Jul 2016.
A sustained bold route. Start below a small diagonal overlap just to the left of the sports wall.
1. 25m 6b Pull up to the overlap, and from its left end, climb directly up into a slight scoop below a bulge (crucial 1 wire). Make hard moves through the bulge to the right end of a horizontal break (gear). Step right and climb a faint diagonal crack to below a bulge (large Cam in pocket). Pull over this to a ledge.
2. 30m 6b Climb up rightwards to a ramp-line which steepens to become a vertical corner. From the top of the corner, make hard moves right. Continue up the gradually easing wall above.
3. 45m 5a Continue up the wall over various bulges to reach easier ground.

CHURCH DOOR BUTTRESS:
The Prentice Pillar   110m   VII,8. Iain Small, Helen Rennard. 14 Jan 2017.
Climbs the obvious fault on the lower front (west) face, just right of *Hoargasm*. The first pitch is partially detached from the rock face behind.
1. 30m Start in a small snow bay and head leftwards to reach a good ledge below steep cracks. Climb these (with an in-situ bulldog from the first ascent at the top of the cracks). Make delicate moves rightwards across a slab followed by strenuous moves to reach the belay.
2. 50m Easier ground leads to the headwall.
3. 30m Climb a stiff corner to a fractured headwall and finish.

The Ninety-Five Theses   105m   IX,9. Iain Small, Simon Richardson. 7 Mar 2017.
The prominent steep groove 10m right of *Gates of Paradise* is the last major continuous feature before the crag tapers to the right. On the first ascent the capping roof was climbed using ice. Start below a deeply recessed V-groove.
1. 15m Climb up to the base of the steep V-groove and climb this with increasing difficulty and exit left onto the top of a projecting fin of rock. This forms the left side of a ledge that runs into the foot of the main corner. From the fin gain a short flake-crack that leads to a good ledge perched on the arete.

2. 40m Follow a flake-crack right into the main corner and climb it to an area of bulges capped by two prominent roofs. Strenuously pull up and left to small foot ledges then pull right around the first roof into a short groove that leads to below the second and largest capping roof. On this ascent the roof was tackled directly by pulling onto its icicle fringe and climbing thin vertical ice above.
3. 50m Finish easily up snow.

CREAG DOIRE-BHEITH:
Vertebrae 30m V.Diff. Kevin Woods, Oliver Skeoch. 19 Jan 2017.
Starting just left of *The Happy Whistler*, this climbs a short wall, then trends up and left, following ramps on a route of least resistance to the easing of angle.

SGORR DHONUILL, Coire Dearg:
Mousetrap 80m I/II. Paul Headland, John Oaks, Tim Hakim. 4 Mar 2017.
From the car park above Ballachulish (NN 048 588), follow the forestry track on the west side of the valley to the head of the track (NN 037 567). Take the path through the woods towards the deep cut gully on the western side of Coire Dearg (NN 030 559). Climb the gully passing a short steepening on the left.

STOB MHIC MHARTUIN:
(NN 208 575) South facing
The crag is just below the summit. Routes by Oliver Skeoch, 20 Jun 2017.

A Wave, An Awesome Wave 30m Severe 4b.
Start just to the right of a scoop. Climb the overhang via a crack, then trend left beneath a suspect block. Climb directly up to a clean wall and surmount this before easier ground leads to the top.

Flakes Of Wrath 30m Severe 4a.
Takes a diagonal line across the buttress. Start to the left of the scoop, climb the slab and pass under the detached block. Continue right here before climbing up to a left-trending ramp. Climb this on solid flakes to the top.

Mellowdrama 20m H.Severe 4b.
Start 2m right of the scoop. Climb a narrow rib that becomes a wider slab. Cross the overlap on its right and at a slanted ledge, step right to a steep juggy wall. Climb this to the top.

I am my Mother's Child 20m VS 4c.
Start at an overhanging scoop beneath the tallest part of the buttress. Climb this directly to beneath a steep slab. Climb the slab to a small ledge beneath a steeper wall. Traverse right to a corner, climb this, step left and finish directly.

BEN STARAV, Stob Coire Dheirg:
Curtains for Mickey 160m II/III . Paul Headland, John Oaks, Tim Hakim. 5 Mar 2017.
From the toe of the central buttress, climb the gully on its right. A short steep section on pitch 3 provides the crux. The route finishes on a sharp subsidiary ridge.

Iain Thow on the immaculate Slabathon (Grade 3), Ben Starav – with Ben Cruachan in the distance. Photo: Noel Williams.

SOUTHERN HIGHLANDS

BEN VORLICH, Summit Crag:
Moral Compass   30m   VII,9 *. Greg Boswell, Guy Robertson. 14 Jan 2017.
On a wall immediately behind and up the hill from *Logical Progression* (SMCJ 1999). Climb straight up the cracked wall staying in the right-hand crack all the way. Deceptively steep and hard higher up!
Note: Greg Boswell later removed all the rotting gear from *Logical Progression* in the hope of a clean ground-up ascent.

BEINN AN LOCHAIN, Kinglas Crag:
Clockwork Orange   70m   V,4. Stuart McFarlane, Brian Shackleton. 13 Jan 2017.
A parallel line to the right of *Bakerloo Line*.
1. 45m Climb the obvious fault-line until thin ice gains access to the upper ramp; belay in a niche.
2. 25m Move left under a roof, step onto a thin ice slab and continue up this to reach snow slope.

East Face:
Alan Brook notes a possible first ascent of the left to right diagonal shelf on 3 Dec 1976, in a party led by Alistair Milner and also accompanied by David Brook, Beryl Milner & Gail Nieman.

BEINN HEASGARNICH, Coire Heasgarnich:
The Wind Horse   70m   III. Simon Richardson. 6 Nov 2016.
The narrow rib immediately right of *Prayer Flag* divides the furthest right of the gully exits from the Basin. Start below the centre of the buttress and move up and left to below a steep wall. Surmount this by climbing up and right (crux) then continue up easier ground near the crest to the top.

Stupa   180m   I/II. Simon Richardson. 6 Nov 2016.
Follow the left side of the broad right-bounding buttress of the corrie. The finest climbing is found close to the left edge overlooking the big snow basin.

LOWLAND OUTCROPS & GALLOWAY HILLS

AYRSHIRE, Loudoun Hill:
Note: Grant Cornwallis climbed *Lambchops* (Lowland Outcrops p161) in 1982.

GALLOWAY HILLS, BIG GAIRY, Telephoto Buttress:
This lies on the right side of Big Gairy about mid-height on the hillside, 200m to the right of the present junction between felled and mature forestry, where the track from Talnotry stops descending and turns further to the right. It is foreshortened and not fully visible until arrival. The best ascent is to start at this junction of forestry and ascend through the mature forestry, up and right then back left, crossing the wall at its top about 25m left of the mature forestry. Continue up and rightwards to a low escarpment, then traverse right for 200m to where a bracken slope leads to the left of the crag, 50mins from the main road at Talnotry.

The main section of the crag is undercut and the following routes start at the two breaks in the overhang.

Through the Looking Glass   40m   HVS 4c **. Ian Magill, Andrew Fraser. May 2016.
A bold outing up the main slab on excellent granite. Micro cams make it slightly less bold. Start at the wide chimney which is the left break, immediately swing right on a spike and pull up onto the broad right-hand slab. Climb the wall on the left to gain the long, thin main slab and pad up this to the overlap. The climbing eases slightly on the upper slab above, but not much. Superb!

Mad Dogs and Englishmen   40m   VS 4c *. Stephen Reid, Chris King. 2 Jun 2016.
Pleasant climbing at the top end of the grade but with excellent protection. Follow *Through the Looking Glass* to the broad right-hand slab, then take the shallow groove above to a steep short wall. Traverse right across the slab until one can step over a slight overlap and continue rightwards, then back up left to a ledge. The steep headwall is climbed via the obvious notch.

Call me a Doctor   170m   E1 5b *. Andrew Fraser, Ian Magill (with Chris King & Stephen Reid for pitch 1). 2 Jun 2016.
The technical crux first pitch forms a fine climb in its own right. While the remainder is good, there are short sections of decomposing heather on pitch 2.
1. 45m 5b The right break in the overhang is gained via a short wall. Desperate moves gain respite at a resting place on the left but the shallow groove and crack above are still puzzling. The final headwall is climbed via a crack on the right. Follow the easier slabs to the right, then left, then heather to a shallow corner at the right end of slabs capped by a roof.
2. 30m 5a Climb the slabs up and left to the right-hand crack through the roof. Move round the right end of the roof on precarious heather into a niche. Pull out of this on the left, onto a desperate slab and heather to below a short cracked slab.
3. 45m 4b A good pitch. Climb the short cracked slab rightwards to the foot of a steeper slab, in the lower centre of which is a grassy groove. Climb the slab to the right of the grassy groove, then slightly left to gain a heathery niche below a cracked corner on an upper slab. Swing out left from the corner onto a slab and continue up this to a heather terrace.
4. 50m 3c Start 6m down the terrace, bypassing the steep start, where it is possible to step right onto the slab. Follow the slab up, then right round the corner. Easier but clean slabs lead up and right.

GALLOWAY SEA-CLIFFS, Southwick Pinnacles note:
Owen Ross notes that access has changed due to a new building and he was unable to find *Lot's Wife*.

FIFE, Limekilns:
Blackjack 13m   E1 5a. Adam Russell. 14 Jul 2016.
An eliminate line directly up the centre of the back wall of the alcove. Climb the centre of the wall between *One Ringer* and *Two Ringer* without recourse to either, through the black section of rock to finish by a short hanging corner.

BERWICKSHIRE COAST, Fast Castle:

Against the Grain   65m   E1 5a/MXS. Adam Russell, Lia Guest. 6 Aug 2016.
A finely positioned esoteric trip through geological time, taking the obvious line traversing through the bands immediately above the lip of the sea cave. Beyond a certain point retreat would involve down-climbing or a swim. Approach as for *Castle Wall*.
1. 40m 5a Start up the slabby corner right of the sea-cave, where the rock bands become much thinner. Traverse hard left across a smooth slab to awkwardly gain a big guano covered ledge. Continue left, following the easiest line around the projecting rib and across the lip of the sea cave to join *Gannet Groove* at its overhanging corner. Pull over this and continue up left on more reliable rock to near the arete.
2. 25m 4b As for *Gannet Groove*.

Ladywell Craig, Ladywell Lower Crag, East Bay:

This is the horseshoe shaped bay immediately to the east of Lower Crag, with clean but slightly friable greywacke and a small stack at its western end. An ancient stake was found set back from the top, suggesting someone may have climbed or investigated the crag before.

Stressed to Impress   18m   E2 5b *. Daniel Carden, Michael Haywood, Cameron Carr. 24 May 2017.
A wide left-trending crack dissects the left end of the main crag. Start 4m left of its base, making thin moves towards a spike in the crack. Cross the slanting crack and delicately ascend the bold wall above, passing a vertical crack.

Notes:

Ladywell Craig, Lower Crag: *Shortbow* was climbed in May 2017. Some other routes look worthwhile but they will all need a good brush to become climbable again, due to a thick covering of furry lichen.
Ladywell Craig, Upper Left Crag: The HVS 5b * right-hand crack is quite good and deserves a name. Good stake in place above.

MISCELLANEOUS NOTES

THE W.H. MURRAY LITERARY PRIZE

As a tribute to the late Bill Murray, whose mountain and environment writings have been an inspiration to many a budding mountaineer, the SMC have set up a modest writing prize, to be run through the pages of the Journal. The basic rules are set out below, and will be reprinted each year. The prize is run with a deadline of midnight on the last day of April each year.

The Rules:
1. There shall be a competition for the best entry on Scottish Mountaineering published in the *Scottish Mountaineering Club Journal*. The competition shall be called the 'W.H. Murray Literary Prize', hereafter called the 'Prize'.
2. The judging panel shall consist of, in the first instance, the following: The current Editor of the *SMC Journal*; The current President of the SMC; and two or three lay members, who may be drawn from the membership of the SMC. The lay members of the panel will sit for three years after which they will be replaced.
3. If, in the view of the panel, there is in any year no entry suitable for the Prize, then there shall be no award that year.
4. Entries shall be writing on the general theme of 'Scottish Mountaineering', and may be prose articles of up to approximately 3000 words in length, or shorter verse. Entries may be fictional.
5. Panel members may not enter for the competition during the period of their membership.
6. Entries must be of original, previously unpublished material. Entries should be submitted to the Editor of the *SMC Journal* by the end of April for consideration that year. Electronic contributions are preferred and should be submitted via e-mail, although double-spaced typewritten hard copies will also be accepted by post. (See Office Bearers page at end of this Journal for address etc.) Any contributor to the *SMC Journal* is entitled to exclude their material from consideration for the Prize and should so notify the Editor of this wish in advance.
7. The Prize will be a cheque for the amount £250.
8. Contributors may make different submissions in different years.
9. The decision of the panel is final.
10. Any winning entry will be announced in the *SMC Journal*, and will be published in the *SMC Journal* and on the SMC Website. Thereafter, authors retain copyright.

THE WH MURRAY LITERARY PRIZE 2017

THE JUDGES WERE UNANIMOUS in awarding this years prize to Steve Hindley for his *Parishes of the Infinite*. Such a simple experience, a gentle walk up a cloudy Beinn Vrackie, but the revelation as the author came above the clouds as one judge described it is 'poetry rendered as prose'. Another thought the piece 'the best hill-walking article' he had read – and that judge is very well read – while a third called it 'a little gem'. Hindley's essay demonstrated that in mountaineering writing it is not the experience which matters but the depth of perception the author brings to it. 'To give air to one's feelings towards a day on the hills in such a personal way is commendable, but to share and include the reader is a rare talent.'

As usual there were interesting historical pieces. Mike Jacob explored Harold Raeburn's ornithological escapades. Delving into the primary source materials and often using Raeburn's deadpan understatements, Jacob describes dangerous ascents of sea stacks and cliffs in Shetland and a raid on an eagle's nest in Angus. This was felt to be a significant piece of research especially since 'Raeburn is one of our greatest ever mountaineers'. Surely a biography must be written one day?

Among the other historical pieces Bill Sproul's examination of the brief life and untimely death of Tom Carruthers attracted favourable comment. 'Sproul writes from the heart and has given us a touching testament to a climber who died far too young.' Graeme Hunter's piece on Ardverikie wall was felt to be 'important' and a 'good celebration' of the climb and of Doug Lang.

In some ways the sadness of untimely death in the mountains ran like a minor theme through the articles and stories. Regular contributor Gavin Anderson's *Requiem for a Climber*, 'short but memorable' was thought to capture the ambience of Creag Meagaidh: 'an uncomfortable tale' but 'realistic'.

Both Ken Crocket and George Allan reflected on near-disasters. Crocket's piece on *The Bullroar Incident* is a model of brevity in which nothing is left out, except the identity of his stubborn partner. Allan, in three miniature essays, reflects on the random nature of fate in the mountains: a view which would not have found favour with Bill Murray.

Another regular contributor, Mike Dixon, focused on the *Ups and Downs* of life, combining social comment with fine descriptions of places as far apart as Fisherfield and New Zealand. Donald Orr's poems contained arresting imagery.

In lighter vein the judges were entertained by Noel Williams's all too credible tale from the CIC: 'fun, short and uplifting,' and by the irrepressible Gordon Smith's account of his first ever rock-climb which might also have been his last. Chris Dickinson's exploration of the wonderful atmosphere and climbing potential of the Island of Soa was 'alive, vibrant, positive and inspiring.' (One of two pieces which benefited from initial rejection in 2016). Raymond Simpson's essay *High on Braeriach* was so fresh it almost had snow on it.

As last year, some pieces of Scottish interest could not be considered by the judges because they missed the **midnight deadline on the last day of April**.

SCOTTISH WINTER NOTES 2016–17

THE 2017 WINTER SEASON was a difficult one, and for many climbers and skiers, it was the worst they could ever remember. The weather was often calm and settled but snowfalls were quickly followed by deep thaws that left the hills bare.

There was no chance for a base to build, and low-angled terrain that would normally be covered in consolidated snow was often left as blank slabs or unstable rubble. Not only did the dry conditions prevent gullies and drainage lines forming ice, it made classic mixed climbs difficult and time consuming.

A recipe of heavy snowfalls and devastating thaws meant the turf was rarely frozen, but there were opportunities for ascents of steep snowed-up rock routes for those poised and ready to climb immediately after the storms. SMC members were in the vanguard, and Helen Rennard had a very successful winter making ascents of five Grade VIIIs, including the first ascent of *Cloudjumper* with Dave MacLeod on Ben Nevis. At the top end of the scale, Iain Small led the way with two new Grade IXs on Ben Nevis and in Glen Coe.

Ben Nevis

As might be expected for such a lean season, Ben Nevis saw the bulk of the pioneering activity, and eight significant new routes were added to the mountain. Iain Small led the way with *The Shape of Things to Come* (IX,9) and *Failure is Not An Option* (VIII,9). Both climbs are situated on the North Wall of Càrn Dearg and are major four-pitch outings climbed on snowed-up rock, although the second route also relied on transitory thin ice. Greg Boswell added one of the most aesthetic lines to the mountain in January when he climbed *Hanging Garden* (VII,8), a direct finish up cracks in the soaring Babylon arête on Number Three Gully Buttress, with Jon Frederick (visiting from the USA) and Stuart Lade. Also of note was the first ascent of *Cloudjumper* (VIII,9) by Dave MacLeod and Helen Rennard. This steep route lies on the East Flank of Tower Ridge, another venue that is becoming recognised for coming into condition quickly after a heavy snowfall.

Conditions improved in late March with a heavy snowfall followed by a helpful cold snap. Iain Small and I added a couple of good mixed routes to Creag Coire na Ciste in the vicinity of Wendigo. *Swift Runner* (VII,7) takes a direct line up the buttress and *Tick Tock Direct* (VII,7) follows the groove system to the right, straightening out the original line of Tick Tock Croc. Intriguingly for such a lean season, both routes relied on thin ice that does not often form.

Iain and I also made a winter ascent of *Tower Face Crack* (VI,6) that lies on the right-bounding arête of Gardyloo Buttress to the left of the icefall of Right Edge. This route was first climbed solo by Brian Kellett in July 1944 and Iain noted that, as in some similar Kellett routes he had done, there were some unusual chokestones in the crack that had possibly been hand-placed. On the other side of Tower Gully, Robin Clothier and I found *Grand Central* (VI,6), which takes the buttress between the Left and Central Upper Tower Cascades.

Iain Small made four trips up the North Wall of Càrn Dearg through the season climbing *Kellett's North Wall Route* (VII,7) with Andy Inglis and making the second ascent of his own route *Days Of Future Past* (VIII,8) with Ian Parnell and Marko Prezelj from Slovenia. Other ascents of note include the second ascent of *Sake* (VIII,9) by Dave Almond and Helen Rennard and two early repeats of *Knuckleduster Direct* (VIII,9) by Dave MacLeod and Helen Rennard, and Iain Small and Murdoch Jamieson. Greg Boswell, Adam Russell and Guy Robertson

Dave MacLeod making awkward delicate moves on the second pitch of Cloudjumper (VIII,9) on Ben Nevis during the first ascent. Photo: Helen Rennard.

The thin ice master at work. Iain Small about to start a 25m unprotected lead during the first ascent of Swift Runner (VII,7) on Creag Coire na Ciste on Ben Nevis. Photo: Simon Richardson.

Dave Almond on the second pitch of The Knuckleduster Direct (VIII,9) on Ben Nevis.

This compelling corner-line on the front face of Number Three Gully Buttress has now seen five or six repeats and is one of the most sought after test-pieces on the mountain.

Photo: Helen Rennard..

added a difficult new link-up on the East Flank of Tower Ridge named *Frosty's Vigil* (VIII,8) that joins Clefthanger, Tripod and The Piecemaker with sections of new climbing between these routes.

The Cairngorms

In the Northern Corries the big event was Greg Boswell's first ascent of *Intravenous Fly Trap* (X,10) with Scott Grosdanoff. This takes the very steep wall left of Daddy Longlegs in Coire an Lochain, and joins a very select group of Scottish Grade X routes that have been climbed on sight (namely: The Greatest Show on Earth, Range War and Messiah all ascended by Boswell in 2015). In early November, Steve Perry made the first ascent of the strenuous *Theory of Relativity* (VII,9) on Lurcher's Crag with Andy Nisbet and Jonathan Preston. Two weeks later the trio were joined by Sarah Sigley for the challenging line of *Wolfpack* (VI,7) that lies to the right. Deeper in the Cairngorms, Roger Webb and I made several additions to Braeriach such as *Shark* (V,7) on Sròn na Lairige and *Forgotten Face* (V,7) in Coire nan Clach, but in general, opportunities for harder climbs in the Cairngorms were few and far between.

Steve Perry on the crux section of Theory of Relativity (VII,9) during the first ascent. This fierce technical problem was one of the most difficult new routes climbed in the Cairngorms throughout the season. Photo: Andy Nisbet.

Iain Small leading the ice-filled corner on the second pitch of The Ninety-Five Theses (IX,9) on Church Door Buttress in Glen Coe. The double roof with its hanging icicle fringe can be seen above. Photo: Simon Richardson.

The story was similar on the eastern side of the massif, and Lochnagar did not have enough build up to bring either the classic or modern test-pieces into condition. Early in the season however, the mountain caught some snow, which resulted in a couple of new additions in the Southern Sector. *Paladin* (V,7) climbs the summer line on The Sentinel and *Columbus Rib* (IV,4) takes the well-defined feature between Resolution Gully and Lunar Eclipse on Perseverance Wall.

Glen Coe and the Southern Highlands

In Glen Coe, activity focused on mixed climbing on the high crags such as Stob Coire nan nan Lochan. The difficult *Unicorn* (VIII,8) saw several ascents and *Satyr* (IX,9) had a spirited third ascent attempt by Ian Parnell and Tim Emmett that was thwarted when sun stripped the final pitch. The higher altitude Church Door Buttress on Bidean was also popular with an on-form Iain Small leading the way on the new route front. In January he made the first ascent of *The Prentice Pillar* (VIII,8) on the lower front face with Helen Rennard. He returned in March to climb the stupendous line of *The Ninety-Five Theses* (IX,9), which takes the impending groove-line and stepped roofs to the right of last year's addition Gates of Paradise. Few Scottish winter routes overhang from the first move to the very last, especially when much of the progress depends on thin ice, and there is little doubt that this climb has set a new level for Scottish icy mixed.

Dry easterly winds meant that the turf was often aerated and unfriendly in the Southern Highlands, although Stuart McFarlane and Brian Shackleton added the fine *Clockwork Orange* (V,4) to Beinn an Lochain, and Greg Boswell and Guy Robertson climbed the short but technical *Moral Compass* (VII,9) on Ben Vorlich.

Northern Highlands and Skye

The warm weather restricted activity in the Northern Highlands.

The second ascent of the steep and technical *Crazy Eyes* (VIII,9) on the Far East Wall of Beinn Eighe by Murdoch Jamieson and Andy Inglis was probably the finest achievement, but for sheer adventure John Mackenzie and Andrew James' new addition to Sgùrr na Muice in Strathfarrar takes some beating. The 280m-long *Globetrotter* (IV,4) was one of the longest new routes climbed during the season and a protracted descent in the dark added to the experience. Further north, John Higham and Iain Young added *Headstone Rib* (III,4) to the rarely visited east flank of Beinn na Fhurain in Assynt in the far North-West. Another good find was *Meshuga* (III) by Andy Nisbet and Steve Perry on Mullach Fraoch-choire above Glen Shiel, but in general the season's mild and unconsolidated conditions favoured steep snowed-up rock routes rather than more traditional middle grade outings.

Skye saw some good ascents during the Winter Festival that later culminated in the first winter ascent of *Canopy* (VI,6) on Blàbheinn by Michael Barnard and John MacLeod. Also of note was an opportunistic early season first ascent of the 235m-long *Silver Fox* (V,5) in Coire Lagan by Mike Lates and Sophie Grace Chappell. Given the poor conditions throughout the winter it was remarkable that any high standard climbing took place at all. Fingers are now firmly crossed for a more helpful and productive 2018 season.

Simon Richardson

Steve Perry on Polar Express (IV,4), Ben Hope. Photo: Andy Nisbet.

John MacLeod making on the first winter ascent of Canopy (VI,6) on Blàbheinn in Skye. The overhanging crux chimney can be seen looming above. Photo: Michael Barnard.

100 YEARS AGO: THE CLUB IN 1917

(*Italics* indicates quotation from the Journal or other named source)

LIFE IN 1917 WAS DOMINATED by what Lloyd George, the new Prime Minister, referred to as 'total warfare'. The Great War might conjure up images of barbed wire, mud and death in foreign fields but some tragic incidents also occurred on home soil. Continuing the nautical theme of last year, I discovered that in January a Royal Navy steam-powered submarine sank on trial in the Gare Loch, with the loss of 32 men. A year later, the submarine, now salvaged and renamed, was part of a large flotilla of British ships engaged in night exercises in the Firth of Forth. The whole venture was a catastrophic disaster, later to be sarcastically referred to as the Battle of May Island. A series of collisions led to the damage or loss of six vessels and the deaths of a further 105 men. The subsequent investigation and court martial were kept quiet until the 1990s. In 2011, sonar images of two wrecked submarines were made during a survey for the proposed Neart Na Gaoithe offshore windfarm.

Also in January, details were published regarding the award of the Edward Medal (a civilian decoration to recognise acts of bravery in an industrial setting) to William Morrison, George Sang (both SMC) and Archibald Young (not SMC) who all worked at the Roslin Explosives Factory near Edinburgh. In June 1916, they had rescued two girls from a blazing building as continuous small explosions took place. Shortly later *the whole building blew up. The medallists are very reticent and deprecatory about their heroic action and the circumstances which led up to it, claiming like all true heroes that they only did their duty. Our members left at home ... prove that they too are ready to maintain a mountaineer's reputation for courage and prompt action in emergency.* But was Young a mountaineer?

German Zeppelins conducted reconnaissance patrols over the Scottish coast and the various curtailments of civil liberty that I outlined last year were now followed by the introduction of bread rationing. The battleship *HMS Vanguard* was blown apart by an explosion whilst moored in Scapa Flow, killing an estimated 843 men. This was the year, too, when the hydropathic hotel at Craiglockhart, Edinburgh was requisitioned by the army as a hospital for officers suffering from the psychological trauma known as 'shell-shock'. The meeting between Siegfried Sassoon and Wilfred Owen, is well-documented. Sassoon was a critic of the war and his confinement in Craiglockhart was a convenient way of dismissing his protests. The alternative, as stressed by his friend Robert Graves, could have been the firing squad. Owen, encouraged by Sassoon, turned his own horrific experiences into compelling poetry. He was discharged in November and killed in action one year later.

It is against this background that one must consider how the participants of sports such as mountaineering viewed the ethics of their leisure activities. Clearly, this was an issue within the SMC for the New Year and Easter Meets were cancelled for the first ever time. The Committee decided that their duty was to heed a Government appeal for the general public to avoid all unnecessary travel, considering that it would have been *unpatriotic and perhaps unseemly* to act otherwise. Nevertheless, an unofficial Easter meet was held by five members (Clapperton, Green, Clark, Garden, Ling – the latter three being President and Vice-Presidents respectively) and a guest (Lyon) at the Loch Awe Hotel, venue for the proposed official Meet. Presumably, the meaning of 'unnecessary' was a matter for personal interpretation and these six men had no qualms about travelling ... an interesting moral question. The familiar tops *all stood out spotless white against the deep blue vault of heaven... a land of peace for the keen-eyed lad with Argyll & Sutherland Highlander on his tunic-strap, son of a Cruachan shepherd, who stepped from the train ... come for a few days' respite from the turmoil of the Somme battlefields, where now for eight long months he assured us he had neither night nor day ceased to hear the roar of the guns.* The various actions of the Somme resulted in over one-million total casualties – I wonder if the young man became one of them?

The 28th AGM of the Club had been held at the North British Station Hotel, Edinburgh, on Friday 1 December, 1916 with the President, W. Inglis Clark, in the chair. The usual sort of club business was discussed and it was reported that the customary monthly get-togethers at the Club Room (12, South Castle Street, Edinburgh) had *practically ceased to exist*. There was no afternoon reception. In his address to the 29 members who attended the subsequent Annual Dinner, the President asked *how far were members, who had the opportunity, justified in pursuing our sport?* His own opinion was that achieving efficiency and mental balance was a personal duty and were *brought to the highest* by a *visit to the hills.*

The Journal

This he did with a week in Strathyre towards the end of January, one morning taking the then-extant train to Killin ... *I had often been before at Killin Junction for it is a very favourite ski-ing resort. Indeed, on more than one occasion I have attached my skis on the platform and returned wearing them to the same spot ...* before walking back to the Kingshouse Hotel (Balquhidder) and praising the delights of Creag M'Ranaich ... *this excursion is one of the plums of the district.* Nevertheless, J.H. Buchanan, writing in the February issue of the Journal with 'Some Memories of Skye', hints at some personal disquiet when he recalled *happy days when one could still indulge in regular holidays with an untroubled mind.*

In the same publication, Rev. Burn wrote extensively, if somewhat cerebrally, about a 25-day holiday, starting in the Loch Arkaig area, during which he climbed 67 hills. His item is illustrated by some of A.E. Robertson's 1906 photos which reveal a landscape free of softwood plantations. The article contains several historical snippets, such as ... *all this glen* [Dessary] *from Morar downwards, plus Glen Pean, Glen Kingie and Loch Arkaig, used to be owned by a self-made man called Coirechoille, from the name of his house (the ruined house is S.W. of Roy Bridge). This man began with one hen and made enough money out of it to be able to buy cattle and finally bought up land wholesale. This was in the days when the right bank of the Dessary alone had twenty houses. Glen Dessary has always been famous for its reivers.* Folklore had it that one of these reivers was shot and killed at the top of Fraoch Bheinn by men from Loch Hourn seeking revenge for the theft of some cattle.

Henry Alexander contributed an article, titled 'Gaick', about a 25-mile bicycle trip from Kingussie southwards to Dalnacardoch via Glen Tromie and Edendon Water. His route partly followed the drovers way from Badenoch to Atholl although they used the Minigaig Pass and Glen Bruar further to the east. The author gives a well-researched account of the Loss of Gaick when, in 1800, an avalanche overwhelmed a bothy and its five occupants, including Captain John McPherson of Ballachroan also known as the Black Officer. The story is made more interesting by the addition of some colourful detail; for example, a certain Mr. Robertson *who was for many summers at the Corrour Bothy told the writer that there were grievances and old scores* against McPherson so that the loss *was not an accident, it was a doom ... becoming one of the great legends of the Highlands*. A small granite memorial stone was erected on the site of the bothy in 1902.

The Rev. Burn continued his walk in the June issue of the Journal, moving northwards via Knoydart, Affric and Mullardoch to finish in Strathfarrar. A fine effort but, as he admits himself with reference to his own article, *nothing on earth would induce me to read it*. I can understand why. To be honest, this could apply to all the articles published that year; there is a lack of gripping story-telling although plenty of semi-interesting rambling, from J.G. Stott's 'The Highlands in June' describing a traverse of the Highlands in 1891 to W.A. Smith's 'Visit to the Cairngorms' in 1875 including a night-time encounter with strangers at the Shelter Stone.

Ernest Baker explored this theme in 'Scansorial Gleanings in Belles-Lettres' (which translates to 'climbing-related pickings in fine writing') in the October issue, writing that *climbing literature ... unless it is utilitarian and meant for practical guidance, is a deadly bore* although he admitted there were exceptions to this *most sweeping generalisation*. A proposition that aroused my curiosity until I read his essay, which I wouldn't include in any of the exceptions.

H.P. MacMillan, K.C. (King's Counsel rather than the Kennel Club) gave a legal summary about 'Rights of Way', all superseded now by more-recent access legislation. The final article, 'Tennyson' by F.S. Goggs, described the great poet's love of walking in the mountains and how his poetry revealed *that in spirit he was truly* a mountaineer. There were no book reviews but there were notes about Cairngorm Club and Fell & Rock Club Journals, where it was recorded that the *fine climber ... and fine officer* L.J. Oppenheimer (author of 'The Heart of Lakeland' and who contributed 'Ben Nuis Chimney' to *SMCJ* 7/37 (1902)) *had died from the effects of poison gas*. An interesting item is a summary of *How I Dropped 'Marjorie' in Loch Scavaig* from the Cornhill Magazine – particularly so for attendees of the SMC Anniversary Yacht Meet. 'Marjorie' was a 15-ton sailing cutter which set out from Ardrishaig on Loch Fyne and met her end in Loch Scavaig ... *that notoriously evil place in bad weather* ... fortunately not repeated in 1997.

The Journal also contained the ongoing 'Roll of Honour' which detailed members' wartime experiences and there was an obituary for Allan Gow Marshall, a Captain in the Highland Light Infantry, who was *the victim of a sniper's bullet* whilst on a solo reconnaissance in February.

Members' Excursions

Where would we be without the diaries of W. Ling? Book 12 has a remarkable 38 entries for mountain trips during 1917, including his attendance at the Easter get-together. He was then in his mid-forties and would normally have included a long alpine season in his itinerary. However, I have a feeling that his activities do not represent those of the majority of SMC members. Ling was unmarried, lived in Cumberland and had easy access to the Lake District, at that time the hub for rock-climbing in Britain and what Harry Griffin remembered, even in the late 1920s, *as a secluded paradise*. The Fell & Rock Climbing Club, whose domain it was, does not appear to have considered that there was anything 'unpatriotic' for civilians to go climbing. Perhaps this was simply down to the compact nature of the Lakes and its proximity to large towns and cities. Like many others, Ling used his cycle (as well as local trains) to access the Lakeland fells and long cycling trips were merely an addendum to a hard mountain day. Uncrowded crags, a small close-knit fraternity of youthful adventurers, unspoilt scenery, hospitable inns ...is it any surprise that he was drawn back there so often?

W.W. Naismith (*SMCJ*, 4/21 (1896), 174) had encouraged SMC members to enjoy the atmosphere of the Lake District:

At Whitsuntide 1896, Mr Douglas and I paid a first visit to Wastdale Head, where were gathered a large number of climbers ... Now that we have seen this climbers' El Dorado with our own eyes, we both confirm heartily all that has been said or sung in its praise. Indeed, the half was not told us. As compared with Sligachan, Wastwater Hotel has a great advantage in being placed in the middle of the best climbing ground, instead of on the edge of it; and as most of the finest climbs are within an hour or an hour and a half of the hotel, one can enjoy a grand day's scrambling, and get back in time for tea, and have a swim in the "beck" before dinner "forbye."

Whilst Ling may not have been at the fore-front of climbing development he had climbed at a good standard for many years. Harold Raeburn wrote (*SMCJ* 6/34 (1901), 132) that *Messrs Glover and Ling have lately* [in 1889] *had the credit of accomplishing the impossible by discovering two new climbs in this thoroughly polished and highly finished climbing region. These climbs are respectively a new variation at the foot of the Eagle's Nest Arête on Great Gable called Ling's Chimney, and a fine new chimney on the Ennerdale face of the same mountain now known as the Engineer's Chimney.* It is noteworthy that Raeburn should have considered that the Lakeland crags were fully developed at that time, for Haskett-Smith's solo ascent of Napes Needle, generally accepted as the start of rock-climbing as a sport in Britain, had occurred only a few years earlier in 1886. The statement itself was typical of Raeburn's self-confidence but it is surprising that his assessment was so wayward.

There is not space to include every entry in Book 12 so I have selected a few:

May 6 Kilpatrick Hills With H. Raeburn. From Bowling to Bearsden. [It would be fascinating to know more. At that time Raeburn was working in Glasgow at an aeroplane factory].

June 16 Criffel With J.H. & Mrs. Bell. Bicycle from Dumfries to New Abbey. Up by Glenburn to summit where we had a fine view of the Lake hills and along the coast. Down the other side skirting round the hillside. Next day cycle to the Nith, ferry over to Glencaple and by Caerlaverock Castle and Ruthwell to Annan.

July 14 Raven Crag Gully, Glaramara Very fine morning. With H. Raeburn from Thorneythwaite. Up into the Combe to Dove's Nest. Into the crack and up to the main cave. We had a candle but no lantern so did not explore to any extent. Up buttress to finish. Then across Combe Ghyll to Raven Crag Gully which was wonderfully dry and we were able to do some of the pitches in the gully itself. At the top pitch, H.R. traversed to the chock stones while I went straight up. [FRCC 1968 guide to Borrowdale describes Dove's Nest as 'unlike anything else in the Lake District ... a great rock face has slipped bodily forwards and downwards; instead of crashing into scree at the base of the cliff, its fall was arrested and it now leans back against the main face, leaving cavities of all sizes ...' providing the opportunity for unique rock-climbing akin to Crypt Route, Church Door Buttress, although less committing].

July 15 Mouse Ghyll & Buttress Same party. Another fine day. Through the woods almost to Grange then up to foot of Ghyll. We climbed up the main pitch but did not like it so went down and made a new route up the buttress. Very steep rock and heather and quite difficult. We then came down the gully and traversed in to the top of the main pitch. HR went down and came up again without difficulty and we then both went down and returned to Thorneythwaite. [Mouse Ghyll is on a broken crag on the NE slopes of Maiden Moor first climbed by Slingsby/Topham in 1897; the direct finish by the Abraham brothers became the first recorded VS in Borrowdale and it would seem that it was easily within Raeburn's ability.]

July 21 _The Screes_ _C Gully (part) & buttress_ With H. Raeburn from Wastwater Hotel. Leave 10. Foot of gully via Wasdale Hall 1215. In spite of the dry weather the gully was still wet and slimy and water was coming over most of the pitches. We started up the left wall and after a number of pitches which were not easy and required care we came to the seventh, a cave which had to be turned on the left by a crack with much water. We had a good look at it and then went out up a slide on the left on to the buttress where we had some steep heather. We traversed back off the buttress above two pitches but the next one looked very severe so we lunched (2.15) and then went out this time on our right (true left) on to the buttress where steep heather and rock took us to the top. A fine view and fine rock scenery in the gully. A good walk along the top (fox and cub) down to the Burnmoor track, a bathe in the river and to the hotel 6pm. [1996 FRCC guide describes the crag as 'generally disappointing but does provide some traditional wet and dark gully climbs' typical of the period. Graded VS. First ascent by O.G. Jones/H.C. Bowen in 1897. Jones described it as 'a deadly place'.]

July 22 _Scawfell_ _N.Climb, Pinnacle from Deep Ghyll_ With H. Raeburn. Fine morning. Leave Wasdale 10.30. Styhead 11.30. Leave rucksacks by Sprinling Tarn. Lunch 12.50. Pikes 1.50. We climbed up by N.Climb, I leading, and then on to Pisgah where we watched three men on Slingsby's Chimney. Then down Deep Ghyll to Jones' Climb [graded Severe in 1996]. HR led and went up easily in rubbers, I brought the boots in the sack but sent them up on the rope over the hard bit above the belay. The rocks were beautifully dry and warm and I got up more easily than last time. The climb took us 50 min. We went down the Broad Stand and had a hot walk back to our sacks. Then went down Grains Ghyll and a fine bathe in a pool near Stockley Bridge and on to Thorneythwaite 7.40.

August 25 _Birkness Combe_ _High Stile_ With H. Raeburn from Buttermere. We joined a large party from Gatesgarth, five Bicknells, two Challoners, Miss Nielson and R. Graham. We went up to the combe. Bicknell, Peter and I on one rope, Raeburn & Graham on another did the Mitre. Then the four did the slabs and the three seniors the Oxford & Cambridge buttress by the ridge finish, very hard, while I went down and took two heavy sacks to the top. After a meal we separated. HR and I by Bleaberry Combe to Buttermere, the others over High Crag to Gatesgarth. Next day was terribly wet and all we could do was to walk to Warnscale Bottom to the falls.

The poignancy of the mountaineering scene is captured in 'Pictures In The Fire' by Lieut. C.F. Holland (_FRCC Journal_, 1916). It is a moving account of a solitary return to the Wasdale Head Inn whilst home on leave ... _nothing seemed changed and the war was if it had never been, the two long years since I was last here, with their vicissitudes, training, the journey to a strange land, the endless fatigues and dangers of active service, the terrible experiences, the sorrow of seeing trusted friends suddenly struck down, were as a day that is quickly passed. In the evening I sat alone and looked at the pictures in the fire ... the happy circle sitting round the fire in this very room ... a succession of climbing memories passes before me_ ... recalling the first ascent of Scafell's Central Buttress with Siegfried Herford and others ...*again I am on the ledge but this time the weather is warm and bright, and I remain on it for seven hours, sometimes alone, sometimes with companions, and that awful crack hanging over my head as bad and awful as anything ever seen in a nightmare. And now the dreaded thing has actually happened and I am trying to climb it ... His memory will always live as long as rock-climbing endures, not only as a great climber but also as a great-hearted gentleman who gave his life for his country ... the finest and bravest man we ever knew.*

Mike Jacob

200 YEARS AGO

1817 WAS A YEAR dominated by unusually severe typhus epidemics in Edinburgh and Glasgow (keeping the gene pool strong) and by literary events – the launch of The Scotsman in January, and of The Edinburgh Monthly Magazine in April (which in October became Blackwood's Magazine), the death aged 41 of Jane Austen in July, and the publication of Walter Scott's Rob Roy – the edition required the entire cargo capacity of the Leith packet to take it to London.

As for mountaineering, little is recorded apart from William McGillivray's rash October ascent of Clisham 'in order to witness a Hebridean snow-storm in all its glory'(see Ian Mitchell's *Scotland's Mountains before the Mountaineers*, p. 156 for more interesting details). However a relevant event, again literary, was the publication by John Thomson of Edinburgh of his New General Atlas, which had as frontispiece (drawn and engraved by Lizars) 'A Comparative View of Heights of the Principal Mountains and Other Elevations in the World'. This was not the first such published Comparative View, but it was certainly the first published in Scotland. It launched a publishing craze, and such views – following a range of formats – continued to appear throughout the century. These are discussed in an entertaining manner on old map internet sites maintained by Kevin Brown (Geographicus), Peter Roehrich and David Rumsey. The 1817 View makes the Ortler the second highest in the Alps (15,430ft.), and features Ben Nevis, Ben Lawers, Ben Wyvis, Ben Lomond, Ailsa Craig and Arthur's Seat in Scotland.

Robin N. Campbell

REFLECTIONS ON JOHN INGLIS, 1962–94

(Killed in a fall from Parallel Buttress, Lochnagar, 19 February 1994)

IN OCTOBER 1992 A HAND-DELIVERED letter lay on my carpet. The writer explained that he had a profound interest in Robin Smith and had heard that I was pulling together a book about him. That was the precursor to regular meetings when John Inglis and I swapped information and talked at length about more than just Robin and mountaineering.

John had already unearthed details of most of Robin's climbing career and recorded each month's activities from 1955 to 1962 onto separate pages of a jotter. Another of John's papers, which I did not see until after his death, was headed 'Biographical Notes on Scotland's finest Mountaineer ever'! He was intrigued with the ethos of the 1950s climbing scene and fascinated by the exploits of those of that vintage, no more so than those of Robin Smith, as his choice of title suggests. Ever aware of how much equipment, clothes and attitudes had changed since those days, he did once question if Robin would have bothered with modern climbing. I immediately thought of John when another contributor to the book later wondered the same, but it was by then too late to extend that line of speculation.

As contributors' letters reached me, all good reads one way or another, I showed them to John. He also became as interested as myself in the contents of Robin's mother's memorobilia box. It pleased him that his own life and Robin's overlapped by a few months and that they had both attended Morrison's Academy, Crieff (John's parents also lived abroad). He also enjoyed speaking to someone who had climbed with Robin and knew him first hand. We never got round to going to the hills together although I showed him what I remembered of the routes Robin and I climbed on Salisbury Crags.

We agreed that he should expand his jottings of Robin's climbing activities and the outcome was a first class review under the title 'Smith's Routes – a Short History', which was printed eight years after his death in the *SMC Journal* (38/193 (2002), 1–14). John enjoyed working on it whilst I liked the concept of Robin being seen through the eyes of a young modern climber. Many quotes from that piece are incorporated in *High Endeavours*.

In February 1994 we agreed that the pub was not the best place for editing. Mornings were better for something like that. The coming Saturday did not suit John as he had a climbing commitment. Sunday was a possibility. Both took a mental note to phone the other, but it wouldn't matter if it was left for a week or two. Neither got in touch and the weekend passed.

It was John's way to joke about danger before setting off for the hills, making out that quips and modern safety gear would assuredly encapsulate him in a cacoon of safety. As usual I had laughed at his patter as we readied to part. On the Monday morning, however, I learned that John and his partner were dead, two of six fatalities on Scotland's mountains that weekend. He was 31.

John and I had discussed the 1962 correspondence and press cuttings connected with Robin's death in the Pamirs, including a letter from the widow of Wilfrid Noyce, with whom Robin died, to the expedition secretary. Left with two young sons, Rosemary Noyce wondered how her husband's death might influence attitudes of climbers with young children:

It may well be that some good may come of Wilf's and Robin's death in the end, though it is hard to see how and what it may be. I do think though that it will have been a bitter blow to other mountaineers with dependents who trust them to come home safely.

We concluded, albeit reluctantly, that most men are unlikely to be much influenced by that sort of thing. Once consumed by an interest, sporting or intellectual, they will carry on regardless. John, father of two daughters aged four and two, was no exception, although his wife Julia fully appreciated his need to climb. Even though he considered himself a careful climber, John nonetheless made the point of phoning home to reassure Julia whenever he came off the hill. At 8 p.m. on that fateful February evening she took it upon herself to initiate enquiries.

A molecular geneticist, John was a genuinely clever fellow whose fulsome obituary appeared in *The Scotsman* on 23 February 1994. Perhaps all it lacked was a note to the effect that he was excellent company. Nor could the writer have been expected to refer to John's unbridled admiration for Robin Smith.

John Inglis will not now take me to view Slime Wall, the location of Robin's famous Shibboleth. Neither will he climb Crack of Doom in Skye to check the accuracy of my recollections of my last climb with Robin in 1956. Perhaps someone will step in to help me on the latter point?

However, such self-centred musings are inconsequential when set beside the loss to his widow, daughters and parents. John's help with the book, as I emphasise therein, was invaluable and hugely appreciated. I'm pretty sure that, had he survived, Robin's biography – *High Endeavours: the Life and Legend of Robin Smith* – would have appeared under our joint names when it came to be published in 2005.

Jimmy Cruickshank

FURTHS: THE EARLY LISTS

Introduction

BEYOND MOUNTAINEERING CIRCLES, the word 'Furths' has little meaning, although its definition to the Munro-bagger is clearly the 3000 foot mountains of England, Wales and Ireland. This name originates from furth (meaning outside) of Scotland, which was first applied to these hills in 1959 by Eric Maxwell of the Grampian Club. Curiously, Sir Hugh Munro never turned his attention to adding this relatively small number of peaks to his celebrated Scottish Tables. As such, there has been a need to undertake historical research of early lists to redress the balance (see Robin Campbell's Variorum Table of the Munros and Tops[1]).

The following work has been influenced by Eric Maxwell's article 'Quod Erat Faciendum' [2], in which he cites the lists of James A. Parker, William McKnight Docharty and Maxwell's son, David Chalmers Maxwell. In short, the purpose of this article is to present these lists to the general reader.

In 1929, Parker published the first (albeit incomplete) list of this genre of hills. While he acknowledged that Snowdonia contained fourteen summits over 3,000 feet, he omitted two, which in his words, 'can hardly be classified as separate mountains, viz., Foel Grach, 3195 feet, and Garnedd Ugain, 3493 feet.' His *List of the Mountains in the British Isles 3,000 feet or over in height* [3] comprised twenty-three for England, Wales and Ireland. It has been suggested that these, combined with the Scottish Mountaineering Club's 1921 list of 276 Munros (plus Beinn Tarsuinn), gave him the arbitrary, but tidy, overall total of 300 mountains.

Docharty's original book of Lists[4], in 1954, was the first to classify hills into 'Independent Mountains' and their subsidiary 'Tops'. Mountains are 'listed as such by virtue of their commanding positions on their ridges and not necessarily bound by the 500-foot [drop all round] rule'. For the Tops Docharty stipulated a minimum requirement of one 50-foot contour on the One-Inch O.S. Maps in England and Wales; and in Ireland a minimum of one 100-foot contour on the Half-Inch Ordnance Survey (Suirbheireacht Ordanais) Maps. This gave a total of 20 and 325 respectively for the three countries [5].

Five years later, Maxwell[6] published (what Dave Hewitt describes as) the 'first formal listing' of the Furths. He used stringent formulae, which involved drop and distance to determine hill status, which resulted in 17 mountains and 32 tops.

As Sir Hugh did not use any criteria to categorize his Munros and Tops, then these two men's lists are not directly comparable. Interested readers should consult David Purchase's excellent article 'On the Classification of Mountains'[7] for in-

---

[1] R.N. Campbell, *The Munroist's Companion*, (SMT, 1999), 167–203.

[2] 'Quod Erat Faciendum', *Grampian Club Bulletin*, 7 (1960), 1–4.

[3] James A. Parker, 'Beinn Tarsuinn and the British "Threes"', *SMCJ*, 18/108 (1929), 336–43.

[4] W.M. Docherty, *A Selection of some 900 British and Irish Mountain Tops*, (privately printed: Darien Press, 1954).

[5] Revised to 21 mountains and 34 tops with the addition of Knockoughter and Caher (now known as Caher West Top) in Macgillycuddy's Reeks, Co. Kerry. See The Supplement to *A Selection of some 900 British and Irish Mountain Tops* and *The Second Selection*, Vol. 1, (privately printed: Darien Press, 1962), pp. 76–7.

[6] D.C. Maxwell, *Tables giving all the 3000-Ft. Mountains of England, Wales and Ireland*, (privately printed: Harley & Cox Ltd., 1959).

[7] *The Munroist's Companion*, (SMT, 1999), 123–54.

depth discussion on this complex and subjective topic. Further reference should be made to Robin Campbell's equally informative 'The Life and Work of William McKnight Docharty'[8].

About one in ten Munroists add the Furths to their tally, but how many others complete a round in their own right – remains an imponderable question. Hopefully, this research will promote further interest in these fine mountains – which tend to be overshadowed by the more popular Munros.

Explanatory Notes
The hills are listed under each country and in height order, in accordance with Derek Bearhop's table on page 92 of Munro's Tables, 1997. (These days, this may be considered to be the official and definitive list.) There are six columns of information.

Column 1 – Hill Number & List
Each hill is uniquely identified by its [Number] listed in the *Database of British and Irish Hills* (ed. Chris Crocker). This can be accessed on Simon Edwardes' online version of the Database: <http://www.hill-bagging.co.uk/Furths.php>.
Lists are identified by the compiler's initials: JAP = James A. Parker; WMD = William McKnight Docharty; DCM = David Chalmers Maxwell; DAB = Derek A. Bearhop.

Column 2 – Name
The Ordnance Survey spellings (generally) of listed summits are given. In the case of Macgillycuddy's Reeks, Docharty acknowledged, in the Supplement (1962), using local names introduced by Claude W. Wall for a number of these mountains and tops. (Knockoughter was Docharty's own 'initiation'.) He also used others from Richard Hayward's book *In the Kingdom of Kerry* and the view indicator erected on the summit of Carrauntoohil. An asterisk (*) denotes a classified independent mountain listed by either Docharty or Maxwell.

Columns 3 & 4 – Height
Imperial heights are taken from Parker, Docharty and Maxwell. A small c. after a height = contour height; ap. = circa or approximate height, usually an aneroid estimation. Those made by Docharty during his second visit (autumn 1956) to Macgillycuddy's Reeks are given here. Maxwell used Six-Inch O.S. Map values, except for thirteen summits referred to in his notes to the Welsh and Irish mountains and/or footnotes to Table 1.
Metric heights are from Bearhop. Heights in square brackets are conversions from the other measurement [3.2808 feet = one metre].

Column 5 – Map Reference
Full six-figure national grid references are given. For reasons unknown, Docharty gave incomprehensible map references for the Irish hills, so these have been omitted. However, conventional six-figure references for Macgillycuddy's Reeks are taken from his article 'Looking Back Over Them All', (*SMCJ*, 29/159 (1968), 29–34).

Column 6 – Map Number
Seventh Series One-Inch to the Mile O.S. map numbers for England and Wales, and those of the Half-Inch Irish Ordnance Survey are included. Bearhop does not provide 1:50,000 sheet numbers for the three countries, so these are given here for completeness.

---

[8] *The Munro Society Journal*, 4 (2016), 24–30.

Table 1: English Furths

No./List	Name	Feet	Metres	Map Ref.	Map No.
[2359]					
JAP	Scafell Pikes	3210	[978]		
WMD	Scafell Pikes*	3210	[978]	NY 216 073	35/20 (1)
DCM	Scafell Pikes*	3210	[978]	NY 215 072	82 (2)
DAB	Scafell Pike	[3209]	978	NY 215 072	89 & 90
[2360]					
JAP	Sca Fell	3162	[964]		
WMD	Sca Fell*	3162	[964]	NY 207 065	35/20 (1)
DCM	Sca Fell*	3162	[964]	NY 207 065	82 (2)
DAB	Scafell	[3163]	964	NY 206 064	89 & 90
[2515]					
JAP	Helvellyn	3118	[950]		
WMD	Helvellyn*	3118	[950]	NY 342 152	"LD" (3)
DCM	Helvellyn*	3118	[950]	NY 341 152	83 (2)
DAB	Helvellyn	[3117]	950	NY 342 151	90
[2362]					
WMD	Ill Crags	3025 c. (4)	[922]	NY 223 074	35/20 (1)
DCM	Ill Crags (5)	3035 ap. (6)	[925]	NY 223 074	82 (2)
DAB	Ill Crag	[3068]	935	NY 223 073	89 & 90
[2363]					
WMD	Broad Crag	3054 (7)	[931]	NY 219 077	35/20 (1)
DCM	Broad Crag	3054 (8)	[931]	NY 219 076	82 (2)
DAB	Broad Crag	[3064]	934	NY 218 075	89 & 90
[2319]					
JAP	Skiddaw	3053	[931]		
WMD	Skiddaw*	3053	[931]	NY 260 290	"LD" (3)
DCM	Skiddaw*	3053	[931]	NY 261 290	82 (2)
DAB	Skiddaw	[3054]	931	NY 260 290	89 & 90

English Furths contd.

[2516]					
WMD	Lower Man	3033	[924]	NY 337 156	"LD" (3)
DCM	Lower Man	3033	[924]	NY 337 155	83 (2)

English Furths – Compiler's Notes and Remarks
(1) 1:25,000 O.S. Sheet Number.
(2) All the English summits can also be found on the 7th Edition 1-inch Tourist Map of the Lake District.
(3) "LD" 1-in. = 1-in. O.S. Map of the Lake District.
(4) Over 3,025 ft. but below 3,050 ft. – O.S. letter, 4/12/48.
(5) Named only on the 6-inch Map.
(6) Aneroid estimation (Eric and D.C. Maxwell). 3000 contour on the 6-inch and 1-inch Maps; 3025 contour on the 1:25,000 Map.
(7) 3,054 ft. – O.S. letter 4/12/48.
(8) 6-inch Map only. 3050 contour on the 1-inch and 1:25,000 Maps.

Table 2: Welsh Furths

No./List	Name	Feet	Metres	Map Ref.	Map No.
[1963]					
JAP	Y Wyddfa	3560	[1085]		
WMD	SNOWDON – Y Wyddfa*	3560	[1085]	SH 609 544	107
DCM	Yr Wyddfa*	3561 (1)	[1085]	SH 609 544	107
DAB	Snowdon	[3560]	1085	SH 609 543	115
[1964]					
WMD	Garnedd Ugain or Crib y Ddisgl	3493	[1065]	SH 610 552	107
DCM	Carnedd Ugain (2)	3493	[1065]	SH 611 552	107
DAB	Crib y Ddysgl	[3494]	1065	SH 610 551	115
[1965]					
JAP	Carnedd Llewelyn	3484	[1062]		
WMD	Carnedd Llewelyn*	3484	[1062]	SH 684 644	107
DCM	Carnedd Llywelyn*	3485 (1)	[1062]	SH 684 644	107
DAB	Carnedd Llewelyn	[3491]	1064	SH 683 644	115
[1966]					
JAP	Carnedd Dafydd	3426	[1044]		

Welsh Furths contd.

WMD	Carnedd Dafydd*	3426	[1044]	SH 663 630	107
DCM	Carnedd Dafydd*	3427 (1)	[1045]	SH 663 630	107
DAB	Carnedd Dafydd	[3425]	1044	SH 663 630	115
[1967]					
JAP	Glyder Fawr	3279	[999]		
WMD	Glyder Fawr*	3279	[999]	SH 642 580	107
DCM	Glyder Fawr*	3279	[999]	SH 642 579	107
DAB	Glyder Fawr	[3278]	999	SH 642 579	115
[1968]					
JAP	Glyder Fach	3262	[994]		
WMD	Glyder Fach*	3262	[994]	SH 656 582	107
DCM	Glyder Fach	3262	[994]	SH 656 583	107
DAB	Glyder Fach	[3261]	994	SH 656 582	115
[1969]					
JAP	Pen yr Oleu-wen	3210	[978]		
WMD	Pen yr Oleu-wen	3210	[978]	SH 656 620	107
DCM	Penyrole-wen	3211 (1)	[979]	SH 656 620	107
DAB	Pen yr Ole Wen	[3209]	978	SH 655 619	115
[1970]					
WMD	Foel Grach	3195	[974]	SH 689 659	107
DCM	Foel-grach	3196 (1)	[974]	SH 689 659	107
DAB	Foel Grach	[3202]	976	SH 688 658	115
[1971]					
JAP	Yr Elen	3151	[960]		
WMD	Yr Elen	3151	[960]	SH 673 651	107
DCM	Yr Elen	3152 (1)	[961]	SH 673 652	107
DAB	Yr Elen	[3156]	962	SH 674 651	115
[1972]					
JAP	Y Garn	3104	[946]		
WMD	Y Garn*	3104	[946]	SH 631 596	107
DCM	Y Garn*	3104	[946]	SH 631 596	107
DAB	Y Garn	[3107]	947	SH 630 595	115

Welsh Furths contd.

[1973]					
JAP	Foel Fras	3091	[942]		
WMD	Foel Fras*	3091	[942]	SH 696 682	107
DCM	Foel-fras*	3092 (1)	[942]	SH 697 682	107
DAB	Foel-fras	[3091]	942	SH 696 681	115
[1974]					
DAB	Garnedd Uchaf	[3038]	926	SH 687 669	115
[1975]					
JAP	Elidir Fawr	3029	[923]		
WMD	Elidir Fawr*	3029	[923]	SH 612 613	107
DCM	Elidir Fawr*	3030 (1)	[924]	SH 613 614	107
DAB	Elidir Fawr	[3031]	924	SH 612 613	115
[1976]					
JAP	Crib Goch	3023	[921]		
WMD	Crib Goch	3023	[921]	SH 625 553	107
DCM	Grib-goch	3026 (3)	[922]	SH 625 552	107
DAB	Crib Goch	[3028]	923	SH 624 551	115
[1977]					
JAP	Tryfan	3010	[917]		
WDM	Tryfan*	3010	[917]	SH 663 592	107
DCM	Tryfan*	3010 (4)	[917]	SH 664 595	107
DAB	Tryfan	[3002]	915	SH 664 593	115

Welsh Furths Compiler's Notes and Remarks

(1) Owing to the change of the Ordnance Datum from Liverpool to Newlyn, eight of the Welsh summits appear in the 7th edition of the 1-inch map as one foot higher than in earlier editions. The new values have been used.

(2) So named on the 6-inch Map. Crib-y-ddysgl on the 1-inch Map refers to the ridge.

(3) 6-inch Map and O.S. information. The 3023 point on the 1-inch Map is at the end of the ridge, about 100 yards E.N.E. of the summit.

(4) O.S. information – no height given on O.S. Maps.

Table 3: Irish Furths

[20001]						
JAP	Carrauntoohil	3414	[1041]		
WMD	Carrauntoohil* or Carrauntual	3414	[1041]	V 804 844	20
DCM	Carrauntoohil*	3414	[1041]	V 804 844	20
DAB	Carrauntoohill	[3409]	1039	V 803 844	78
[20002]					
JAP	Beenkeragh	3314	[1010]		
WMD	Beenkeragh*	3314	[1010]	V 801 853	20
DCM	Beenkeragh	3314	[1010]	V 802 853	20
DAB	Beenkeragh	[3314]	1010	V 801 852	78
[20003]					
JAP	Caher	3300 ap. (1)	[1006]		
WMD	Cahernaveen*	3300 ap.	[1006]	V 794 838	20
DCM	Cahernaveen (2)	3285 ap. (3)	[1001]	V 795 838	20
DAB	Caher	[3284]	1001	V 792 839	78
[20004]					
JAP	Macgillycuddy's Reeks	3200 ap. (4)	[975]		
WMD	Knocknapeasta* (5)	3250 ap.	[991]	V 836 841	20
DCM	Cummeenapeasta* (2)	3260 ap. (3)	[994]	V 836 841	20
DAB	Cnoc na Peiste	[3241]	988	V 835 841	78
[20005]					
WMD	Caher	3200 ap.	[975]	V 789 840	20
DAB	Caher West Top	[3199]	975	V 790 840	78
[20006]					
WMD	Barrabwee (6)	3200 ap.	[975]	V 832 838	20
DCM	Barrabwee (2)	3185 ap. (3)	[971]	V 828 834	20
DAB	Maolan Bui	[3192]	973	V 832 838	78
[20007]					
WMD	Knockoughter	3160 ap.	[963]	V 799 848	20

Irish Furths contd.

DAB	Knockoughter (7)	[3146]	959	V 800 847	78
[20008]					
WMD	Knockacuillion (8)	3141	[957]	V 823 834	20
DCM	Knockacuillion (2)	3141	[957]	V 823 832	20
DAB	Cnoc an Chuillin	[3143]	958	V 823 833	78
[20009]					
JAP	Brandon Mountain	3127	[953]		
WMD	Brandon*	3127	[953]		20
DCM	Brandon Mountain*	3127	[953]	Q 464 117	20
DAB	Brandon Mountain	[3123]	952	Q 460 116	70
[20010]					
WMD	Crom Cruach* or Crom Cruagh (9)	3100 ap.	[945]	V 841 845	20
DCM	Crom Cruach (2)	3110 ap. (3)	[948]	V 841 845	20
DAB	The Big Gun	[3081]	939	V 840 845	78
[20011]					
WMD	Cruach (10) or Cruagh	3062	[933]	V 841 848	20
DCM	Cruach (2)	3062	[933]	V 841 848	20
DAB	Cruach Mhor	[3058]	932	V 840 848	78
[20012]					
JAP	Lugnaquillia	3039	[926]		
WMD	Lugnaquillia*	3039	[926]		16
DCM	Lugnaquillia* (Percy's Table)	3039	[926]	T 030 916	16
DAB	Lugnaquillia	[3035]	925	T 032 917	56
[20013]					
JAP	Galtymore	3018	[920]		
WMD	Galtymore*	3018	[920]		22
DCM	Galtymore Mountain* (Dawson's Table)	3018	[920]	R 879 240	22
DAB	Galtymore	[3015]	919	R 878 238	74

Irish Furths – Compiler's Notes and Remarks

(1) The highest point of the Caher Ridge I made to be about 3,300 feet, the Ordnance Survey point, 3,200 feet, being a lower point at the extreme west end of the ridge.

(2) Not named on O.S. Maps. The names used here…are supplied by Mr W.M. Docharty, who is in turn indebted to Irish friends for guidance.

(3) The heights are from aneroid measurements by Mr Eric Maxwell.

(4) Only two definite heights are marked on the Ordnance [1-inch] Map, namely, the eastern end, 3,062 feet, and the western end, 3,141 feet; but I made the height of the middle top, which is certainly the highest point, to be about 3,200 feet.

(5) Alternative names Cummeennapeasta, Slievenapeasta, Moylaun Bwee.

(6) Alternative names Barna Ruadh, Knockgrin, Ballaghageeha.

(7) There is some uncertainty as to the correct name for this summit.

(8) Alternative name Foilnagower.

(9) Alternative name Lackagarrin.

(10) Alternative name Foilnabreachaun.

Errata and Updates

(1) [DCM] Table 1. Typo: The two prefixed letters of the English grid references, SD should be NY.

(2) Carnedd Llywelyn. [DCM] Typo: Northing 664 should be 644.

(3) The Big Gun. [DAB] Typo: Northing 848 should be 845.

(4) Garnedd Uchaf. Renamed Carnedd Gwenllian by The Princess Gwenllian Society, in September 2009.

(5) Tryfan. 917.5m. (surveyed by John Barnard, Graham Jackson and Myrddyn Phillips using a Leica 530), on 24 June 2010.

(6) Glyder Fawr. 1000.9m. (surveyed as above), on 16 August 2010.

(7) Glyder Fach. 994.3m. (surveyed by Myrddyn Phillips using a Trimble GeoXH 6000), on 16 May 2014.

Acknowledgements

My sincere thanks to Robin Campbell for his patience and invaluable advice given throughout the preparation of this article. I am also indebted to Myrddyn Phillips for kindly providing up-to-date survey data. Finally, to the late Ben Horsburgh (Munroist No. 12 and Scottish Mountaineering Club member) to whom Docharty presented his trilogy of books, which I have had the good fortune to acquire.

Simon Glover

MULLARDOCH OPEN DAY

ON THE 21 MAY 2016 one of our members John Hay hosted an open day at Mullardoch with the intention of forming a link between the mountaineering community and some other users of the hills.

We met in the garage adjacent to the deer larder which all the Cannich estates share. John welcomed everyone and began by explaining his involvement with Mullardoch over the last 36 years. His ground lies on the south shore of loch Mullardoch forming the north faces of Toll Creagach and Tom a' Coinnich. He recounted how he had purchased the ground from the Forestry Commission when they had harvested all the accessible timber subsequent to the dam being built and flooding the glen. The beautiful remnant Ancient woodland was not in good condition with most trees approaching 200 years old and no new growth.

He soon became aware that deer were the greatest threat to regeneration and began the task of controlling them by culling them himself and erecting exclosures to protect the remaining seed stock. In order to do this work he built simple wooden bothies along the rugged and inaccessible five kilometre south shore of the loch, accessing the sites by small boat and carrying materials on a pack frame! Although he had help with the fencing and "casual" labour from members of the club he has achieved his goal largely by his own herculean efforts over the last 36 years. Extraction of carcases is particularly difficult on this ground where no ponies or vehicles can operate. As some club members will witness it involves dragging deer down to the loch where they can be picked up by small boat and a sometimes exciting journey down the loch, often in the dark! The results are that the ancient native woodland is now in a much healthier state and there is a continuous corridor of trees along the loch side and creeping up the hill.

As the rain hammered on the roof of the garage we retreated to the deer larder where Dr Linzi Seivewright, late of SNH now an independent ecologist, explained the current Scottish Government's plans in the context of the 2016 Land Reform Act. This Act challenges all land owners to deliver social, economic and environmental benefit from the land which they manage. Grazing pressure is a major issue and in the absence of sheep this means that deer management is now a major concern of Holyrood.

As deer range freely across many estates it is now incumbent on landowners, often with diverse and conflicting objectives, that they must collaborate with their neighbours in formal Deer Management Groups. There are 44 such groups covering upland areas in Scotland and by the end of 2016 they were expected to provide Deer Management Plans of a standard acceptable to SNH scrutiny. If they fail to do this the Government may introduce statutory measures to enforce compliance.

A DMP is a substantial document covering a comprehensive range of ecological and social issues; it is no longer simply a matter of deer population density and cull targets. Annual habitat assessments are required to establish the impact of herbivores on different vegetation, woodland, blanket bog, fertile flushes and other montane environments. To do this random plots are sampled on each habitat and compared over time to assess damage or recovery. Deer numbers and movements are established by sweeping the ground with teams of observers, helicopter counts over 'white ground' in winter and dung pellet clearance counts. This information provides an estimate of density which is a rough guide to survival or recovery of various habitats. Despite all this information local conditions and seasonal pressures can affect deer impact.

The DMP also needs to consider the diverse social and economic interests of neighbouring land owners and users: forestry, agriculture, other wildlife, conservation, sporting and recreational tourism including of course mountaineering.

This is an exciting and for some an uncertain time and Linzi's presentation stimulated a lively Q and A session to which most people contributed. Also present were members of SNH, RSPB, JMT and Scottish Mountain Rescue.

John treated us all to a generous lunch at the main bothy and we went for a walk through the nearest exclosure to view the slow but steady progress of regenerating Scots pine, birch, rowan and juniper on this wet acid north facing slope. Linzi demonstrated how to set up a 4m square vegetation sample and how to code herbivore impact, vegetation types, damage and growth, trampling and erosion. Q and A continued covering a wide range of topics affecting the Highlands from deer densities and welfare to access, windfarms, cost of pathworks, mountain bikes (which came in for a bit of criticism because of erosion on and off track) and how to fund repair or regeneration of landscapes.

The day proved to be a unique opportunity for diverse land users to share their experience and opinions. Many candid views were expressed and some very contentious issues aired in a respectful and constructive manner. We were fortunate to have access to such authoritative sources of answers to the many questions which were raised.

We are indebted to John for his generous hospitality and the prodigious efforts which he has made to preserve and expand the natural habitat and also to share his understanding and appreciation of it with other hill users.

As hill walkers and mountaineers are far greater in number than any other users of the mountain landscape, It is to be hoped that the SMC or Mountaineering Scotland may contribute to future public debates on land use or even become involved in Deer Management groups as stakeholders in the Scottish Landscape and representatives of the wider community.

A post script to this event occurred at the Easter Meet where John rather modestly gave me the latest Deer Management Plan for West Affric and Kintail and recent SNH habitat survey. Careful scrutiny of these documents showed that Mullardoch had not only achieved its cull targets and had one of the lowest deer densities but was one of the few properties to have a clean bill of health in terms of all habitats showing low impact of herbivores.

I think the club can be proud of the achievement of one of its members who has quietly done so much in a practical sense to preserve and restore the beauty and ecology of the Mountains which we all too often take for granted.

Raymond Simpson

SCOTTISH MOUNTAINEERING TRUST – 2016
Scottish Charity Number SCO 09117

THE TRUSTEES MET on 8 April and 14 October 2016. During the course of these meetings, support was given to:

Nevis Partnership – Polldubh; SCNP – National Parks Project Phase 3; Mountaineering Scotland (then Mountaineering Council of Scotland) – Access and Conservation; Mungo Ross – Calton Athletic Recovery Group; John Muir Trust – Footpath Officer; Scottish Avalanche Information Service – Be Avalanche Aware; R Crawford – Dundee Mountain Film Festival; Doug Scott – Community Action Nepal; JMCS – Coruisk Hut; Jonathan Conville Memorial Trust – Scottish Winter Courses 2016/2017; J Robbs – Staunings Alps; B Leatherland – Hill Tracks; G Cohen – Des Rubens and Bill Wallace (John Muir Trust); John Muir Trust – Suilven.

The present Trustees are DN Williams (Chairman) (*Ex Officio* Immediate Past President of the SMC), ER Allen, R Anderson (*Ex Officio* Convenor of the Publications Sub-Committee), PJ Biggar (*Ex Officio* Editor of the SMC Journal), JAP Hutchinson, AM James, SD Pearson, CR Ravey, SM Richardson (*Ex Officio* President of the SMC), and RG Ross. JM Shaw is the Trust Treasurer and JD Hotchkis is the Trust Secretary. The Trustees wish to record their gratitude and appreciation for the valuable input of JRG MacKenzie over the previous 4 years, Trustee and as the Chairman of the Trust.

CR Ravey and JAP Hutchinson (who are both Directors of the Publications Company and Trustees) provide valuable liaison between the Publications Company and the Trust.

The following grants have been committed by the Trustees during 2016:

Nevis Partnership – Polldubh (£5,000 per annum over 2 years)	£10,000
SCNP – National Parks Project Phase 3	£500
Mountaineering Scotland – Access and Conservation	£4,000
Mungo Ross – Calton Athletic Recovery Group	£4,500
John Muir Trust – Footpath Officer (£2,500 per annum over 2 years)	£5,000
Scottish Avalanche Information Service – Be Avalanche Aware	£1,500
R Crawford – Dundee Mountain Film Festival	£750
Doug Scott – Community Action Nepal	£6,000
JMCS – Coruisk Hut	£2,300
Jonathan Conville Memorial Trust – Scottish Winter Courses 2016/17	£1,000
J Roberts – Staunings Alps	£500
B Leatherland – Hill Tracks	£2,000
G Cohen – Des Rubens and Bill Wallace (John Muir Trust)	£12,000
John Muir Trust – Suilven (£5,000 per annum over 2 years)	£10,000

James Hotchkis (Hon. Sec. SMT)

MUNRO MATTERS

by Dave Broadhead (Clerk of the List)

This report covers 1 January to 31 December 2016. The five columns below give number, name and year of Compleation of Munros, Tops and Furths as appropriate. *SMC member, **LSCC member.

No.	Name	M	T	F	No.	Name	M	T	F
5901	John Darling	2015			5951	Patricia Donald	2016		
5902	W. Roger Parry	2015			5952	Beverley Smith	2016		
5903	Dave Cann	2015			5953	Nathan Crossley	2016		
5904	Robin Mackenzie	2015			5954	Alistair K. Smith	2016		
5905	Sue Pugh	2015			5955	Judith Borup	2016		
5906	Dave Pugh	2015			5956	Peter M. Kyle	2016		
5907	David Jamieson	2015			5957	James C. I. Smith	2016		
5908	Keith Monaghan	2014			5958	Fraser Campbell	2016		
5909	Matt Blackham	2016			5959	Adrian Matthews	2016		
5910	Diane Winnard	2014			5960	James A. Robertson	2016		
5911	Simon Cocker	2014			5961	Linsey McQuillan	2016		
5912	Alistair Sneddon	2015			5962	Andrew McQuillan	2016		
5913	Kathleen McCutcheon	2015			5963	Alexander Kelso	2016		
5914	Donald Mackenzie	2015			5964	Chris Firth	2016		
5915	Richard Catlow	2015			5965	Jon Mark Winderbank	2016		
5916	Shane Younie	2016			5966	John Irvine	2016		
5917	Noel R. Ayling	2015			5967	David Mowat	2016		
5918	Nicholas W. Wilson	2015			5968	Chris Boothman	2016		
5919	Terry Sheldrake	2015			5969	Sheena McKie	2016		
5920	Shaila Rao	2016			5970	Stuart McKie	2016		
5921	Owen Brown	2016			5971	Fraser Russell	2016		
5922	Linda Grant	2011			5972	Derek Coleman	2016		
5923	Patrick Grant	1999			5973	Judy Taylor	2016		
5924	David R. Roberts	2016			5974	Peter Blair-Fish	2016		
5925	Michael McCann	2016			5975	Tracey A. Grant	2016		
5926	May Roushdy-Genie	2016			5976	Trevor Sturmy	2016		
5927	Ian C. Smith	2016			5977	Dougal Goldring	2016		
5928	Kevin Joss	2013			5978	Harry Haworth	2016		
5929	Howard McKee	2015			5979	Valerie Allen	2016		
5930	Barbara Brodie	2016			5980	Karen Ward	2016		
5931	Ruari Greer	2015			5981	Anita Bottomley	2016		
5932	Maisie Mackenzie	2015			5982	Stephen Nolan	2016		
5933	Hugh Mackenzie	2015			5983	Christine Bailey	2016		
5934	Michele Reason	2016			5984	John Bailey	2016		
5935	Mark Lampard	2016			5985	Andrew Waugh	2016		
5936	Ian Baverstock	2016			5986	Catriona Urquhart	2016		
5937	Roy Lake	2016			5987	Anne Bradbury	2016		
5938	Geoff Cooper	2016			5988	Alec Mamwell	2016	2016	2016
5939	Jeanette Knibb	2016			5989	Robert Dawson Scott	2016		
5940	Michel Van Herck	2016			5990	Karen Best	2016		
5941	Garry Minors	2016			5991	Lloyd Best	2016		
5942	Rhona Adam	2016			5992	Conan Fischer	2016		
5943	Alan J. McClelland	2016			5993	Stuart Anderson	2016		
5944	Victoria Morris	2016			5994	Alexander H. Swanson	2016		
5945	Gil Carling	1993			5995	Jonathan Middleton	2016		
5946	Dan Cornell	2016			5996	Pauline Henderson	2016		
5947	Richard Ker	2016			5997	Martin Beswick	2016		
5948	Jeff Dickens	2016			5998	Colin Watson	2016		
5949	Tom Litterick	2016			5999	Rachel Wilson	2016		
5950	David Nightingale	2016			6000	Ian Haigh	2016		

No.	Name	M	T	F	No.	Name	M	T	F
6001	John Featherstone	2016		2016	6052	Tom Thomson	2016		
6002	William Rae	2016			6053	John Hunston	2016		
6003	Stacey Hearl	2016			6054	Mick Bates	2016		
6004	Robert Osborne	2016			6055	David Jinks	2016		
6005	Gerhard Mors	2016			6056	Ian Morris	2016		
6006	Daniel Lewis	2016			6057	Keith Helliwell	2016		
6007	Joyce T. Wilson	2016			6058	Julie McLean	2016		
6008	Brian P. Cruickshank	2016			6059	Ian Wilcock	2016		
6009	Michael G. A. Will	2016			6060	Alan Clayton	2016		
6010	Ian Folly	2016			6061	Vania Kennedy	2016		
6011	Ken Durose	2016			6062	Chris Jepson	2016		
6012	Simon Wurr	2016			6063	Peter J. D. Roberts	2016		
6013	Gill Cairney	2016			6064	James R. Plant	2016		
6014	Chris Gooch	2016			6065	Allan P. Plant	2016		
6015	John Paterson	2016			6066	Allan Plant	2016		
6016	Catherine M. Smith	2016			6067	Steve McEwen	2016		
6017	Derek Sharp	2016			6068	Robin Dunn	2016		
6018	Neil Sharp	2016			6069	Alan Welsh	2016		
6019	Charles G. Metcalfe	2016			6070	Jim McLuggage	2016		
6020	Alex Barbour	2016			6071	John Norton	2016		
6021	Maureen Stevenson	1992			6072	Allan Brown	2016		
6022	Christine Johnston	2016			6073	Alistair Macwilliam	2016		
6023	Robin Green	2016			6074	James Murdoch	2016		
6024	Stephen T. Wells	2016			6075	Stuart M. Young	2016		
6025	Stuart Wallis	2016			6076	Thomas P. Wright	2016		
6026	Kaye Cantlay	2016			6077	Moira C. Thomson	2016		
6027	Philip Kammer	2016			6078	Derek Thomson	2016		
6028	Sorrel Hopkins	2016			6079	Derek Muir	2016		
6029	Iain Mitchell	2016			6080	Stephen Kerr	2016		
6030	Gary A. Holtby	2016			6081	Moira Hamilton	2016		
6031	Michael Gray	2016			6082	R. F. Withington	2016		
6032	John B. Robertson	2016			6083	Jim Coxhead	2016		
6033	Brian L. Holmes	2016			6084	Graham Ritchie	2016		
6034	Gordon S. Paterson	2016			6085	Marion Johnston	2016		
6035	Davd Atherton	2016			6086	Gordon Johnston	2016		
6036	Graham S. Macnab	2016			6087	Brian Smith	2016		
6037	Gary Butler	2016			6088	Anthony Kane	2016		
6038	Neil Christie	2016			6089	Jane Watts	2016		
6039	Marlene Baillie	2016			6090	Richard Reid	2016		
6040	Lindsay Donald	2016			6091	Eric Hindmarsh	2016		
6041	Stephen Wool	2016			6092	Alasdair Raffe	2016		
6042	Alastair Maclean	2016			6093	*Stuart Bauchop	2016		
6043	Robert Wilson	2016			6094	Nigel Pike	2016		
6044	Justin Dunn	2016			6095	David J. Hartley	2016		
6045	Gordon Dowling	2016			6096	Carrie L. Craig	2016		
6046	Domokos Gyore	2016			6097	Charles Hutchinson	2012		
6047	Colin J. Campbell	2016			6098	Eric Dawson	2016		
6048	Sara C. Jeyes	2016			6099	Les Hobbs	2016		
6049	Andrew T. Jeyes	2016			6100	David Traynor	1999		
6050	Robert Davie	2016			6101	John Galt	2016		
6051	Neil McCluskey	2016			6102	Stuart Graham	2016		

Comparing this year's data with last year (in brackets): New Munroists 202 (217); males 77% (80%); resident in Scotland 66% (64%); couples 13% (12%); average age 55 (55); size of Compleation summit party 13 (10); average Compleation time 24 (24) years; Golden Munroists 10 (8).

Clerk of the List hits the headlines

Early in 2016 I was invited by Peter Evans (4999) to feature as Clerk of the List in the regular 'Working in the outdoors Q&A' which appeared as a full page in the Spring/Summer 'Active Outdoors' colour supplement issued with all the Scottish Provincial Press local papers. With social media currently getting a bad name for some less than accurate reporting I thought it would be appropriate this year to highlight my review of the correspondence with some good old fashioned attention grabbing headlines. No fake news here!

Children climb Munros

As ever, some Munroists remembered being introduced to the hills by their parents. Alasdair Raffe (6092) began his Round aged 6 and was delighted that his mother who encouraged him on that occasion was able to join him again on his Compleation on Mount Keen. Kevin Joss (5928) remembered 'aged only 8, kitted out in a pair of wellie boots and a less than watertight blue kagool, I made my way to the summit of Mayar in Glen Clova in the driving rain and snow with my Dad, William G. J. Joss (1978) and a couple of school friends.' Rhona Adam (5942) climbed Ben Vorlich (Loch Earn) in 1964 with her father, Duncan H. McPherson who had joined the SMC in 1929. Chris Gooch (6014) 'tagged along on my Dad's walking trips with his friends in my teens. The one you may have heard of is the late Jim Rennie, who used to draw the maps for SMC guides.'

Happy families

Alistair K. Smith (5954) joined his two brothers Barry K. Smith (1652) and Jonathan M. Smith (2904) on The List. Father and son Derek (6017) and Neil Sharp (6018) Compleated together on Ben More (Mull) and proudly requested joint certificates. Young Neil had introduced his Dad 'to climbing and hillwalking when I was aged 42 and extremely unfit.' James R. Plant (6064) his brother Allan P. Plant (6065) and Allan P's son Allan Plant (6066) Compleated together on Bla Bheinn while brother and sister Moira C. Thomson (6077) and Derek Thomson (6068) finished on different hills a few weeks apart but ended up with sequential numbers. Alastair MacLean (6042) Compleated on Ben Challum 'chosen because my eldest son is called Callum! Not to upset my daughter Iona, my second last hill was Ben More on Mull, overlooking Iona!'

Ben Nevis the hard way

Howard Mckee (5929) claimed 'I never intended to 'do' the Munros, my interest is in the scenery and peace of the mountains' but then went on to recall 'probably the best day was to meet friends staying for a weekend at the CIC hut to winter climb, when I couldn't arrange a lift, so got the night train from Preston, got off at Corrour, walked in plastic boots along the Grey Corries and glissaded at 11p.m. down a long snow-filled gully in the moonlight from Carn Mor Dearg, arriving at the hut about 11.30pm to the astonishment of my friends and the grudging admiration of the SMC residents. An off-day ascent of North Gully on the Sunday, down to the Fort & back on the train to work in Preston…'

Bagger nearly came a cropper

Munro Rounds do not always go smoothly. Keith Monaghan (5908) a rare Munroist from Northern Ireland admitted that he 'fell off Fionn Bheinn going through a cornice in a whiteout.' Luckily, he 'was able to climb 100 feet or so back over the top' despite a couple of broken ribs. I also have to own up to cracking a rib on the same hill some years ago when I slipped climbing over the roadside gate!

Beinn Dorain mystery solved

Explaining her choice of Compleation hill, Barbara Brodie (5930) explained that 'my Dad grew up in Tyndrum (Brodie's store was my Grandfather's, then my Uncle's and is now my cousin's) and it's where he met my Mum; when we were young if we lost anything and asked where it was the answer was always the same 'the top of Beinn Dorain.'

Belgian bagger admits to spending money

Michel Van Herck (5940) from Mol in Belgium was the only overseas Compleater this year. He sent a delightful letter, introducing himself as '57 years old, married and have a nice and lovely wife who gives me two beautiful children.' He then explained 'I have been in Scotland 18 times, all this times I came by van which I use for my work….I drove thousands of kilometers, I spent a lot of money on fuel and scottisch outdoor shops!!! ….I became wet, cold, white out, almost eaten by midges, pain in legs and knees, all kinds of weather you can get and so much more!!! But also very nice views. But? It was worth it.'

Arts & books

The Munro Society JOURNAL No 4 (2016) arrived in the post, literally bursting out of its envelope. Expanded to an impressive 182 pages with a striking colour photo of Suilven on the front cover, this publication has gone from strength to strength thanks to the editorial skills of Derek Sime (685) and his team. Inside, 34 concise articles cover a worldwide range of mountain related topics, interspersed with photos, illustrations, poems and member's short anecdotes. Plenty here to interest anyone who enjoys going to the hills. Highly recommended.

Jim Coxhead (6083) noted that 'I am more than following in the footsteps of my aunt, Elizabeth Coxhead who wrote a couple of climbing novels and presented me with my first pair of climbing boots.' This reminded me how much I enjoyed reading 'One Green Bottle' many years ago, a classic of the genre whose heroine obtains her first pair of climbing boots by more dubious means! Google for more details.

Keeper tribute

In July 2016 I was very sad to learn of the death of Gordon A. McAndrew (450), Keeper of Regalia. Following his Compleation in 1986 Gordon decided to produce a more tangible celebration of this achievement and designed a distinctive tie and brooch. With the approval of the Court of the Lord Lyon, this incorporates major features from the Arms of Sir Hugh T. Munro, a red stylized heraldic eagle's head encircled by branches of laurel and oak, all subscribed by the numeral 3000. Although not an SMC member, for the next 30 years Gordon supplied ties and brooches to Munroists with great efficiency. To allow this tradition to continue, his family agreed to sell the remaining stock to the Club and Chris Huntley has taken over as Keeper of Regalia.

Munros a mere warm-up

Munroists are invited to share future plans when they report. Victoria Morris (5944) 'has arranged an 8-month sabbatical from work in 2017 to walk from John O'Groats to Land's End via the highest point of each of the mainland historic counties. Currently the route is about 3500 miles!' Sorrel Hopkins (6028) had 'a trip to the Himalayas planned for next year to ensure that I keep my motivation.' Travelling from Cambridgeshire, Stephen Wool (6041) worked out that his 7 year Round required 27 journeys to Scotland totaling circa 30,000 miles and declared ' I will definitely not attempt a second Round. As I kept a journal for every climb and have a photo of every summit I may write a book for my grandchildren.' Tom Thomson (6052) reported 'my interest in Munros sparked a general interest in mountaineering and I have now completed Kilimanjaro, Mont Blanc, Gran Paradiso, Stok Kangri, Toubkal and Aconcagua.' Moira Hamilton (6081) 'plans to go to the Atlas Mountains in Morocco – meanwhile she noted 'I did spot an SMC Grahams and Donalds book the other day and have put that on my Christmas list.'

Munificent Munroists

Fraser Campbell (5958) was prompted by 'the thousands of gallons of rain which drenched me, my boots and equipment' to raise over £12,000 for Water Aid. Alan Clayton (6060) celebrated his Compleation with donations to the Scottish Mountaineering Trust, Mountain Rescue and the Mountain Bothies Association and finished his letter 'thank you and all at the SMC for the wonderful work you do on behalf of us all.'

First compleat woman minister?

Apart from First Munroist Rev A. E. Robertson (1) The List has traditionally been egalitarian and avoided titles. Valerie Allen (5979) aka Rev Dr. Valerie L. Allen wonders if she is 'the first woman Church of Scotland minister to climb the Munros?' The first such ordinations were made in 1969 so I think she probably is.

Munro mix ups

Stacy Hearl (6003) organized a large celebration of her Compleation on Meall Buidhe (Glen Lyon) but 'unfortunately we were 8 people down on the day as they had attended Meall Buidhe the Corbett also in Glen Lyon!' Fortunately, Fergus the piper climbed the correct hill.

With only two summits left, David Atherton (6035) struggled up Knoydart's Luinne Bheinn in horrendous weather 'and a record number of midges for company.' Careful preparations followed for Compleation in the Northern Highlands a few months later 'only to discover that Beinn a' Chlaidheimh, the target hill is no longer a Munro!'

Star letter

From the many fantastic letters received each year I like to share part of my favourite. Like many others, Gill Cairney (6013) experienced highs and lows in the course of her Round and finished by writing: 'Apologies for the long letter, but I am always amazed by my own achievement. Doing this has been a journey, not a long one as such, but I have learned, confidence in myself and my abilities has grown. I know my wee Dad would be proud of me, not necessarily for ticking off a list, but for getting out there and doing it. I genuinely do feel, compleat.'

Lost and found

Iain Mitchell (6029) reported losing 'a camera on Beinn a' Clachair, several walking poles, a sit mat and a small tripod' but was lucky 'to find a ten pound note near ski slopes on Meall a' Bhuiridh!' Domoskos Gyore (6046) reported losing a tent but finding an ice-axe and a full bottle of champagne!

Curious coincidence leads to spooky compleation

Devastated by the death of his wife in a road accident in 1998, well-meaning colleagues of John B. Robertson (6032) persuaded him that 'a day out in the hills could only help the healing process I was going through. My first tiny hill was Ben A'an in the Trossachs and I was hooked from the first day.' 18 years later he planned to Compleat on Ben Avon (Leabaidh an Daimh Bhuidhe) and admitted 'as a spooky aside I only realized a few weeks before that Ben A'an was my first hill and Ben Avon (pronounced the same way you will be aware) was my last Munro, a totally unplanned coincidence.' A final supernatural twist to the tale came 'on the day before climbing Ben Avon we all visited Craigievar Castle and while in the haunted room I was tapped twice on the shoulder with no one behind me. As a total sceptic I attach no significance to this but it remains unexplained nevertheless. My more superstitious colleagues reckon it was a sign of approval for what I was about to do the next day.'

Wedding bells for baggers

In October Thomas P. Wright (6076) chose his Compleation on top of the Inaccessible Pinnacle as the moment to propose to his partner Alfiya. Their guide for this happy event was Jonah Jones who had notched-up 63 ascents of the In Pin so far that year!

Golden guys and gals

Prolonging the pleasure of their Rounds over 50 years or more, Golden Munroists this year were W. Roger Parry (5902) 50 years, Donald Mackenzie (5914) 50 years, Richard Catlow (5915) 52 years, Geoff Cooper (5938) 51 years, Rhona Adam (5942) 52 years, Fraser Campbell (5958) 50 years, James A. Robertson (5960) 54 years, Conan Fischer (5992) 51 years, Jim Coxhead (6083) 50 years and David J. Hartley (6095) 50 years.

Club Corner

Clubs continue to play an important role in encouraging and supporting Munroists through their Round. Mentioned this year were Aberdeen Mountaineering Club; Banbury Mountaineering Club; Blantyre Hillwalking Club; Cairn Ban Mountaineering Club, Glasgow; Chester Ramblers; Capricorn Mountaineering Club; Colmcille Climbers Club, Londonderry; Deeside Hillwalking Club; Glasgow Holiday Fellowship Walking Club; Glenrothes Hillwalkers; Grampian Hillwalking Club; Highways Hillwalking Club, Edinburgh; Inverness Highland Hillwalkers; Lylecraigs Hillwalking Club; Jacobites Mountaineering Club, Edinburgh; Milgavnie Mountaineering Club; Ochils Mountaineering Club; Paisley Hillwalkers Club; The Pill Ptarmigans, Bristol; Scottish-hills; XXL Hillwalking Club, Aberdeen.

WEEKEND SUPPLEMENT aka AMENDMENTS

No.	Name	M	T	F	C	G	D
2968	David Paterson	2003			2012	2015	
2874	Anthony Dyer	2001			2015		
3518	Ron Bell	2005	2005	2005	2015		
4108	Charles Kilner	2008	2015	2009			
4033	Donald F. Irvine	2002	2002	2008	2015		2016
1806	Ross Gervis	1997	2012	2011	2010	2016	2011

No.	Name	M	T	F	C	G	D
		2013					
1279	Nigel P. Morters	1994	2009		1999	2015	
		2008					
690	*David J. Broadhead	1989			2016		
4519	Mark McKain	2010			2015		2016
3552	Martin Richardson	2006		2003	2016	2016	2009
1609	Robert J. Ferguson	1996	1996		2004	2014	2016
5105	Tamsin Bird	2012		2016			
5106	Andrew Bird	2012		2016			
4483	*William A. Forbes	1986	1995	2002	2002	2006	2014
		2009					
		2016					
5506	Alistair Deering	2014	2015		2015		2016
5930	Barbara Brodie	2016			2016	2016	
2454	**Mary Webster	2000	2009		2005	2016	
		2014					
4897	Norma Bisset	2011			2016		
4898	Ron Bisset	2011			2016		
1807	Alan J. Black	1997			2013		2016
4396	Mark Gibson	2009	2013	2016	2015		
3526	Michael O'Donnell	2005		2016	2012		
1041	David Park	1992	1992				
1042	Rod Harrison	1992	1992	1999			
1043	Mark Douglas	1992	1992	1999			
5886	Bengt Karlsson	2015	2016				
4564	James A. Anderson	2010			2012	2016	
3767	Alan Hinchliffe	2004		2016			
3183	Barry Smith	2004		2014	2016		
1990	Alan Fraser	1998			2016		
614	George Bruce	1987		2016	1998	2014	
1891	Dave Marshall	1993					
		2010					
		2014					
		2016					
2628	Rob Pearson	2001	2001	2002	2012		2016
2629	Margaret Pearson	2001	2001	2002	2012		2016
1351	Margaret Beattie	1994			2007	2016	
		2000					
		2005					
1897	Alan M. Ure	1996			2016		
1898	Karam A. Ure	1996			2016		
3059	Alex Mackenzie	2003			2016		2012
2346	David Allison	2000	2003	2002	2008	2016	2011
		2012					
3438	Hazel Strachan	2005					2011
		2008					2012
		2010					2012
		2012					
		2013					
		2014					

No.	Name	M	T	F	C	G	D
		2015					
620	Norrie Muir	1988	2002		1997	2014	2014
3112	Bert Barnett	2001	2002	2002	1998	2000	2012
		2001	2009	2007	2007	2009	2013
		2009	2015	2015	2013		
		2012					
		2016					
2774	Howard Jones	2002			2008	2014	2016
2862	John Edward Casson	2002		2007	2010	2014	2016
3987	Colin Lees	2004	2012	2013			
		2007					
		2011					
		2016					
4704	Kirsten Paterson	2010			2016		
602	Irvin John Cushnie	1988	1988	1991	1994		
		2006					
		2016					
2110	Alexander J. L. Stalker	1999			2016		
3440	Campbell McGee	2005		2007	2016		
4062	*Michael G. Barnard	2008	2008		2016		
613	*Andrew Tibbs	1988					
		2016					
3785	Jim Robertson	2007	2013				2016
2122	Ron Hilditch	1999	2016		2012		
2832	Richard A. Lloyd	2002			2010		
		2016					
2161	Donald Brown	1999			2016		
		2003					
		2010					
3783	Alan Taylor	2006		2016	2009	2013	
4728	Stephen Peatfield	2011			2016		
747	Leonard J. Thomson	1990	2009		2016		
1796	John L. Robinson	1997		2003	2016		
3120	William John McAllan	2004					
		2015		2015			
4775	Alexandra Macleod	2011			2016		
1533	Graeme Morrison	1995			2009	2016	
		2009					
		2014					
		2015					
		2016					
1874	Bryan Rynne	1997	1997	1997	2009	2016	2009
1341	David Bonham	1994					
		2016					
3789	Stewart Watson	2007		2011			
		2016					
4438	Lionel S. Foreman	2009		2009	2016		
2989	George Smart	2003	2016		2016		
		2016					
1911	Martin J. Almond	1997	1997	2014	2012	2015	2013

No.	Name	M	T	F	C	G	D
		2006					
		2016					
2377	K. Clarke	2000			2016		
1160	Peter E. Collins	1993		1994	2008		2011
2624	**/*Lisa Silver	2001		2007	2013		
1746	James King	1997	1997	2014	2003	2014	2014
2893	Tommy Hunter	2003		2007	2016		
2991	Ewan J. Lyons	2003	2009	2012	2009	2016	
		2012					
4120	Frank Johnstone	2003		2016	2011		
		2013					

In 2016 I heard from 75 (88) Munroists requesting to amend entries on our Lists (last year's figure in brackets) as follows: New Munro Rounds 14 (19); Tops 6 (10); Furths 11 (10); Corbetts 40 (29); Grahams 11 (17); Donalds 12 (12). Full House 4 (6) total now 44.

Corbetteers confused

The irrepressible heighters were busy again, establishing Cnoc Coinnich 764m near Arrochar as a new Corbett, bringing the total to 222. This confused some would-be Corbetteers such as Alexander J. L. Stalker (2110) who 'thought I had finished them a month or so earlier on Ainshval on Rum but then noticed the list had changed.'

Royal notes

'Queen of the Munros', Hazel Strachan (3438) reported Round 8 but still has some way to catch 'King' Steve Fallon (1045) with 15 Rounds. The effusive tone of her letter made it clear that familiarity has not diminished her enthusiasm. Her latest Round involved 113 days of walking and was almost thwarted by a heavy fall of snow on the Cuillin – in June! 'I was wearing a pair of Marigolds covered with a pair of gardening gloves.' How's that for 'chasing the ephemeral' President Richardson? More seasonally, in January she 'caught a lovely sunrise as I climbed Fionn Beinn, happy that I had snowshoes on my feet.' Hazel seems to have a knack with the weather and noted 'it has been years since I've had a truly soggy day.' On her penultimate day, in the Northwest Highlands (where else?) she 'rather enjoyed myself in 9 hours of constant drizzle and rain because it was such a novelty.'

Not that Donald again

Enthusing about the Donalds, John Edward Casson (2862) noted 'whilst they do not have the grandeur of the Highlands, they do have the attraction of being unfrequented by other walkers. In fact, you have more chance of bumping into a wind turbine than another walker.'

Ticking in Tasmania

Thanks to the wonders of the world-wide web I had a fascinating exchange of emails with Dr Louise Fairfax of Launceston, Tasmania. Louise maintains a list of bush-walkers who have climbed all the Tasmanian Abels and was preparing a magazine article about Munros. With 160 summits of height exceeding 1100m the Abels sound a much tougher proposition requiring long approaches through challenging terrain. She noted that a recent Launceston Abelist, Malcolm

Waterston, is the son of Robert Waterston (4321) who still holds the record, at 69 years, of the longest Munro Round. Malcolm is apparently also close to his Munro Compleation, so I look forward to hearing from him.

Income tax inspector dodges list

Writing to correct a small error in his entry, Chris Andrews (280) explained that his late father and SMC member Christopher Andrews was an early Compleater who chose not to register, unlike his friend and fellow Income Tax Inspector John Dow (5) though his Round was acknowledged in his 1953 *SMCJ* obituary.

Metric baggers form new society

Distracted some years ago into climbing Marilyns (British hills with 150 metres of separation) your Clerk subsequently registered in the Marilyn Hall of Fame, having climbed more than 600 of the 1556 listed hills. This has revealed a whole new world of bagging beyond our familiar Imperial lists. To cater for this growing interest the Relative Hills Society was formed in 2016 to support those climbing not just Marilyns but also Humps, Tumps, Simms, Sibs, Ultras, Ribus, Majors and the Switzerland Finest 50. For further details please visit <www.rhsoc.uk>.

Apologies

In last year's *SMCJ* (2016) I mistakenly congratulated Bert Barnett (3112) on equaling what I thought was a record 17 entries in the Lists, established by Hamish Brown (62). An eagle-eyed correspondent quickly pointed out that with a remarkable 26 entries, Stewart R. Logan (327), currently President of the Munro Society remains well ahead. Apologies to all concerned.

Better late than never

Munroists who finally got around to registering in 2016 include Garry Minors (5941) from 2008, Gil Carling (5945) who finished the original List in 1993 and the Revised List in 1999 while Maureen Stevenson (6021) finished back in 1992. Remember it is never too late to add your achievements to our six Lists by writing to Dave Broadhead, 17 Drumdyre Road, Dingwall, IV15 9RW. For a Munro or Corbett Compleation certificate please enclose an A4 sae (with correct postage please). Check <www.smc.org.uk> for further details and to view the picture galleries of Munroists and Corbetteers celebrating on their final summit.

　　Enjoy your hills.

Dave Broadhead (Clerk of the List)

IN MEMORIAM

ROBERT J.F. (BOB) BROWN j. 1999

BOB DIED FROM A stroke at the age of 81 in June last year. This brought to a close a life that was lived to the full to the very end and, as his son, I have been asked to write on the areas and times outwith his later decades of Scottish climbing.

Born in 1934, Bob grew up in Oxford. Bird nesting, egg collecting, fishing and scouting set him on the outdoor path. One impressive skill acquired in these days was his ability to identify birds from their song alone, this was developed out of necessity due to being unable to afford binoculars. He was a university college choirboy and his sharp mind did well at school, seventy years later he could still put to use the Latin from those days. An engineering apprenticeship at Lucy's was combined with competitive cycling at a high level with the Oxford City Road Club, laying down impressive time trial performances and riding in every English county in a single year. We can trace his climbing to these days, when a weekend might consist of cycling to North Wales, climbing a route on Cloggy and then back for work.

Bob's National Service was spent as an armourer with the RAF in Germany, where he loaded planes during the Suez crisis and participated in nuclear tests on Christmas Island. He then returned to Oxford and work in research and development for Pressed Steel at Crowley. Work, however, was only a means to an end for Bob, and his favourite end was climbing. In 1962 he was a founder member of the Oxford Mountaineering Club, where lifelong friendships, and his

later marriage to Fay, were forged around climbing, most often in North Wales. The club still has the hut at Pentrefoelas which Bob and friends converted from the shell of a farmhouse. A friend of the time recalls Bob always neat in his breeches, red socks and Dolomite boots and, with his sociability and enthusiasm, never struggling to find a partner. Forays were also made north of the border, one memorable ascent was of Point Five Gully, where the party managed to get off the hill in daylight – the next day's daylight. Partners in these days included Brede Arkless, Eric 'Spider' Penman, Richard McHardy and Al Harris (Bob said that riding pillion behind Al was far hairier than any route they did together).

The Alps beckoned and an early route was the traverse of La Meije with frequent partner of the time Chris Hirst, featuring an unplanned stormbound bivi under a tarp with two Italians. This didn't blunt his enthusiasm however, and there followed many trips to the Dolomites and the Alps. Routes climbed in the former included: the Traverse of the Vajolet Towers; Cima Piccola di Lavaredo, Spigolo Giallo; Crozzon di Brenta, Asti Diedre. And in the latter: Aiguille Dibona, S.Face Direct; Grépon, S.W. and Mer de Glace Face; Charmoz – Grépon Traverse; and the N.Face of the Matterhorn (an early British ascent on which Bob and his partner moved together for most of the route).

In the late 1960s Bob and Fay moved to Burghead, where he took the post of mountaineering instructor at the Moray Outward Bound Sea School. Many days of work and pleasure were spent in the Cairngorms, Glen Affric and further afield. Finally, in the 1970s, he and Fay acquired a dilapidated croft near Dingwall. His practical skills came to the fore in its wholesale renovation, although the project was much delayed by the suitable prioritisation of other pursuits. A young family did not stop his climbing and he forged a long-term partnership with John Mackenzie, finding, cleaning and putting up routes at Strathconon, Camas Mor, Stone Valley and across the North. Plus, there was always an old mate to meet for a route during the family camping holiday to Cornwall, Wales or the Isles. Bob's activities and outlook on life had a profound effect on his growing sons, what now seem to us normal pastimes, weekends and holidays are looked on as high and extreme adventure by friends and colleagues.

In later years Bob exhibited the fitness and enthusiasm of one much younger. When one young gun commented 'I hope I'm climbing at your standard at your age', Bob, typically, replied "then you'll have to get a hell of a lot better between now and then, won't you?" The winter was often escaped by visiting Calpe with friends such as Ian "Pin" Howell, where he enjoyed the sun, cold beer and company as much as he did the climbing. He was also a member of the Highland CTC, cycling large distances in Britain and the Alps. Notable birthdays were suitably celebrated: 60th – Old Man of Stoer, 70th – Old Man (no chance!) of Hoy, 80th – cycling a loop of 100 miles, and grudgingly cycling the 26 more that he overlooked when planning the route.

Bob's final months were packed with good times: climbing at home and abroad, walking in the Lakes, a dip in the winter sea. His trip to Wales featured a retreat in torrential rain and low visibility via an overhanging abseil that came up short, followed by a long walk out. One hundred friends old and new joined his family to say farewell to Bob at his home in Lochussie. There were reminisces of snow and rock but above all of Bob himself: irascible and opinionated, sometimes tactless, humorous, great company and, though sometimes well hidden, kind.

Peter Brown

John MacKenzie writes: Bob died on 10 June from a stroke aged nearly 82. He and I had been climbing at Glenmarksie less than two weeks before where he had led a tricky Severe with no problems at all. If all of us can be still climbing at that age, then I think we would be happy at whatever standard we could manage. His drive, his thirst for rock, lasted all his life and when he started to show some small signs of frailty in his later years, despite doctors telling him 'to act his age, watch telly' his riposte was to tell them to do that themselves, but he would carry on climbing. That was Bob right through, cutting straight through the waves of mediocrity, rebutting popular opinion and probably being deliberately controversial just to see the reaction.

I first climbed with Bob in 1978 and I soon found that if I said 'black' he would say 'white' and that was just fine. I had no problems with opposite views and enjoyed the invariably lively conversations because Bob was more than just a crag rat, he had a wealth of interests and these included birds, cycling, politics, music and cooking. He was a pretty rounded person and having served in the RAF before becoming an outdoor instructor, had seen just about every type of human possible. Once you became a friend there was absolutely nothing he wouldn't do for you.

We both had a similar view on climbing: simply the most important activity you could do, bar none, all else sort of fitted in around it, a nucleus of perceived perfection at least to the true believer. Unclimbed crags in particular appealed, a Holy Grail that rarely lived up to hoped-for expectations but nevertheless, Don Quixote like, we charged on expecting the best. A good example of these intentions was when, some years ago, we spotted a fine head of rock peering above the heather, obviously some distance off. Without consulting the map and regardless of the many years of combined experience, we tussled over bog and heather, past lochans and heading due north arrived unexpectedly at the main road, the A894 with our crag, Creag a' Bhadaidh Daraich a little beyond. We could have driven to the same spot. The crag as it turned out was loose, just to add insult to injury, but we had a good laugh at ourselves.

More successful were exploits on the West Buttress of Creag Ghlas with cleaning as well as climbing gear, resulting in good routes such as Salamander and Bob's Hall of Mirrors, a most unlikely route for the grade, where he had spent a long time over several days cleaning out the grass from the cracks. Once, having topped out of a route we spied a huge but dangerously perched rock the size of a small piano overhanging the crag. It didn't take much effort to move the boulder, which after clearing the crag in a single bound, proceeded down slope at a great pace so that 300m below it went through the old fence as if it wasn't even there before mowing down several poor quality trees. This was, of course, all done for safety reasons having previously ensured no one was around. Further, this was when the new estate owners were renewing the deer fence and felling the trees anyway, such was our excuse for a good trundle. Bob years later often reminded me of the way the fence parted like the proverbial Red Sea with a great twang and the sulphurous smell that wafted up the crag.

The 1990s and early 2000s were fun with spells of good weather. Bob's discovery of the Camus Mor crags, unaware of Kevin Howett's original route, was a masterstroke. He had taken the long boggy walk in, spied the extensive crags and being Bob had reasoned that the Ardmair fish farm would have a boat which could, in theory, take one directly to the foot of the crags, thus saving a very long walk. With complete confidence he approached Robin Bradley the then owner and asked if we could use his boat next Wednesday, this being Monday. Amazingly, Bob had met a similar thrawn character to himself who said yes. Bob phoned me up that evening and asked what I was doing on Wednesday. I said I was working. 'Well, delegate', he said, 'You're going climbing'. That was that then, so we went, took the boat, landing at a perfect little bay complete with waterfall and did a cracking route, Dreadnaught, the start of a long summer in which Robin took us repeatedly to the crag in the early morning and back again in the early evening. The moral of this little story is if you don't ask you don't get!

Stone Valley near Gairloch was another one of Bob's chance discoveries though a couple of the routes had in fact been climbed before by locals though we didn't know that at the time. When we arrived it was May and unseasonably cold, so cold in fact that the top pitch of a nice Hard Severe called Open Secret was being covered in snow, but such was the keenness that we carried on, surely the first and last 'winter ascent' on that crag. With other friends like Graham Cullen and later Blyth Wright and Graeme Ettle, lots of routes were done but it was always with Bob that initial discoveries were made and huge fun achieved. Graham often joined us in other escapades, including White House Crag near Diabeg and routes in the far north-west as well as in Skye.

The Strathconon crags were evening haunts, often accompanied by our numerous friends, the midges. Glenmarksie crag, once cleaned gave good technical routes in the middle grades and deserves to become more popular, more so if others could help clean it occasionally as the rock is superb with good protection. What was then the hardest route, Man O' War on the top crag took something like 17 leader falls before eventual success. Bob and I took turns, dropping off on a No 4 Friend in an almost casual manner eventually, with swarms of midges forming an unholy halo around our heads, such that we were reduced to wearing a balaclava when belaying. We must have been keen.

Bob's knowledge of the Cuillin was extensive and together we made sorties whilst checking routes for the guide, his many previous trips there saving much effort in what has to be the UK's most complex range. Just occasionally we visited the Cairngorms. Later with Fay his wife, he made a thorough exploration, and these hills would become a very special area for them.

Trips to other parts of the UK followed and Bob had a fine knowledge of Wales, having climbed with the likes of Pete Crew and other redoubtable worthies of that era both there and in the Lakes and the SW granite crags of Cornwall. I remember doing the classics of Tremadog with him in very close weather, staying at Eric Jones's barn; being hot and sticky on Vector, cooler on a free ascent of Tensor, windier in the Pass when Bob seconded Cenotaph Corner whilst his chalk bag was being emptied by the up draught. His enthusiasm was totally infectious, almost anything was possible.

Before I met him, Bob used to go to the Alps and Dolomites where he had climbed good routes but I always felt that rock rather than snow was his thing and thus we used to go to areas in Europe for 'hot-rock' holidays, in particular to Spain and Sardinia with a group of friends including Charles White and Ian (Pin) Howell. Many, many good routes were done, as well as longer trad climbs that punctuated the usually shorter bolted ones. On one occasion, later on in our overseas trips, Charles and I fancied a trad route called Rock Dancer 2, a long single pitch. Bob at this stage was getting on a bit and we didn't think he would be that keen so was handed the camera. When Charles and I were at the top discussing the possibility of Bob getting up this or how and what photographs he had taken, a strong voice from 50m below demanded that the rope be taken in smartish. He climbed the route well and emerged at the top beaming, putting our doubts to shame and proving just what a tough old man he really was.

Our climbing like our friendship was solid and dependable. Though we both had a friendly competitive edge which ensured extra effort to avoid the other taking over the lead, this was tempered by the knowledge that if the going ever really got tough, you could always feel that 100% concentration from below, willing you on, almost ensuring that success would inevitably follow.

Likewise, when back in the flatlands, he could be both sage and mentor, never one to allow you to wallow but always there in support. He often told me how lucky he was to have met Fay and how she was the best life partner and wife he could have had. They formed a good team and when Bob was finding the hill too much at times they cycled extensively, covering huge distances. My sympathies and those of a vast number of friends go to her and to their three fine lads, Alexander, Peter and Thomas. They have inherited much of their father's grit and determination and I most certainly wish them success and happiness in all that they do.

Our active years together had an innocence about them, a single minded focus, free of the vicissitudes of life's other cares and worries. There is usually a period in a climber's life when aspirations and ability come together and with Bob the timing was perfect, you could say we seized the moment, 'Carpe Diem' literally (though Bob would have deliberately mistranslated it as 'whinge daily') and we took huge joy in the process. So, farewell old pal, the best and truest friend any man could have asked for.

John MacKenzie

Peter Biggar writes: he was like a cheeky sparrow fluttering on my doorstep demanding tea and, if the day was sunny, 'Why aren't we climbing?' He always came just when I was in the middle of something, but I was always glad to be interrupted. Why he wanted to climb with me was something of a mystery, our standards were poles apart. He introduced me to the climbing wall which I suppose brought about some limited improvement. He dragged me up his beautiful route Salamander. I was frightfully nervous:

'I wish you'd stop farting!' he said.

He hauled me up Little Chamonix in the Lakes. The crux appalled me:

'Just stand there and get over your grip.'

We went on a truly dreadful club meet to Wales. In between torrential downpours and violent gusts we clambered up most of Creagh Dubh Wall at Tremadog, but on the ledge below the last pitch his chalk ball was blown clean out of his bag and we abseiled back down to the muddy trees.

Nothing daunted Bob went in search of a piece of steak for our dinner. There was a rumour current in Tremadog that day that the world was going to end at two o'clock. Looking down the dismal village street in the black rain it seemed all too plausible. We tried another butcher:

'Got any Popeseye?'

'No boyo, never 'eard of it.'

'Oh well,' said Bob, hearing the village clock strike, 'at least the world's not going to end!'

'Oh yes,' said the butcher grinning, 'Big disappointment!'

We had a plan. Bob had never climbed Ardverikie Wall; something had always gone wrong. One May day the sun shone and a gentle breeze blew. Warm, dry rock. We climbed in shirtsleeves. Pitch flowed into pitch, Bob led them all. He was 78 at the time.

'I feel a pint coming on,' he said.

He was a man of contradictions. One day the climbing wall was full of promise, the next he'd never go there again. In groups he liked to provoke argument. He was at his best when you got him on his own. There always seemed to be a yearning for something else: but Bob was always seeking and he found a great deal. No matter where he went he was always glad to get back to his home at Lochussie where his heart was.

JAMES EDWARDS j. 2003

IN AUGUST 2016 the club lost one of its most enthusiastic and versatile members. James Edwards was an accomplished mountaineer and polymath. James was a man with whom you could forget to go climbing because the conversation was so interesting and the discussion all consuming whether it be the environment, God, comparative education systems, the merits of the Apache, Spartan or Persian way of life, climbing ethics and grades, politics or just stuff. Why was the P51D better than a Spitfire? Was the birth of democracy related to the development of the phalanx? What's the best glacier travel system? There was never a dull walk in.

James slipped and fell in the Fisherfield mountains. He was setting up a radio relay station for the Wilderness Challenge on behalf of the Dundonnell Mountain Rescue Team, who then had the unenviable task of rescuing one of their own. The rescue was successful, but tragically James died a few days later in hospital.

James studied Environmental Geology at Sheffield University and soon discovered he was a natural at winter climbing. Although he later climbed many

testing routes such as The Citadel (VII,8) on the Shelter Stone and The Rhyme of the Ancient Mariner (VII,7) on Ben Nevis, from the very beginning James was looking beyond the classics. His first significant new routes took place with Gareth Hughes in January 2003 in Coire an Laoigh in the Grey Corries where he found Choc-a-Block (VI,6) and The Epithany (V,6). A week later, he was back with fellow Sheffield University climber James Thacker to add The Alternate (IV,5) and Chaf Direct (IV,6).

The following season, James really got into his stride with first ascents of Turf War (V,6) on the Douglas Boulder and the difficult Under The Weather (VII,7) on the West Top of Bidean, both with Gareth Hughes. By this point, James was taking Scottish winter climbing seriously, and the previous summer he made a reconnaissance visit to Coire nam Fhamhair on Beinn Bhan. The intention was to scope out the wall right of Die Riesenwand for a possible repeat of The Godfather, but James noticed a couple of lines left of Genesis on the left side of the crag. He returned at the end of December with Sam Barron and climbed Revelations (VI,6), a superb natural line of weakness near the left end of the cliff. Three weeks later he was back with Hughes to add Biblical Knowledge (VI,5), which takes the left edge of the fault-line taken by Genesis. These ascents were noteworthy and turned heads. This was well before the mixed climbing leashless revolution and few people dared to conceive new lines on one of the most impressive and feared walls in the Highlands.

James made his home near Inverness and the North-West quickly became his local hunting ground. Little known terrain perfectly suited his enquiring mind and exploratory nature. He climbed regularly with Roger Webb, Neil Wilson, Gary Kinsey and Martin Hind pioneering many new routes from Finlay's Rise (V,6) on Beinn Dearg to Enigma Variations (VII,8) on Stac Pollaidh, and Finny's Cave (V,6) on Beinn Dearg Mor to Roseroot (V,6) in the Fainnachs.

James was also a strong alpinist, and early in his climbing career he climbed a number of grandes courses including an icy ascent of the Walker Spur. James drew heavily on his alpine and Scottish expertise when he spent a year in New Zealand on a teaching exchange and immediately set his sights on exploring new ground. During the winter of 2004 he climbed a new route on the 800m west face of Mt. Huxley (2505m) with Sam Barron, spending a night in a snow hole near the summit. James also teamed up with Steven Fortune and Paul Warnock for an 1100m route on the south-east face of Mt. McKerrow (2650m) – Fortune Favours the Bold (TD). His most impressive first ascent took place on Mount Aspiring (3033m), the 'Matterhorn' of New Zealand, in January 2005. After an attempt the previous spring, James climbed 24 Hour Party People (ED2), a direct line on the South Face with Kevin Neal and Ollie Metherell involving thin icy mixed up to Scottish VII and bold climbing on 'weetabix rock'. These climbs were remarkable achievements for a visiting climber and represent the most important alpine ascents by a British mountaineer in the Southern Alps in modern times.

After flirting with becoming a guide he returned to his first career as a primary school teacher, here he was outstanding: his enthusiastic and robust style making admirers out of doubters providing the children of his school with a solid anchor point in an often insecure world. Like many he loved the work and hated the paper work and the hills provided a welcome break.

With his wife, Tanya, whom he met when he was 18, and two young boys, Finlay and Ruben, James was very much a family man and greatly enjoyed taking them to the hills and wild places, from family hillwalking to going new routing with Finlay on Mull and visiting a new island each year. Keen to expose the boys to different cultures he and Tanya took them on epic cycling holidays in Europe that would have been challenging without children. Combining that with an active climbing life requires compromise and having climbed some of the longest and most remote routes in Scotland he applied his inherent enthusiasm to shorter days and took a great pride in producing such easy access high quality winter routes as 'Once were Alpinists' (II,6) and 'Now winter bouldering' (III,6). In summer, taking advantage of its proximity, he became a devotee of Moy rock, sadly he will never now be able to complete his personal battle with the last three moves of 'Little Teaser' but may remain the airtime record holder.

A member of Dundonnell Mountain Rescue Team his irreverent sense of humour, indomitable spirit and extensive technical knowledge made him a good man to have around on long and often miserable days or nights. In that role he is greatly missed.

The breadth of James's character and his influence on others was illustrated by the spread of groups that attended his funeral, family, teachers, pupils, mountain rescue teams, guides, climbers and friends. One story summed him up, he met a family looking to buy a child's bike, they were appalled by the cost, within an hour or so he had befriended them, identified a suitable bike and located one on gumtree.

A man who would not knowingly walk past on the other side, he is a loss to us all and in particular to Tanya and the boys.

Roger Webb and Simon Richardson

DES RUBENS j. 1979

ONE EARLY MORNING IN 1972 drivers going north across the Forth Road Bridge must have been a little bemused to see a banner slung between the piers high above them proclaiming 'FOR SALE'. An intrepid band of Edinburgh students, including Ken MacDonald, George Gibson and Des Rubens had climbed to the top of the piers either side of the road under cover of darkness and then abseiled down and fixed the banner 20m below the walkway. They made their news splash for the students' charities week, but needless to say the police were not amused!

In July 2016 drivers going along the busy Great Junction Street in Leith may have been equally bemused to pass a peloton of brightly coloured cyclists following a wicker coffin lying on a wheeled frame attached to a cycle tandem. This time the police were in escort for Des Rubens' funeral cortege. For over 30 years Des had been a teacher of outdoor activities at Craigroyston Community High School in north Edinburgh. The school's ethos, under inspiring head Hugh Mackenzie, had been to open up as many opportunities as possible for children from a very deprived area. It was a testament to Des's huge contribution to this mission that so many tributes poured in from the community when his sudden death was announced. Within hours there were hundreds of messages on Facebook with comments such as 'Mr Rubens was the best teacher I ever had'. In the forty-four years between these two dates my best friend Des lived out his many-faceted mountaineering life.

Des was born in Perth and brought up in Carnoustie. He was educated at Dundee High School where he excelled at running. Around age 15 he was the second fastest 400m runner in Scotland, beaten only by David Jenkins (who later went on to gain an Olympic medal).

Des began climbing when he entered Edinburgh University in 1970. It was within the university mountaineering club (EUMC) that he made many of the friends, including his wife Jane, who stayed close to him for life. In the 1970s we often found ourselves climbing, not on beautiful warm sun-baked rock (a rare treat in Scotland!), but on wet, slimy, vegetated rock in hideous weather conditions. It was all part of the fun, and our 'Vile Rock' escapades were a counterpoint to the 'Hard Rock' trendsetters like Cuthbertson and Hamilton. Our first climb together was in Arran with David Geddes, on an unfinished route on Beinn Tarsuinn (Brobdignag) that had been twice attempted by our friends Ian Rowe, Sandy Trees and George Gibson. It involved almost vertical grass and loose rock as well as some technically difficult and absorbing moves on good rock. But though we added some new sections we too were unable to complete the route; we had to escape by squirming through a hole in a chimney to one side. Naturally the day ended in a long descent in the dark, precursor of many such days and nights to come.

A couple of years later, after an EUMC Dinner, Des, George and I made a memorable ascent of Shadbolt's Chimney, a particularly vile and vegetated route in Glencoe, which is probably rarely repeated since its first ascent in 1908. We had somehow obtained a barrel of beer left over from the Dinner and after a soaking ascent of Clachaig Gully and an evening in the pub had repaired to the Dray (the tiny hut in Glencoe built by the Edinburgh Squirrels in the 1960s). On the Sunday the weather continued absolutely foul and we spent all morning pretending to want to go climbing. The game was to score points by making absurd climbing proposals which the others would be too 'feart' to agree to, thus establishing one's own greater commitment. Finally we ventured out in the mid-afternoon, in clothes still saturated from the day before, and climbed this deep chimney filled with loathsome green slime and tottering blocks, while the weather threw hail and even snow at us (Scotland in May!) Coming back we just waded the river, too wet to bother with a bridge.

Another time we went to Ben Nevis in October, to climb Slav Route and thus emulate our hero, W.H. Murray who had written of the same climb that 'it passes my understanding how it is possible for October rain water on Nevis to be so cold and remain liquid'. In those days we had not joined the SMC, and so we were camping in the Allt a' Mhuilinn where Des, as was his custom, prepared a fine haggis for our tea after a suitably soaking ascent of the climb. On the Sunday Des excelled himself climbing a horrible wet groove on Left-Hand Route which I could barely follow. On the North Face of Aonach Dubh, Fingal's Chimney was only conquered thanks to a superlative performance by Des on greasy, cold rock, and Deep Gash Gully, with its remarkable 'mud finishing hold', provided a further masochistic exercise in appalling weather.

But it wasn't all 'vile rock'. Particularly in winter Des was in his element. He did magnificent leads on the Central Chimney of The Brack and on Bidean's Diamond Buttress. On each of these the ice was so steep that he took a slight fall but immediately recovered and demolished the difficulties with astonishing speed and skill. On perfect winter days we did fine climbs like Cumming-Crofton on Beinn a' Bhuird, and new routes on Foinaven and Liathach. With his powerful chest and bold approach Des was a natural ice climber. In later years he enthusiastically adopted more modern ice techniques and took many 'ice-cragging' holidays in Norway and the Alps.

In 1972 Des took part in his first Asian climbing expedition, exploring the Bashgal valley in Afghanistan on a trip organised by Ian Rowe. Typically he took advantage of the opportunity to visit the famous Buddhist statues at Bamiyan that have now been destroyed by the Taliban. Three years later, five of us drove overland to Pakistan and climbed in the Thui range. Des was the first to reach our highest point (6400m unclimbed subsidiary top of Thui I) and several other peaks.The fascination of the travel through so many countries and the exploration of unknown mountain country was so thrilling that all of us became more or less hooked on expeditioning. In 1977 Des and I enjoyed a solitary fortnight trekking in the mountains of Kashmir before joining Rob Collister for an expedition to Zanskar, which had only recently been opened to foreigners. It was our first experience of the Buddhist Himalaya and we were all affected, but apart from our moderate successes on two new peaks Des's abiding memory was of the iron rations imposed by Rob's austere regime - food was always very important for Des! After a return trip to Zanskar thirty-five years later Des wrote movingly (in the Alpine Journal and the Scottish Mountaineer) of these two expeditions and the changes wrought in the area over these years.

Des and I had a trip with Dick Isherwood in 1980 to the then largely unexplored Charakusa glacier, involving an exciting five day failure on K7 west and a satisfying success on Drifika (6447m), and culminating in our arrest for unauthorised wanderings beyond the 'inner line'. Des's loyal unflappability was ideal for both unplanned bivouacs and unexpected arrests. Then in 1985 we organised a more ambitious expedition, to attempt a new line on Gasherbrum III (7952m) which had only had one previous ascent. In company with Clive

Rowland and Paul Nunn we enjoyed the unparalleled marvels of the trek up the Baltoro, and joined a crowded Gasherbrum base camp. But we were soon on our own, penetrating a dangerous icefall that had been climbed only once in 1958 by the legendary Italians Cassin, Bonatti and their team. Unfortunately Des suffered a painful tooth abscess, but he recovered sufficiently to plough up to about 7500m with me before we were defeated. Des suffered frostbite and had to be extremely careful to avoid infection on the long walk out (Balti villages not being known for cleanliness); eventually he lost only a part of one toe, leaving an unsightly stump which did not affect his climbing but served to repel his small children at bedtime.

The 1988 SMC Centenary expedition to Shiwakte on the eastern flank of the Kongur range was an enjoyable trip for Des, again as much for the adventures in unfamiliar cultures (yurts and camels) as for the climbing in totally unexplored terrain. His account of the trip in SMCJ 1990 is worth re-reading.In 1992 he reached 7500m on Nanga Parbat with Aly Kellas before altitude and weather took their toll.

Apart from Asia Des enjoyed many successful climbing trips to Canada, USA, Peru and the Caucasus, as well as the Alps. Following his retirement we had a succession of splendid Alpine holidays. Knowing each other so well and enjoying the same approach to mountaineering, it was a constant pleasure to be in his company.

Des had a fabulous sense of humour. One aspect was his kindly exaggerated introductions to speakers at the Eastern District meetings – 'we are enormously honoured to have Murdo MacTavish with us, he has made a huge sacrifice to share his extraordinary experiences in far-flung lands etc etc'. Another was his love of pretending that England and its people were a faraway place of which we know little. George Gibson and Des became friendly with Ben Humble in Ben's later years; Des loved to chuckle at reminiscences of Ben's eccentricities, and was particularly fond of Bill Murray's story about the 'Humble kipper'. His enjoyment of favourites like Miles Kington's 'Middle Laners', or Iain Smart's 'Rounding Cape Horn' was so infectious that it enlivened our journeys together. On our many travels there was always an inexhaustible banter. In recent years much of it concentrated on Munros, Corbetts, Grahams etc, prompted in part by the sterling efforts of our good friend Dave Broadhead, the Clerk of the List. We would come up with ever more bizarre suggestions for mountain records and feats. By contrast Des's own Munro collection proceeded at a very leisurely pace. He had only four left to do, one of which, An Socach, was my last one. We had an idea of finishing together, but I always told him there was no hurry. Interestingly, a few years ago while we were enjoying John Hay's wonderful hospitality at Loch Mullardoch, where Des had Beinn Fhionnlaidh still to do and I had to tick Mullach na Dheiragan, Des revealed that in his early hill-walking days he had traversed from Sgurr nan Ceathreamhnan to Mam Sodhail, and had passed within a few metres of An Socach but in his teenage naivety had not bothered with the summit (or was this the wisdom of unmaterialist youth?).

Des had an immensely comforting physical presence. His great bear hugs were loved by child and adult, man and woman alike. They were the utterly natural outflow of his affection for his friends. His warmth was physical too as well as emotional. Many's a time he would be sweating in a tee shirt while I was struggling with three or four layers. Sometimes I would just put out my hands to enjoy the warmth radiating from him as one might from a fire!

He also had a certain lack of self-consciousness that only made him more lovable to his friends. Whether it was his gallus sunglasses in the Alps, his baseball cap in America or his shalwar kameez in India, he just kept us amused by the way he carried it off with no thought or care of how others saw him. His approach to food had some parallels too. He would be quite capable of finishing off a communal packet of biscuits over a brew without even being aware of the regular back and forth of his hand from packet to mouth, all the while providing genial company. His commitment to vegetarianism was rarely able to withstand the attractions of salami when in the company of carnivore friends such as Stan Pearson or Steve Kennedy. These last were his companions in ski touring and (more recently) big wall climbing – fields of adventure where I did not participate but Des's enthusiasm carried him forward.

How impossible it is to sum up a human being in a few words. Everyone who knew him will have their own Des. For me what stands out are his warm-heartedness, humour, patience, good-natured guilelessness. I never saw Des flare up in anger; he was so rarely even grumpy that on the rare occasions when he became slightly tetchy it was so out of character that it was hard to take him seriously.

It is fitting to recall his pride at serving as the Club's President, a duty he carried out with both modesty and skill. His sterling work in reviving the fortunes of the Eastern District deserves mention too. By moving the lectures to a much more suitable location in Princes Street, by combining forces with the JMCS and AC, and most importantly by putting much thought into selection of good speakers and enthusiastically promoting them he breathed new life into a dormant aspect of club activities, and inspired the Northern District to follow his example.

On 28 June 2016 we left the Oberaarjoch hut on a perfect morning, crossed an easy glacier bowl and climbed a very loose rib to gain the south-east ridge of the Finsteraarhorn. There was not a soul about, the air was still, the sun shone from a cloudless sky and on all sides the snow-clad Alps stood forth silently. We were on an easy section of ridge when suddenly I turned around to see Des fall 400m to the glacier on our right. I can only assume that a loose rock gave way and caused him to overbalance – he was carrying quite a heavy sack. The traumatic sequel is hard to relate; one minute my closest friend was a few metres behind me, the next minute he had passed to another world, though it took many more hours before my mind would accept this. I will miss him intensely for the rest of my days.

Geoff Cohen

Dave Broadhead writes: Saturday 16 October 1971. Edinburgh University Mountaineering Club Freshers Meet, Glencoe. 'Hello, my name's Des. Would you like to do North Face Route?' So began a lasting friendship and a wonderful climbing partnership, tragically cut short almost 45 years later. This was also my first real rock climb and although the meet report noted tersely that we 'battled our way up' the route, thanks to Des I look back on this as the first of many great adventures together. Thanks to his good judgment and determination, we finished the climb, despite terrible weather. Thanks to his patience there was no grumbling when I had to reverse and re-climb a couple of pitches because I forgot to pick up the shared rucksac. Thanks to his good rope-management I only dangled ignominiously a few times when my feet slipped off wet holds and thanks to his route finding skills we managed to climb down Curved Ridge, having reluctantly given up trying to reach the summit of the Buachaille.

That same weekend Des also met Jane Sokolic, an American exchange student

from St Louis who 15 months later became Mrs Rubens. Active in the EUMC we all became good friends though Des and I only managed a few climbs together over the next 4 years, all memorable in different ways. A fantastic round of the Beinn Dearg range in early January, my first taste of the NW Highlands; Parallel Gully A on Lochnagar, my first proper ice climb; a spring ascent of The Chasm in Glencoe with gaping bergshrunds below each pitch; backing off The Sutor at St Abbs Head after riding there and back on his Honda 50 moped despite petrol rationing in the 'three-day week' crisis.

During these years we developed our climbing skills and experience with other partners until the 1975 EU Hindu Raj Expedition brought us together for three months and introduced us to Geoff Cohen, a lecturer at the University who shared our enthusiasm, spirit of adventure and sense of fun. On our return from Pakistan, Des and I both did teacher training at Moray House College and with the freedom afforded by school holidays, our climbing together suddenly flourished. New Years in bothies or cottages with ex-EUMC friends, Easter and October depending on weather and conditions, longer trips in the summer and as many weekends as we could manage in-between.

In July 1978 we drove out to the Alps, climbing in the Bregaglia before moving to the Ortler where Jane and my then partner, Anne Macintyre joined us. To begin with our objectives and achievements were modest but we were starting to get more enjoyment out of being in bigger mountains and more confident and better organised with our climbing. These overseas trips were always more than just climbing, with the added bonus of seeing new places, experiencing different cultures, meeting new people and eating different food. Returning from one of our Alpine trips we visited his Auntie Margaret, who lived in Argenteuil near Paris. Des had not seen her for over 20 years and it took a long time to find the house but we received a fantastic welcome and sat down to an enormous meal before bed. Next morning, after a short walk around town we were fed another huge meal before continuing on our way to the Channel ferry. We returned to the Alps in 1982 with improved skills and ambitions, culminating in an ascent of the magnificent Walker Spur on the Grandes Jorasses, climbing the top part of the route plastered in fresh snow, conditions which Des relished. Next on our list was Route Major on the Brenva Face of Mont Blanc. Unfortunately, the weather was against us and we did the Frontier Ridge of Mont Maudit instead. The guardian of the Trident hut recognised Des immediately as he had stayed there three years before and soloed the Old Brenva!

Des regularly accompanied Jane on visits to her family back in St Louis and in 1981 suggested combining this with a climbing trip. We met up in Boulder, Colorado and climbed every day for 30 days, wearing the ends off our fingers in the process. Our fantastic tour of several major rock-climbing areas with Dick Williams and Dick DuMais, two well-known US climbers, all happened thanks to Des's networking skills. After experiencing 'the land of the free' it seemed natural to look behind the 'Iron Curtain', so in 1984 we applied to join an 'International Mountaineering Camp' in the Russian Caucasus, part of the demonised Soviet Union. This stands out as the most enjoyable and most successful trip we ever did together, in terms of the quality of the climbing and the friendliness of the people we met, even though Des did get a telling off one afternoon in Moscow's Gorky Park for putting his feet up on a park bench. Our ascent of the North Peak of Ushba, the so called 'Matterhorn of the Caucasus' was possibly only the second British ascent since the first in 1888 by John Garford Cockin and his Swiss guide Ulrich Almer.

In 1979 Des moved from teaching Physics into outdoor education, to which he devoted the rest of his career until his retirement in 2011. At that time Lothian Region were rolling this out in all their secondary schools and many teachers with an interest in the outdoors leaped at the chance to do what was considered a dream job. Des soon moved back to Craigroyston High School where he had started teaching and where he seemed to relish the challenges presented by youngsters from the notorious housing schemes in the north of the city, many from very deprived backgrounds. Significantly, after years of cutbacks and economies, Des was the last such teacher in the city, as outdoor education was gradually cut to extinction. From the stories he told over the years I have no doubt that Des did a remarkable job, demanding all his considerable patience, good humour and understanding, to the benefit of a large number of young people.

Family responsibilities increased in 1986 with the birth of Andrew, followed a few years later by Catriona but fatherhood did not diminish Des's enthusiasm for climbing. We met up again in California in the summer of 1989 to climb in the Sierras, the high point of which, literally, was an ascent of the Keeler Needle, finishing on the summit of Mount Whitney. This was our last overseas adventure together but we still managed plenty of short climbing trips closer to home. In August 1994 we enjoyed six active days in Northern Ireland, helped once again by Des's network of contacts and the following summer had three brilliant days on Beinn a' Bhuird, camping high in the Garbh Choire. In 2005 Des and I were both honoured to be Vice-Presidents of the Club, so looking for something useful to do we decided to attend our first Easter Meet in Dundonnell. Over the years the average age on this event seemed to be going up and numbers going down, so we were welcomed with open arms and nicknamed 'the teenagers'. We had such a great time that we also became regulars and encouraged an infusion of younger blood into what is now a popular gathering once again.

In his early climbing days Des was notorious for his rather basic gear and could give the impression of being a bit disorganised. His favoured winter attire was a donkey jacket and woollen balaclava, relying on the old red one-inch OS maps long after metrication and few could manage to pack their rucksac into such an uncomfortable looking shape! One Easter, with darkness fast approaching, he walked in from Achnasheen railway station to meet me at Nest of Fannich bothy. Not realising that his map pre-dated the building of the Loch Fannich dam, he was left wondering where all the water had come from as the long inundated Cabuie Lodge track he was following disappeared into the loch. Stung by accusations of 'gear lag' he eventually realised the benefits and became quick to embrace newer and invariably lighter and more effective equipment. Naturally left-handed, I never ceased to be intrigued by the way he tied his laces!

Through teaching he soon learned that good organisation is the key to staying on the right side of the fine line between success and shambles and as ever, Des used his increasingly effective organisational skills to the benefit of others. He always co-ordinated and booked winter weekends on the Ben for our small group of CIC enthusiasts, latterly emailing a few days beforehand an inventory of gear stashed in the hut loft. In 2005 he instigated an autumn reunion of our ex-EUMC contemporaries at Lagangarbh which was a great success and has been repeated every year since, at various locations. November was the traditional month for Munro bagging which evolved into the annual 'bothy meet', a get together with some of the 'Aberdeen office', usually arranged at the last minute. Ironically, this year Des started the email exchange in June to try and agree a date and venue before he went off overseas again, with four unclimbed Munros remaining. His greatest organisational achievement was in revitalising the Eastern District lecture programme. With a lot of hard work behind the scenes he was able to attract a variety of top class speakers and with his unique blend of relaxed gravitas and good humoured enthusiasm was successful in advertising and introducing them to ever increasing audiences as the JMCS and the Alpine Club also became involved.

When Des and I got together, like all teachers and parents we inevitably talked shop and families, but Des also had a wide range of other interests which made him great company, with a sharp and often self-deprecating sense of humour, especially when sharing a dram or two. When he phoned it was seldom a quick call, particularly if we had not seen each other for a while. Like all teachers in their late 50s, retirement became a popular topic for discussion. Unlike myself, Des was always adamant that he planned to work on past his 60th birthday, so it came as a great surprise when, aged a mere 59 he phoned to say 'Guess what I am doing tomorrow?' The authority having made him an offer he could not refuse, Des embraced the opportunities of retirement with an enthusiasm undiminished after 5 years. Ironically the last time we saw each other was at a fantastic party in

Edinburgh at the end of April 2016, arranged to celebrate Jane's last day at work. Family and friends, we will all miss Des enormously. His friendship enriched my life immeasurably since that fateful day all those years ago. Thanks Des.

IAIN HUGH MURRAY SMART   j. 1951

Iain Smart self-medicating on Menanders Island (1960)

IAIN SMART, AMONGST many other things, was born with a hankering to probe into the boundless expanse of our wild natural world in order to sustain his inner most being and to cultivate his philosophy of life. Over the years he embarked on many unique personal experiences which seeped into his soul and often gave a freaky winsome interpretation to his personal world; to wit, those wandering journeys alone across the blazing fading autumnal glories of the arctic tundra, or trustingly embarking on a hazardous voyage in a small open boat through confused drifting pack ice to attempt to climb what was once considered to be the highest mountain in Greenland, and on lonely heathland sharing companionship with another living creature who too bore the scars of time and up which he passed the night perched in its twisted branches to savour the sleeping world with all around the infinite sky of eternity.

Iain, with other fellow students at Edinburgh University, began to roam and explore his native land in all its aspects. There were episodes too of some uniqueness, such as the time on a past hard winter when while staying at the remote Faindouran bothy in the Cairngorms he became unable to escape on his frostbitten frozen feet and had to be ignominiously carried out to a roadhead for further attention. In later days he went with Tom Weir in pursuit of many home grown pleasures and so it came about that Iain often appeared in Tom's My Month piece in the Scots Magazine as Scotland's foremost foreground. It was also back to his true love at the arctic summer's end when with John Hay in a high-power inflatable they zipped around the intricacies of Scoresby Sund or dwelt quietly in the glory of the fall on remote islands.

In the late Fifties, with his long time friend Malcolm Slesser and others of note on an Anglo-Scottish junket, he made his first expeditionary sally to the Stauning Alps in east Greenland, and from henceforth the boreal bug of the Arctic Riviera had bitten him. Wishing that others should share the clear pristine purity of the aura of peace he began to take Margaret and family to camp and potter on the summer tundra, probing at the idiosyncrasies of terns eggs, gathering musk ox wool for spinning into threads to be made into a stylish society pullover, sketching and reading, digesting the weighty concepts of the thinker Gramsci or the evocative poems of Donnchadh Ban but always to absorb the sparkling atmosphere of the Northland.

His wish to let others enjoy the same delights that the Arctic had given to him led to his role in the founding of the Scottish Arctic Club where at the annual supper topical information could be exchanged and recent pictures of so-called epic deeds be briefly shown, each speaker being limited to six slides at Iain's insistence that the occasion was meant for fraternal chat not personal projection.

Initially his career began as the visiting medical man who sailed in a fishing boat to visit the isolated roadless villages dotted along the east coast of Newfoundland, then he moved to an isolation hospital in the dry interior of British Columbia, before holding an academic job in Vancouver where we first met. However most of his career hinged around the Department of Anatomy in Dundee University where his teaching role involved creating on the old-fashioned blackboard his highly acknowledged and aesthetically pleasing multicoloured and detailed drawings of choice items such as the lesser intestinal convolutions. For a change of scene he entered into the microscopic wonders of peering into, noting and understanding the intricate design and evolution of the unborn bird brain sliced out of slides and how we humans represent a few stages down the line. He had little patience for protracted committee meetings and had evolved a masterful technique for dealing with their boredom: he had created a standard answer suitable to reply to most situations where his opinion was been asked. When he was addressed he could awake from his rewarding reverie of sailing his charter yacht through the Western Isles, piloting his hired aircraft on a tour of the beloved hills, scuba diving to sensible depths at off St Kilda, or swishing stylishly down a groomed ski piste dreaming of the Snow Maiden alias the chalet girl getting dinner ready: snapping awake he willingly provided his stored gem of incomprehensible wisdom that was needed to satisfy his stupefied colleagues.

His pleasure was to claim that in our era we had found a discreet academic niche out of the chill wind. In any other later time we would have been rejected as inadequate material belonging to the scrapheap of over produced studenthood.

In 1965 the students of the neighbouring St Andrews University decided to run an expedition to the Sukkertoppen mountains of west Greenland, and since in those days it was not a requirement to be covered by search and rescue insurance the alternative was to bring along a qualified doctor to administer the appropriate rites, and my friend from those distant Vancouver days Dr Iain Smart fitted the bill. Strange to say, and haloed with luck, his services were never seriously needed except for excess mosquito puncturing on one innocent who believed in arctic sun bronzing on naked flesh, and if there had been more problems then my experience was to show that the standard reply was to "Give the man an aspirin." On the other hand we learnt some of his useful survival points, such as to bring along your own spoon with a hole drilled in the handle and a string attached to tie on and store in the back pocket, an old Slesser tip to prevent starvation induced by ravenous fellow mountaineers intent on scoffing any uneaten dinner scraps from the unfortunate who had mislaid his spoon. He also saved his eyesight by wearing his old fashioned snow goggles while being flown in a beat-up DC3 plodding slowly over the barrier of dazzling pack ice drifting offshore.

Once established in the Sukkertoppen fjords and on our way to scale our first peak we diverted our canoes to a bird colony on a small skerry to pursue his interest in the binary nature of terns' egg sizes but unfortunately there was only a single egg on its ownsome amongst all the nests : the locals had cleared it out for a big feed of omelettes. A brief sentence in the subsequent report described the research undertaken but stated that 'the results were not of statistical significance.' Well, we tried..

One day three of us set out to traverse a long jagged ridge of a hill we called the Gorgon, it was to take twenty one hours on the trot. Initially with wisps of sunlit mist wafting across the wandering erratic approach he rightly displayed little faith in the navigational skills of his companions and pointedly proceeded to erect miniature stone cairns to secure our line of retreat, a useful precaution amongst unknown complexities, if rather unpopular in his native hills. My diary writes of 'a formidable problem, a great sloping slab with an unclimbable edge up to the ridge. In my mind I work out what has to be done, it's the sort of thing one reads about but have never done before. I will have to finger traverse/layback half way up the edge, put in a peg, and do a tension traverse left across the slab weakness towards the sunset…a fine route being worked out in the midnight.. Iain comes up quickly on the ropes, and then leads down a broken dyke, hurling off debris, and disappears up "a chimney" except when I follow it is a finger traverse on an iced slab to a straight pull on a holdless wall which I hardly make without a good rope tug…the night has gone, a quarter moon is rising above the ridges, a solitary first star has appeared..'

This was just one of those days that Iain relished, a bountiful store of memories to be recalled at leisure sitting by the barrel shaped wood burning stove in their old manse of Auchanleish up in Glenshee.

It was there that Iain and Margaret spent many years. When the family was small they abandoned the high terrace house in Dundee that overlooked the extensive green open ground to the rail bridge running across the Tay estuary and took to the remote but friendly peace of the glen. It started as a weekend second house in the country but became a home to be savoured. No matter if it became snowbound or the chill spring winds shrank hopeful flowers trying to show their heads. This was better than the curtailing city life. You could sup your coffee sitting in the sitooterie and watch the woodpeckers hammering at the bird feeder or the red squirrels scampering up the truck to pinch their share. Down below by the birch fringed banks, cut deep by the river Ericht flowing southward, the quiet murmurings of the river drifted up to the house. This bank when snow covered sloped adequately but not excessively and gave a challenging schuss down through a tricky gap in a stone wall, a dubious pastime hardly suitable for a post Hogmanay recovery.

All in all Iain had a good, well fulfilled life such as others might envy and appreciate. A life like that is a worthy ambition.

Phil Gribbon

Phil Todd writes: we'd sailed that morning from Loch Skavaig: Duncan, Iain and myself from Anatomy and Hannah from America. We were checking in with officialdom on Rum.

'What climb do you intend to do?'

Iain muttered the name of a route on Askival.

'You need to have a rope.'

Iain had one round his shoulders.

'Gear?'

I pulled a sparse rack of hexes out of my pack.

'Guide book?'

We didn't have one. It looked like the checklist was going to win until Iain interjected.

'I think if you look at the guide book you'll see my name on the first ascent.'

Of course, when we got to the base of the crag, Iain couldn't remember where the climb went, and the false starts this entailed put us back on the yacht having dinner at midnight. Over post-prandial drams, Iain told the story of the first ascent and how he and Malcolm Slesser were landed surreptitiously on the forbidden isle by fishing boat and spent a fugitive fortnight hiding from gamekeepers by night and climbing by day.

The wind picked up overnight and I was awakened in one of the wee small hours by Iain and Duncan stomping around on the deck and launching the dinghy. They rowed across to a neighbouring boat, knocked on their hull and informed the drowsy inhabitants that either we had moved upwind, or they were dragging their anchor. This revelation seemed to have no immediate consequence, and all went back to bed. When we woke in the morning, however our neighbours had gone.

We cruised the small isles, climbed and were grounded by the tide (along with the ferry) at Eigh, and anchored in the inlet immortalized as 'Camusfearna' in Ring of Bright Water. Iain revealed he had signed on to work in Gavin Maxwell's basking shark fishery. However the venture was defunct before Iain reached its base on Soay.

At the Anatomy Department, Iain cultivated an air of amiable eccentricity. My first impression of him at work was sitting at a drawing board using an eraser which dangled from a daisy chain of elastic bands attached to the ceiling. He mystified his colleagues by his repeated success at winning substantial Medical Research Council grants and publishing in prestigious journals. The secret, according to Iain, in grant work is to declare a modest but achievable goal, while in fact working towards a more ambitious objective. That way you can't fail to deliver, and may surpass expectations.

He applied the same approach to expeditions. My first trip to Greenland with Iain and Slesser was grandly titled: 'The Kaiser Franz Joseph Fjord Expedition'. In fact the objective of the expedition was Peterman Peak, but Iain felt confident we could actually reach the fjord, even if the mountain thwarted us. I recall, on our return voyage, we encountered a midden from a previous expedition whose uneaten marmite jars attested to the presence of both Slesser (the jars) and Smart (the fact they were uneaten). It also highlighted for me the exuberant lack of environmental concern of these early explorers.

On another occasion Iain and I took a side trip to an island where he had once spent the summer with his family. The campsite, complete with driftwood furniture was preserved by the arctic stillness as if abandoned days rather than years before. Traces of Iain seem to litter the lonely coasts of Northeast Greenland. The other thing that stands out in my memory of the return trip is Iain's method of lighting a damp wood fire when primus fuel is plentiful.

The same technique cost me my eyebrows a couple of decades later when he persuaded me to apply it to the wood stove in Tilly Jane Ski Hut on the northeast flank of Mt Hood. We'd rafted the Owyhee in the empty quarter of southeastern Oregon the previous year and seen nobody for a week with the improbable exception of a cowboy who appeared across the river from the hot spring where we were soaking and intermittently plunging into the cold stream. The cowboy was complete with cowboy hat, horse and rifle. I wondered about the cowboy attitude to skinny-dippers, but he seemed oblivious to us as he dismounted, examined the ground in front of his horse, remounted and rode off up a side canyon. Iain said you could expect this sort of thing from time to time when the fabric of space-time developed small tears.

Our objective this year would be the Rogue in the southwest corner of the state, and a couple of evenings later, we lounged at Big Windy Camp laying on sleeping bags spread out on the bench above the entrance to Upper Black Bar Rapid. As the stars wheeled above, and the G&Ts contributed an impressionistic blur to the conversation, Iain reminisced about his early career in Canada.

It was perhaps the same romantic notion that had attracted him to Maxwell's shark fishery which took him as a newly graduated doctor to Newfoundland where sick coastal dwellers would row out to his surgery on an itinerant steamer, address him as 'Doccie boy' and be prescribed pills out of bottles labelled, in Latin, 'medicine for the ague'. Work in a TB sanatorium, an attractive specialty for a mountaineering doctor, took him to British Columbia, but penicillin nipped this promising career in the bud, and Iain found himself in McGill University in Montreal learning the autoradiographic techniques with which C.P. Leblond discovered the function of stem cells, and which Iain later applied at Dundee University to study the embryonic development of the cerebral cortex. By the time the limes ran out for our G&Ts the pauses for reflection and contemplation of the constellations and of the star-gaps caused by the looming trees lengthened until they eventually merged into sleep.

The next night, by contrast, we were joined in luxury's lap at the aptly named Paradise Lodge by Roddie Cameron who had travelled upstream by jet-boat. The lodge is part hotel, part working ranch and the fact that the ranch hands and guests intermingled at dinner appealed to Iain's egalitarian streak. Roddie had been the third man in the tent in Utah when, in a freak accident, a tree was blown down and a branch scythed through the tent impaling Slesser's sleeping bag but missing the man. The three of them had been expedition mates on the Scottish East Greenland Expedition in 1958, and a couple of years later in Sir John Hunt's Greenland Expedition, where Roddie's talents as a raconteur and entertainer were undoubtedly appreciated. At Paradise, he informed the management there would be a concert that night, produced guitars and fiddles, and put on a show.

It was my idea to binge-watch Greek tragedy at the fringe one August. Between performances, we stretched our legs, Iain's long strides leading us up Arthur's Seat, by the Salisbury Crags where he did his first rock climbs, down past his boyhood home, in our minds traversing gas-lit prewar streets, round the castle crag where he was apprehended for illicitly climbing into the castle: this at the time of the Stone of Scone Caper and a heightened sensitivity to student pranks. Trojan Women was our last play and just as it reached its tragic climax in an ancient cubby off the Royal Mile, the tattoo ended and the fireworks went off with a crescendo of noise and light. We took this as a sign of divine approval and joined the crowds heading down the High Street for a pint. Iain pointed out the place where Montrose was hanged.

Bob Aitken writes: (A few words from the chauffeur).
I felt I knew Iain long before I met him, from his own extensive, masterly, and self-revealing writings in the Journal and from the illuminating sketches provided by old comrades such as Tom Weir and Malcolm Slesser – *Red Peak* and *Friends in High Places* offer particularly piquant vignettes. But my contacts with him were limited to pleasant brief encounters at Club functions until about five years ago, when I fell by happy chance into the unofficial role of chauffeur to the Honorary President, collecting Iain from Blair and conveying him to Dinners, Meets and the occasional funeral of SMC worthies. Admiration ripened rapidly into profound affection.

Listening to Iain provided a liberal education as well as a most enjoyable distraction from the longueurs of the A9, though I was always aware of the limitations of my capacity to engage with the full breadth of his erudition and insight. He passed lightly over my intellectual deficiencies, and would focus his discourse on areas where I could share his enthusiasm if not his expertise, such as Scottish literature and poetry. I was pleased to find that our world views converged in key areas: I was, for example, more than happy to accept his argument that our mutual lack of high climbing achievement could readily be attributed to excessive imagination, rather than simply to cowardice and clumsiness. By way of exchange, in defending what he liked to call his 'cultivated obscurity', Iain appreciated a quip I'd picked up forty years ago from a cheerful young Church of Scotland minister in New Zealand: 'Blessed are the meek, for we shall inherit the Earth – if that's all right with the rest of you.' He also enthusiastically adopted one of my own favourite axioms from Thoreau: 'Beware of all enterprises that require new clothes.' He applied that to buttress his dogged reluctance to accept the Polar Medal for his extensive bold explorations and diversified scientific studies in the Arctic, and especially to his unwillingness to undertake the formalities attendant upon a Royal investiture. Despite all that modesty, Iain did quietly enjoy praise for his writing.

We had modest fun out on the hill too. Iain would not let advancing age and infirmity, which he was of course able to explain in full physiological and neurological detail, to inhibit him. It was a pleasantry between us, albeit I think not entirely frivolous for Iain, that as Honorary Members of the Club we were under a particular moral obligation to continue to 'push, attack and foray' within our limits. After one Fort William Dinner I drove him up to the top car park in Glen Nevis in unpromising weather, ostensibly merely to look at the mountains; but Iain tottered rather alarmingly up through the gorge to Steall meadows, where, he confessed, he had never expected to go again. We navigated the bridge to gain tea and cake at the hands of the President in the hut. On the return we had to wait while a young woman wearing a full via ferrata kit tentatively negotiated the bridge in both directions, clipped to the side cables. She dismounted gingerly at the far end and proclaimed to a couple of admiring friends that she'd been waiting for years to do that. Iain was close behind her, ambling over in his wellies.

In similar vein, returning from another Dinner he insisted we take an instant chilly soaking from the wildest excesses of a wet westerly gale to make a visit of inspection to the Drey, just to fill a gap in his knowledge of Glen Coe. In 2015, on the Easter Meet at Inchnadamph, we managed to make the circuit of Stac Polly by dint of my carrying a pair of folding picnic chairs on a pack frame, a practical arrangement that Iain and Margaret had contrived to allow them to continue to take country walks. We stopped often, but fortunately the weather was tolerably kind. From our chairs we admired at our leisure the famous view across Assynt to the north, the peaks, as Iain said, like mighty sandstone battleships ploughing westwards across a Lewisian ocean. His final stop was just inside the fence above the road; neither he nor I were confident that he would manage the last few yards to the tarmac. But after a good rest, he did.

In the spring of last year, after Margaret had died, we made another expedition-with-chairs around the sun-dappled bluebell woods at Kinclaven, an exercise in total immersion in a serene haze of woodland azure. In an article long before, Iain had said that even by moonlight this wood seemed always benign. Most of us mountaineers probably like to think we have a developed appreciation of place and landscape, but Iain had a special capacity for intimate engagement, whether in remotest Greenland or in rural Perthshire.

In his last year Iain was wont to joke that he was now the oldest person he knew. He was a bit miffed at the failure of the key comrades of his youth, Dutton and Slesser, to fulfil their pact to pre-prepare each other's obituaries for the *Journal* – he had checked whether the Editor had anything on file for him. 'Just typical', he grumbled cheerfully. For me he embodied the particular ethos of the SMC and its *Journal* since the 1950s, to which he and his two old friends contributed so much by word and deed: profound passion for mountain country, distinctive wry humour, sardonic and sceptical intellectualism, and concern for the exploration and effective expression of the Club's fourth dimension.

We're very fortunate that as well as our memories of his distinctive rangy figure, cheerfully rugged face, and his shock of white hair, Iain has left us a substantial legacy of extraordinary writing: writing about landscape, and our relationship with landscape, which at its best is as refined, penetrating, and perception-enhancing as anything in the literature of mountaineering, and underpinned by that deliciously quirky independent mind and gentle, quintessentially Scottish, self-mockery.

The old tribute, 'we shall not look upon his like again', was never more entirely apposite.

Robin Campbell writes: Iain[1] Smart was born in Edinburgh on 2 May 1928. His father managed a bamboo plantation in India, and the family came home briefly for Iain's birth, before returning to India. When Iain was five years-old, his mother brought him back to Edinburgh to begin his education. He attended George Watson's Boys College: an institution which, he felt, drove him 'along intellectual tramlines.' His teenage years coincided with the tail end of WW2 and the brief spell of enthusiasm for global socialism that followed, well rendered in some of Iain's stories, especially the excellent An Encounter with Gramsci, in which 'twa wee Edinburry shites' meet Glasgow servicemen celebrating leave at McCook's Cottage with Sten guns, poached trout and venison, and revolutionary discourse.[2]

Iain studied medicine at Edinburgh University. He met his wife Margaret

---

[1] registered as 'Ian'.

[2] See *The Big Eye of Summer*, (Papyngay Press, 2004).

Iain at Whitewell (2015)

Kennedy there, and they both moved to Canada after graduation, and married there in 1953. In Canada he worked as a doctor in Newfoundland and Kamloops before switching to University work at UBC in Vancouver and then McGill University in Montreal. Their three daughters Robin, Lesley and Jinty were all born in Canada. In 1960 Iain returned to Scotland to a post in the Anatomy department at Dundee University, living in town and in an imposing but challenging house in Glenshee – Auchenleish. Although he took early retirement from Dundee in the early '80s, he continued to work there, and with a research group at the Université de Lyon, on a part-time basis until around 2000. His academic work was focused on the anatomy of the mouse brain and its development, with occasional detours into avian biology and archaeology. His last scientific paper in 2007 – in typical Iain fashion – gave his academic address as the Neurology Centre, Bridge of Cally, Blairgowrie.

Iain was one of the post-War generation of climbers who went to Edinburgh University and established the climbing club there. Included in this group were his close friends Geoff Dutton, and Malcolm Slesser – all three distinguished scientists, mountaineers, and members of our Club – despite involving themselves at least as cheerleaders in the firing of postboxes bearing the legend 'E II R', deemed to be insulting to Scotland, that went on at that time. For Iain was an enthusiastic republican and nationalist throughout his life. You may easily imagine his embarrassment and discomfiture when Her Majesty awarded him a Polar Medal for Arctic exploration in 2015. Besides feeling that he did not merit such an Honour, he could not countenance an obedient visit to Buckingham Palace to receive it, and so it was delivered into his hands at the bottom of his stairs in Blairgowrie by Royal Mail. Iain then mischievously tried to use his Medal as a lever to prise out belated recognition for William Speirs Bruce's Scottish National Antarctic Expedition of 1902.

Iain's exploratory climbing was very much a form of escape. He had no interest in technical prowess on rock and ice, but soon mastered all the necessary crafts of mountain travel – bush-whacking, camping, ski-ing, canoeing and sailing, sledge-hauling – and used these skills to get himself to places where Nature held the upper hand. Although his abiding love was for Scotland, he had a long adulterous affair with Greenland, beginning in 1958 with the first Staunings Expedition. He told me he had made 19 visits to that mountainous coast. On many of these visits he was content with one or no companion, and often carried out the scientific duties required of all well-funded expeditions, such as the many weeks spent on Menanders Island in Kong Oscars Fjord measuring the volume and shape of tern's eggs with Tom Weir.

Iain's involvement with the management of the Club began with work for the Journal around 1971. For many years he was responsible for the 'Miscellaneous Notes' section, and other small print sections, including the Keeping of the List of what he called 'Clan Munro' until Bill Brooker took a firmer grip of this. Like insufficiently many others, he took a poor view of the repeated attempts by the 'testosterone-poisoned' to introduce women to membership, and at the 1989 Dinner at Nethy Bridge after the fateful vote, he amused me by making a tape of the last all-male rendering of the Club Song. Unfortunately, he spoiled this valuable relic by recording an episode of 'Piping Times' on top of most of it, so that only one Chorus survives. He became our President in 1990, replacing the pre-Dinner slide lectures with Symposia dealing with weighty matters such as Access to Mountains and the Philosophy of Sport Climbing. One of his after-dinner Presidential speeches introduced the bemused members to Iain's heroes: Genghiz Khan, J.R.R. Tolkien, and the Latin poet Horace, whose Odes he was particularly fond of quoting. In 2012, he became our Honorary President and – no doubt for the best of reasons – persuaded the Club to rotate this post and the Honorary Vice-Presidents periodically, thus burdening our Treasurer with extra costs and our Secretary with extra administration. Besides these official duties, Iain was a strong supporter of the Club's Meets, and he was one of the many stalwarts whose regular attendance helped keep going the fragile unofficial Skye Meet which I revived around 1990.

Iain died in Blairgowrie on 24 December last year, after a short period of illness. With his passing, the Club has lost a very distinctive voice, a voice that spoke consistently on behalf of our wild and romantic fringes, geographical and political. According to Iain's daughter Jinty, it was a romantic poem by Ratcliffe Barnett – minister for many years at Greenbank Church in Morningside – that first stimulated his interest in getting away to the wild and mountainous West. It is too long to quote in full, but the last verse gives its flavour well, and the student of Iain's works and words will detect many affinities, perhaps even a fingerpost that directed his life:

So I leave the Highland highway, and I hoist the brown sail
For the summer isles of Tir-nan-og, from Barra to Kintail
And there upon the snow-white sands and machars of the West
I seek and find the lost things – the things that I love best.

Obituaries for Miles Hutchinson, Drew Somerville and Stan Thompson will appear in 2018.

PROCEEDINGS OF THE CLUB

At the committee meeting in October 2016 the following mountaineers were admtted to the Club. We warmly welcome:

GEOFFREY ASHTON (71)
JEFFREY BANKS (69)
HANNAH R. GIBBS (29)
AMY GOODILL (33)
CYNTHIA M. GRINDLEY (67)
KEVIN HALL (28)
ANDREW J. HOWISON (46)
MARTIN K. MCKENNA (26)
HENRY W. O'BRIEN (26)
JOHANNES PATERSON (35)
ADAM RUSSELL (28)
EMILY WARD (29

And at the April meeting in 2017:

PETER S. DAVIES (33)
ALASDAIR FULTON (33)
PETER HERD (23)
Donald M. ORR (67)
ALEX REID (27)
ELSIE RILEY (37)
JEREMY WINDSOR (45)

The One-Hundred-and-Twenty-Eighth AGM and Dinner

3 December 2016

After our venture to the east in 2015, the Club were back at the Ben Nevis Hotel in Fort William for our 128th AGM and Dinner. Despite the favourable bright and dry weather, the afternoon talk by Martin Moran was well supported and provided an inspiration to all those that consider the over sixties might be easing off in the grade that they climb at.

The AGM was business-like and informative for the members. The secretary did make a plea for members to consider if they could fill any of the vacant positions and provide help with the work load. Currently many club officials are taking on more than their original remit.

We were informed that the MC of S has changed it's name to Mountaineering Scotland and our representative noted that there did seem to be a high percentage of expenditure on Sport Climbing. The club was informed that there are plans for more national parks to be created. Concerns expressed included questioning of the true benefit of multitudes of National Parks.

For many years the SMC Journal has contained the Accident Reports. However more recently obtaining the details from the Police has proved difficult. The Journal Editor had contacted the Police at an appropriate level to explain our interest and requirement for the data. He awaits a reply.

Possible changes to the method of booking for the Dinner were discussed. The existing system of sending a cheque and receiving a ticket as a receipt, may be becoming outdated in this digital age. Other options were mentioned and views canvassed at the AGM and later in the bar. The Dinner secretary did note that a few members did say they liked to keep the ticket from each Dinner.

At the Dinner the hotel wined and dined us with the usual high standard of service and food we have become accustomed to. Club President, Noel Williams gave a brief summary of the highlights from the year and also extended his thanks on behalf of the Club to Tom Prentice who after 18 years in role of Publications Manager has now given notice that he would like to handover the reins. During this time the climbing guides have continued to set the high standard that all other publishers aspire to.

Our guest speaker, Stuart Pedlar, was an inspired choice. Stuart already has a successful career as a Musical Director for stage shows, but over the last few years he has undertaken a very fruitful search for historical information concerning the early exploration of the Cullin of Skye. The actual speech was a Tour de Force – almost a performance in itself. Stuart related his early puzzle of what could have happened to the Sligachan Hotel visitors and climbs book. Its existence had been referred to in articles, including some in the SMCJ. However its current whereabouts was unknown. His diligence took him to the Skye Museum where to his amazement and delight, a typed copy was found in storage. Then further searches turned up the original in Sconser. These papers date back to the late 1800s and record routes up until 1970.

The start of the President's Walk, Glen Nevis. Photo:Chris Huntley.

On Sunday the newly appointment President, Simon Richardson, proposed a scrambling ascent of Meall Cumhann from Glen Nevis. The popularity of the outing meant we almost filled the road head car park. With quite a number of club

On the President's Walk: perhaps a little more difficult than usual?

Photo:
Chris Huntley.

guests joining us. Simon ensured all went smoothly by placing a rope on certain short exposed sections. The route up, skirted a mean looking rock crevasse which we all peered down but none ventured into, despite a solid looking abseil metal stake already in position. Within a few hours we were all at the top and could enjoy a rather sociable lunch stop.

Chris Huntley

Lakes Meet, Robertson Lamb Hut, Langdale

2–4 September 2016

It is rumoured (translation : it was on the SMC Facebook page) that upon seeing reports of last year's SMC Lakes Meet in Langdale, a certain ex-president sped down to the lakes to climb a particular climb. Questions were asked through the book of face – 'what is that climb?' It was

The Jean Genie lives on his back
The Jean Genie loves chimney stacks
 He's outrageous, he screams and he bawls…
Jean Jeanie; VS 4c; Trowbarrow; South Lakes Limestone.

The great man died earlier in 2016 (David Bowie that is, not the ex-president). So it provided added reason to squeeze in this visit. The Main Wall at Trowbarrow stands as an affectionate, off-the-wall tribute. But, perhaps more important to this

*Duncan Reid
(CAF) on Jean
Jeanie (VS 4c)
Trowbarrow,
South Lakes
Limestone.*

Photo: Bob Reid.

visit, it also dries exceptionally fast. A more entertaining entrée to the weekend could not have been imagined, with several teams visiting on the Friday night, climbing said *Jean Jeanie* before pub closing time. The gentle breeze off Morecambe Bay and soft South Lakes light were memorable. Other routes including *Harijan*, *Coral Sea* and *Jomo* were climbed – leaving the rest of the album (Cracked Actor, Major Tom, Aladdin Sane et al) for future meets.

Despite the unfavourable weather outlook our group of SMC Members had gathered at the excellent Wayfarers Robertson Lamb Hut in upper Langdale on the first weekend of September. We came from far and wide – including a couple of meet guests who were CAF members.

Saturday was definitely a day for Wainwright bagging though the hutzpah shown by Brian Shackleton and Chris Ravey attempting *Crescent Climb* on Pavey Ark in a downpour has to be noted. They enjoyed some great abseiling practice.

The new Lakes bumper fun book* came into its own directing much activity toward a nearby 'dries fast after rain' location – namely Black Crag and its near neighbour Long Scar. Members climbed three or four routes here and the aforementioned intrepid pairing of Brian Shackleton and Chris Ravey (fresh from Alpine efforts) managed six routes between them! Other members chased Wainwrights.

The numbers are going up. The meet is proving popular. Do join in.

Members: Dave Broadhead, Ian Crofton, Simon Fraser, Lisa Hutchison, Pat Ingham, Andrew James, Chris Ravey, Bob Reid, and Brian Shackleton.
Guests: Guillaume Breuil (CAF), Duncan Reid (CAF), and Nick Walmsley.

Bob Reid

* Lake District Rock – by FRCC Guidebook Team, 10 Jun 2015, Paperback – Part of the WIRED series of guides designed to have your climb also available on a smart phone. Will it catch on? The Publications Committee are working on our own Scottish version of this Wired Guide.

Rjukan

16–20 February 2017

A successful Meet, despite the weather causing problems: often warm and damp at times with little falling snow. The lack of early snow in the Vemork Gorge especially, made access to the many popular routes more difficult this year. Although the river was sufficiently frozen, enormous blocks of rock in the gorge made travel to the ice routes quite awkward. Certain routes were suspect with melting ice, and there were some retreats due to dangerous conditions.

However, the 'Saboteurs' were not put off, and despite some lost 'effective' days due to conditions, very few team members complained, and as always, made good decisions as to locations. Where access was less problematic and better conditions prevailed, sometimes softer, more 'wet' ice would result in excellent climbing. The afternoon sun also caused some anxiety, with several large rockfalls from popular routes. Climbers had to be prudent.

However this paints a poor picture, but with experience, skills, good decision-making and some adventurous attitudes, many of the twenty-six member team were very satisfied with the climbing, and came home pleased. Others headed for the Gausterblikk Ski Centre and were equally happy.

The team included 14 CC members, 4 FRCC members, 5 were AC or AC aspirants, and 3 were AAC members. The numbers don't add up to the 27 Meet members, as many were in two, or even 3 mountaineering Clubs. We were delighted to have a visiting DAV team, including my brother Pete (also DAV), joining the Meet. The German climbers, all living east of Stuttgart, were all friends and members of the celebrated German Alpine Club.

After various uneventful short-term flights from several UK airports, and a flight from Stuttgart, all to Oslo Gardermoen, we were all soon ensconced in (often uprated) hire cars and off across the surprisingly lightly snow-clad countryside to Rjukan. Conditions did seem fairly dry, with little snow around, and although giving quite easy driving for a change, scenes of less than usual ice on the approach roads gave uneasy thoughts.

Richard Jolley after the difficult start to Top Hat. Photo: Smiler Cuthbertson.

Richard Jolley on Kong Bore at Kong Vinter. Photo: Smiler Cuthbertson.

Once again we enjoyed the much improved hostel facilities provided by the Gjestegård staff and Torbjørn, who after organising everything so well slipped on ice in the town and broke a leg! Peri organised a get-well card, signed by everyone on the Meet and this was delivered to Torbjørn in his hospital bed. We trust he has made a full recovery. That's two Meets in a row he has had the same incident (next visit we must take him some non-slip shoe grips)!

In spite of early arrival concerns in the warmer conditions, team members often found adequate or near-perfect conditions (softer or more plastic ice). However, higher climbing regions provided rock-hard ice with winds that kept days cool.

The Mountain crag referred to as Gaustatoppfossene was visited on several days by various teams of 'Saboteurs'. The lure of colder conditions and better ice did persuade teams to this higher crag, but in reality the wind and often inclement weather, the rock-hard ice, and some alpine-style belays being required, made it an arduous destination for most. The Germans and Pete, however, breezed up everything.

There were days when the temperature had risen overnight, giving some routes a 'wet' nature, but conversely, temperatures often dropped overnight and this only enhanced the moods of team members in searching for good routes.

The Vemork Bridge routes surprised a couple of teams, one pair (Richard and Smiler) topping out on Vemorkbrufoss Est (WI5) just twenty minutes before a deluge of water engulfed the line. It is still an unexplained occurrence, this spasmodic releasing of water from tanks above the gorge and down certain routes. The well-known (regular?) releasing over the famous and much sought-after route, Rjukanfossen (WI4), in the Upper Gorge, didn't occur (or wasn't seen to?) for some reason, although this area did produce several unfortunately warm and wet (route) days. Most routes climbed in this Upper Gorge area were manageable though, with care.

Conditions in the Rjukan Gorge as a whole were more difficult than usual due the lack of snow, resulting in much time-consuming and awkward scrambling over uncovered boulders (some very large), the lack of snow giving none of the usually easy (and well tracked) level ground.

However, several bold teams ticked off various steep and difficult routes, like Sabotofossen (WI5), Verdons End (WI5, Trappfosse (WI4) and Juvlesayer (WI6), the latter route giving CC members, Robin and Paul, an unpredictably slow climb due to a party above them. This resulted in the only real concern for the Meet organiser and several team members not in their beds at 8p.m. A small team did drive down to the Vemork Bridge car park, but just in time to avoid serious night time searching, while crossing the bridge looking for headtorch lights, the installed rescue (call) system worked and the required mobile call to the hostel relieved the anxiety.

The climbing continued on all of the days available, resulting in good, single and multi-pitch routes, with many teams enjoying short and easy access to popular crags.

Our German guests were very strong, both in their climbing standards and stamina, completing more routes per day than most teams, and usually all of high quality, notably, in the Kongvinter basin, where a trapped rope in the notorious crack caused Richard and Smiler a fair delay, while a climb was done by two of our guests, and the trapped rope released.

Geoff and Brian (both CC) did what they always do, quietly and without fuss, ticking off of several notable routes a day, although Trappfoss, and then Rjukanfossen, proved a distinct problem (too much water on the routes) on one day.

A large contingent of CC and other Club members had a good day on the superb Tjonsonnstadbergfossen (WI4), above the town. Climbing almost as long as it takes to type the route name, Richard and Smiler, in front of Tim and Brian S. picked the more solid direct line.

Helen (AC) and Alex (CC) followed a more vegetated line sometimes to the right of the ice, and when Smiler and Richard past them while abseiling through the trees, Helen and Alex took a wise decision to join the group of team members descending. It was getting very warm, indeed, a substantial fall of ice occurred an hour later, somewhat further to the left of our route.

Several of the independently working teams, were climbing and socialising at various locations, taking slightly less-able climbers or newcomers to Rjukan, into their teams to achieve many wonderful ice climbs, having fun outings as threesomes. Any (so-called) rest days taken, usually turned into strenuous and (for some) less-than skillful days, Langlauf touring and on downhill skis.

Steve and Michael Jenkins had purposely brought their own skiing gear this trip. They had a few great skiing days and good days climbing as well, enjoying both activities. Peri and Astrid climbed well, but were frustrated with the conditions, and also hired skis on some mountain days, often accompanied by Lewis. A notably quiet but effective team, Keith and Kate, worked all week through the Heavy Water guidebook, including many, very successful ascents.

With the warmer conditions, melting had accessed the bottom section of Top (WI5) in the Lower Gorge, causing it to break off, as it regularly does, and gave Richard Jolley a chance to shine with several consecutive dead-hangs on alternate axes until knees came to his assistance. Climbing throughout the Meet with Richard, Meet Leader Smiler was doing pretty well, seconding most routes due to his unfortunate recent health problems, but he opted out of this difficult challenge, and Lewis took up the mantle of repeating and cleaning the few screws from this well known (now WI6) challenge. This difficult exercise was to be one of Lewis's final ice-climbing days with the 'Saboteurs', before heading off into the wastes of Norway with his Ski Club for a further week.

No serious injuries or scares occurred. Thanks must go to my fellow would-be rescuers on a very cold and dark night at the Vemork Bridge rendezvous.

At the hostel, the new annexe being built for us was not ready. This was being provided to avoid any possibility of us destroying the hostel kitchen, so we were again allowed to use the highly superior facilities of that kitchen, and I felt, throughout each evening mealtime, the team held their heads up high and didn't let the Club(s) down.

With the roads clear of snow (although it was coming soon) a more relaxed travel back to Oslo for most members was taken, on the 25th. This followed a morning's (or longer) climbing before returning to the hostel to shower, pack and depart. Richard and Smiler had a rapid 2-hour return trip via Ozzimosis (the superb and steep WI4). Starting out early, they had the crag to themselves for most of the short time there.

All members flying out the next morning, on arrival at the airport, headed for the comfortable doss behind the restaurant opposite Arrivals. An uneventful return flight left most members very satisfied with a great Meet.

Smiler Cuthbertson

Ski Mountaineering Meet, Lagangarbh

18–19 February 2017

Friday 17 February 2017 members from across Scotland converged on the club hut at Lagangarbh for the annual Ski Mountaineering Meet. Ann, Brian and Dave bravely walked up Meall nan Tarmachan(1044m) breaking their journey with a wet ascent. On arriving at Lagangarbh, they found that the drying room was out of commission. An unfortunate finding in view of the wet conditions they had endured that day. The forecast presaged poor weather next morning so discussions continued long into the night.

Next morning David and Ole headed west to Glenfinnan to have a round of the two Munros Sgùrr Thuilm (963m) and Sgùrr nan Coireachan (956m). Hard work in the rain, and the wind did not make it any better. Views were grey and extended 30 metres. They did see patches of snow within 30m from the path but as they had not taken skis along, they by-passed them all. Of their kit, it was safe to say it did not perform well; Gore-Tex® did not breathe! Navigation was easy, simply by following one another, assuming they knew where they were going, or what they were doing, for that matter. Hard fact: 6 hours 49 mins, 22.24km, 2045m total ascent.

Ann, Brian, Chris, Colwyn and Grant climbed the mighty peak Meall na Gucaig (616m). The original plan to traverse the rolling lump from east to west was dumped in favour of a simple out and back approach from Inchree taking in the impressive An Drochaid waterfall.

Amy, Gill, Hamish and Robin opted for the relative comforts of the Kinlochleven climbing wall, returning to Lagangarbh over the Devil's Staircase to give them a taste of the wet conditions underfoot experienced by the other two parties.

On 19 February an intrepid crew did carry skis up onto the northern summit of Buchaille Etive Beag, Stob Coire Raineach (925m) where enough activity was undertaken to be able to say they had been skiing! To celebrate the modest ascent coffee and cake at Glencoe ski centre followed shortly afterwards.

Gill, Hamish and Chris made a sociable and not too cold or wet ascent of Curved Ridge, even resorting to the use of an ice axe on the final 100m snow slope to the summit where the sun was shining!

Starting in Kinlochleven, Grant mountain biked over the Devil's staircase and, immediately opposite the hut, Robin did an ascent of the Corbett, Beinn a' Chrulaiste (857m).

So yet another SMC ski mountaineering meet where the shortage of snow precluded skiing, but not fine hill days out!

Members: Robin Clothier, Amy Goodill, David Crookes, Gill Irvine, Hamish Irvine, Colwyn Jones, Ole Kemi, Ann MacDonald, Stan Pearson, Chris Ravey, Brian Shackleton, Grant Urquart, Anthony Walker.

Colwyn Jones

Skye Winter Meet, Glen Brittle Hut

24–26 February 2017

After the superb weather and conditions of the previous year this meet proved anti-climactic. Roger Robb and Pete Biggar were fortunate in having a good day in a snowy Kintail on the way to the island, but then mild wetness set in. Dave Broadhead and Geoff Cohen were very unlucky in suffering a double puncture near Invergarry which meant being relayed back to Dingwall. For a variety of reasons no one else turned up.

Roger and Pete dodged most of the rain falling on the Cuillin on Saturday by heading north and exploring the Quiraing in sunshine and showers: it was very scenic. The stove and a dram or two made the evening very pleasant.

On Sunday they walked up to Coire Lagan until the rain became so heavy that further progress was deemed unnecessary. Let us hope for better luck next year.

Roger Robb and Pete Biggar looking cheerful despite the downpour on the Skye Winter Meet. Photo: Roger Robb.

PJB

Ski-Mountaineering Meet, Nevache, Hautes-alpes, France

March 2017

Chris Dickinson, Richard Bott and Gavin Swinton joined Anthony Walker for a week's ski-mountaineering/touring based in Nevache at 1620m in the French Southern Alps near Briançon. With the hot dry weather continuing from the previous week, it seemed certain that southern France would have the edge over Scotland in terms of sun-bathing, if not skiing.

On the Sunday we drove to the end of the cleared road above Nevache in the upper Valley of the Clarée, where we were somewhat alarmed by the number of cars whose passengers had clearly made a much earlier start than us. The day's destination was La Grande Manche, a wild and dramatic valley hemmed in by spectacular limestone ridges and towers. The early morning frost gave way to a cloudless sky as we skinned up the summer path through the trees to the open snowfields by the Chardonnet refuge. Then it was first on the left and on up through the well covered boulder fields into the enclosed valley itself. Despite our earlier misgivings, there was not another soul to be seen, the silence being broken only by the swish of skins on fresh snow, and the occasional expletive as balled-up soft snow had to be scraped off. The snow pack varied from solid, in the shade of the rock walls, to hollow sugar in the full sun at the foot of the final 300m ascent. Anthony and Gavin continued on up, undaunted by the soft conditions, and on to much firmer snow as the gully steepened and narrowed, to reach the col at 2823m. A brilliant ski down the 35 degree slopes soon regained the more prudent members of the party, and found Chris sitting by a large test pit of air and sugar. The fine firm snow-pack below with a fresh dusting on top gave good varied skiing down to the harum-scarum path where several unscheduled high-speed excursions into the trees added extra excitement. Chris, meanwhile, missed the path and took another adventurous route straight down through the rocky bluffs to the road. A four star outing in a stunning location.

Monday was a slightly easier day, following 2km of the ski de fond piste towards Les Fonds de Cervieres, south-east of Briançon near the foot of the Col d'Izoard; and then up the pleasantly straightforward ridge to the first summit of the Crete de Dormillouse. This follows the frontier and allows a quick bite with one foot in Italy and the other in France. The descent varied from icy hard-pack with pockets of powder higher up, via sections of agreeable 'moquette' (is there an English word for this?), to bottomless sugar lower down. Avoiding head plants when one plunges suddenly into 18 inches of mush is not easy. And so back along the 2km of track - to Richard's dismay, as he had been overruled on his devious plans to avoid it. Only three-star skiing today, but the excellent Hotel de l'Izoard at Cervieres, which serves good beer and out-of-hours food on a sunny terrace, surely added an extra half-star.

With the hot weather continuing, Tuesday's plan for the ascent of the Pic Blanc de Galibier from the Col du Lautaret had to be abandoned. Even at 8a.m. and at 2000m the snow was too soft on the southern faces, and the north-east facing Col de Laurichard at 2654m seemed a better plan. Chris, Richard and Gavin headed up, with ice axe and crampons coming in handy on the steeper sections while conditions were already softening up near the col. Despite this being a popular area, there was no one around except a high-speed local, who raced up the col and whizzed straight back down with barely time for a 'Bonjour'. Firm snow with icy patches gave a good descent back down to an early pint at the local hostelry at the Col du Lautaret, with splendid views of the Meije (and no skating involved!)

On Wednesday we were joined by John Peden, with Mandy and Jamie Peden as guests. They had arrived late the previous night for a 24-hour break from their chalet-hosting stint in the Three Valleys, and were disappointed to discover that a 6 a.m. start was planned, rather than a cosy lie-in. The day's objective was the tour of the Pointe de Buffere in the upper valley of Nevache. A somewhat strung out party contoured round the base of the rock spire of the Pointe de Buffère, and, with little communication soon became three distinct groups. Chris, Gavin and Richard in the advance group,having noted some avalanche activity higher up, were suspicious of the south gully behind the rock spire, and continued up to the Col de Buffère. From there Gavin and Richard traversed round to the Col du Grand Area, and enjoyed excellent skiing down to the Refuge de Buffère, while Chris took a more direct route. Anthony, meanwhile, disappeared off up the lower part of the south gully, hoping someone would follow. John, Mandy and Jamie had been obliged to make a re-fuelling stop, but rejoined Anthony just as he was beginning to wonder if the whole project had been abandoned. Having decided that the sloughing seen from below was old material from rocks heated by the strong sun, the party continued up steep loose snow and old debris, with Anthony trying a variation on to scree, rock and even worse snow, to reach the flat, commodious and wind-free col at 2652m. The reward was a superbly enjoyable descent down the north facing gully – definitely the pièce de résistance of the week: 400m of delectable fresh snow on a firm base at an entertaining angle. Christened 'Hero's Gully' later by the rest of the party, it was definitely a tour de force (do the French have a word for that too...?) Further down, flat light and soft patches added an extra challenge. All were reunited at the Refuge de Buffère, for a warm welcome and a chilly beer: a fitting finale to a five star outing.

Unfortunately the weather decided that we had had enough superb days out. Rain followed by fresh wet snow pushed up the avalanche risk from 1 or 2 to 4, so Thursday to Sunday saw the group skiing at Montgenèvre and Sansicario (Milky Way) and sight-seeing in Briançon. The few off-piste endeavours varied between good and more-pain-than-pleasure. On Saturday Chris, Gavin and Richard made a snowy and blowy sortie up to the Col d'Izoard, followed by beer and optional tarts at the excellent Refuge Napoleon.

A great week sampling a small part of this fine area was enjoyed by us all, and it is to be hoped that we can return in the near future.

Anthony Walker

Easter Meet, The Corrie Hotel, Isle of Arran

20–23 April 2017

An historic date for a Meet as the SMC have visited the Island sporadically as follows – New Year 1892 Brodick and again in 1922, New Year 1907 Corrie and again in 1950 and 1979 so the longest gap was 38 years until this particular Easter Meet (details thanks to Robin Campbell).

Members and guests all arrived by ferry most to Brodick but the Aberdeenshire and North-west groups disembarked at Lochranza, a windy trip with some lack of visibility over the hills and higher peaks. Plans were made in the evening as we enjoyed staying in a hotel right by the sea with views of Holy Island through the windows.

Friday dawned disappointingly as all the hills were selfishly holding on to the clouds again, a windy day with intermittent showers. Some members got very wet and wind-buffeted on Bheinne Bharrain or attempting the round of Glen Sannox while others meekly opted for the standing stones on Mauchrie beach and the King's Cave. By late afternoon the clouds fell away, the sun appeared and the hills were revealed in all their glory.

Saturday was a bright and beautiful day filled with a variety of pursuits, climbing, walking, scrambling and even painting in the sun. Among the summits visited in many combinations were Cioch na h-Oighe, Mullach Buidhe by its north-west ridge, North Goatfell, Goatfell, A'Chir and the outlier, Bheinne Bharrain. Climbing took place on the Lower Slabs of Coire na h-Uaimh with *Slapstick Wall* the route of choice for most. The Witch's Step proved tricky for some!

The evening saw us gathered near the sea for the group photograph with thanks to David Stone (Image Archivist) where a few people were conspicuous by their absence, not murdered on Goatfell but waylaid by the Witch's Step. A fine Dinner with some nods to Fawlty Towers as orders for a few arrived fiendishly late or not at all. Noel Williams kindly and professionally provided us with an excellent illustrated lecture on the eccentric Clement Wragge describing his weather recording epics on the Ben and his attempts at weather forecasting in the Antipodes.

Sunday homewards for most, via climbs waiting to be done. A group sailed over to Holy Island and spent some tranquil hours there appreciating the wanderings of wild Eriskay ponies and Soay sheep with lambs near the seashore. Interestingly enough there are no foxes, moles or grey squirrels on Arran. A well

Easter Meet 2017 - Arran

L to R : Tom Prentice, Peter Macdonald, David Stone, Simon Fraser, Noel Williams, Colin Stead, Eve Mackenzie & Lucy (guests), Dave Broadhead, Cynthia Grindley, Bob Aitken, John Fowler, Helen Forde, John Mackenzie, Nancy Kennedy (guest), Steve Kennedy, Colin Moody, Roger Robb, Campbell Forrest, Bill McKerrow, Mike Watson, John Hay not in photo : Simon Richardson, Geoff Cohen, Gordon Macnair, Raymond Simpson. Photo D. Stone

Peter Macdonald triumphs on the Witch's Step (not a scramble!). Photo: Noel Williams.

over-subscribed meet but much enjoyed by those present especially with it being held in more unfamiliar countryside with a pleasant ferry ride over the sea. Thanks to John Fowler for the organisation.

Attending were: R Aitken, DJ Broadhead, G Cohen, C Forrest, HGS Forde, JRR Fowler, S Fraser, CM Grindley, JYL Hay, SD Kennedy, PF Macdonald, JRG Mackenzie, WS McKerrow, G McNair, CA Moody, RT Prentice, SM Richardson, RJC Robb, GR Simpson, AC Stead, D Stone, ML Watson and DN Williams.

Our guests were G Fellows, N Kennedy and E Mackenzie.

Helen G S Forde

Skye Spring Meet, Allt Dearg Cottage

10–17 June 2017

L to R: Dave Broadhead, Alan Smith, Peter Wilson, Simon Richardson, Tom Prentice, John Mackenzie and Eve Mackenzie. Photo: Noel Williams.

After last year's superb weather we hoped for the same again, but didn't get it. The week was dismal and wet. Despite the precipitation parties ventured out every day and managed to bag lots of Marilyns as well as snatch a few climbs.

Dave Broadhead started his tally on the Saturday by heading out to Aird of Sleat and crossing Sgùrr nan Caorach before returning via Dalavil and Gleann Meadhonach by bike. Meanwhile Alan Smith and Peter Wilson traversed The Storr. On the Sunday Dave was joined by Simon Richardson and Tom Prentice when he added the two Marilyns on the north side of Loch Eynort. Alan and Peter paid a visit to the crags at Suisnish.

The next day Dave cycled to Fiskavaig and through Huisgill to Talisker Bay. He then returned via Loch Eynort, An Cruachan and Glen Brittle. Alan, Peter and Tom ascended Sithean a' Bhealaich Chumhaing north of Portree. John Mackenzie and Noel Williams went mineral hunting on the shore of Moonen Bay below Waterstein Head while Simon went stack hunting on Waternish.

On Tuesday ascents were made of Beinn Tianavaig and three hills on Sleat. In a short dry interlude John and Simon helped Noel complete a project on a prow of rock on the shore near Earlish, south of Uig.

The Wednesday saw Peter and Simon climb a couple of routes at Neist before rain stopped play. Dave bagged two Marilyns on Waternish and Noel traversed Suidh' a' Mhinn via Loch Sneosdal. Tom ascended Sgùrr an Fheadain from the cottage, continued over the north peak of Bidean Druim nan Ramh and returned via An Caisteal and Bruach na Frithe.

Ruadh Stac was bagged on Thursday and on the Friday Dave, Peter, Simon and Tom managed to ascend Pinnacle Ridge on Sgùrr nan Gillean.

The meet organiser on the first pitch of Prowler (E1 5a) on the coast at Earlish, near Uig.
Photo: Simon Richardson.

Members present: Dave Broadhead, John Mackenzie, Tom Prentice, Simon
Richardson, Alan Smith, Noel Williams and Peter Wilson.
Guests: Willie Jeffrey and Eve Mackenzie.

Noel Williams

JMCS REPORTS

Edinburgh Section: over the past year two Club members have notched up significant achievements at home and abroad. Our Treasurer, Bryan Rynne, became one of the few folk (less than fifty recorded, I understand) to have climbed all the Munros and tops and Furths, the Corbetts, the Grahams and the Donalds. Bryan has managed to combine his hillwalking with rock climbing at a high standard in the UK and abroad. If only he would take up winter climbing, I am sure that the contents of Cold Climbs and Chasing the Ephemeral would soon all be ticked. On the international stage, Ruairidh Finlayson completed the Seven Summits, a feat particularly notable as he did them all in the company of his brother Fionnlagh – not many sets of brothers can have been up them all together.

We welcomed Ian Sykes as the guest speaker at our AGM and Dinner in Crianlarich. If you are ever offered a ticket to hear Ian read out the first thousand number of π, I recommend you take it – he is a naturally enthralling and entertaining speaker and gave us a fascinating account of a few of the many episodes of his life in and around the mountains, concluded by a Patey song accompanied by his own banjo playing. Next day many members accompanied Stewart Bauchop up the snowy Buachaille Beag, his last Munro, in superb winter sunshine above a temperature inversion which filled the glen below with a layer of cloud. (This was just after the snowfall in November 2016, when we still dared to dream of a great season!) Days like that inspire you to keep going to the hills and, despite protestations to the contrary, I am pretty sure that Stewart is Corbetteering now.

If you want someone to blame for the poor winter of 2016/17, blame us. Last year we paid for a Ben track key; this year we laid out more money to get two keys, and look what happened – not exactly value for our investment!

As is usual these days, lots of members have had climbing and ski mountaineering holidays abroad, quite apart from their exploits in the UK. You can read more about our various foreign and domestic adventures, in places well known and also some less travelled, in the lavishly illustrated Annual Newsletters which can are in the Library section of our website.

If you are interested in joining the Edinburgh JMCS, we always welcome new faces. Please come along to our Monday or Wednesday night activities and meet and climb with some of the existing members. We climb indoors during the winter on Monday and Wednesday evenings, usually at Ratho on Wednesdays and at Ratho and/or Alien Rock on Mondays. During the summer we will be inside or out, depending on the weather; you can see where we are going by looking at our website which also lists our forthcoming weekend meets. Just Google 'Edinburgh JMCS'. It is probably best to contact Nils Krichel, the Membership Secretary, beforehand to make sure there has been no last minute change of venue.

Our huts are available for booking by kindred Clubs; please contact the Custodians whose names are shown below. We have the Cabin in Balgowan, between Laggan and Newtonmore, and the Smiddy at Dundonnell in the North West.

The present committee includes: Honorary President: John Fowler. President: Ruth Love. Vice President and Smiddy Custodian: Helen Forde (30 Reid Terrace, Edinburgh EH3 5JH, 0131 332 0071). Secretary: David Small (5 Afton Place, Edinburgh, EH5 3RB, secretary@edinburghjmcs.org.uk). Treasurer: Bryan

Rynne. The Cabin Custodian: Ali Borthwick (01383 732 232, before 9 p.m. please). Membership Secretary; Nils Krichel <nils.krichel@gmail.com>.

David Small

Glasgow Section: the Glasgow Section enjoyed another very successful, busy and varied year in 2016. Club membership currently stands at 85 members in total; 44 ordinary members and 41 life members in 2016. The new Member Secretary is Simon Taylor. You should contact Simon if you want to go on a meet or find out more about the club. (newmembers@glasgowjmcs.org.uk). Guests are very welcome to come along to all of the club meets which are active and popular.

Reflecting the enthusiasm within the club, throughout 2016 there were 21 official weekend meets including the annual work meet to the club hut at Coruisk on the late May bank holiday 28–29 May. In addition to general maintenance of this fine hut, roof void insulation was installed; the chimney was re-rendered; a pre-filter and water UV steriliser unit were fitted (supported by a grant from Highland Council) and new mattresses installed largely funded by a grant from the SMT. Coruisk provides simple, cheap and ferry accessible accommodation in a most beautiful setting; see <http://www.glasgowjmcs.org.uk/coruisk.php> for details, or to book the hut e-mail Coruisk Hut Bookings – Iain Sneddon <coruisk@glasgowjmcs.org.uk>.

JMCS meets were held across Scotland and the Lake District. Many were held in the SMC huts: CIC, Lagangarbh, Raeburn, Ling and Naismith.

The indoor wall of the Glasgow Climbing Centre hosts an indoor Thursday evening meet every fortnight, with cappuccinos available in the Balcony Café (other hot drinks available!) Midweek meets are held at local outdoor rock climbing venues in the central belt over the summer; please see the club website for details http://www.glasgowjmcs.org.uk/index.php .

The long winter season allowed members to climb winter routes from mid-November 2015 in Glen Coe (Crypt Route), until 30 April 2016 on Ben Nevis (Astral Highway). A team who had previously found a Camalot 6 (head sized) abandoned on a sea cliff hoped that this would be the key to a stylish ascent of Piggot's route on Beinn Eighe, but were disappointed to find the crux chimney was verglassed so that the usual thrutch and struggle were required.

The many fine winter climbs, especially late season on the Ben included Orion Directissima and Astral Highway Link Up, Indicator Right-Hand, Hadrian's Wall Direct (two ex-presidents and an SMC member) and Jacknife. Others were Ménage à Trois (Beinn an Dothaidh), Tainted Elixir (Ben Cruachan, a day before another strong Glasgow JMCS pair climbed the same route); Scabbard Chimney, Twisting Grooves and Chimney Route (Stob Coire nan Lochan), Moonlighting (Lost Valley) and Deep Throat (Coire an Lochain). In late January two members (both ex-presidents) climbed Route 1 on Ben Nevis The best and by far the most memorable winter route was however Eagle Ridge (Lochnagar) – huge respect to the early ascensionists who went up without modern tools and gear.

In mid-march an ex-president climbed a short new route on Ben Nevis with an SMC member which they entitled *Aquatherapy* (II,3) a modest route perhaps but in view of the melting snow, wet slab avalanche risk and potential cornice collapse, it was felt to be the best that could be safely achieved!

In early January 2016, two members joined an SMC member living south of Munich and went icefall climbing in the Sellraintal in Austria. An excellent winter climbing venue with good road access and accommodation ensuring it is popular.

Two members enjoyed climbing the sea stack A' Chailleach in April 2016, where a considerable sea swell made the Tyrolean access interesting.

In summer ascents included Torro (Ben Nevis) and Lost Pinnacle (The Cobbler), which few people know about, but there really is a hidden, tall pinnacle on The Cobbler, with a nice VS line on it. In May the Fiddler's Nose was picked and ticked!

At the end of April, two ex-presidents plus the current president were ski-mountaineering with a larger group in Switzerland. Despite some poor weather, they had successful ski ascents of the Strahlhorn and Allalinhorn from the Brittania Hutte.

In May two ex-presidents were in Umbria where they climbed on a number of excellent bolted limestone crags in the area (Ferentillo, Foligno) mainly single pitch. One memorable route was Mal Di Denti (toothache) an aspiration for a dentist to conquer toothache.

Climbing in the Picos de Europa, included long and nice lines up the smooth (some times not so smooth) walls of Naranjo de Bulnes and Torre de Cerrado.

In August two ex-presidents were based in Leysin where they climbed on a number of bolted limestone peaks in the area. The most significant climb was a superb day on the Directe route of the Miroir d' Argentine. This is a fantastic 500m, 13 pitch route graded 5a. It follows a big corner for four pitches to a large shelf, a move left onto the main slab and then direct to the notch in the skyline in another eight excellent pitches; very highly recommended.

Other overseas activities included a +6000m summit in Bolivia's Cordillera Real range: the East Face of Huayna Potosi.

The North ridge of the Piz Badile had two separate ascents by teams of members, one with the president, and the Piz Bernina was ticked. This August trip also saw presidential ascents of the Bugeleisen, the Via Meuli on the Pta Albigna, the Via Classica on the Bio Pfeiler, and the Westkante on the Torre Innominata.

The A.G.M. and club dinner were held on 19–20 November 2016 at the Glen Hotel, Newtonmore where 26 members and guests met to celebrate this annual event of the club. On the afternoon before the 2016 AGM three members made an early season ascent of Stirling Bomber (V,7), a sterling effort; two others climbed the Seam, and Savage Slit had a club ascent the next day, before the snow all disappeared again!

Office Beaerers: President Mark Gorin; Secretary Charles Craig; Treasurer Justine Carter; Meets Secretary Neil Wilkie; Newsletter Editor Ole Kemi; Coruisk Hut Custodian Iain Sneddon; New Member Secretary Simon Taylor.

Colwyn Jones

Lochaber Section: 2016 started with a well attended slide show from former club member Sandy Kane on his trips and ascents of routes in a variety of locations around the world, including some of the clubs trips to Europe as well as closer to home. There were many fascinating stories from both sides of the floor, with interest from current members for a trip to the Dolomites in the future.

There were organised weekend meets to Muir of Inverey near Braemar, Ling hut in Torridon, Naismith hut in Elphin and Inverardren Cottage in Crianlarich. A first for the club was to attend the impressive Elphin Music festival which took place directly below the hut and which just happened to coincide with our meet to Elphin. There were some reserved members enjoying the music early in the evening after various outings during the day, but who, after consuming some loosening up liquid, were almost recreating the moves of their miss-spent youth. I did say almost recreating!! All the meets were very well attended and enjoyed some particularly good weather, especially the meet to Crianlarich, with ascents of Ben More and surrounding hills, as well as routes on the Cobbler, while bathed in some hot, late August sunshine.

Bookings for Steall Hut continued the strong growth pattern from the previous two years at the start of the year, however by the end of the year, due mainly to the poorer weather and more especially, to the landslide closing the path through Steall Gorge, bookings took a dip, as well as some cancelling the bookings. Takings for Steall were still double what they were three years prior, although down slightly on the previous year. Almost all interest in Steall is generated through the website <www.steallhut.co.uk> and the Mountaineering Scotland Huts Directory.

The club dinner and AGM closed the year making a return trip to the Cairndow Inn and again being well attended on both evenings, with one of the members managing to make a trip over from his home in Germany.

President: Simon Fraser; Secretary: Iain MacLeod (ia.macleod@btinternet.com); Treasurer: Ken Scoular; Hut bookings: Ewen Kay; Hut Custodian: John Matheson

Iain MacLeod

London Section: in 2016 meets took place in Scotland, North Wales, the Lake District, Peak District, Wye Valley and in South Pembroke. Mostly, the activity was a mix of rock climbing and hill walking. Abroad, members were active in the High Atlas, the Dolomites, the Mont Blanc area, Stubai Alps and on the other side of the world in Queensland, Australia.

A winter foray into the Scottish Hills is a permanent fixture in our programme but the weather in Assynt was cruel. A blizzard defeated a traverse of An Teallach but a few munros were 'bagged'. The banter and the cuisine of our chef David Hughes compensated adequately for the soaking on the hill.

Over 20 members experienced the hospitality of the Wayfarer's Hut in Little Langdale in March, with several routes done on Gimmer Crag and various rounds of the valley. Other memorable days out in the summer took placed on the cliffs at Gogarth on Anglesey, on Dinas Mot in the Llanberis Pass and a surprisingly sunny meet in Arrochar in late May! Several members also enjoyed sailing in the Hebrides including some rough walking on Jura during a circumnavigation of the island.

The year ended with a well-attended Section AGM and dinner at Losehill Hall, Castleton. We are grateful to the guest speaker, Mateo Cabello, who described the preparation and themes from his book Of Mountains and Men.

Our club hut in Bethesda shines brightly now the exterior walls have been painted and the number of block bookings by guest clubs increased in 2016 helping the Section's finances. We continue to struggle to recruit new members especially from the younger generation. However, while the average age rises inexorably, our spirits remain willing, at least for now!

Officers for 2017: President: Andy Hughes; Secretary: John Firmin (07845

732189); Treasurer: David Hughes; Glanafon Hut Bookings: Dave L Hughes
(davidlewishughes@hotmail.com).

John Firmin

Perth Section: over the years the Perth Section has evolved into The Perth
Mountaineering Club but we remain proud of our roots in the JMCS. We are a
small club with between 70 and 80 members though much of our membership is
no longer active on meets for a variety of reasons. However the active contingent
had a busy and enjoyable year.

We continue to enjoy the privilege of access to huts maintained by the SMC
and kindred clubs. Milehouse in February was very stormy with less than ideal
snow conditions but we still managed ski touring on Geal Charn and some brave
souls bypassed the frustrated skiers to battle their way to and from the corrie but
no routes were possible. Lagangarbh again provided a memorable weekend
particularly the traverse of Bidean on hard névé with a cloud inversion.
Unfortunately I along with too many others did not make it to the Steall hut but
the scrambly traverse of the Ring of Steall was enjoyed despite severe midge
conditions in August.

Other highlights included the traditional Burns Supper meet at Invergarry
complete with piper and an expert address of the haggis. Despite the poor snow
conditions we enjoyed good skiing on the Ben Lawers meet in March. An
innovative meet involved kayaking across Loch Quoich and ascending Ben Aden
and Sgurr a' Choire Beith in April. The May trip was to Glenbrittle hut in Skye
and we had an enjoyable but midge ridden trip to Knoydart in June. We generally
have one whole weekend and one day meet each month.

Climbers were active too with many classic routes ascended including the photo
competition winning climb of Final Selection on Stag Rocks in Am Monadh
Ruadh. The Wednesday evening sessions continued with good attendance at
various local crags. During the winter months we still meet in the evenings usually
at Dundee climbing wall but more recently at the new Perth College wall. An
entertaining illustrated talk on the history of the club was given at the joint lecture
with the PSNS was given in January by Dr Iain Robertson. It was our turn to
organise the Mountain Mind Quiz and a very successful competition took place
in Birnam in March.

Sadly we have to report the death of two former presidents. Bob Milne joined
the club in 1948 and was a key member of the club in the '50s and '60s. He was
very fond of Derry Lodge and knew Bob Scott of Luibeg well. Ray Lee joined
the club in 1984 and was very active with the club for the next 20 years. He was
a great companion on the hill and afterwards in the hut or campsite and he will be
much missed by those of us who new him.

We met for our annual dinner at the Clova Hotel in November. Over 20 attended
and we were blessed with crisp clear weather to enjoy walks on the surrounding
plateau. At the AGM in the same month the following office bearers were
confirmed.

President: Alasdair Dutton, Vice President: Dennis Underwood, Secretary Tim
Storer, Membership Secretary Wendy Georgeson. For more information and
contact details visit: www.perthmountaineering-club.co.uk.

Alasdair Dutton

SMC ABROAD

MONT BLANC RANGE, GRANDES JORASSES – DIAMOND RIDGE

About ten years ago I spotted a new line on the Italian side of the Grandes Jorasses. The Diamond Ridge (as it became called) follows a prominent spur up the right side of the Tronchey Wall before joining the Tronchey Ridge high up below its third tower. Over 1400m high, the Tronchey Wall is the highest face in the Mont Blanc Range and home to only two routes. Both are unrepeated – a fearsome reputation and exposure to stone fall has put off all subsequent suitors, but the Diamond Ridge itself looked almost benign in comparison. And most importantly, it appeared to be objectively safe.

At first I could not believe that the Diamond Ridge was unclimbed. It seemed left over from a bygone age, but when a French-Italian team attempted a new line up the deeply-cut gully to its left in 2010, topos in the climbing press confirmed that it was indeed untouched. By early last year I could wait no longer. It was too good an objective to ignore so I made it the primary objective for a visit to Chamonix in July 2016. My partner was Michael (Micha) Rinn from Germany. We climbed together in January during the BMC International meet at Glenmore Lodge and had instantly clicked. Micha shares my love of adventure and the unknown, and despite the atrocious weather during the meet, we sealed our partnership with a new route on Lochnagar.

But of course, there was a glitch. The Diamond Ridge starts at the head the chaotic Pra Sec Glacier (untrodden until 1972 and impassable in summer) and is severely undercut at its base. The obvious way to bypass this was to start 200m lower down the mountain, climb the small peak of Punta Grassi on the right (one of the last summits in the range to be climbed in 2006), and then traverse left to gain the ridge just above the initial overhangs. Unfortunately our photos showed the traverse threatened by a hanging icefall originating from the left branch of the Tronchey Glacier, and it looked potentially dangerous. As always, the only way to resolve this was to go and have a look.

On 16 July I flew to Frankfurt. Micha drove to Chamonix and we walked up to the Envers des Aiguilles Hut that evening. Over the next two days we climbed the modern classics Children of the Moon and Subtitles Dulferiennes on the Aiguille du Roc, and then carried our bivouac kit (there was no room in the hut) up the more traditional Mer de Glace Face of the Grepon. So a good start, but then the weather became poor and Micha picked up a nasty bowel infection. Once he was recovered we went up to the Torino Hut and climbed the elegant pinnacle of the Roi de Siam in the Vallee Blanche and then joined the crowds on the Dent du Geant. It was all very laid back and relaxed, but crucially, our time up high was allowing us to acclimatise.

After another night in the hut we spent the day in Val Ferret scoping out the route. It became clear that the best way of accessing the Diamond Ridge was to climb the left flank of Punta Grassi to gain a crossing point in the couloir below the icefall. The hanging glacier didn't look too bad. Glacial recession had worked in our favour here, and the overhanging icefall in our photos had relented to more of a rounded snout. It was still a worry, but it didn't look excessively dangerous. Beyond the couloir was an easy-angled snowfield that would quickly take us out of danger onto the crest of the ridge itself.

We bivouacked in Val Ferret and started the approach just before dawn on 28 July with food and fuel for two nights. The weather forecast promised two dry

7 July 2014 Mont Gruetta, The Tronchey Wall on the Grandes Jorasses. The 1600m-long Diamond Ridge follows the sunlit crest just right of centre.
Photo: Simon Richardson.

and cloudy days before bad weather swept in on the third. So not perfect, but good enough. We reached the foot of Punta Grassi at 2600m and started climbing at 9a.m. The line up the left flank slotted together well – there was a blank slabby section leading past a cave and then onto the easier ground leading to the couloir below the hanging glacier snout.

It was awkward climbing down into the couloir, but we were across it in seconds and soon moving across the snowfield to the safety of the Diamond Ridge itself. We started this about midday and climbed 10 pitches to a notch in the ridge. The rock was marvelous. It reminded me most of the east side of Mont Greuvetta – perfect granite with loads of excellent features. Whenever you reached up there was a perfect hold just where you needed it.

There was not a bivouac site big enough for two but we found separate ones about 15m apart. The cloud had been swirling around all day, but it cleared and we spent a comfortable night. Next morning, a steep step above the notch proved to be the crux of the route and we used three points of aid before continuing up the crest of the ridge for another 16 pitches. We thought we'd be drawn rightwards towards the Tronchey Ridge, but the natural line took us straight up to the base of the Second Tower.

Here things began to get a little awkward. There was significant snow banked up on the ledges, so there was lots of changing out of boots into rock shoes and taking crampons on and off mid pitch. We crossed an icy couloir and climbed a steep wall left to gain the prominent right traverse below the imposing Third Tower. We expected easy ledges here, but instead we found smooth unprotected slabs that were soaking wet with dripping snow. The belay was poor and Micha led a full 50m ropelength before coming back saying he couldn't make the final moves because the final slabs were covered in ice. There was no foothold big enough to stop and put on crampons, so Micha had to repeat the entire traverse in crampons so he could climb the ice at the end. It was now getting dark, so it was a pretty tense time for both of us, and an outstanding lead by Micha. We bivouacked immediately afterwards by digging into a snow bank on top of the Second Tower.

The next day we continued up the original route of the Tronchey Ridge, by traversing above the top of the steep section of the East Face to join the upper crest. We were on the 4208m summit of the Grandes Jorasses at midday just as the forecasted bad weather was sweeping in from Mont Blanc. The descent went smoothly and we reached the Boccalate Hut at 17.00 to a great welcome from guardians Franco Perlotto and Roberta Cutri. The hut was empty because of the poor weather, and at first, they couldn't understand where we'd come from or what we'd climbed. Once we explained they both became very excited, and Franco immediately contacted the Italian Alpine Club and also the well-known Italian climbing historian Luca Signorelli who is based in Courmayeur.

It snowed hard that night, almost to the level of the hut, and after a leisurely breakfast we walked down in the rain and were met by Luca halfway up the hut trail. Luca was charming and enthused about our ascent. 'You have made history,' he said. 'This is only the third time the Tronchey Wall has been climbed, and each time by a separate route!' Until that point I hadn't really considered our climb to have anything but personal significance, but a 1600m-high new line on one of the most important peaks of the Alps was not going to pass unnoticed. As we sped back up the motorway to Germany later that afternoon, the Internet hummed as news of our ascent on the CAI website spread fast. In a climbing world where technical difficulty is often king, it was rather refreshing that a route that could have been climbed a hundred years ago could still capture the wider imagination.

Simon Richardson

SLOVAKIAN TATRY

The High Tatra mountain range has attracted mainly eastern European climbers in both summer and winter since early 20th century – this is, after all, the closest mountain range to Estonia, Lithuania and Latvia. Few British have spent much time there, especially in winter, with the exception of individuals like a friend of mine from south of the border, whose introduction to the mountains was through the exercising of a random opportunity: meeting Hungarians in the 1990s and taking up their offer to go there for climbing, and returning regularly since then.

In February 2017, Fiona Murray and I joined six other folk on a trip to the Slovakian Tatry. The main leg was a flight from London Luton to Poprad, Slovakia (we added an Edinburgh to Luton leg), then by taxi to the trailhead at Biela Voda (in 2017 it was 20 euros and about a 20 minute drive; bring a map to show the taxi driver where it is). From there a 2½ to 3 hour walk on a well-signposted path through forest takes you very pleasantly up the 7.5km and 600m height gain to the hut, at 1551m.

Fiona Murray in front of the hut (Chata Pri Zelenom Plese). There are summer routes on the crag behind the hut but the winter routes are on the facets of the crag facing left. All photos: Susan Jensen.

Chata Pri Zelenom plese (the Hut by the Green Lake) is owned by the Slovakian Mountaineering Association, and is currently (perhaps always) operated by teams who are fantastic and generous cooks. If you are vegetarian let them know when you arrive. The hut sleeps 55 in the main building in both alpine platform and bunk-bed rooms. There is no wifi at the chata but there is a strong mobile data signal, which is good because the printed weather forecast didn't get updated very often in the hut. There is a big dining area with huge windows that that look out on to the main crag that is the north face of Malý Kežmarský štít, so you can spend hours either memorising the lines of the crag, trying to figure out where you were earlier that day, or watching another team have an epic (binoculars advised) while you get through a pivo.

The climbing is very Scottish in style; a Polish lad at the hut told me that it was the only place outside of Scotland where warthogs are used (when I told him that Japan also does, he looked crestfallen at the loss of the sole kinship). The area is primarily for mixed climbing on frozen turf and snowed up granite – and the rock doesn't have to be white to be in condition – but it has to be cold, because if the turf isn't frozen you'll be stuffed. The winters generally stay quite cold and there is little build up of neve. While there are gullies, they tend to have rocky sections, and a climber really should be going at Scottish grade IV at least to have a decent choice of routes. Scottish VI would give you access to most of the crag, and the routes vary from 2 to 15 or so pitches in length – most of the routes done commonly in winter are 3–5 pitches. The popular routes have lots of pegs and in situ gear and even bolt belays, and abseiling off routes when finished is fairly common. Walk-offs are often quite straightforward as well. Combine that with a 30–40 minute walk from the hut to the base of a route (after a very well stocked breakfast at the hut, starting at what feels like an obscenely late 7 a.m.), a fairly easy return to the hut and copious beer and cake to be had when you get there, and the whole thing becomes a holiday as well as a solid climbing trip.

There are also a small handful of icefalls in the corrie, mainly single pitch and ranging from Scottish III–V. There are quite a few ridges that take you from peak to peak around the cirque should you want a mountain day rather than the cragging. There appears to be some ski touring available, but not sure where one goes except up into the higher corries and back down. There is even a series of south facing buttresses on Kozi štit (again, 30 minutes from the hut) that have sun-soaked winter rock climbing, with bolted belay/abseil stations. The highest peak in the Tatry is 2657m, so no altitude issues.

The only currently existing guidebook for the area, available from the chata, is pretty hard work to use. Compiled by a local activist, it seems to have been simply a compilation (rather than an authorship) of the route drawings that have been entered in the hut's new routes binder. There isn't usually an indication of length of route (just the hours that it took on the first ascent), and the grades are UIAA Roman numerals. The sketches can be inaccurate in the direction the lines go, although there is a reasonable set of features drawn on that can make pretty good sense once you are on the route. The photodiagrams are of decent quality but the crags are so big that each page has quite vague detail, so time is well spent in the hut's dining room, sucking down a pivo and gazing at the crag. All in all, it contributes to the sense of adventure and exploration.

On this trip, four of the group stayed from Sunday to Friday, two from Sunday to Saturday and two from Monday to Monday. Weekends are definitely very busy at the hut, so the Sunday to Friday may be the best bet if you want to be there for less than a week. The weather was quite good while we were there, and climbing was possible (and enjoyable) every day; there was one morning where we waited until 9 or 10 a.m. to leave the hut because it was snowing (would have been considered an ok day in Scotland) but that still left plenty of time to get a good route in and be back in time for tea/beer and cakes.

A turfy line at about Scottish VI; this pitch was protectable only with warthogs.

A dark corner line centre-right in the lower tier of buttresses rising vaguely left–right is the classic of the area: five pitches at VI/VII. It is apparently in condition either when there is no ice or a lot of ice; not to be climbed when there is only a little ice!

The gear required for climbing here is pretty much identical to climbing in Scotland – bulldogs and warthogs are handy, plus the usual wires (double set 1–8, small wires are very useful), hexes and full set of cams (less likely to have iced up cracks). Ice screws are necessary if you are planning on icefalls, obviously, and occasionally on the mixed routes as well.

Leaving day – it is entirely possible to walk out in the early morning (leave the hut by 7.30), get to the road and to the airport for a flight at 12.30, especially if you take the path to Tatranska Matliare and get a taxi to the airport from there. Otherwise, for a more leisurely exit, have a good hill day and then walk down to either the Biela Voda trailhead you came up from (then hitch a lift or catch the bus to Tatranska Lomnica), or take the above turn to Tatranska Matliare and continue walking to Tatranska Lomnica – a couple of kilometres' walk from where you get to the road. This will be utterly miserable if the path is clotted with soft snow and it is raining, but fine in cold and sunny weather. Overnight in Tatranska Lomnica gives you a chance to catch up on that food and alcohol that you might have missed at the hut (if that is possible) and have a lie-in before you get the train or taxi to Poprad airport the next morning.

Susan Jensen

TREKKING IN GARHWAL AND KINNAUR, INDIAN HIMALAYA

Hamish and Gill Irvine had long been planning an autumn trip to India with Geoff Cohen and Des Rubens when the latter's tragic death lead Geoff to drop out and I was persuaded to step in two months prior to departure. With more emphasis on trekking and covering new ground rather than establishing a base camp and climbing peaks, three is a good number to share a tent, stove, cooking gear and costs. We duly arrived in Delhi on the morning of 25 September 2016 to be met by a car and driver who drove us straight up to Dehradun where three young Nepali porters were awaiting our arrival. Our transport and personnel were arranged by a local agency, Rimo Expeditions, which we had used before, to good result and Pasang, Pemba and Nangnang went on to give outstanding support. In their early twenties, the two brothers were younger than my own children, and though slightly older, Nangnang was only half my age, so we looked a rather unlikely group but thankfully seemed to hit it off immediately, despite our limited common language.

I had spent some time in Dehradun in 1980 and remembered it as a quiet backwater. Now as capital of the relatively new state of Uttaranchal it had become frantically busy and overwhelmingly noisy with constantly tooting traffic a background to our last-minute preparations. Buying kerosene for Hamish's shiny new MSR Dragonfly stove proved the main problem. After much frustration dealing with official sources, the boys managed to procure an impressive volume of uncertain provenance in a variety of dodgy looking containers. Our woes continued when Hamish discovered the rubber washers on his impressive collection of shiny red Sigg bottles had all perished and once again we were saved by eastern ingenuity and improvisation.

After two sleepless nights and a day scouring the bazar it was a relief to continue our drive north, into the mountains at last, to the village of Sankri (1450m) in the Tons valley, at the end of the motorable road. With the help of a variety of dubious sources of information we had a vague sport-plan which involved leaving a stash of food and gear and doing a warm-up acclimatisation trek for 10 days or so here in Garhwal, before carrying everything across the mountains into Kinnaur for further adventures.

Sankri is the starting point for the Har Ki Dun trek, popular with Indian nationals, and after putting the word out for a local guide there was no shortage of applicants. With a winning grin and claiming 25 years of guiding experience we were immediately won over by Batar Singh, sporting homespun tweeds and a traditional hat rather than the flash western-style gear favoured by younger candidates and he proved to be an excellent choice.

Refreshed by a good night's sleep at last, a short jeep ride next morning took us to Taluka (1900m). Two days walking took us to scenic Har Ki Dun (3566m) before back-tracking a short distance and leaving the trekking crowds to walk a further 3 days up the beautiful Ruinsara Nala to a high camp at about 4000m below the Bali Pass (4890m).

To the north we had a fantastic panorama of the snowy Swargarohini peaks rising to over 6000m while our route lay south, into the Yamuna River catchment. So far the weather had been mixed, with regular afternoon rain, usually after we had pitched camp. Now heavy hail turned to snow and we were a bit concerned about our route over the pass, until the stars came out and the temperature dropped. With a dusting of snow on scree the pass had more of a Scottish than a Himalayan feel and although Batar sported a pair of boots our boys were relying on trainers. Pemba's had already disintegrated and he was now using Gill's spare hill-running shoes. On the crux section of the crossing, involving a short traverse across an alarmingly steep and exposed scree slope, there was a heart-stopping moment when Pasang slipped, gingerly regaining his footing a moment later. Thanks to Batar's route-finding skills we were soon enduring a long steep descent down some very spectacular terrain, gleefully guided around a particularly steep buttress down which an unfortunate Korean lady had apparently fallen and broken a leg.

Eventually we joined the popular pilgrimage route up to the Yamunotri Temple and spent the night in a nearby ashram having first freshened up and gained considerable merit by joining fellow pilgrims bathing in the hot spring. Along with the temples at Gangotri, Kedarnath and Badrinath, the Char Dham Yatra, a pilgrimage to worship at these most holy Himalayan sites is highly auspicious for any Hindu, with scheduled package tours departing weekly from most major Indian cities through the season.

Next morning there was no let-up for our poor leg muscles as we continued our descent, exchanging enthusiastic greetings with the stream of pilgrims toiling slowly upwards on foot, on ponies or uncomfortably on the shoulders of four sweating carriers of a dandy chair. We finally reached Hanuman Chatti (2400m) by lunchtime, leaving the afternoon to relax despite the prospect of regaining all that lost height in the back of our minds. As we started our climb next morning we were passed by dozens of immaculately uniformed children streaming down to school from the village above, before being overtaken by the Vodaphone engineer striding up to do some maintenance on the local phone mast. Higher up we were treated to the spectacle of dozens of vultures soaring effortlessly close around. By now the valuable potato crop had been harvested and the grazing animals moved down from the high summer pastures and so we hardly saw a soul over the next few days as we worked our way along a series of grassy ridges and across the Phachu Kanta Pass, returning eventually to Taluka and thence Sankri.

Refreshed by a rare hot shower, the following morning we hired a jeep, or rather the ubiquitous Mahindra Bolero which took us and all our stuff a few kilometres down the Tons valley and up the lower section of the Rupin river to Dhaula, starting point for our trek across the Rupin Pass (4625m). Batar had other commitments, so we now had Harwill to guide us and carry a share of the loads. Lacking any English, he failed to inspire much confidence through overuse of the phrase 'pani nay' (no water) when discussing possible campsites, though thankfully he was happy to carry a large load.

By now we were enjoying perfect weather with plenty of blue sky and a waxing moon. Over the next five days we continued up the valley, passing several interesting villages whose inhabitants were mainly busy gathering winter fodder, twisted into thick braids and hung from the branches of convenient trees. We also became aware of the popularity of this route with Indian trekkers when we passed several fixed Indiahike camps, eventually catching up with a group of more than 20 below the pass. Mostly young graduates with good jobs in various big cities down in the plains, they were very friendly and enthusiastic about their trekking experiences. Judging by the predominance of Quechua gear, Decathalon has clearly made inroads into the growing Indian market. As an angrezi (foreigner) who has seen enormous changes to the Himalaya over 40 years, through climate change and particularly human pressure, it is encouraging to see so many educated young Indians enjoying and hopefully appreciating this fantastic environment whose future lies in their hands.

Descending from the pass, we had great views north across the Baspa valley to the snowy peaks of the Kinner Kailash range. The Tons river, our starting point, is a tributary of the Ganges, flowing east and eventually into the Indian Ocean. Now we were on a tributary of the Sutlej, flowing west to join the Indus before draining into the Arabian Sea, so it felt like we had crossed a significant watershed. A long knee-challenging day took us down to the fleshpots of Sangla (2600m), the rapidly growing hub of this area. Anxious about our rapidly dwindling rupees,

Hamish saved us any embarrassment with his debit card as Indians now seem to be very well provided with ATMs, even in remote spots like this.

We made full use of our rare rest day to visit the amazing old fort and temple at Kamru, perched on the hillside high above the town. Next morning we were all up and away before dawn to catch the first bus down to Rekong Peo. I made the mistake of getting an offside window seat looking down the awesome drop thousands of feet to the river as the bus crept precariously down the narrow road carved out of the vertical walls of the very impressive Baspa gorge. Part way down we stopped at a small Hindu shrine perched at the edge of the cliff and were all happy to receive individual blessings from the priest officiating. At the bottom, we crossed the Sutlej river, briefly joining the route we had followed in 2014 on our journey to Spiti (*SMCJ*, 43/206 (2015), 366–70). On that occasion, from our overnight stop in nearby Kalpa, we had admired the Kinner Kailash peaks opposite which had encouraged us to now attempt the parikarama, a circuit of the range, crossing a high glacier pass down to Chitkul and back to Sangla.

Alas, the best laid plans - our proposed route lay close to the India-Tibet border but in recent years an Inner Line Permit had not been required. Typically for India, having just missed the morning bus to our starting point at Thangi, when we tried to hire a jeep the drivers warned us that due to increasing border tensions, the Indian military were taking a harder line with foreigners and demanding permits. Being Sunday the permit office was closed and the minimum group size was four, so we took out the map and quickly came up with an alternative, driving in the opposite direction to the road end at Kilba and trekking back towards Sangla on the south side of the Baspa valley. Our Leamann map was sketchy, to say the least, but there were plenty of locals to ask for directions and this turned out to be a memorable and varied trek. After a delightful homestay in Sapni village followed by a dramatic camp on a steep grassy ridge, we enjoyed a couple of nights at a high camp below the Barun Ghati pass from which we climbed Point 5145m. Little more than a hill-walk cum scramble, blighted by moraine and loose rock, we were rewarded with a fantastic view and the lack of any cairn suggested a first ascent.

Back in Sangla, with insufficient time for another trek, we bade a fond farewell to our porters who were happy to be heading home in time for the festival of Diwali, while we decided to spend a few days in Sarahan. Perched high above the Sutlej River and famous for the magnificent Bhimkali temple, we had overnighted here in 2014. As well as revisiting the temple, we spent a day walking up the forest clad slopes of Bashar Peak above the town, another excellent viewpoint. In reading about this area, we came across many references to the delights of the Hindustan-Tibet road. Created at the end of the nineteenth century to facilitate the passage of visiting British officials and immortalised by Kipling in Kim the route linked the older towns and villages like Sarahan, so we decided to try to locate and follow a short section. Everyone we asked recognised the name immediately, but when we tried to follow the route north, our way was immediately blocked by a large army training camp, while in the other direction we ended up following a bus route and could only conclude that the road is now just history.

During the 1960s the Indian military began a major road-building programme, following aggressive border incursions by the Chinese and a modern road now follows the Sutlej, clinging precariously to its crumbling gorge. As well as improving national security, this has also enabled engineers to harness the considerable hydro-electric potential. Side roads now connect the older towns and villages above and allow export of valuable produce such as apples and potatoes. Since my first visit to India in 1979 the population has doubled to 1.2 billion people and many of the towns and villages we visited were clearly growing, and looking relatively prosperous with attractive new homes and temples built with stone and local timber. Most had electricity and satellite TV and access to schools and healthcare, every sign that development is making a real difference. On our way back to Delhi we spent a couple of nights in Shimla where there are still plenty of interesting, if rather dilapidated relics of the Raj amid the vibrant bustle of this state capital of Himachal Pradesh and popular tourist honeypot.

Dave Broadhead

PERU 2016 – ALPINE CLUB OPEN EXPEDITION

On 4 June 2016 I joined nine other Alpine Club members in Lima on my first visit to South America. The trip was organised by Derek Buckle whom I knew from a successful trip to India two years previously. This was his fifth visit and once again he had arranged what turned out to be excellent logistical support from Peruvian Andes Adventures, a local company based in the town of Huaraz, gateway to the Cordillera Blanca, our destination at the end of a long drive the following day. This involved an altitude gain of 3000m so we were happy to spend the next couple of days with a visit to the hot springs at Chancos and a gentle walk up to the idyllic Laguna Shallap, which gave us the chance to get to know each other and start the gradual process of acclimatisation before walking in to our first base camp at 4225m in the Quilcayhuanca valley.

This is often called the Valley of Condors and we soon enjoyed the first of many

The South-west Ridge of Jatunmontepuncu '...easier to climb than pronounce.'
Photo: Dave Broadhead.

sightings of these magnificent birds. Looked after by Antonio, our excellent cook and the ever willing Urbano and Iban who helped carry gear up to high camps, we continued our acclimatisation with a couple more day hikes which also provided an opportunity to get the lay of the land and a better idea of the climbing conditions. The previous rainy season had seen very little snow-fall, leaving some peaks looking distinctly bare and uninviting as climbing objectives.

At last, on 11 June we walked around to the neighbouring Cayesh valley to attempt our first peaks. Early next morning Rafal Malcyzk, Melanie Windridge and I endured a very long and tedious climb from a low camp in the valley up through a succession of vegetation, moraine and scree to reach a col from which a gentle rocky ridge lead at last to ice and snow, giving an interesting climb to the summit of Chopiraju Oeste (5475m).

Across the valley, our companions toiled up to a higher camp, hoping to get a closer look at the impressive San Juan (5843m). The impressive NW ridge of this peak has become a much prized classic, first climbed in 1958 by Myrtle Emslie, Derek Fabian, Hugh Simpson and our former President Bill Wallace. Too early in the trip for a realistic attempt, Phil Leadbeater and Chris Petraukas climbed neighbouring Quimarumi (5455m) instead, while Derek Buckle and Nick King were frustrated when the soles of both the latter's rather venerable plastic boots peeled off almost simultaneously, causing an early retreat. As a group we were a diverse mixture of age, gender and experience sharing a sense of humour and a willingness to co-operate which meant that we all got on very well together on and off the hill.

After a rest day at base camp, Nick headed back to Huaraz to replace his boots so Derek joined Rafal, Melanie and I, walking up to a high camp at about 4900m below the Huapi Pass while Chris and Phil with Nick Berry and Catriona Clunas went up to investigate the long approach to Chinchey (6309m). On 15 June the four of us had a delightful day on Jatunmontepuncu (5421m) whose SW ridge proved much easier to climb than pronounce. Highlight of the route was a single airy step around from beneath the awesome cornice overhanging the SE slopes onto easier slopes on the W side.

Back in base camp some of us endured a very windy rest day while Derek and Nick K, in replacement boots, headed up towards Chinchey, meeting Nick B. and Catriona descending, forced back by the wind. Chris and Phil were still hanging in and climbed the W face of Chinchey in an arduous 18-hour day from a high camp on the glacier. Meanwhile John Hudson joined Nick B, Catriona, Melanie, Rafal and myself walking back round to an atmospheric camp at the head of the Cayesh valley, surrounded by ice-cliffs and waterfalls. From here five of us had another enjoyable climb up the W flank of Maparaju (5424m), once we found the zig-zags of the old mule track leading up to the glacier.

Back at base camp and now well acclimatised, the four younger members just had time for a morning jog up and down the unpronounceable JP, as we now called it, before the donkeys returned to start the journey back to Huaraz for a couple of nights. Sometimes described as the 'Chamonix of the Andes' the town was a much more colourful and bustling place.

We stayed at the Morales Guest House on the outskirts, enjoying a fantastic view of the surrounding snowy mountains from their roof-top terrace. At dusk we would stroll down to the busy town centre and eat at one of a number of excellent restaurants. With their three weeks of leave almost finished, three members of the party returned home while the rest of us headed back into the mountains on 23 June, to a new base camp in the popular Ishinca valley, slightly further N.

Dominating the head of the valley, the fine snowy pyramid of Tocllaraju (6032m) looked very inviting, so next morning we packed our sacs and climbed the moraine, to establish a camp at about 5300m on the glacier above. Chris and Phil had their eyes on the W face and made a very early start while Derek, Nick K, Rafal and I left slightly later for the easier NW ridge. With perfect weather and no other parties on the route we were lucky to enjoy a particularly fine climb, returning to our glacier camp for another night before descending. Reaching the moraine again, we learned the Brexit result, which took the wind out of our sails a bit. Fortunately, close to our base camp, the Ishinca refugio sold remarkably cheap beer, so spirits were soon revived. We were briefly joined by a few more AC members, coinciding with a few days of rare poor weather, which improved again just in time for Chris, Phil, Derek, Nick K and myself to enjoy the traverse of Ishinca (5530m) before starting the long journey home.

Dave Broadhead

SOUTH GEORGIA 2016

Last autumn I was very fortunate to take part in an expedition to the sub-Antarctic island of South Georgia. On 17 September we left the security of the yacht Pelagic Australis anchored in the lonely bay of Trollhul on the wild south coast, and began the long haul up to the Graae Glacier. Our team consisted of Stephen Venables, Caradoc (Crag) Jones, Skip Novak, Henry Chaplin, David Lund and myself, and we were attempting a 15-day ski traverse across the rarely visited Salvesen Range in the southeastern part of the island.

The expedition was the brainchild of Stephen who had visited the area in 1990

Travelling up the Harmer Glacier on the way to Starbuck Peak. All the mountains in the picture are unclimbed. Photo: Simon Richardson.

and made the first ascent of Mount Carse (2331m), the third highest peak on South Georgia. Since then, Stephen had yearned to return to attempt the spectacular unclimbed peaks deep in the range, but his 2010 trip was a pure ski traverse and when he visited with climbers in 2014 they were thwarted by strong winds. For Skip and Crag it was a return trip too. In 2005 they had traversed the range with Richard Haworth and Julian Freeman-Attwood and made the first ascent of the beautiful Mount Pelagic (1731m) after a valiant attempt on Mount Baume (1912m), the highest named unclimbed peak on the island. Stephen, Skip and Crag hold a long-term fascination with South Georgia and have more first ascents on the island to their names than anyone else. For Henry, David and myself, it was our first visit to this mythical island of majestic icy peaks rising straight out of the turbulent South Atlantic.

The weather was ominously overcast when we left the boat, and as we gained the glacier it started to snow. We pitched two tents at the junction of the Harmer and Jenkins glaciers just to the south of Starbuck Peak (1434m), our first objective and the dominant summit of the area. Disappointingly, the wind increased overnight and developed into a five-day storm. Our days were spent talking, reading and digging out our tents that were battered by 160kph winds and buried in 150cm drifts. On the fifth night the snow turned to rain and next morning we woke to a spectacular sight of pristine white mountains shedding their storm clouds and wide open glaciers covered in perfect neve. Starbuck Peak rose 900m above us – a beautiful rime-encrusted spire that looked more fantasy than reality. We had been on South Georgia for a week and this was the first time we had seen any mountains. It was tempting to dash up the unclimbed peaks adjacent to the tents, but Stephen wisely suggested we push on, so we could be in position to attempt Starbuck Peak the following day.

We were a classic case of a team being stronger than the sum of its individual parts. South Georgia demands a wide variety of yachting, small boat, skiing, survival, mountaineering and technical climbing skills, and although not all of us were experts, between us we covered the spectrum of requirements. Having never sailed before, and with only rudimentary skiing ability, I was very much a passenger until it came to putting on crampons. With South Georgia's reputation for having the worst weather in the world, we knew that we would be extremely fortunate to climb any peaks at all, and throughout the five-day voyage from the Falkland Islands, it had been made clear that if we were lucky enough to find ourselves in a position to attempt Starbuck Peak, then the team would initially look to me to find a route.

Of all the skills however, siting and erecting the tents was the most crucial. Many expeditions to South Georgia have had their tents destroyed in the first days of their trip by ferocious winds and have had to retreat to their support boat with their plans and tents in tatters. We took specially made dome tents with triple thickness fabric and twin sets of double gauge poles. The trick is to pitch in flat open spaces so the wind howls past and does not bury the tents with drift. Setting up camp was a job for the experts, so once we arrived at camp, Henry and I were given the task of scoping a line up Starbuck for the following day.

As we skinned up to the broad shoulder on the mountain's north-west flank we were irresistibly drawn towards the virgin snow peak to the north. Although it was late afternoon, the weather was calm, and for all we knew, this could have been the last climbing opportunity we would get, so we set off at pace towards the summit. A final easy ridge of wind-blown rime took us to the summit of P1318m, which lies 600m south of 'Black Crag South' (1245m) climbed by the

Starbuck Peak (1434m) from the Novosilski Glacier.

The route spiralled around the mountain starting along the ramp traversing the west face on the right.

Photo: Simon Richardson.

1955–56 Carse survey expedition. We drank in the view, relishing our perch so close to the sea and looking northwest along the spine of South Georgia towards the dominant Mount Paget. On the descent we noted that a spiral ramp up the north and west faces could be the key to climbing Starbuck, and on the east face there was a steep tapering gully leading to the top. If these features connected we might be in with a chance.

Next morning (23 September), we roped up as two ropes of three and set off from the shoulder towards the start of the ramp on the north face. A left, then right, dogleg avoided the steep icefield below and we were soon at the start of the rising ramp cutting across the west face. This gave five pitches of exposed snow and ice climbing, interspersed with an awkward mixed section of Scottish Grade V, and

Mount Baume from the east. The route up the North-east Face follows the rocky ridge right of centre, keeping left of the seracs in its lower half. Photo: Simon Richardson.

led to a sharp notch on the southwest ridge. Fortunately a narrow ledge led around the south face to within sight of the tapering gully on the east face. Until this point the climbing had been relatively straightforward, which was just as well because the soft metamorphic rock was very friable, and the few cracks expanded when pegs were placed. The only reliable protection were Bulldogs (ice hooks) placed in narrow cracks, or better still, our Pecker hammered into a blank seam.

The way ahead now looked very difficult and the gully was out of reach. Our only option was to downclimb to reach a ramp of 70 degree poorly consolidated snow that led up and right to the mushroom-encrusted summit ridge. With little hope of finding any worthwhile protection (our single Pecker was the key belay anchor) I tried four different lines until I found a streak of snow that had been hardened from occasional drips from a rocky overhang above. I wriggled up a hidden ramp below the overhang to emerge below the summit mushroom, which succumbed to massive excavation. The 40m-long pitch would not have been out of place on the crux of a Grade VI thin face route on Ben Nevis. I dug a hole on the other side of the ridge, and one by one, the rest of the team (except for David who had elected to wait for us below) came up and climbed the spectacular final 20m of rime to the tiny summit. The much-coveted Starbuck Peak had finally been climbed!

We descended through the night and reached our camp at 1 a.m. Later that afternoon, Henry, Stephen and I made the first ascent of the attractive twin-summited snow peak (c1000m) that lies 2km south-east of the shapely 'Avalanche' peak (717m) marked on 1955–56 Carse survey map. The following day we moved camp to the broad col at the head of the Spenceley Glacier to the east of Mount

Baume. Next morning, Stephen, Henry and I climbed 'Icing' peak (1461m) which lies just east of the col, and was first climbed by the 1955–56 Carse survey expedition, whilst Skip and Crag reconnoitred the approach to Mount Baume.

Crag, Skip, Stephen and I decided to attempt Baume by the northeast face, the line of the 2005 attempt, and we started climbing at midnight on September 27 with a view to reaching the snowfield that comprises the upper two-thirds of the face at first light. Unfortunately the climbing on the lower rock spur, that neatly bypasses the hanging seracs on the right, was more difficult than expected. Crag led several Scottish Grade V mixed pitches and we emerged on the snowfield in the full heat of the day. After a careful ascent of the steep convex face in bottomless unconsolidated sugary snow using buried axes as anchors, we gained the summit ridge mid afternoon with the 30m-high summit tower resembling the nose cone of a rocket ship looming ahead.

We felt on the edge of all things with steep drops to the Novosilski and Spenceley glaciers on two sides and the deep blue of the ocean, peppered with icebergs, behind. Fortunately a huge flake of rime had curled around to create an icy tunnel up the back of the tower, and we took turns to stand carefully on a tiny pointed apex of snow. It was a spectacular climax, and Stephen declared, with absolute conviction, that it was a finer summit than Everest. The descent took all night and we arrived back at the tents after a 27-hour push. Unlike Starbuck that was very Scottish in nature, the climbing on Mount Baume was more alpine, and we rated the 700m route TD. Meanwhile over on Mount Pelagic, Henry and David made its second ascent, following the 2005 line up the north ridge on skis, before Henry skied off the summit.

Supplies were running low, but the weather was still perfect, so Henry and I left camp at 6 p.m. on 28 September for a night time attempt on the attractive 1800m-high peak that lies 4km southeast of Smoky Wall on the north side of Spenceley Glacier. After climbing four pitches of bullet hard ice to gain the northwest ridge, we found it was severely corniced and not the casual snow climb we were expecting, so we returned to camp. Next day we skied down the Spenceley Glacier and over the Ross Pass. Rather than continue down the detritus of the lower reaches of the Ross Glacier, we spent three more days (including one storm-bound in the tents) traversing the Webb and Cook glaciers to reach St Andrews Bay where the Pelagic Australis met us on 2 October.

The expedition had been extraordinarily successful. We travelled 65km over 16 days and climbed four unclimbed peaks and repeated two others. Starbuck and Baume are amongst the most technical summits climbed on South Georgia. Undoubtedly we were lucky with the weather, but it took Stephen's genius to organise the trip for early in the spring when glacier travel is easier and the weather gods are most likely to be benign.

Simon Richardson

REVIEWS

Walking the Song: Hamish Brown (Sandstone Press, 2017, paperback, 290pp, ISBN978-1-910985-58-8, £8.99).

Mysterious title? What is it all about? Is it that every step that Hamish Brown took around his widely travelled world is done with joy singing in his heart? Could be, yet when the reader dips into the Good to be Young section of the contents page another more logical answer appears. Your guess, please?

Yet this song could be true for Hamish with his long and fruitful career through life. Much of this material has already appeared in print, from which this brief book is a well chosen selection and a record of events. His foreword says as much, by explaining it is a potpourri or literary medley of evocative events that have been his lot, so that in some ways it reads like a chopped up autobiography with tantalising snippets brought out to be savoured and possibly either to instil some envy in those of us who only relate infrequently to the great outdoors or make us wonder what sort of a person could relish embarking on Munro round after Munro round.

It is always worthwhile to read about the places you know, because it brings back your own memories and the passing acquaintance you have had with their delights and difficulties, but sometimes it taxes the brain to link this plentiful roll call of well-kent Scottish hills with your own days spent wandering the self-same highland heights. These days all ring true and score better than the big ones that can be everyone's objectives, whether Matterhorn, Meije or Mont Blanc, where blow-by-blow endeavours on complex routes pall beside the familiar hills of home.

The chosen topics are covered fully but not excessively, and are permeated by the author's personal ethos, abounding in well-honed aphorisms and phrases to be stored away. The selection of 43 tales are wide-ranging, from his schoolboy days in the war-fretted Far East to incarceration beside the Great Bitter Lake awaiting improbable official telephone orders while creepy crawlies, flies, ants and cockroaches dropped from on high, or kipping down on the rough floor of one of the houses of the street on St Kilda, to skipping though the apertures piercing the bladed crests of Corsican cliffs, ending up short in Ethiopia on the edge of a deep hole hewn out of the bedrock, into which was squeezed a Christian church created in situ— all these and many more snippets keep the interest going.

This absorbing little book is an anthology to be sampled at random as it ranges far and wide; more a late-lie-in-bed dip-in browser than a serial book to wade-through at bedtime.

Phil Gribbon

The Sky's the Limit – the story of Vicky Jack and her quest to climb the Seven Summits: Anna Magnusson (Luath Press Ltd, 2016, 208pp, paperback, ISBN 978-1-910745-79-3, £11.99).

When Vicky Jack reached the summit of Mount Everest on 16 May, 2004, she became the first Scotswoman to complete the Seven Summits (the highest peak on each of the seven continents) and the oldest British woman to reach the top of Everest. The completion of this challenge occupied almost seven years of her life and is all the more remarkable because until Vicky embarked on her journey, she had very little technical climbing experience.

This book by Anna Magnusson tells the story of the challenge that Vicky sets herself having 'compleated' the Scottish Munros. Initially she climbs the highest mountain in Europe, Mount Elbrus, but during the descent decides she is going to climb all of the Seven Summits! The book outlines how Vicky builds up the mental, physical and technical abilities to tackle each successive summit, albeit with inevitable difficulties and setbacks along the way but with an increasing realisation that much more preparation would be required for success on Everest itself.

This is a relatively short book of around 200 pages, divided into eleven chapters plus prologue and epilogue by Anna Magnusson, along with a foreword and afterword written by Vicky Jack herself. There are two opening chapters outlining Vicky's early life, growing up conventionally in Kilmalcolm and then making her way into a successful business career whilst escaping to the Scottish hills at weekends to climb the Munros. On compleation of the Munros on Slioch in 1996, she embarks upon her Seven Summits challenge. There is a chapter given over to each summit prior to Everest, although some of these chapters do seem quite short. The final three chapters cover the particular challenge of Everest and the two attempts required for her ultimate success in reaching the summit in 2004.

The book is an interesting and easy read about an extremely motivated individual who is constantly setting herself fresh goals and challenges. In no way does this book try to describe in detail the ascents of the Seven Summits, but there are nevertheless some interesting insights into what may be encountered by anyone considering any of the ascents. When reading the chapter on the Vinson Massif in Antarctica, I found that some of Vicky's recollections such as the blue ice runway at Patriot Hills, the unforgettable vastness of the white continent ,and the extreme cold when there was any wind, were similar to my own memories of climbing Vinson in 2000, the year after Vicky. The chapters on Everest are particularly absorbing and poignant, when all Vicky's preparation and strength of character are necessary to bring her safely down again after two summit bids.

In the first of the three Everest chapters, there is an interesting reference to the visit by Edmund Hillary and Tenzing Norgay in the summer of 1953 to Balquhidder (where Vicky subsequently lived) following their successful ascent in June of that year. Their visit was to see Edwin Ker (not 'Kerr' as in the book), a climber (and early skier) and member of the SMC, who was godfather to Charles Evans the deputy leader of the 1953 expedition. Ker would have been familiar to the Everest team members, having himself been in the Himalayas with Evans prior to 1953, though he is not a well known figure within the SMC or generally in Scottish mountaineering circles.

Finally, this book was originally published by Black & White in 2007. This new edition, published by Luath Press in 2016, has been updated in respect of the acknowledgements by Anna Magnusson along with the addition of the afterword by Vicky Jack herself. The new edition is dedicated to Anna's late parents, Magnus and Mamie Magnusson.

Brian Shackleton

Second Man on the Rope: Ian R. Mitchell (Luath Press Ltd, 2016, 153pp, paperback, ISBN 978-1-910745-23-6, £7.99).
The Last Hillwalker: John D. Burns (John D Burns, 2017, 302pp, paperback, ISBN 978-0-9955958-0-4, £9.99).
Mons Graupius: M. G. Anderson (Boyle & Dalton, 2015, 326pp, paperback, ISBN 978-1-633370-55-5, £11.75).
Each of these books, in its own idiosyncratic way, spans a period a few decades

ago that the reader will recall with nostalgia or revere as history, according to his own age and outlook. Ian Mitchell's two earlier climbing books, Mountain Days & Bothy Nights and A View from the Ridge, were co-written with his climbing companion Dave Brown, who now appears as the truculent leader in Second Man on the Rope. (Our self-effacing author is, of course, the eponymous Second.) With the exception of a nasty winter accident on Beinn a' Chreachain, their exploits in the Scottish hills and bothies during the 1980s are hardly high adventure, but Mitchell has a talent for spicing the dullest fare and holding the reader's interest. Whether crossing a swollen river or bedding down in a frost-bound Jacksonville, the pair keep up a Doric banter that seldom palls, and their couthy humour is shot through with much climbing lore and a worldly-wise grasp of the human condition. A Sunday newspaper bizarrely described Mitchell as 'Chris Bonington crossed with Jim Kelman', but these yarns (first published 25 years ago and now re-issued) are surely the non-fiction progeny of Dutton's Doctor stories and Munro's Para Handy.

John Burns, too, has a fondness for bothy nights, when Horatian logs are heaped high and the amber liquid is amply dispensed. His book is sub-titled 'a sideways look at 40 years in Britain's mountains', and it traces his abiding love of the hills – and of camp and bothy life – from boyhood days on the Lakeland fells to winter routes in the Highlands and Canada. He sets his life's story against a well-painted background of three-day weeks, miners' strikes, food-free smoky pubs and puritanical youth hostels, and he reminds the reader how unsatisfactory yet scarcely affordable was so much of our climbing equipment in the '70s and early '80s. Having grown up on Merseyside, he made frequent trips as a young man to Scotland and presently took up a social-work post in Inverness, which allowed him to indulge his enthusiasm for ice-climbing.

Burns's treatment of his material is mostly light-hearted, but he recalls how on joining the Cairngorm Mountain Rescue Team he was '… immediately impressed by how professional their attitude is… One of the many things I learn from taking part in rescues is just how inaccurate press reports are… They report the wrong mountain, the wrong events, and misquote team members…. [and] delight in calling folk who get into difficulties "idiots." In all my time in mountain rescue I never came across an idiot.'

Like Mitchell, Burns is as much scholar as jester. Having researched Aleister Crowley's life he staged a one-man Fringe play about this sinister individual, whom he describes – with slight exaggeration, perhaps – as 'one of the foremost mountaineers of his generation.' Given the wry humour that characterises The Last Hillwalker, it should not surprise us to learn that Burns in recent years has also performed as a stand-up comedian. 'In stand-up,' he writes, 'I find something that replaces the adrenalin rush of climbing.'

'Nivver spyle a story wonderin gin its true,' says Mitchell, but while neither he nor Burns is above embroidering a tale, their narratives are solidly based on real events. In this they differ from M. G. Anderson, whose novel Mons Graupius is too outrageously implausible to be mistaken for fact. Set in the 1960s, it tells in the first person the story of an Edinburgh lass, Moira Fiorelli, the expensively educated daughter of a fish & chip shop proprietor, who improbably combines the characteristics of Jean Brodie and Lara Croft. Her mountaineering progresses from walks in the Pentlands to rock climbs on the Cobbler and a winter epic on the Ben; but never are the ups and downs of her rocky love-life neglected, and indeed an uncharitable reader might offer Mons Veneris as a more apposite title.

Though the author has lived for many years in the USA, his youth was spent in

Scotland where he kept company with the Squirrels, so the cognoscenti may be able (for all I know) to identify the real-life prototypes of some of the novel's grotesque protagonists. Other characters seem to have been borrowed from the cartoon section of the Sunday Post, complete with the excruciating 'help-ma-boab' vocabulary that was surely rare even in Mr Anderson's distant dancing-days. If however the reader can turn a blind eye to the caricatures and a deaf ear to the dialogue, he will be rewarded with some entertaining episodes and even a smattering of social history.

As someone wistfully remarked, 'nostalgia is not what it used to be.'

Graeme Morrison

Nowt but a fleein' thing — A History of Climbing on Scafell: Al Phizacklea and Mike Cocker (Fell & Rock Climbing Club, 2016, 398pp, £35).

This huge tome is devoted to the history of climbing on the buttresses of Scafell, from Coleridge's descent of Broad Stand in 1802 to the present day. It follows a natural progression, dividing the chronology into logical periods depending on the main activists and major ascents, and is profusely illustrated throughout. Scafell was one of the crags favoured by the very earliest climbers, so this book is not just a history of a crag but also a history of the origins of our sport, and the rather curious title comes from a remark made by the local inn-keeper on being told that someone had climbed a route up a particular part of the crag previously considered unassailable.

An entire book devoted to the history of climbing on just one crag is not a new idea, of course (*The Black Cliff* by Wilson, Soper and Crew, and Crocket & Richardson's *Ben Nevis* spring immediately to mind) but this surely has to be (at one foot square and over an inch and a quarter thick) the largest volume ever devoted to a single cliff. Weighing over 6lbs, it's not an easy thing to peruse in bed, though the resulting arm exercise may be useful if you are inspired as a result of reading it to scale any of the climbs described. The point of such a large format is to do justice to its fantastic collection of photographs, both historical and contemporary, and when one opens it for the first time one can see why — it works well, especially when one gets to a section of photodiagrams illustrating almost every line and variation on the crag. Many of the more recent pictures have been taken by Phizacklea himself, and they demonstrate nicely what a fine photographer he is, both in his ability to frame a good image and in his dedication in putting himself in the right place at the right time to capture subject, light and atmosphere to perfection.

The chapters on the early years have been written by Mike Cocker, who is something of an expert on climbing history having previously written *The Wasdale Climbing Book* (also published by the FRCC), which will have provided a great deal of the material used here. Phizacklea (who penned the last three Scafell climbing guides and has put up more new routes on the crag than anyone else) has contributed the remainder of the book, with the exception of two chapters on winter climbing that were the work of Brian Davison, and a chapter on geology by John Moore. All these authors can be considered experts in their respective fields, and this shows in the quality of their work. As a book, it is both easy to read and very entertaining, for the text is relieved from being just the annotated first ascents list that it could so easily have been by numerous tales and anecdotes woven amongst the historical facts — many of which have not to my knowledge appeared in print before, the result of both in-depth archive research and personal interviews with climbers. The immense amount of unpaid labour required to gather all this information together can only be wondered at, and it is not at all surprising that the book (which was originally intended to be published in 2014 to coincide with the centenary of the first ascent of Central Buttress) did not actually hit the shelves until late last year.

There are, it has to be said, quite a few small proof-reading errors that have somehow escaped notice, and which the authors will no doubt be kicking themselves about. These though are of little consequence compared with the major sin of omitting to provide a serious reference work such as this with an index!

In summary, this is an extensively researched, well written and very entertaining book on the history of one of the most important crags in the development of British mountaineering, and the authors and their assistants are to be congratulated on producing such a fine homage to such a fine crag, and the FRCC for taking the financial plunge in publishing this important volume of record and selling it at a price that effectively means it is a non-profit making venture.

Anyone who is interested in the history of climbing in our islands is recommended to buy one quickly before the limited print run is exhausted — and at £35 it's cheaper than many climbing guides.

Stephen Reid

Chasing the Ephemeral – 50 routes for a successful Scottish Winter: Simon Richardson (Mica Publishing 2016, 256pp, ISBN 978-0-9560367-9-7, £25).

Sitting idle through the snowless January of 2017, I was delighted to receive a book that with its superb photos and smart layout instantly re-awakened my passion for winter climbing. As our current Club president, Simon Richardson needs no introduction to enthusiasts of the Scottish winter sport. His pioneering and guide-book writing activities have spanned more than 30 years. With Chasing the Ephemeral Simon has made a further valuable contribution to the pursuit he has done so much to develop and promote.

The book categorises 50 representative winter climbs by reference to the type of conditions and stage in the season in which they are best attempted. Simon's aim is that the user will select appropriate objectives and be more productive in climbing achievement as a result. The section titles – Early Bird, Cold Snaps, Lean Times, Top Nick and Late Season – cover every conceivable aspect of winter conditions except the unmitigated thaw. Each climb gets a detailed write-up with notes on history, style, approach and nearby alternatives together with a map and photo-diagram. On Ben Nevis the selected climbs are marked with pinpoint accuracy as overlays on topographic maps of the cliffs.

The photographic quality is consistently excellent, with some stand-out scenic shots that made me gasp with new yearnings. The brilliance of Scottish winter climbing compared with any other branch of mountaineering sport is self-evident. Viewing shot after shot of such steely beauty, older climbers can justify their past obsessions. More importantly, young climbers will be inspired as well as informed. The introductory pages are a valuable complement to the route descriptions, containing a massive amount of explanation and advice on preparations, hazard assessment, equipment and tactics.

The grade range is wisely pitched between III and VI, with the addition of a couple of lead-in VIIs. This gives the book appeal to the greatest number of aspiring climbers as they progress through the middle grades. In geographical spread, the selection shows a definite bias towards Lochaber and the Cairngorms. In Simon's own words: 'there are some areas I know better than others … this book is a synthesis of my own experience.'

There are only three picks in the whole of the North-West Highlands and none at all on Skye, and there is limited fair in Glencoe and the Southern Highlands. By contrast there are 20 routes featured on Ben Nevis and the Aonachs. How could Beinn Eighe with its wealth of brilliant climbs be excluded? Had Simon adopted a more representative selection from each area the book would be standing proud and unchallenged as the new Cold Climbs. Maybe a revised edition could redress the balance.

Chasing the Ephemeral should become a standard bible on every winter climber's bedside table. However, I fear that the choice of a cerebral title, whilst clever in its way, may serve to deflect the potential purchaser's attention towards more overtly practical guides and textbooks. Perhaps Simon, in his modesty, has not realised just how great is the potential appeal of his beautiful book. I, for one, will be promoting it enthusiastically to all the winter aspirants who cross my path in coming years.

Martin Moran

Whatever Title: Iain Smart (Papyngay Press. 2016, 457pp, softback, ISBN 9781517726348 £16.40 available from Amazon).
This is a strange book. To those brought up on Iain's contributions to the Journal over many years it will seem very strange indeed. The work appears to have grown gradually, very much at its own pace, out of earlier work. The tales entitled 'Midnight on the Capel Mounth', 'High Noon,' 'Autumn Glory' and 'Crossroads at Midnight' all appear in the expanded version of The Big Eye of Summer but not in that work's first incarnation. Just as the expanded version of the Big Eye grows out of the earlier one, Whatever Title grows out of the expanded version, for this work starts with 'Midnight on the Capel Mounth' and works its way via 'High Noon' (now on Tap O' Noth), 'Autumn Glory' and 'Crossroads at Midnight'. One of the minor themes of the present work, the prolongation of youthful life is explored in 'Disobeying the Rules' and in 'Far Out on the Far Cuillin' which appear even in the earlier more slender volume of The Big Eye. This latter theme is never satisfactorily resolved in Whatever Title.

Although the narrator of the work is named once or twice he is not commonly referred to by name and I think we can safely assume that this is Iain or some imagined version of himself. He is a retired doctor, seems very like Iain in terms of urbanity, erudition and thought and he enjoys intellectual argument, climbing, sailing and flying aircraft.

When we first meet Nicholas, Iain's great protagonist and companion through much of this book, there is the real possibility that he is the Devil himself. Iain is partly taken in by the Satanic aura which surrounds him. By p.69, however, Nicholas is revealed as 'a fallible human,...a lonely one with a mysterious history' having 'the mixed attributes of a teen-age tearaway and a sage with a long history'.

Iain and Nicholas continue to meet and have discussions in diverse places: in a bothy on the south side of the Torridon hills (Coire Fionnaraich?), in sheltered bays on the NW coast and by burns and lochs (one of them sinister). They climb on the crags of Sgòrr Ruadh (Academy Ridge and Raeburn's Buttress? Not named), they go fishing and camp in idyllic spots where it seems there is always just the right amount of breeze to keep the midges at bay. Gradually mountaineering fades into the background: indeed, like the other main activity in the book, sailing, it really only functions as background to the real meat of the book: intellectual exploration.

If there is one idea which lies at the heart of this book it is the relationship between what Iain calls the core programme in the brain and the superabundant circuitry. The core programme is what ensures our survival: makes a falling man clutch for holds, makes us snatch our hands from fire, makes us run from danger and so on. The superabundant circuitry goes beyond instinctive reaction and is concerned with rational thought and control, everything intellectual and all things emotional and artistic.

Two lengthy cruises in the good ship Periplus take up a lot of the book; there is an interlude in which Iain attends a Latin class which becomes a seminar on the Book of Kells and finally the work concludes with Iain's being given insight into the neo-religious order based at Letterallan of which Nicholas is the most senior member and enfant terrible. Involved discussions are carried on at all times.

Iain and Nicholas undertake the first cruise of the Periplus alone and at the winter solstice. In some ways it is a dangerous undertaking and causes alarm to the Letterallan community who collectively own the vessel. On the voyage it is revealed that Nicholas had been a prisoner of some fanatically religious group in Beirut. He had been kept chained to a radiator and in constant fear of his life. This partly explains his odd behaviour in the earlier chapters and earlier works. Now he is seeking to exorcise fearful memories.

Taking advantage of a settled spell of high pressure the friends sail as far out as the Flannan Isles. Nicholas is drawn to Eilean nan Tighe and with misgivings Iain rows him ashore.

'Westwards the last flush of the setting sun was leaving us in a spooky half-light....I wished I was back on the little yacht waiting below....Nicholas, on the other hand was in a fearful ecstasy....if it had been anyone else I would have thought he was trying to see Tir nan Og on the far horizon....Then he raised his arms as if in a prayer of thanksgiving. Nicholas in a state of prayer! This was a strange evening.'(pps. 178–9) But Nicholas, no longer a Satanic figure, provides an explanation:

'During the long nights of despair chained up in darkness and heat and unpredictable cruelty I dreamed of doing this.....I thought I would do it in High Summer but...I am here in High Winter and it is even more healing.' And the one-time Devil goes on to echo the Prayer Book: 'Even here in Winter there is the sure and certain hope that dawn will come...' Then somewhat to Iain's relief, 'he returned to normal...and said "As I keep telling you we are all emotional beings. Now let's get out of here." '

If this work had been conceived as a conventional novel it could have finished here. We have been intrigued by Nicholas seen as "His Satanic Majesty" but now the heart has been plucked out of his mystery; a rational explanation of his oddness has been given. We feel sorry for him and pleased at his recovery, but he is no longer intriguing. But, of course this is not an ordinary novel, indeed to call it a novel at all is rather misleading: it is much more like a series of dialogues with, at times, convincing and appropriate backgrounds. (The potential wildness of the sea is a good background for Nicholas's state of mind and its mid-winter calm suggests returning order and coolness).

Why does Iain continue the work past its emotional climax? I think the answer is simple. In the Preface to his earliest published book The Big Eye Of Summer he says:

'I have written about things that happened to interest me without regard to whether they interested anyone else.' He wanted to go on writing about things which interested him and he does. In some writers this would have been mere self-indulgence, but to an extent Iain gets away with it because of the lucidity of his prose, his urbanity and charm. For all its seeming abstruseness this is not a difficult book to read.

What are we to make of the much discussed relationship between the Core Program and the Superabundant Circuitry (how weary one becomes of these phrases)? Do these seemingly explanatory titles really add anything to Plato's divisions of the soul or Freud's division of human consciousness? Thinkers tend to agree that when base self-protective passions take over things go awry. Plato talks about the soul, Freud about the unconscious mind and Smart about the brain: but so what? The effects are just the same. Does it really matter if the religious fanatics persecute Nicholas because of the dominance exerted by the appetitive elements of their souls (Plato), of their Ids (Freud) or their Core Programs (Smart)? Are not these just different ways of speaking about the same thing? If it be objected that Smart at least locates the mental causes accurately in the brain, surely the reply is: where else would one expect to find them? The brain is always there as a cause but its relationship to consciousness is not understood.1

In the later parts of the work there is social comment as well as neurological discussion. On the rather strange trip to the alpine ski-resort and on the second cruise of the Periplus (this time minus Nicholas but with Alice the Abbess of the Letterallan Order at the helm), Iain and friends come into contact with some dodgy high-society figures and their underlings who have the feel of the underworld about them. To give a flavour:

'There was a disturbance as Charlie Gowan arrived with partner Robert Malone.....Ramon welcomed them civilly enough but as a well-fed, tolerant lion might welcome a couple of jackals.

Charlie was too insensitive to notice.' (p336)

Nothing happens of course. Nobody is seduced or murdered, nothing is stolen, though dodgy dealings off-stage are hinted at. One could say nothing of consequence apart from Nicholas's redemption, happens in the whole book. Action, Smart leaves to other writers: his forte is reflection.

There is, however, one more unexpected twist at the end of the work. Iain always regarded himself as a 'cradle Calvinist'; he was religiously agnostic. But at times in this work he is soothed by religious music. He takes pleasure in attending evensong at the Letterallan Community. This strain of deeply suppressed religious sensitivity is actually brought out in one of Iain's earlier essays:

Landing on one of the Western Islands, Iain comes across 'a statue of a young Madonna and Child.'

As he says: 'a disturbing experience for a hard-bitten, rational agnostic brought up....under the baleful shadow of the psychopathic Calvin. Nevertheless I left some buttercups of my own. There was a remote possibility that it might be remembered.' (*The Big Eye of Summer* first ed. p.76)

In the present work a few paragraphs from the end of the book Alice the Abbess '...led me to the wall behind the cross...and drew back the curtain to reveal Christ crucified. It was horrifying in its detail. In front were two soldiers...one looked bored the other slightly amused.' Alice makes the point that this cruelty is what people are capable of. But the work ends on a calm, redemptive note:

'She stood and bade me rise. "On a morning as fine as this," she said, "Let's go and sit in the cloister.'

The last words should be Iain's not mine: 'We sat there companionably in silence in the mellow sunshine listening to the gentle whisper of a fountain. A couple of hours passed without my noticing. I believe I was meditating; something I have never done before.'

PJB

Highland Scrambles South: Iain Thow (SMT Publications, 2017, soft covers, 415pp, ISBN 978-1-907233-23-4, £25).

This is the eagerly awaited companion to Highland Scrambles North, which appeared in 2006, and it covers not only the Highlands south of Inverness but also Galloway and the islands of Rum, Arran and Mull. Besides the better known areas, the author has included routes in such unfamiliar localities as Morar, Appin and the Loch Lochy hills, so that in total over 200 excursions are described. One's admiration for this beautifully produced book is therefore tinged with regret at the laying bare of not a few undiscovered crags. Consolation comes however from the matchless competence with which Thow and the SMC have discharged their task, and from knowledge that the revenues will be charitably disbursed.

The book is sub-titled 'Scrambles & Easy Climbs...', though paradoxically the old Easy grade of climb is not used; instead the system (as in HSN) comprises numerical grades 1, 2 & 3 for the simpler scrambles, together with the familiar adjectival grades of Moderate, Difficult and (rarely) Very Difficult for the rock climbs. In defining these grades, and in his section on Weather, the author stresses how the prevailing conditions and type of rock may dramatically affect difficulty – a point that, while obvious to the rock climber, may be less apparent to a hillwalker unaccustomed to reverses.

Preceding the route descriptions, which are lucid and remarkably detailed, there are admirable introductory chapters on History, Wildlife, Weather and Geology, the last being a masterly contribution from Noel Williams. Arguably the passages on climbing history should have been distributed among the regional sections, not relegated to a separate chapter, but this is perhaps a matter of personal preference.

The style of writing tends towards the conversational, and would surely have attracted the blue pencil of a rock-guide editor of the old school. 'The fun continues!' 'Breathe a sigh of relief.' 'You haven't finished yet, however!' These ejaculations will irk as many readers as they amuse, though perhaps in a guide to carefree scrambling the author may be forgiven for occasionally smudging the line between objective description and exclamation.

In addition to 27 maps there are almost 100 photo-diagrams, on which the scrambles and graded climbs are indicated by dashed and dotted lines respectively – a nice touch that typifies the close attention to detail in this book. The colour photographs are excellent, and will serve to remind you that our native crags are invariably blessed with bright sun and cloudless skies. So pull on your shorts, dispense with the rope, and romp up sun-warmed rock, untrammelled by belays or hesitant leaders!

Graeme Morrison.

Wild Country – The Man who made Friends: Mark Vallance (Vertebrate Publishing, 2016, paperback, 240pp, ISBN 978-1-910240-81-6, £14.95).

I read Mark's book from cover to cover, fascinated, over two days. I knew he was a very talented mountaineer who had been one of the early British climbers on the big walls in Yosemite Valley in the 1970s. There he had mated up with Ray Jardine, who had designed the first reversed cams that ultimately became known as Friends. Ray had kept the design very secret, the original homemade samples always hidden under his jacket. How Mark took the design and developed Friends in the UK is a captivating tale in its own right, but the book tells a much deeper story.

Early days learning to climb and becoming an outdoor instructor were followed by a two-and-a-half year spell at Halley Bay in Antarctica. Mark gives a vivid description of life under the ice, dog-driving, and the life of men living in a very isolated world.

His account of returning to America, and then the trials and tribulations of setting up 'Wild Country', the company he started in order to make and distribute Friends, is a brilliant portrayal of the early days of the climbing industry. His dream was to create and sell high-quality, innovative, climbing equipment; and Friends were followed by Rocks – beautifully designed curved nuts – and then Fire rock shoes with the first sticky rubber soles.

With his friend Dick Turnbull he started 'Outside' in Hathersage, one of the best climbing shops in England, and they then set up 'The Foundry', which may have been the world's first proper indoor climbing wall. Battles with dissenting business partners and law suits over patent rights with powerful competitors such as Yvon Chouinard followed, and these are all recounted here, speckled with a good dusting of climbing stories.

A few years ago he was diagnosed with Parkinson's disease, which he describes as a nightmare that he learned to live with while being determined to keep climbing. The book is an inspirational tale of a very determined man who has without doubt altered and enhanced the climbing world. Absolutely a 'must-read'.

Ian Sykes

Exploring the Landscape of Ben Nevis and Glen Nevis: Noel Williams for Lochaber Geopark (Nevis Landscape Partnership, 2017, 64pp plus detailed map, £15).

This excellent slim guidebook and accompanying comprehensive map introduce the reader to the rocks and landscape of Ben Nevis and Glen Nevis through eight walks. It is not exclusive to the geologist, rather it is aimed at the interested layman, but even as a professional geologist I found some 'I never thought of it that way' moments. There are simple textual and diagrammatic explanations of the most significant geological concepts of the region such as glaciation, mountain building, volcanism and caldera formation.

The eight excursions vary in length and seriousness. There are three Munro days, namely the Ben itself and two in the Mamores, while the Allt a' Mhuilinn walk should enliven a trip to the CIC, and the walk by Nevis Gorge to Steall is included too. Thus, the walks should appeal to a range of abilities or, put another way, there is something for any weather.

Each walk is described in the book, accompanied by an extract from the geological map and including between nine and seventeen locations of geological interest. An excellent innovation is that each locality is given an eight-digit grid reference (i.e. 10m) for use with a GPS (if preferred) and many have a photograph of the point of interest. If you have ever followed complex geological itineraries, wondering if you are at the outcrop described, you will be glad of this. Indeed, the author's directions are crystal-clear throughout, and the photographs and diagrams superb. There is a glossary of geological terms, covering most of those used, and a short glossary of Gaelic place names.

The map appears to be printed on the same tear-resistant, 100% waterproof polyethylene as the excellent Harvey's British Mountain Maps. It is cleverly designed, with the 1:25,000 scale geological map, sections and technical information on one side and details of each walk on the other side, so that the user can fold it to show the details of one walk without a major on-hill re-fold. Information on each walk contained in the map includes an excellent satellite photograph, a rather basic topographical map and a topographic cross-section of the walk, all with the localities marked.

The technical information on the map is excellent, with text, diagrams and photographs explaining mountain building, caldera formation, metamorphism, glaciation, erratics and a geological timeline. The two geological cross-sections are also very clear. Perhaps inevitably there are a few places where the terminology used on the map differs from that in the book.

My one significant gripe would be with the geological map supplied by the British Geological Survey. As on the British Mountain Maps, the geology is overlaid on a map with shaded relief. This shading overpowers the colours so that it is difficult on the key to distinguish between the various pinks, the yellowish browns and the brownish yellows. I wonder what was wrong with standard geological map format, in which the relief is not shaded and geological units are further identified by a letter on map and key. Fortunately, it is easier to read the geological map extracts and key that are included in the book.

There is some overlap between book and map, but they are slim and I think it would be better to take both on the hill. They look reasonably weather resistant and are supplied with a plastic folder.

This excellent guide will be useful to me for my own interest and also as a resource with clients. I can't wait to put it in my sack and head for the hills; and if you want to understand our mountain landscape, so should you! I hope that other districts will be given a similar treatment.

Andy Heald

******

ERRATA

'.......this Errours den,
A monster vile, whom God and man does hate:'
(Edmund Spenser, The Faerie Queene, Canto I, xiii)

In the 2016 edition of the Journal: the description of the photo on p.227 is wrong as the climb is on Craig an Eilte, not Buchan Hill.

On p.255 Craig an Eilte, and its new routes, has appeared as a buttress of Buchan Hill's Black Gairy, when actually it is a substantial crag in its own right already featured in Lowland Outcrops and is miles away from Buchan Hill. Logically, the Buchan Hill routes should be after the route description of *Mental Block* on p.226.

On pp.138–9 in connection with the Soa Island climbs Anthony Walker should replace Alastair Walker.

ORDERING THE SMC JOURNAL

Members should automatically receive a copy of the Journal when it is published. Members wishing to order extra copies or non-members wishing to place a regular order should contact the Distribution Manager, Roger Robb, by **e-mail** <journal.distribution@smc.org.uk>.

SMC JOURNAL BACK NUMBERS

Back numbers of the Journal may be obtained from Clifford Smith:
16 House o' Hill Gardens, Edinburgh, EH4 2AR.
e-mail: <journal.archive@smc.org.uk>
tel: 0131-332 3414   mob: 07748 703515

The following years are available: post and packaging are extra.

	Year			Year
£5.00	1972		**£12.95**	2000
	1977			2001
	1978			2002
	1979			2003
	1980			2004
	1983			
			£13.95	2005
£5.50	1985			2006
				2007
£5.70	1986			2008
	1987			
	1989		**£14.95**	2009
	1990			2010
	1991			2011
	1992			2012
				2013
£6.95	1993			2014
	1994			
	1995		**£16.95**	2016
£8.95	1996			
	1997			
	1998			
£11.95	1999			

SCOTTISH MOUNTAINEERING CLUB HUTS

Bookings can be made to stay at any of the five Club Huts by contacting the relevant Custodian.

CHARLES INGLIS CLARK MEMORIAL HUT, BEN NEVIS
Location: (NN 167 722) On the north side of Ben Nevis by the Allt a' Mhuilinn. This hut was erected by Dr and Mrs Inglis Clark in memory of their son Charles who was killed in action in the 1914–18 War.
Custodian: Robin Clothier, 35 Broompark Drive, Newton Mearns, Glasgow, G77 5DZ.
e-mail <cic@smc.org.uk>

LAGANGARBH HUT, GLEN COE
Location: (NN 221 559) North of Buachaille Etive Mor near the River Coupall.
Custodian: Bernard Swan, 16 Knowes View, Faifley, Clydebank, G81 5AT.
e-mail <lagangarbh@smc.org.uk>.

LING HUT, GLEN TORRIDON
Location: (NG 958 562) On the south side of Glen Torridon.
Custodian: John T Orr, 8 Fleurs Place, Elgin, Morayshire, IV30 1ST.
e-mail <ling@smc.org.uk>.

NAISMITH HUT, ELPHIN
Location: (NC 216 118) In the community of Elphin on the east side of the A835.
Custodian: John T Orr, 8 Fleurs Place, Elgin, Morayshire, IV30 1ST.
e-mail <naismith@smc.org.uk>.

RAEBURN HUT, LAGGAN
Location: (NN 636 909) On the north side of the A889 between Dalwhinnie and Laggan.
Custodian: Clive Rowland, Inverene, Links Place, Nairn, IV12 4NH.
e-mail <raeburn@smc.org.uk>.

SCOTTISH MOUNTAINEERING CLUB GUIDEBOOKS

Published by THE SCOTTISH MOUNTAINEERING TRUST

HILLWALKERS' GUIDES
The Munros
Munros GPS data sets – from
The Corbetts and other Scottish hills
The Grahams & The Donalds
The Cairngorms
Central Highlands
Islands of Scotland including Skye
North-West Highlands
Southern Highlands

SCRAMBLERS' GUIDES
Highland Scrambles North
Highland Scrambles South
Skye Scrambles

CLIMBERS' GUIDES
Scottish Rock Climbs
Scottish Winter Climbs
Scottish Sports Climbs
Inner Hebrides & Arran
Ben Nevis
The Cairngorms
Glen Coe
Highland Outcrops South
Lowland Outcrops
North-East Outcrops
Northern Highlands North
Northern Highlands Central
Northern Highlands South
Skye The Cuillin
Skye Sea-Cliffs & Outcrops

OTHER PUBLICATIONS
Ben Nevis – Britain's Highest Mountain
The Cairngorms – 100 Years of Mountaineering
A Chance in a Million? – Scottish Avalanches
Hostile Habitats
The Munroist's Companion
Scottish Hill Names – Their origin and meaning

e-BOOKS
Cairngorms Scene and Unseen
A Century of Scottish Mountaineering
A History of Glenmore Lodge

APPLYING FOR MEMBERSHIP OF
THE SCOTTISH MOUNTAINEERING CLUB

The following notes are provided outlining the principles by which climbers may be admitted to membership of the Club.

The Committee does not lay down any hard and fast rules when considering applications but considers each case on its own merits. Candidates must be over 18 and have experience of mountaineering in Scotland in both summer and winter. This experience should have extended over a period of at least four years immediately prior to application and should not be confined to just a single climbing district.

The normally expected climbing standards include:

- Experience of winter climbing including several routes of around Grade IV standard and the ability to lead climbs of this level of difficulty.

- Rock climbing experience including climbs of Very Severe (4c) standard and the ability to lead routes of this level of difficulty. In considering applications, emphasis will be placed on multi-pitch climbs in mountain locations.

- The ascent of at least 50 Munros of which at least one third should have been climbed in snow conditions.

In short, the candidate should be able to show – by producing a detailed list of climbs – that they are competent to lead a variety of outings in the mountains of Scotland in both summer and winter. The technical standards specified refer to applicants currently active and may be varied at the discretion of the Committee for older candidates provided that the applicant's routes reflect a reasonable standard for their time. Climbing in the Alps and elsewhere is taken into consideration. Candidates who do not fulfil the normal qualifications listed above but who have made special contributions to Scottish mountaineering in the fields of art, literature or science may receive special consideration.

It is essential that each candidate, before applying, should have climbed with the member proposing the application. It is also desirable that a candidate should be introduced to a member of the Committee before the application is considered. Application forms must be obtained on behalf of candidates by members of the Club who may not propose or support candidates for election during their own first two years of membership. The annual membership fee is £40.00 (£30.00 for those aged 65 and over) which includes the Club Journal.

A fuller version of these notes for members wishing to propose candidates is available from the Club Secretary who is happy to advise candidates and members on any aspect of the application process. Please contact John R R Fowler, Honorary Secretary at:

e-mail: <jrrfowler@tiscali.co.uk>
tel: 0131 226 4055.

OFFICE BEARERS 2016–17

Honorary President: Neil Quinn
Honorary Vice-Presidents: Robert T. Richardson and Robin N. Campbell
President: Simon M. Richardson
Vice-Presidents: Helen G.S. Forde and Chris M. Huntley

Honorary Secretary: John R.R. Fowler, 4 Doune Terrace, Edinburgh, EH3 6DY. **Honorary Treasurer**: J. Morton Shaw, 7 Kirkbrae Terrace, New Deer, Turriff, AB53 6TF. **Honorary Membership Secretary**: Geoff Cohen, 198/1 Grange Loan, Edinburgh, EH9 2DZ. **Honorary Meets Secretary**: John R.R. Fowler. **Honorary Editor of Journal**: Peter J. Biggar, Hillhead, Craigton, North Kessock, Inverness, IV1 3YG. **Honorary Librarian & Honorary Archivist**: Robin N. Campbell, Glynside, Kippen Road, Fintry, Glasgow, G63 0LW. **Honorary Custodian of Images**: David Stone, 30 Summerside Street, Edinburgh, EH6 4NU. **Honorary Reporter on Accounts**: David Small, 5 Afton Place, Edinburgh, EH5 3RB. **SMC Website Manager**: Tony Stone, 43 Woodbank Crescent, Sheffield, S8 9EF. **Convener of Publications Sub-Committee**: Rab Anderson, 24 Paties Road, Edinburgh, EH14 1EE. **Convener of Huts Sub-Committee**: Andrew M. James, 41 Urquhart Road, Dingwall, IV15 9PE. **Representative to the MCofS**: Brian R. Shackleton, 4A Campbell Road, Edinburgh, EH12 6DT. **Committee**: Richard K. Bott, Simon Fraser, Alison J. Coull, Colin A. Simpson, Fiona J.L. Reid and Simon Yearsley

Journal Information

Editor:	Peter Biggar, Hillhead, Craigton, North Kessock, Inverness, IV1 3YG. **e-mail** <journal@smc.org.uk>
New Routes Editor:	Andy Nisbet, 20 Craigie Avenue, Boat of Garten, PH24 3BL. **e-mail** <newroutes@smc.org.uk>
Photos Editor:	Ian Taylor, 15, Pulteney Street, Ullapool, Ross-shire, IV26 2UP. **e-mail** <itandtf@hotmail.com>
Reviews Editor:	Graeme Morrison, 42 Orchard Drive, Edinburgh, EH4 2DZ. **e-mail** <g.d.morrison@btopenworld.com>
Distribution:	Roger Robb, Blaven, Upper Knockbain Road, Dingwall, IV15 9NR. **e-mail** <journal.distribution@smc.org.uk>
Back Numbers:	Cliff Smith. **e-mail** <journal.archive@smc.org.uk>

INSTRUCTIONS TO CONTRIBUTORS

The Editor welcomes contributions from members and non-members alike. Priority will be given to articles relating to Scottish mountaineering. Articles should be submitted **by the end of April** if they are to be considered for inclusion in the Journal of the same year. Material is preferred in electronic form (.txt, .pdf, .odt, .rtf or .doc/docx) and should be sent by e-mail direct to the Editor.

Those without access to e-mail can send hard copy (typewritten and double-spaced) by post to the Editor's home address. Illustrations not relating to an article should be sent to the Photos Editor. Photographs should be high resolution and must be accompanied by explanatory captions including the photographer's name.

Books for review should be sent to the Reviews Editor by the end of April, though they can sometimes be sent later by prior arrangement.

The Editorial team reserves the right to edit any material submitted.

INDEX NOTES

Page numbers with *italic* type denote illustrations.
Page number runs in **boldface** contain text and in-text illustrations.
The content of Meet Reports, Obituaries and Reviews is not indexed.

INDEX OF AUTHORS

INDEX OF PEOPLE mentioned in text

INDEX OF PLACES mentioned in text

INDEX OF PHOTOGRAPHERS AND ARTISTS

INDEX OF OTHER SUBJECTS

INDEX OF REVIEWS (Reviewers in brackets)